The Poetical Works of

JOHN KEATS

*Edited with an Introduction
and Textual Notes*

By

H. BUXTON FORMAN, C.B.

London

OXFORD UNIVERSITY PRESS
HUMPHREY MILFORD
1926

Oxford University Press

London   Edinburgh   Glasgow   Copenhagen
New York   Toronto   Melbourne   Cape Town
Bombay   Calcutta   Madras   Shanghai
Humphrey Milford Publisher to the UNIVERSITY

Printed in England at the OXFORD UNIVERSITY PRESS
By John Johnson Printer to the University

India Paper.

PREFATORY NOTE

THE whole of Keats's known works in verse are included in this volume ; and the foot-notes contain a large selection of variorum readings. Sixteen lines of *The Eve of St. Mark*, found by the Editor in a Keats scrap-book lent to him by Mr. Frank Sabin, and given in the Introduction, have not been printed in any other edition. The Editor has endeavoured, in the Introduction, to acknowledge all obligations.

CONTENTS

POSTHUMOUS AND FUGITIVE POEMS   PAGE

   Sonnet written at the end of "The Floure and the
     Lefe" 292
   Sonnet to Haydon, with the following . . . 293
   Sonnet on seeing the Elgin Marbles . . . 293
   Sonnet on a Picture of Leander 294
   To—— ["Think not of it, sweet one, so ;—"] . 294
   Lines ["Unfelt, unheard, unseen,"] . . . 295
   Sonnet on the Sea 295
   Sonnet on Leigh Hunt's Poem "The Story of
     Rimini" 296
   On Oxford : a Parody 296
   The Poet : a Fragment 297
   Modern Love 297
   Fragments of The Castle Builder . . . 298
   A Song of Opposites ["Welcome joy, and welcome
     sorrow,"] 300
   Sonnet to a Cat 301
   Lines on seeing a Lock of Milton's Hair . 301
   Sonnet on sitting down to read King Lear once
     again 302
   Sonnet ["When I have fears that I may cease to
     be"] 303
   Sharing Eve's Apple 303
   A Draught of Sunshine ["Hence Burgundy, Claret,
     and Port,"] 304
   Sonnet to the Nile 305
   Sonnet to a Lady seen for a few moments at Vauxhall 306
   Sonnet ["Blue ! 'Tis the life of heaven,"] . . 306
   Sonnet to John Hamilton Reynolds . . . 307
   What the Thrush said : Lines from a Letter to
     John Hamilton Reynolds 307
   Sonnet—The Human Seasons 308

   Extracts from an Opera

      "O ! were I one of the Olympian twelve," . 308
      Daisy's Song 309
      Folly's Song 309
      "Oh, I am frighten'd with most hateful
        thoughts !" 310
      Song ["The stranger lighted from his steed"] 310
      "Asleep ! O sleep a little while, white pearl !" 310

   Faery Song ["Shed no tear—O shed no tear !"] . 311
   Faery Song ["Ah ! woe is me ! poor silver-wing !"] 311
   Sonnet to Homer 312
   Song ["Spirit here that reignest !"] . . 312
   Teignmouth : "Some Doggerel," sent in a Letter
     to B. R. Haydon 313

ILLUSTRATIONS

INTRODUCTION

The chief aim in the present edition of Keats's poetry is to supply in a handy form an authoritative text of the whole body of his work in verse. The edition differs from those which I have prepared in past years, in that it is neither an exhaustive *variorum* edition nor a mere unannotated text, but a text illustrated by readings and cancelled passages selected from the great mass of manuscript and printed material. These illustrations are offered as likely to be helpful to those who would form a conception, not only of the results which Keats arrived at, but also of the steps by which he attained them, so far as those steps may be said to have a true literary or psychological value.

The more notable the effort on which the poet was engaged, the better has it seemed worth while to indicate the lower rungs of the creative ladder by which he ascended to the final result. Hence, the comparative fulness of annotation in the case of, say, *Lamia, Isabella, The Eve of St. Agnes,* the *Ode to a Nightingale,* and *Hyperion,* is to be attributed either to the intrinsic interest of the variations themselves or of that leap of the poetic mind which they serve to mark ; while the comparative freedom from foot-notes in the case of such work as *Otho the Great* and *The Cap and Bells* does not point to the absence of manuscript sources on which to draw, or to any failure to consult any or every source, but to the conviction that the variations are of little general interest, the works themselves being in the main of inferior texture.

In settling the text I have of course refrained from abandoning what is authorized, in any particular of the slightest consequence, without recording the counter-authority ; but I have not, as in my LIBRARY editions, sought to record every comma, capital, or typographical eccentricity (perhaps not Keats's after all), which I or the Press authorities have found it needful to amend for the sake of reasonable uniformity. "If these delights thy mind may move," the LIBRARY editions can be consulted in public libraries or picked up second-hand at a high price ; or, for a very small price, the "COMPLETE" *variorum* edition which I prepared for Messrs. Gowans and Gray of Glasgow may still be had. One not unusual editorial freedom, however, I have not permitted myself : when a reading is quoted from a manuscript, it has been my endeavour to cite the manuscript with the minutest accuracy ; and I trust it may not be found that I have in any instance been betrayed into representing Keats, or his brothers, or others of his transcribers, as having written anything but what they actually did write. If in the notes it has been needful to quote a word misspelt in the manuscript, I hope I have always got it printed with due inaccuracy ; and if I have so much as supplied a single letter obviously omitted by accident, I trust that the liberty has been duly indicated by the orthodox method of enclosure within brackets. But we are only mortals—the printers and I.

It seems to me that, in an edition of Keats intended to meet a popular demand among the educated classes, an attempt should be made to record precisely how and in what forms the text has come through the nineteenth century and reached his lovers and admirers in the twentieth.

As to the main body of printed authority for the text, the books had better be here mentioned with the customary bibliographical details. The volumes which Keats himself issued through the press are three. The contents of the first reappear in Keats's own order of arrangement as the text of the first fifty-three pages in the present edition ; and the book is cited in the foot-notes as *Poems 1817*. It was early in that year that this small volume was published.

The book, though worked in fours, is a foolscap octavo, each sheet of paper being cut in halves. It was issued in drab boards, with a back-label reading

"Keats's | Poems," and consists of a blank leaf, fly-title "Poems" in heavy black letter, with imprint on verso, " Printed by C. Richards, | No. 18, Warwick Street, Golden Square, London," title-page as given at the end of this Introduction, Dedication with a note on the verso, and pages 1 to 121 including the fly-titles to the Epistles, Sonnets, and *Sleep and Poetry*. There are head-lines in Roman capitals running throughout each section, recto and verso alike, (1) " Poems," (2) " Epistles," (3) "Sonnets," and (4) "Sleep and Poetry." The note after the Dedication is as follows :—

" [The Short Pieces in the middle of the Book, as | well as some of the Sonnets, were written at an | earlier period than the rest of the Poems.] "

Keats's second venture was the far more ambitious work *Endymion*, forming pages 55 to 168 of the present volume. There was talk of making the poem a quarto, with a portrait of Keats by Haydon ; but ultimately it appeared without a portrait, as a handsome octavo volume. It was done up in thick drab boards labelled at the back, "Keats's | Endymion. | *Lond. 1818*," and consisted of (1) fly-title "Endymion : | A Romance " with imprint at foot of verso, " Printed by T. Miller, Noble street Cheapside," (2) title-page (with its motto adapted from Shakespeare's seventeenth Sonnet), which will be found reproduced at the end of this Introduction, (3) the dedication reprinted as lines 3 to 6 of page 55 in the present edition, (4) the Preface (pages vii to ix), (5) an erratum leaf with sometimes one and sometimes five errata printed on the recto, and (6) 207 pages of text including the fly-titles to the four books. The head-line throughout is "Endymion" in Roman small capitals, the number of the Book being indicated in smaller letters at the inner corners, and the pages in Arabic figures as usual at the outer corners. The full page consists of twenty-two lines ; and the lines are numbered in tens in the margin, not every ten lines of verse, but every ten lines of print, so that when a fresh paragraph begins with a portion of a verse, that particular verse counts for two

lines. In numbering the lines for the present edition
I have of course counted by lines of verse.

The poet's third and last book of poems, the contents
of which, arranged in the order adopted by Keats,
occupy pages 169 to 279 of this edition, was issued in
12mo in the summer of 1820, put up in stout drab
boards like those of *Endymion*, with a back-label
"Lamia, Isabella, | &c. | — | 7s. 6d." It consists of half-
title, reading "Lamia, Isabella, | &c.," with imprint on
verso, "London : | Printed by Thomas Davison, White-
friars," title-page, as given (*post*) following that of
Endymion, Advertizement, Contents, and pages 1 to
199 including the half-titles to *Lamia, Isabella, The
Eve of St. Agnes*, the miscellaneous Poems, and *Hyperion*.
There are head-lines in Roman capitals running throughout each section, recto and verso alike: (1) "Lamia," (2)
"Isabella," (3) "Eve of St. Agnes," (4) "Poems," and (5)
"Hyperion." The pages are numbered in the usual way
with Arabic figures ; and in *Lamia* and *Hyperion* the
Parts and Books are marked at the inner side of the
head-line in smaller Roman capitals. On the verso of
page 199 the imprint of Davison is repeated ; and there
are eight pages of Taylor and Hessey's advertizements,
beginning with one of *Endymion*. A large part of the
contents of the volume still exists in the poet's manuscript ; and Professor Sidney Colvin possesses Richard
Woodhouse's Common-place book, described later on,
the contents of which bear largely on the poems in the
1820 publication. The following title for it, by the
way, is sketched in pencil on a blank page of the
manuscript book :

LAMIA

Hyperion, a Fragment,

ISABELLA

ST. AGNES' EVE,

and other poems.

The Advertizement prefixed to the published volume

(page 170 in this edition) appears to have been supplied by the publishers. In a copy shown to me by the late Canon Ainger, Keats had drawn his pen through and through this advertizement, writing at the head, "I had no part in this ; I was ill at the time." The statement about *Endymion* he had bracketed off from the rest ; and beneath it he had written " This is a lie ! " In connexion with this unusual vehemence of expression, it is no more than fair to mention that the Woodhouse Common-place book, used by the publishers when considering which of Keats's unpublished poems they would issue in 1820, records a vote against *Hyperion* ; and the inference is that they were induced by Keats's friends to publish the fragment after all.

In regard to the remainder of Keats's Poetical Works, those, namely, which are not to be found in the three volumes published by himself, an endeavour is here made to arrange the whole under one chronology, although it is not possible to adhere literally to the scheme, in view of the fact that, while *Otho the Great* was being composed, other poems were also written, and must not, obviously, be inserted between the scenes of the tragedy. We have not, however, yet completed the tale of the *editiones principes* of Keats's Poetry, seeing that his *posthuma* have from time to time been issued in substantive volumes as distinguished from the mere extension of editions of his works. The first in importance, as in date, of these posthumous *editiones principes* is the late Lord Houghton's invaluable contribution of 1848. In 1833, at the villa of Walter Savage Landor " on the beautiful hill-side of Fiesole," Lord Houghton, then Mr. Richard Monckton Milnes, had met Charles Armitage Brown, whose name is now universally associated with that of Keats ; he had previously learnt much about the poet from Joseph Severn, then still (as to the end) at Rome ; and he now found that Brown, having carefully guarded the literary remains of Keats, intended to publish them in two or three years on returning to

England. Brown returned, got forward with his preparations, wrote his biographical account of Keats, and had arranged for publication, when he suddenly decided to emigrate to New Zealand. This he did, leaving his material for Lord Houghton to make use of, "for the purpose of vindicating the character and advancing the fame" of Keats.

Charles Cowden Clarke, Edward Holmes, George Felton Mathew, and Henry Stephens, helped the biographer and editor with their recollections; John Hamilton Reynolds "contributed the rich store of his correspondence"; Charles Wentworth Dilke and William Haslam supported the undertaking with letters and reminiscences; to John Taylor and James Augustus Hessey, Keats's friendly and helpful publishers, and Charles Ollier, who in a less friendly and helpful manner had preceded them in that office, Lord Houghton was "indebted for willing co-operation"; and Mr. Jeffrey, who had married George Keats's widow, contributed, in a very slovenly and misleading way, a great mass of letters and *data* which, notwithstanding his lack of judgment, of experience, and of thoroughness, were of quite extraordinary value. The result founded on all these aids and communications was given to the world in the year 1848, in two of those handy and agreeable volumes which, printed by Messrs. Bradbury and Evans, issued in a steady stream for some years from the house of Edward Moxon of Dover Street—the volumes which we associate with the names of Shelley, Wordsworth, Landor, Hood, Tennyson, and the Brownings.

When the book made its appearance, one of the main literary supporters of the undertaking, who had known intimately both Keats and Brown, was amused as well as nettled at the *rôle* claimed for Brown as the "generous protector" of Keats, and left a somewhat caustic note on the subject in his copy of Lord Houghton's work, the title-page of which he decorated with the following couplet from *The Rosciad*:

Appearances to save his only care ;
So things *seem* right, no matter what they are.

Charles Wentworth Dilke, in quoting thus epigram-
matically from Churchill, did not of course mean
to apply the couplet literally ; but the inscription and
other notes show how advanced his views of editorial
obligation were ; for Lord Houghton can scarcely be
said to have carried editorial licence beyond the limits
then usual.

Lord Houghton's first contribution to Keats literature, published in the best of company, may be
bibliographically described as consisting of two
volumes, foolscap octavo, bound in purple-brown cloth,
upright-straight-grained, blind-blocked on the sides
with the same severe floral-scroll design that appears
on the fourth edition of Tennyson's Poems (two
volumes, 1846), *The Princess* (1847), *In Memoriam*
(1850), Landor's *Hellenics* (1847), and many others.
The colour is the same as that of the cloth used
for several editions of *In Memoriam*. The Keats
volumes are gilt-lettered across the back, "Life |
Letters &c. | of Keats. | Vol. I.[II.]" The title-pages
are as follows :—

LIFE,
LETTERS, AND LITERARY REMAINS,
OF
JOHN KEATS.

EDITED BY

RICHARD MONCKTON MILNES.

IN TWO VOLUMES.

VOL. I. [II.]

LONDON:
EDWARD MOXON, DOVER STREET.
1848.

The half-titles read "Life, Letters, &c. | of | John Keats." Their versos are blank; but those of the titles have the central imprint "London: | Bradbury and Evans, Printers, Whitefriars." In volume I, pages v to vii contain a dedication to Francis (afterwards Lord) Jeffrey, page viii is blank, the preface extends from page ix to page xix, page xx is blank, and page 1 starts with a dropped head reading "Life and Letters | of | John Keats." There are 288 pages of the text, with head-lines reading "Life and Letters of" on the versos and "John Keats" on the rectos, save on page 288, where the legend appears in full: the printers' imprint is repeated at the foot. The volume has for frontispiece a print from a steel plate engraved by H. Robinson after the well-known half-length portrait of Keats by Severn, three-quarter face, seated behind a table with an open book before him, the right hand resting on the book, the left supporting the chin and cheek (fingers closed), while the elbow rests on the table. An eight-page catalogue of Moxon's publications is generally found in perfect copies, inserted within the glazed primrose end-paper of the recto cover.

Of volume II the text also starts with a dropped head worded as in volume I, with which it is uniform as to head-lines up to page 108. Then there is a half-title, "Literary Remains," dividing the posthumous poetry from the Life and Letters; and the poetry itself occupies the remainder of the volume, ending on page 306, and bearing distinctive head-lines. At the foot of page 306 the printers' imprint recurs; and facing it is a list, headed "Poetry," of volumes sold by Moxon: the verso of this is blank. The frontispiece to this second volume is a well lithographed fac-simile of a holograph manuscript,—the song "Shed no tear— O shed no tear."

These fascinating volumes have no index of any kind, or even so much as a table of contents; but besides the Literary Remains forming the bulk of the second volume, many poems and fragments are scattered through the first volume, some embodied in letters, and some appended at the close of the volume, after the Notes on Milton there reprinted from the scarce American periodical *The Dial*. A list of these poems is proper to this place. The page column indicates the position in Lord Houghton's volumes.

POEMS IN VOLUME I

POEMS IN VOLUME II

(in the continuation of the Life, &c.)

Moxon had already in 1846 reprinted, in his delightful paper-covered 24mo. series of Poets, Smith's edition
of Keats's *Poetical Works* (1841) with a trifling change
of order in the contents ; and he now proceeded to
publish a reissue in foolscap octavo to accompany
the *Life, Letters, and Literary Remains.* The 1851
issue of this book (" a new edition ") has no biography,
but contains the same portrait print as the *Life &c.*
Since that time no substantive volume of fresh poems
by Keats has been published ; but additions have been
made in one issue after another until the mass has
grown very considerably.

One more posthumous *editio princeps* remains to be
dealt with. In the long journal-letter which Keats
wrote to his brother and sister-in-law in America in
December 1818 and January 1819, occurs the following
passage, headed " Friday " simply, but belonging probably to Christmas Day 1818 :—

" I think you knew before you left England, that my
next subject would be ' the fall of Hyperion.' I went
on a little with it last night, but it will take some time
to get into the vein again. I will not give you any
extracts because I wish the whole to make an impression. I have however a few Poems which you will
like, and I will copy them out on the next sheet."

This no doubt relates to the fragment of *Hyperion*
in direct narration, as ultimately published in 1820.
The poem in that form, it will be remembered,
was abandoned finally in August 1819 ; but by the
end of the year he was at work on an attempt to recast it in a wholly different form. This took place
at Wentworth Place: in the morning he sat with
Brown and worked at *The Cap and Bells*: in the

evening, *fide* Brown, he had a room to himself "and was deeply engaged in re-modelling the fragment of *Hyperion* into the form of a vision."

This remarkable production (pages 443–457 of this edition) was mentioned in the *Life, Letters*, &c. (1848) as a recast, but remained in manuscript until Lord Houghton contributed it to the third volume of the *Bibliographical and Historical Miscellanies* of the Philobiblon Society (1856–7), in doubt whether it was a recast or a draft. A few copies of it were also printed in pamphlet form apart from the *Miscellanies*. The fragment was afterwards published in the Appendix to Lord Houghton's new edition of *The Life and Letters of John Keats* issued in 1867 by Moxon & Co. On that occasion it was said to be without doubt the first draft. But Lord Houghton must have failed to consult again his manuscript memoir by Charles Brown, wherein the "Vision" is distinctly said to be a late reconstruction. It will be seen that, although a great deal of the "Vision" is special to the new poem, there are large passages from the epic version of *Hyperion*. A comparison of passages which are substantially identical while varying in detail perhaps affords the most astounding instance on record of the loss of artistic power and perception under physical decay and mental agony. The conception of Moneta, though not artistically on Keats's highest level, has a touching grandeur of its own, and, apart from the detrimental treatment of the *Hyperion* fragment, is highly notable. As regards the holograph manuscript of the "Vision," Lord Houghton told me in 1883 that a mystery attached to its fate: it was lent for some purposes of the 1867 reprint; and the owner failed to recover it. I have attempted to trace it further, but in vain.

The Philobiblon Society's separate print of course ranks among the *editiones principes* of Keats's writings; and it is perhaps the scarcest of all. It is a pott quarto pamphlet of twenty-four pages printed on Saunders's unbleached hand-made paper, water-marked "1856."

There is no title-page ; but there is a half-title reading
" Another Version of Keats's ' Hyperion '." Pages 3
and 4 are occupied by the following note :—

> " Another Version of Keats's
> ' Hyperion.'

" The MS. of the following Poem was given to me by
Mr. Brown, the friend and protector of John Keats,
together with the other *Literary Remains* which I
published in 1848. Is it the original sketch out of
which the earlier part of the printed poem was composed, or is it the commencement of a reconstruction
of the whole ? I have no external evidence to decide
this question ; but it seems to me that, in either case,
this fragment well deserves preservation. If it is the
first composition out of which a portion of the printed
poem was selected, it is most remarkable, as showing
the affluence and self-command of the genius that could
afford to lay by passages of so much originality and
splendour as, on this supposition, have here been
cancelled. If, on the other hand, it is the beginning
of a new version of the whole Poem, we may equally
admire the imagination which was not content with
what had been already accomplished, and, not satisfied
with completing the work as it stood, desired to
improve its scope and enlarge its proportions. There
is, indeed, no lover of the writings of this wonderful
youth who will not be glad to see this production for
its own sake, and apart from all discussion as to
its intention ; but the problem of the priority of the
two poems—both fragments, and both so beautiful—
may afford a wide field for ingenious and critical conjecture. R. M. MILNES."

The poem starts on page 5 with a dropped head
reading "Hyperion, a Vision" ; but the head-lines, from
page 6 to page 24, read on the versos, " Another version
of," and on the rectos "Keats's Hyperion." Concerning
the title of this reconstruction, I do not find much
evidence properly so called. As we have seen, Brown

is the authority for the now established fact that Keats
attempted the task of "re-modelling the fragment of
Hyperion into the form of a Vision"; but it does not
appear that he called it "Hyperion, a Vision." Lord
Houghton contributed it to the Philobiblon Society's
Collections as "Another Version" of the fragment, and
used the description "A Vision" on one page. The
almost invariably accurate Woodhouse calls it "The
Fall of Hyperion, a Dream"—not casually or descrip-
tively, but as the title of an unpublished work from
which he inscribes some extracts in a collection of
quotations from various authors prefixed to his interleaved copy of *Endymion*.

Many of Keats's poems appeared first in periodicals;
and mention should here be made of *The Examiner* (in
Leigh Hunt's time), *Annals of the Fine Arts* (1817–20),
Hunt's *Literary Pocket-Book*, his *Indicator*, *The Gem*,
a *Literary Annual*, edited by Thomas Hood, *Hood's
Magazine*, *The Dial*, *The Athenæum*, *Notes and Queries*,
and *The Century Guild Hobby Horse*, all of which are
among the textual sources laid under contribution for
the present edition. And it should also be mentioned
that, in the year 1877, a great mass of new material,
mixed with old and frightfully garbled, appeared in
the New York *World* (June 26 and 27). The Manuscript source of most of it is now in what may
properly be called the HOUGHTON-CREWE KEATS COL-
LECTION.

Passing now from Printed to Manuscript material
in this survey of authorities and their history, I
think I may say that the sources of the present edition
include practically everything that is known. In
giving a somewhat full account of this material it will
be necessary to compromise more or less as between
the order in which the material was gradually un-
earthed and the order in which the final results
obtained from it appear in this edition.

First and foremost, Lord Houghton, always generous,
not only allowed me to make free with all his Keats

publications for the purposes of my previous editions, but tendered the use of his manuscript papers also, though at the time I was not able to make the full examination of them at Fryston Hall which he offered to allow. His generosity, however, has been continued by his son, the Earl of Crewe, who has permitted a free use of the papers by Professor Colvin, Mr. Ernest de Sélincourt, and myself; and between us three workers there has, of course, been reciprocity of accommodation. The HOUGHTON-CREWE KEATS COLLECTION is now much increased in value both by addition and by rearrangement.

Sir Charles Dilke's collection includes many things, of the utmost consequence, both to the text of the writings of Keats and to the completeness of illustrative detail. Letters from the poet, books formerly possessed by him, numerous letters from George Keats, Severn, and Brown, and a great mass of related documents, were placed unreservedly in my hands by Sir Charles, and figure conspicuously throughout the volumes of my previous editions.

Important papers of Severn fell some twenty-four years ago into the hands of Mr. Henry Sotheran of Piccadilly; and I had the advantage of going over them all and making full collations, either by Mr. Sotheran's kindness or by that of later owners of such as passed from the Piccadilly establishment before I examined the collection. To one or two of these papers it will be necessary to recur later.

A document of exceptional interest used at that time was a copy-book into which Tom Keats had copied, before publication, a number of the poems forming the 1817 volume. This book contained transcripts of the *Specimen of an Induction*, *Calidore*, *On receiving a Curious Shell*, *Imitation of Spenser*, and several of the Sonnets. It had passed into the hands of John Scott, editor of *The London Magazine*, who was killed in a duel with a Mr. Christie arising out of the abominable "Cockney School" articles in *Blackwood's Magazine*.

Tom Keats had visited Scott in Paris ; and it may have been on that occasion that the copy-book came into Scott's possession.

A more important document acquired by myself about the same time, and still in my collection, was a curious volume originally used for writing fair copies of poems in—poems from various hands. At a later stage it was converted into a scrap-book—newspaper cuttings and other curiosities being stuck over pages of George Keats's writing ; and in one part several of George's copies from John's poems are inserted, having at their head the autograph manuscript of the sonnet to Mrs. George Keats (when Miss Wylie), whom I suppose to have been the owner of the book, seeing that it contains among its curiosities the original parchment commission of James Wylie, as adjutant of the Fifeshire Regiment of Fencible Infantry, signed by George III. in 1794.

The numerous letters to and from Haydon, preserved in the journals of the painter, filled up important blanks and supplied a great number of additions and corrections for Keats's Poetry as well as his Letters.

Most of Keats's principal works and a great mass of the minor poems have been revised by me from manuscript sources ; and not the least of the fortunate chances attending my efforts was the discovery of Richard Woodhouse's copy of the published *Endymion*, in which were noted, not only the variations of the final manuscript from the printed text, but also those of the first draft, which had not itself come to the surface. Woodhouse was an ardent admirer of Keats and an enthusiastic student of his works, as well as an excellent scholar and most judicious adviser. His copy of *Endymion* was interleaved, seemingly while Keats was still alive, and the textual differences were noted down in the most business-like and elaborate manner, while the pages bear many remarks and hints of a learned and acute kind, whereof I have not scrupled to avail myself. So far as regards the largest of

Keats's poems, this book has been of more service than either of the other printed copies of *Endymion* used by me, namely Sir Charles Dilke's copy and one in my own possession with a number of autograph corrections. But Sir Charles Dilke's copy has a quantity of manuscript poems bound up at the end ; and these have yielded a good deal of assistance in textual work. Numerous readings marked *Dilke* in the foot-notes are from that volume.

In Woodhouse's copy of *Endymion*, there is a note against the passage " so I will begin " &c., line 39, Book I, to the effect that the poem was begun in the spring of 1817 and finished in the winter of 1817–18 ; and in the title-page he has inserted *April* before 1818. The statement corresponds with Keats's own record of May 1817 that he was busying himself at Margate with the commencement of *Endymion*. This reference cannot of course be to the same *Endymion* ("I stood tip-toe upon a little hill ") that he expected to finish in one more attack when he wrote to Clarke in December 1816. Probably the conception referred to by Lord Houghton (ALDINE edition, page xvii) as "long germinating in his fancy " really took bodily form and substance, and that substance was wholly rejected, when Keats came within the radius of Haydon's heroic art propaganda, for the design on an ambitious scale which the next spring was to see in print. Woodhouse records that at the end of the first draft is written " Burford Bridge, Nov. 28, 1817." His statement as to the month of issue scarcely does more than confirm the record of the series of documents bearing on this point published by Lord Houghton. Thus, the first book was in the publisher's hands by January 1818, and the last was copied out by the 14th of March ; the original Preface, rejected upon the unfavourable verdict of Reynolds and others of Keats's friends, is dated the 19th of March ; the Preface as published is dated the 10th of April, and went, it seems, in a letter to Reynolds of that date.

The title-page originally devised was as follows :—

ENDYMION.

A ROMANCE.

By JOHN KEATS.

"The stretched metre of an antique song."
Shakespeare's Sonnets.

In favour of the simple dedication as printed in the book, the following had been rejected :—

INSCRIBED,

WITH EVERY FEELING OF PRIDE AND REGRET

AND WITH "A BOWED MIND,"

TO THE MEMORY OF

THE MOST ENGLISH OF POETS EXCEPT SHAKESPEARE,

THOMAS CHATTERTON.

The original preface referred to above reads as follows:—

ORIGINAL PREFACE REJECTED ON CONSIDERATION.

IN a great nation, the work of an individual is of so little importance ; his pleadings and excuses are so uninteresting ; his "way of life" such a nothing, that a Preface seems a sort of impertinent bow to strangers who care nothing about it.

A Preface, however, should be down in so many words ; and such a one that by an eye-glance over the type the Reader may catch an idea of an Author's modesty, and non-opinion of himself—which I sincerely hope may be seen in the few lines I have to write, notwithstanding many proverbs of many ages old which men find a great pleasure in receiving as gospel.

About a twelvemonth since, I published a little book of verses ; it was read by some dozen of my friends who lik'd it ; and some dozen whom I was unacquainted with, who did not.

Now, when a dozen human beings are at words with another dozen, it becomes a matter of anxiety to side with one's friends—more especially when excited thereto by a great love of Poetry. I fought under disadvantages. Before I began I had no inward feel of being able to finish ; and as I proceeded my steps were all uncertain. So this Poem must rather be considered as an endeavour than a thing accomplished ; a poor prologue to what, if I live, I humbly hope to do. In duty to the Public I should have kept it back for a year or two, knowing it to be so faulty : but I really cannot do so,—by repetition my favourite passages sound vapid in my ears, and I would rather redeem myself with a new Poem should this one be found of any interest.

I have to apologize to the lovers of simplicity for touching the spell of loneliness that hung about Endymion ; if any of my lines plead for me with such people I shall be proud.

It has been too much the fashion of late to consider men bigoted and addicted to every word that may chance to escape their lips ; now I here declare that I have not any particular affection for any particular phrase, word, or letter in the whole affair. I have written to please myself, and in hopes to please others, and for a love of fame ; if I neither please myself, nor others, nor get fame, of what consequence is Phraseology ?

I would fain escape the bickerings that all Works not exactly in chime bring upon their begetters—but this is not fair to expect, there must be conversation of some sort and to object shows a man's consequence. In case of a London drizzle or a Scotch mist, the following quotation from Marston may perhaps 'stead me as an umbrella for an hour or so : "let it be the curtesy of my peruser rather to pity my self-hindering labours than to malice me."

One word more—for we cannot help seeing our own affairs in every point of view—should any one call my dedication to Chatterton affected I answer as followeth : "Were I dead, sir, I should like a Book dedicated to me."

TEIGNMOUTH,
March 19*th*, 1818.

On the 27th of April, Keats wrote to Taylor apologizing for giving him "all the trouble" of *Endymion*, and adding, apparently in allusion to that poem, "The book pleased me much. It is very free from faults ; and, although there are one or two words I should wish replaced, I see in many places an improvement greatly to the purpose." The measure of Keats's fluency in composition may be judged by observing the alterations recorded in Book I. Of that Book there appears to have been but one manuscript, written on sheets of quarto foolscap paper, and considerably altered before going to press. The other three Books were written into a blank book and afterwards copied on quarto foolscap uniform with that used for Book I. Hence the printer's copy (the quarto manuscript) shows much more revision in Book I than elsewhere. The quarto manuscript remained in the Taylor family till 1897, when it was sold at auction by Messrs. Sotheby, Wilkinson and Hodge, and was bought by a bookseller. With that manuscript I collated the printed text throughout before issuing the Library edition, the precious holograph being courteously lent to me by Mr. Taylor ; but the variations given in Books II, III, and IV from the draft, I took from Woodhouse's manuscript annotations, not having yet traced the holograph draft of these three books. The manuscript of the rejected Preface (first published by Lord Houghton in 1867 in the *Life and Letters of John Keats*) was formerly in the collection of Dr. John Webster, sometime M.P. for Aberdeen. It was attached to the rejected title-page and dedication, the whole consisting of six quarto leaves evidently detached from the Taylor manuscript, which, if I remember rightly, did not begin in Keats's autograph, but had at least one leaf in another hand. The rejected Preface, when I saw it in 1890, showed some cancellings; but I have mislaid any notes I may have taken of them; and, since I saw it, it has been sold by auction and gone I know not whither.

Keats's holograph manuscript of *Lamia*, from which the poem was actually printed, consists of twenty-six leaves, foolscap folio, generally written upon one side only. It is a carefully finished manuscript, finally revised for the press. The extract from Burton does not figure in it; but there is the following foot-note on page 1 :—"The ground work of this story will be found in Burton's 'Anatomy of Melancholy' *Part* 3. *Sect.* 3. *Memb.* 1*st Subs.* 1*st.*" It was lent to me for use in connexion with the Library edition of Keats, having remained in the Taylor family; and it was disposed of by public auction at the same time as the manuscript of *Endymion*, namely in 1897. The fragment in the HOUGHTON-CREWE collection referred to at pages 182 *et seq.* consists of two leaves from a draft of Part II of *Lamia*.

Of the bulk of *Isabella or the Pot of Basil* I had no manuscript authority before me in preparing the library edition of 1883 and only Woodhouse's transcript for the reissue of 1889 : nevertheless, that is the next poem to be dealt with now.

In a letter from Teignmouth to Reynolds dated the 27th of April, 1818, Keats says, "I have written for my folio Shakespeare, in which there are the first few stanzas of my 'Pot of Basil.' I have the rest here, finished, and will copy the whole out fair shortly, and George will bring it you. The compliment is paid by us to Boccace, whether we publish or no . . ." As the folio Shakespeare, now in Sir Charles Dilke's hands, contains no stanzas of *Isabella*, it is to be presumed they were only loose in the book. Again on the 3rd of May 1818, Keats writes to Reynolds, "I have

written to George for the first stanzas of 'Isabel.' I
shall have them soon, and will copy the whole out for
you." And, in a letter to Bailey dated the 10th of
June, he says, "I want to read you my 'Pot of Basil.'"
This all points to the recent completion of the poem ;
and Lord Houghton records on the authority of Brown
that it was only just completed when the friends
started on their Scotch tour in June 1818. On the 14th
of February 1819, he promised to send the poem out
to his brother George, with other recent work. It is
necessary to be particular about this point, because
Leigh Hunt when reviewing the 1820 volume, made
the unaccountable statement that the poems in this
volume "were almost all written four years ago, when
the author was but twenty." The allusion to Boccaccio
is connected with a project of Keats and Reynolds
to issue a volume of tales versified from that author.

No doubt Keats fulfilled his promise to send the
manuscript of *Isabella* to Reynolds before he started
on his Scotch tour with Brown. After his return he
appears to have met Reynolds and discussed the poem
with him ; for, in a letter dated "Wedn. morn." and
post-marked "Oct. 14," Reynolds speaks of having seen
Keats "yesterday." The contents of the letter point
to the autumn of 1818 ; and, though the year-date of
the post-mark was torn off (with a few words of the
text) in opening the sealed letter, the almanac tells us
that the 14th of October was a Wednesday in 1818.
The holograph is said to be in the possession of
Mr. W. H. Arnold of New York, who allowed the
letter to appear in *The Century Magazine* for October
1895, where it reads thus :—

"My dear Keats : I was most delighted at seeing you
yesterday, for I hardly knew how I was to meet with
you, situated as you are and confined as I am. I wish
I could have stayed longer with you. As to the poem,
I am of all things anxious that you should publish it,
for its completeness will be a full answer to all the

ignorant malevolence of cold, lying Scotchmen and
stupid Englishmen. The overweening struggle to
oppress you only shows the world that so much of
endeavour cannot be directed to nothing. Men do not
set their muscles and strain their sinews to break a
straw. I am confident, Keats, that the ' Pot of Basil '
hath that simplicity and quiet pathos which are of
sure sovereignty over all hearts. I must say that it
would delight me to have you prove yourself to the
world what we know you to be—to have you annul
The Quarterly Review by the best of all answers.
When I see you I will give you the Poem, and pray
look it over with that eye to the *littlenesses* which the
world are so fond of excepting to (though I confess,
with that word altered which I mentioned, I see
nothing that can be cavilled at). And let us have the
Tale put forth, now that an interest is aroused. One or
two of your sonnets you might print, I am sure. And
I know that I may suggest to you which, because you
can decide as you like after[ward. You] will remember
that we were [to print?] together. I give over all
intention, and you ought to be alone. I can never
write anything now—my mind is taken the other
way. But I shall set my heart on having you high,
as you ought to be. Do *you* get Fame, and I shall
have it in being your affectionate and steady friend.
There is no one I am more interested in, and there is
no one that I have more pleasure in communicating
my own happiness to. You will gratify me much by
letting me have, whenever you have leisure, copies of
what you write; for *more than myself* have a sincere
interest in you. When shall I see you, and when
shall I go with you to Severn's ?

      Your ever affectionate

Wedn. morn.   J. H. REYNOLDS."

Two of the tales from Boccaccio versified by
Reynolds were published in *The Garden of Florence*,
&c. (1821). In view of the unachieved scheme of

joint authorship, the following sentences from the
Preface to Reynolds's volume should stand associated
with his letter and with *Isabella*:—

"The stories from Boccaccio (The Garden of Florence
and The Ladye of Provence) were to have been associated with tales from the same source, intended to
have been written by a friend; but illness on his part,
and distracting engagements on mine, prevented us from
accomplishing our plan at the time; and Death now,
to my deep sorrow, has frustrated it for ever! He,
who is gone, was one of the very kindest friends I
possessed, and yet he was not kinder perhaps to me,
than to others. His intense mind and powerful
feeling would, I truly believe, have done the world
some service, had his life been spared—but he was of
too sensitive a nature—and thus he was destroyed!
One story he completed, and that is to me now the
most pathetic poem in existence!"

The holograph of *Isabella* in the British Museum
volume (Egerton 2780) is called simply *The Pot of
Basil*. It is probably the one sent to Reynolds and
duly returned by him. Mr. R. A. Potts formerly
possessed what would seem to be two fragments of
the original draft. This manuscript, which was
collated for the LIBRARY edition of 1883, is of stanzas
xxx to xl, exclusive of stanza xxxii; two leaves, one
shorter than the other by the length of a stanza,
written upon both sides of the paper, and probably
having lost stanza xxxii with stanza xxix at the back
of it by a stroke of those generous scissors wherewith
manuscripts of Keats were distributed by Severn,
formerly the owner of these fragments. The readings
marked *MS. fragment* are from this.

In Woodhouse's "Common-place book" is a transcript from an autograph manuscript of *Isabella* with
notes and corrections, some in the poet's writing and
some in other handwritings. It would be almost safe
to assume that any variation of Woodhouse's version
from the printed text is a genuine reading incidental

to the stage of the composition which had been reached when the holograph was transcribed; but as a matter of fact the transcript was clearly made from the very holograph now in the Museum. At the close of the Woodhouse transcript are inscribed the words "Written at Teignmouth in the Spring of 1818 at the suggestion of J. H. R."

The Eve of St. Agnes is the next poem to be dealt with. In a letter to George Keats and his wife dated the 14th of February [1819], Keats says that he took with him to Chichester, where he had been staying in January, "some of the thin paper, and wrote on it a little poem called 'St. Agnes' Eve,' which you will have as it is, when I have finished the blank part of the rest for you." Lord Houghton says the poem "was begun on a visit in Hampshire, at the commencement of this year [1819] and finished on his return to Hampstead." On the 5th of September 1819, Keats wrote to Taylor from Winchester that he was "occupied in revising 'St. Agnes' Eve,' and studying Italian."

A manuscript of *The Eve of St. Agnes*, wanting the first seven stanzas, was in the Locker-Lampson collection. It was among the relics which passed from the late Joseph Severn to a Dr. Valeriani, and which were afterwards bought and sold by Messrs. Sotheran of Piccadilly (see *ante*). This manuscript, collated for the LIBRARY edition of 1883, is written in double columns on both sides of very thin oblong paper, presumably that taken to Chichester, and shows abundant and extensive revisions and corrections. Nothing could be more interesting as a study of a great poet's way of work. It is possible that the opening stanzas were separated to be sent to Mr. Taylor in support of Keats's complaint that a liberty had been taken with the text of the seventh stanza; but, as the Woodhouse Common-place book, containing a transcript of the poem, was in use at the publisher's house and could have been appealed to, it is perhaps more probable that Severn cut the stanzas off for an autograph collector. Fortunately the Woodhouse transcript seems to have been made from the Locker-Lampson holograph before it was mutilated, and may be held to supply for critical purposes the missing seven stanzas. It also supplies a suppressed one between the published stanzas iii and iv. Woodhouse's divergences from the final state of the holograph are, generally, of a trifling kind. The holograph is difficult to read completely; and there was room for two interpretations of the author's final meaning here and there. Moreover, Woodhouse was in communication with Keats, and may have got an oral change or two, as for instance in the matter of the hero's name, which he gives as Lionel in his transcript and never writes Porphyro, though the holograph shows Keats to have been wavering between Lionel and Porphyro.

The transcript in the Museum Keats manuscript book, made by George Keats, was evidently from a different holograph. Hence it may be presumed that, when Keats was "occupied in revising" the poem in September 1819, he was making a fresh copy from the very rough draft already described. In collating the whole of these manuscripts with Keats's published text, I have noted many variations of no great consequence in themselves in order to give a reasonable insight into the composition of this deservedly much-prized poem.

The Pocket Dante mentioned at page 349 in connexion with the Sonnet *On a Dream* &c. is in my own collection: it contains a holograph draft of that sonnet and a copy by Miss Brawne of Keats's last sonnet.

A holograph manuscript of the Stanzas beginning "In a drear-nighted December" was sold at Sotheby's in June 1876 and purchased by Mr. Charles Law, who lent it to me at the time for collation: it is the manuscript referred to at page 338.

The letters of Keats to his sister, which form so large a proportion of the letters first published by me in 1883, threw a flood of new light on his character, and had also their contributions to and bearings on the mass and text of his verse. These were lent to me by Señora Fanny Keats de Llanos for the purposes of my edition of that year, and, though not bequeathed by her to the nation as a memorial of her illustrious brother, were — all but three or four — presented after her death to the British Museum by her daughter, Señorita Rosa Llanos y Keats.

Thus far my survey has been mainly of the material available up to 1883. After the LIBRARY edition of that year was published other workers put forth books by and about Keats based more or less on original material. First came an American issue of Lord Houghton's edition of the poetry, together with a volume of letters, superintended by Mr. J. G. Speed, who, being a grandson of George Keats, had access to some of the papers formerly preserved at Louisville in Kentucky, and was enabled to publish one new letter of considerable interest as well as several passages omitted from previous printed versions, and a *fac-simile* of the holograph draft of the lines, "Unfelt, unheard, unseen."

Later still Mr. Colvin's admirable volume for the MEN OF LETTERS SERIES was written and brought out. It first appeared in 1887. Not only is it, as an appreciation of Keats's character and works, highly valuable ; but it is based upon material of which much had not then (and some has not yet) been published. Of much of this material Mr. Colvin gave me the benefit of consultation at first hand for the purposes of a revision of my Library edition published in 1889 and of the volume entitled *Poetry and Prose by John Keats* published the next year.

The following is Mr. Colvin's own account of the special material used by him with which I am now particularly concerned.

" In addition to printed materials I have made use of the following unprinted, viz. :—

"I. Houghton MSS. Under this title I refer to the contents of an album from the library at Fryston

Hall, in which the late Lord Houghton bound up a quantity of the materials he had used in the preparation of the 'Life and Letters,' as well as of correspondence concerning Keats addressed to him both before and after the publication of his book. The chief contents are the manuscript memoir of Keats by Charles Brown, which was offered by the writer in vain to *Galignani*, and I believe other publishers; transcripts by the same hand of a few of Keats's poems; reminiscences or brief memoirs of the poet by his friends Charles Cowden Clarke, Henry Stephens, George Felton Mathew, Joseph Severn, and Benjamin Bailey; together with letters from all the above, from John Hamilton Reynolds, and several others. For the use of this collection, without which my work must have been attempted to little purpose, I am indebted to the kindness of its owner, the present Lord Houghton.[1]

"II. Woodhouse MSS. A. A common-place book in which Richard Woodhouse, the friend of Keats and of his publishers Messrs. Taylor and Hessey, transcribed—as would appear from internal evidence, about midsummer, 1819—the chief part of Keats's poems at that date unpublished. The transcripts are in many cases made from early drafts of the poems: some contain gaps which Woodhouse has filled up in pencil from later drafts: to others are added corrections, or suggestions for corrections, some made in the hand of Mr. Taylor and some in that of Keats himself.

"III. Woodhouse MSS. B. A note-book in which the same Woodhouse has copied — evidently for Mr. Taylor, at the time when that gentleman was meditating a biography of the poet—a number of letters addressed by Keats to Mr. Taylor himself, to the transcriber, to Reynolds and his sisters, to Rice, and Bailey. Three or four of these letters, as well as portions of a few others, are unpublished.[2]

[1] Now Earl of Crewe.

[2] This statement was left standing, no doubt through oversight,

"Both the volumes last named were formerly the property of Mrs. Taylor, a niece by marriage of the publisher, and are now my own. A third note-book by Woodhouse, containing personal notices and recollections of Keats, was unluckily destroyed in the fire at Messrs Kegan Paul and Co's. premises in 1883 . . . "

Woodhouse's book of transcripts has been called a Common-place book because it happens that he used for his purpose a book published in 1811 by Taylor and Hessey for use as an ordinary Common-place book. This publication was a quarto volume of blank paper with a printed introduction, bound in brown grained calf; and it was entitled *The Literary Diary; or, Improved Common-place Book.* The preliminary matter consists of an explanatory treatise, an abridgment of the "Aurifodina" of Drexelius by Bishop Horne, and an "Index, formed with some variations, on the celebrated plan of Mr. Locke." All this machinery was of course wasted in the circumstances of the case ; but the book is of good paper ; and Woodhouse produced very workmanlike copies. The Common-place book contains transcripts of no fewer than thirty-two minor poems by Keats, besides those of *Isabella, The Eve of St. Agnes,* and *Hyperion.*

Under the title "A Shelf of Old Books," Mrs. Fields contributed to *Scribner's Magazine* for March 1888 an account of some books of personal interest owned by the late Mr. James T. Fields. One of these was a volume containing the poems of Coleridge, Shelley, and Keats, annotated in manuscript by Leigh Hunt. Inserted in this were a letter from Coleridge, a tiny business note from Shelley, and a fragment of Keats's holograph draft of "I stood tip-toe upon a little hill." It seems to follow line 37, and is duly described with all its cancellings set out in the COMPLETE edition, Volume I, page 208.

in the later issue of Mr. Colvin's book ; but both he and I have, since 1887, published the letters and passages referred to.

By 1889 Mr. Colvin had in his hands the holographs (which had been so badly dealt with in the New York *World*) of some of the most important of Keats's letters to George and Georgiana Keats in America, showing portentous variations from published texts and a surprising mass of unpublished or imperfectly published matter. Of these also I had the use in 1889. Since then (1891) Mr. Colvin has used the same material in his *Letters of John Keats to his Family and Friends*; and I myself published in a single volume in 1895 the whole of Keats's then known letters, chronologically arranged. These included several discovered after 1891.

In *The Athenæum* for the 23rd of January 1891, Professor Jenks of Melbourne in Victoria announced the discovery of that highly interesting little volume of Keats manuscripts, formerly belonging to George Keats and now in the British Museum. It contains holograph copies, by the poet, of *Isabella*, the Mermaid Tavern lines, and *The Eve of St. Mark*; and also transcripts of "Hence Burgundy, Claret, and Port," *The Eve of St. Agnes*, the Odes on Melancholy, to a Nightingale, and on a Grecian Urn, "Welcome joy, and welcome sorrow," "Where's the Poet?" the Ode to Autumn, the Robin Hood lines, some lines by L. E. L. on a portrait of Keats, three stanzas of *Adonais*, and a sonnet by the Honorable Mrs. Norton. Placed loosely in the volume were a transcript of the *Lines written in the Scotch Highlands* and some verses addressed by "an unknown bard" to one of George Keats's daughters. The book proved on careful collation to be most valuable. From it are the readings marked *Holograph* in the foot-notes to *Isabella*.

Why it has been suggested that the poems in George Keats's book not in the autograph of the poet are in that of his sister-in-law, it is difficult to imagine. Apart from the easily verifiable fact that all but one of them are in George Keats's writing, it is obvious on internal evidence that the hand is that of a man, and of that particular man who signed his name as George Keats on the first page. From the fact that he put the date 1820 under his signature, it is not very unsafe to deduce that, during the three weeks which the brothers passed together in January of that year, George got together all he could of John's unpublished work, taking such holographs as were available, and copying from his brother's or Brown's book when no detached copies were at hand. From the almost rustic appearance of the little volume, I judge that he got the papers bound together in Kentucky on his return. The binding is of strong brown leather (cowhide, I should say), roughly worked; and the book opens badly. The loose papers have now been fastened in at the end of the book, the Egerton arms have been stamped upon the original rough cover, and the book is officially known as Egerton Manuscript 2780.

The following data bear upon the manuscript authority for *Otho the Great*. Keats and Brown went to the Isle of Wight for a summer sojourn in 1819; and during the months of July and August the tragedy was written at intervals under very peculiar conditions. Those conditions are thus described by Brown in a note given by Lord Houghton in the ALDINE edition of 1876 :—" At Shanklin he undertook a difficult task; I engaged to furnish him with the title, characters, and dramatic conduct of a tragedy, and he was to enwrap it in poetry. The progress of this work was curious, for while I sat opposite to him, he caught my description of each scene entire, with the characters to be brought forward, the events, and everything connected with it. Thus he went on, scene after scene, never knowing nor inquiring into the scene which was to follow, until four acts were completed. It was then he required to know at once all the events that were to occupy the fifth act; I explained them to him, but, after a patient hearing and some thought, he insisted that many incidents in it were too humorous, or, as he termed them, too melodramatic. He wrote the fifth act in accordance with his own views, and so contented was I with his poetry that at the time, and for a long time after, I thought he was in the right." There are numerous references to this undertaking in Keats's published letters; but one in particular should be quoted here. It is in a letter to Mr. Dilke dated "Shanklin, August 2, 1819," and is as follows:— "Brown and I are pretty well harnessed again to our dog-cart. I mean the tragedy, which goes on sinkingly. We are thinking of introducing an elephant, but have not historical reference within reach to determine as to Otho's menagerie. When Brown first mentioned this I took it for a joke; however, he brings such plausible reasons, and discourses so eloquently on the dramatic effect, that I am giving it a serious consideration." This joke no doubt got to Brown's ears, even if Keats did not show it to him; for in *The Papers of a Critic* (1875), Volume I, page 9, Sir Charles Dilke gives the following extract from a letter dated ten days later (August 12, 1819), in which Brown, writing from the Isle of Wight to Mr. Dilke retorts with yet more boisterous jocularity:—" Keats is very industrious, but I swear by the prompter's whistle, and by the bangs of stage-doors, he is obstinately monstrous. What think you of Otho's threatening cold pig to the newly-married couple? He says the Emperor must have a spice of drollery. His introduction of Grimm's adventure, lying three days on his back for love, though it spoils the unity of time, is not out of the way for the character of Ludolf, so I have consented to it; but I cannot endure his fancy of making the princess blow up her hairdresser, for smearing her cheek with pomatum and spoiling her rouge. It may be natural, as he observes, but so might many things. However, such as it is, it has advanced to nearly the end of the fourth act."

From the fact that Keats wrote to Taylor on the

5th of September 1819 of having finished *Lamia* after
finishing *Otho the Great*, we may fairly regard the
Tragedy as having been done before the end of
August, even if it was taken out again and touched
up after that month. Brown certainly made at least
one copy of the whole play ; and it may be that Keats
touched up one transcript or more of his colleague's
making. George Keats wrote to Dilke in 1833 a
letter which has bearings on this subject, and of which
passages will be found in the General Appendix of the
Library edition of Keats's Works (Volume IV, pages
416–17). He had no reason to love Brown, though
he was grateful to him for befriending Keats. On the
Otho topic, George, who, by the bye, wrote much better
than he spelt, says :—

"When I left Hampstead I thought I had a
complete copy of *Otho*, John took some pa[ins] to
get the sheets together, copied what was deficient and
[made] the whole, as he said perfect, when I arrived
home I fo[und] many sheets missing, I suspected
Brown had abstracted [them]. I may not perhaps
do him justice, I may be meeting [out the] same
measure to him that he meeted [*sic*] to me, and
regret that any cause should have occur[r]ed to sever
so long a friendship between you. . . .

"I belive I must retract the above severity against
Brown, since writing it, I have been looking over
John's correspondence in which he dwells so much
on his kindness that I must perforce acquit, and *try*
to like him. Has any one got a copy of John's, unpublished works ? I suppose I must suspend my
curiosity untill I can cross the broad Atlantic."

In a later letter he says :—

"I have an imperfect copy of *Otho* much of it the
original composition, Brown has a perfect copy, and
has I believe some ownership right to it, perhaps one
half, will he furnish a copy, or sell his interest ? "

Some eight or ten years ago, a large fragment of
what is probably the holograph produced in the con-

ditions described by Brown was sent over from
America and passed into the hands of Mr. Thomas
Wise. It consisted of the first three acts and the
first scene of Act IV ; and, when I saw it, it was
bound as a separate volume. Among the papers of
the late Joseph Severn were the remains of a
manuscript from which he had cut some pieces,
to give away as specimens of Keats's handwriting.
The greater part of these remains were (1) the
second scene of Act IV, almost complete, and (2)
Act V, also almost complete : these are, no doubt,
substantially the complement of the bound manuscript ; but there was also among the Severn papers
a short fragment from the first scene of Act I, beginning with Conrad's speech (line 23) and ending with
line 44. Lord Houghton's text, first published among
the Literary Remains, varies greatly from the dis-
membered manuscript, as may be seen in the COMPLETE
KEATS from the results of collation. The small manuscript fragment of Act I, scene i, corresponds with
the first printed text ; but it may safely be assumed
that that is because Brown's copy so corresponded
and that it was from Brown's copy, handed over with
the rest of the Keats papers, that Lord Houghton
printed the play. Also, it seems quite clear that
there were other reasons than those found in Keats's
letters for acquitting Brown of the particular charge
of meanness retracted by George Keats : his brother
must have unwittingly taken the missing portions
of *Otho* to Italy with him. Hence, so far as that
affair is concerned, however much Brown may have
misjudged George Keats, he " leaves the court without
a stain upon his character."

The appearance of the large folio fragment from
America, which must be what George took back
with him in 1820, responds perfectly to Brown's
graphic description of the way in which the colla-
borators worked. Keats's writing generally goes boldly
and freely across the pages—the iambic line being

usually enough for the width of the paper. The names of the speakers are as a rule inserted on the verso of the leaf preceding that on which the dialogue is written upon the recto, so that an inch or so is thus added to the width of paper available for speech and name of speaker. In some instances Keats omitted to put the names: for example, at the beginning of the long variant of lines 16 to 121 in the first scene, the speakers' names had to be inserted in square brackets for seven speeches in the COMPLETE edition, where all *minutiæ* of the kind are recorded.

In collating the manuscript and printed texts I have adopted readings from each. The list of persons of the drama, printed by Lord Houghton, is not in the holograph Manuscript, in which GERSA and GERZA both stand as the name of the Prince of Hungary. Presumably the list was furnished by Brown.

Concerning the fine fragment *King Stephen*, Lord Houghton gives in the Aldine edition of 1876 the following note by Brown:—" As soon as Keats had finished *Otho the Great*, I pointed out to him a subject for an English historical tragedy in the reign of Stephen, beginning with his defeat by the Empress Maud and ending with the death of his son Eustace. He was struck with the variety of events and characters which must necessarily be introduced, and I offered to give, as before, their dramatic conduct. ' The play must open,' I began, ' with the field of battle, when Stephen's forces are retreating '——' Stop,' he cried, ' I have been too long in leading-strings ; I will do all this myself.' He immediately set about it, and wrote two or three scenes—about 170 lines." Brown's estimate was considerably within the mark, as there are about 193 lines. The manuscript fragment, which is in the HOUGHTON-CREWE collection, consists of eight leaves—three quarto leaves in the writing of Charles Armitage Brown and five folio leaves in Keats's writing. This manuscript I first examined in 1889. Brown's first leaf has on the recto the title—

King Stephen.
a fragment
of a tragedy,
by
John Keats
Novr 1819—

while the verso bears the following list of

Dramatis Personæ.

King Stephen.
Duke of Glocester
Earl of Chester.
Earl Baldwin.
The Empress Maud, or Matilda.

In Keats's text, however, Glocester is the Earl of
Glocester. So far as Scene I is concerned, Brown's
transcript corresponds with the published text save in
line 35, where he reads " Not twenty Earl of Chesters."
From the appearance of this manuscript it would seem
that, in November 1819, to throw off poetic utterances
in the finest and freest style was as easy to Keats as
the breathing of his native air.

Between the times at which the LIBRARY editions
and the COMPLETE edition appeared I obtained what is,
as far as I am aware, the only known authority for the
Sonnet beginning—

Before he went to feed with owls and bats.

This was preserved by Henry Stephens in a little
manuscript volume consisting of Keats's published
Poems of 1817 copied out with the addition of eight
fugitive pieces of which this Sonnet alone was still unpublished when the little volume, written by Stephens
in 1828, came into my hands. The Sonnet is doubtless
authentic, although poor, obscure, and possibly corrupt
in the last line.

It was during the same interval that I had an
opportunity of examining a holograph manuscript of
The Cap and Bells, wanting stanzas ix to xvi and lxxxii

to lxxxviii. I think it possible that Keats got it out to
work on it, after throwing it aside—for on the margin
of one of its pages is written the clearly late fragment
(page 486) beginning—

This living hand, now warm and capable ;

but he may have had it in his hand again merely to
lend to Hunt for *The Indicator*, in which a few stanzas
were printed. The variations and rejected readings
recorded in my foot-notes are of course from this manuscript. It is written with unusual inaccuracy: the
first stanza, for example, shows the forms "sleight" for
"slight," "woing" for "wooing," "warn" for "warm,"
and "smoth" for "smooth." Errors of this kind are
not recorded as a rule in the notes to this poem in
the COMPLETE edition, where however the results of a
scrupulous examination of the holograph are given.
This manuscript was sold by auction on the 5th of June
1902 ; and I examined it again : it had been further
mutilated since my previous examination, as I pointed
out in *The Athenæum* for the 14th of June : the sheet
containing the latter part of stanza xlv, stanzas xlvi
to li, and, I believe, the fragment "This living hand,"
had been removed in the interim ; but who now owns
either that sheet or the rest of the manuscript, I
cannot say.

Up to the time when the COMPLETE Keats was published, no holograph manuscript of *Hyperion* had yet
come to light ; but Woodhouse had had one copied into
his Common-place book before it was revised finally for
the impression of 1820, and had marked or got marked
in pencil some of the subsequent omissions and alterations. The transcript was made in what one would
feel confident in describing as the writing of a lawyer's
young clerk (Woodhouse was a lawyer): it is very
carefully made, and, I did not doubt, preserved much
of Keats's spelling, punctuation, and capitalling. It
may be noted as a measure of the transcriber's educa-
tion that *Mnemosyne* is invariably spelt *Muemosyne*

(Keats's *n*'s and *u*'s being more or less indistinctive).
In one case, Woodhouse found his boy out, and altered
the *u* to an *n*. There is scarcely any doubt that this
transcript was the "copy" sent to the printer in 1820
to set the poem up from. It has the usual indelible
printing-house finger-marks, and, as touched up with
the pencil, does not vary from the printed book in a
greater degree than would be likely, if we allow for the
usual amount of printing-house punctuation and a not
undue revision of proofs by the author. The rest of the
Common-place book was kept clean and secret while
Hyperion was thus "at press," by some arrangement of
sealing up ; for the remains of the sealing-wax are still
there on the pages before and after *Hyperion*.

Since the Complete Keats was published very little
unknown poetry by Keats has come to light, and none
of any consequence except a suppressed passage of *The
Fall of Hyperion* and a passage of *The Eve of St. Mark*,
to be mentioned presently. Of *Hyperion* as published
by Keats, however, the holograph manuscript, almost
complete, has been recovered and added to the British
Museum collection ; and a further examination of Lord
Houghton's papers by the Earl of Crewe has revealed
the presence of a transcript of *The Fall of Hyperion*,
made by Woodhouse's clerks and corrected by Woodhouse himself. The recovery of these two documents
—the holograph of *Hyperion* and the Woodhouse transcript of *The Fall of Hyperion*—formed together an event
of capital importance in relation to the text of Keats's
works ; and that event was signalized by the issue of a
large folio volume from the Clarendon Press, under the
editorship of Mr. Ernest de Sélincourt. The volume
contained a *fac-simile* of the holograph and a print of
the Woodhouse copy of *The Fall*, together with admirable introductions and notes by the editor.

In the meantime, on the 13th of May 1901, some
Keats manuscripts were disposed of in the autograph
collection of the late Townely Green. The Keats
items included (1) a holograph copy of the Sonnet on

first looking into Chapman's Homer, headed in another hand "To Mariane Reynolds," and catalogued as "Autograph Verses to Marianne Reynolds" [*sic* ; but her name was really Mariane with one *n* only], (2) the draft of the Nightingale Ode now in the HOUGHTON-CREWE collection, headed "Ode to the Nightingale," not "a Nightingale," (3) a beautiful copy on quarto paper of the Ode to Psyche, and (4) a rough sheet of note-paper bearing fair copies of the lines "Unfelt, unheard, unseen," and the Hymn to Apollo. All of these manuscripts I examined carefully: by far the most important was the *Nightingale* draft, fully described by Professor Sidney Colvin in No. 30 of *The Monthly Review* (March 1903), which contains a fac-simile of the manuscript.

With special reference to this important lyric, Benjamin Robert Haydon, in one of his letters to Miss Mitford (*Correspondence &c.*, Volume II, page 72), says of Keats—"The death of his brother wounded him deeply, and it appeared to me from that hour he began to droop. He wrote his exquisite *Ode to the Nightingale* at this time, and as we were one evening walking in the Kilburn meadows he repeated it to me, before he put it to paper, in a low, tremulous under-tone which affected me extremely." Lord Houghton says the Ode was suggested by the continued song of a nightingale which, in the spring of 1819, had built its nest close to Wentworth Place. "Keats," says the biographer (ALDINE edition, 1876, page 237), "took great pleasure in her song, and one morning took his chair from the breakfast-table to the grass plot under a plum tree, where he remained between two and three hours. He then reached the house with some scraps of paper in his hand, which he soon put together in the form of this Ode." The anecdote as told in the *Life, Letters, &c.* (Volume I, page 245 of the 1848 edition, and page 207 of the 1867 edition) represents Brown as detecting the poet in the act of thrusting the scraps of the Ode away

" as waste paper, behind some books," and names Brown as the person who put them together. I presume Lord Houghton thought afterwards that Brown must have mistaken the bearing of Keats's action, inasmuch as the other evidence does not square with the carelessness implied. It is well to put the two forms of the story together, because the earliest version is still a favourite " literary anecdote," and the HOUGHTON-CREWE draft does not appear to me to dispose finally of the question. This draft clearly shows Keats in the act of composition—or *recomposition*; but I do not think Professor Colvin proves conclusively that those two leaves were the very scraps Brown saw Keats bring in and hide. It is quite conceivable that the poet, after hiding—perhaps forgetting where he hid—the scraps, found himself in the mood to give one of the Reynoldses a copy of the ode, sat down, and recomposed it, mainly, of course, from memory.

In December 1903, Messrs. H. Sotheran & Co., of 37 Piccadilly, lent me for collation a beautiful holograph manuscript of lines 1 to 96 of the poem beginning

I stood tip-toe upon a little hill,

the complement, no doubt, of the manuscript in the ROWFANT collection with which I had previously collated the poem from line 97 to the end. At the same time they lent me a holograph manuscript of the sonnet *On leaving some Friends at an early Hour*, on the back of which were some lines of or connected with " I stood tip-toe," and, further, a holograph of the stanzas *To some Ladies* (pages 15–16 of this edition).

It was from the Woodhouse section of the HOUGHTON-CREWE papers that Mr. de Sélincourt was enabled to give for the first time the trifle of 1814, " Fill for me a brimming bowl " (pages 283–4 of this edition), and the early sonnet on Peace (page 284); for at the end of *The Fall of Hyperion* Woodhouse's clerks had copied for him a small collection of minor poems mostly long familiar to Keats's readers, but including one or two which Lord Houghton had not thought it worth while to print.

Lord Crewe also discovered in 1904 a fragment of the manuscript of Keats's Ode to Fanny, of which Mr. de Sélincourt gave an account in *Notes and Queries* for the 4th of February 1905. And the Woodhouse transcript of the Sonnet "The day is gone" (pages 437–8 of this edition), now found in the same collection, varies from the Houghton text, hitherto adopted, by the transposition of the second and third quatrains. Mr. de Sélincourt gives the Woodhouse transposition in full, though only in his notes ; but, as he pronounces the general effect of the whole sonnet "immeasurably enhanced" by the change, I presume that he would have adopted the new arrangement in the body of his book if he had had it in time. No other manuscript being then available, the choice lay between two hypotheses, (1) that Woodhouse's copy was made from a rough holograph which left a doubt and that the Houghton version was derived from a better holograph, and (2) that Lord Houghton himself transposed the quatrains from the Woodhouse copy. I think the sequence from line 12 to line 13 better than that from line 8 to line 13 ; and would leave the Sonnet as it is. Since the body of the present edition was printed I have had in my hands what is probably the holograph draft copied by Woodhouse, and have illustrated some remarks on it in *The Bookman* for October 1906 by means of a reproduction of the manuscript. Mr. de Sélincourt can quite properly claim this manuscript as evidence on his side ; but it leaves me unconvinced. I can hardly suppose that Keats did not copy the Sonnet fairly for Miss Brawne ; and I should expect her copy, if it were found, to show the quatrains arranged as in the Houghton text, and the reading *light whisper* in the third line as against the more significant but distinctly cacophonous *tranc'd whisper* of the newly discovered manuscript. The holograph is in the scrap-book lent to me by Mr. Sabin, of

118 Shaftesbury Avenue. In that book is a beautifully written manuscript of the Sonnet to Spenser (also "fac-simile'd" in *The Bookman*), which has great value in that it clears Keats of responsibility for the ridiculous line describing Phœbus with "a golden quill": it turns out to be "a golden quell," wherever Keats may have got that bold and picturesque noun—whether from *Macbeth* ("our great quell") or out of his own head. He used it also in *Endymion* (II, 537, "a sovereign quell"); and he was quite capable of evolving the noun *quell* from the verb *to quell*, in sheer emulation of Leigh Hunt's liberties with the English language—the liberties of the "loved Libertas"!

Mr. Sabin's book contains a third holograph—a leaf from a rough copy of *The Eve of St. Mark*, or of a part of that fragment. It is of very high interest, though the sixteen lines which I think it authorizes us to add to the fragment are not of equal quality with what we had already, and may have been specially rejected, not merely dropped with the whole scheme of the unfinished poem. The newly recovered passage deals with the essential legend which Dante Gabriel Rossetti told me he was convinced that Keats was going to treat as the back-bone of the poem—the legend about the wraiths of people who were in peril of death trooping into church on St. Mark's Eve. Rossetti identified the fragment with the poetic scheme mentioned in a letter to Fanny Brawne (COMPLETE edition, Volume v, page 185), and was of opinion that Bertha in *The Eve of St. Mark* had trifled with her lover and, now that he was sick, was to go to the cathedral porch and watch the wraiths going in, with the view of ascertaining whether her lover's wraith came out again—for those who were to die that year would not come out; but those who were to get well would. Keats simplified the legend: for him, all whose wraiths went in would die: here are the sixteen lines, which immediately precede line 99,

Als writith he of swevenis,

at page 342 of the present edition.

> Gif ye wol stonden hardie wight—
> Amiddes of the blacke night—
> Righte in the churche porch, pardie
> Ye wol behold a companie
> Appouchen thee full dolourouse
> For sooth to sain from everich house
> Be it in City or village
> Wol come the Phantom and image
> Of ilka gent and ilka carle
> Whom coldè Deathè hath in parle
> And wol some day that very year
> Touchen with foulè venìme spear
> And sadly do them all to die—
> Hem all shalt thou see verilie—
> And everichon shall by the[e] pass
> All who must die that year Alas

There is a rejected reading of the last couplet, which joins more perfectly than the final version does with line 99—

> And everichon shall by the[e] go
> Truly mine auctour says it so

of which the last three words seem to me to have been carelessly written for *sayeth so*. *Appouchen* in the fifth line is plain enough ; but it seems likely that Keats meant to write *Approchen*. The British Museum holograph (Egerton 2780) shows, of course, no trace of this new passage ; but it is not clear which was written last, the draft whereof the new passage is a fragment, or the Museum copy which is also a much revised draft. I have not been able to ascertain what bearing the copy sent to George Keats in the Winchester journal-letter of September 1819 has on the status of the new passage, as I do not know in whose possession that letter now is. But this is clear :—both copies are drafts, showing Keats in the mood of composition and revision ; and in both alike, for example, the first word in the line

> Gif that the modre (God her blesse)

was first written as *If* and then altered to *Gif*, or, literally, to *GIf*. If he could be drafting *The Eve of St. Mark* twice, why not the *Nightingale* Ode? The beautiful draft of the Houghton-Crewe collection is astonishingly mature.

Of work attributed to Keats in former editions and here excluded from the text there is very little; but of such rejection as has been necessary an account should be rendered. The poem and sonnet given in Lord Houghton's Aldine edition (and others) as of doubtful authenticity are both omitted because I do not think that Keats had anything more to do with the poem than with the sonnet ("Pleasures lie thickest where no pleasures seem"), which is to be found among Laman Blanchard's works, and is assigned to that author in several anthologies, as for instance in Leigh Hunt's *Book of the Sonnet*, Dr. Mackay's *A Thousand and One Gems of English Poetry*, and Mr. John Dennis's *English Sonnets*. Lord Houghton has recorded his belief that the sonnet was "one of George Byron's forgeries" (Aldine edition, page 493); but at page 326, the poem commencing with the words "What sylph-like form before my eyes," is introduced by a suggestion that there were genuine pieces among the forgeries sold at the George Byron "autograph" auction. My own belief is that, so far as the actual documents are concerned, all were forged; but that many of them were copies, in assumed hands, of genuine documents. Some of the Shelley letters certainly were; and I think it is only a question of time how soon this particular piece of verse shall be traced to the source outside Keats's work from which George Byron copied it. The song "Stay, ruby-breasted warbler, stay," given at page 6 of the Aldine edition, was probably sent to Lord Houghton from America. I omitted it because, in the scrap-book mentioned at page xxiv, containing a mass of transcripts by George Keats from his brother's poetry, this poem is not only written in George's hand but signed "G. K." instead of "J. K."; and indeed it seems to me more

likely to be one of the effusions which George is
recorded to have produced than an early poem by
John. The occurrence of the song among the lately
found Woodhouse papers of the HOUGHTON-CREWE
collection induced Mr. de Sélincourt to enter it once
more to the credit (or discredit) of Keats's account with
the Muse, against the evidence of George Keats. I still
think that George's claim holds good; but here are
the verses, for those who wish to form an opinion on
the subject.

SONG.

TUNE—"*Julia to the Wood-Robin.*"

Stay, ruby-breasted warbler, stay,
    And let me see thy sparkling eye,
Oh brush not yet the pearl-strung spray
    Nor bow thy pretty head to fly.

Stay while I tell thee, fluttering thing,
    That thou of love an emblem art,
Yes! patient plume thy little wing,
    Whilst I my thoughts to thee impart.

When summer nights the dews bestow,
    And summer suns enrich the day,
Thy notes the blossoms charm to blow,
    Each opes delighted at thy lay.

So when in youth the eye's dark glance
    Speaks pleasure from its circle bright,
The tones of love our joys enhance
    And make superior each delight.

And when bleak storms resistless rove,
    And every rural bliss destroy,
Nought comforts then the leafless grove
    But thy soft note—its only joy—

E'en so the words of love beguile
    When Pleasure's tree no flower bears,
And draw a soft endearing smile
    Amid the gloom of grief and tears.

From the same George Keats scrap-book a sonnet
attributed by George to his brother John was extracted
for the LIBRARY edition in 1883. It is the sonnet
beginning with the line

> Brother belov'd if health shall smile again,

and passed without public challenge as Keats's till
I observed it by chance among Mrs. Tighe's posthumous poems, and of course withdrew it at once from
my current editions of Keats and made confession of
the mistake into which George Keats had unwittingly
lured me. No doubt Keats had copied it at some time
from the volume containing *Psyche* (which he greatly
admired in early days before his taste was mature) and
some minor poems, and thus deceived his brother
without intending to do so.

Another piece which I was led to attribute to Keats
was a delightful set of couplets issued by Leigh Hunt
in *The Indicator* for the 19th of January 1820, headed
Vox et Præterea Nihil, and opening with the lines

> Oh! what a voice is silent. It was soft
> As mountain-echoes, when the winds aloft
> (The gentle winds of summer) meet in caves.

After some discussion with Dante Gabriel Rossetti,
I concluded that these beautiful lines had been written
by Keats as a part of *Endymion*, in one of the foot-notes
to which I inserted them with the suggestion that they
had been intended to come between lines 853 and 854
of Book II and had been rejected by Keats as over-
weighting the passage. This suggestion also passed
unchallenged for thirteen years, after which, through
the courtesy of Mr. Bryan Charles Waller, author of
The Twilight Land and *Perseus with the Hesperides*, I was
made aware that *Vox et Præterea Nihil* was to be found
in a volume of poetry by his uncle, Bryan Waller
Procter (" Barry Cornwall ").[1] Of this false ascription

[1] *Marcian Colonna, an Italian Tale, with Three Dramatic Scenes and
other Poems*, published by John Warren and C. & J. Ollier in
1820. In this volume the title is enlarged to *A Voice—Vox et
Præterea Nihil*.

also due confession was made ; and the couplets were
cancelled in my current editions of Keats's poetry.
How they had betrayed me and others, may be judged
from the single sample—

> Like the low voice of Syrinx when she ran
> Into the forests from Arcadian Pan ;

strongly resembling a couplet in *Endymion*—

> Telling us how fair, trembling Syrinx fled
> Arcadian Pan, with such a horrid dread.

There has been some temptation to add to Keats's
poetic fragments the following lines forming a part of
a letter sent to Fanny Brawne :

> To see those eyes I prize above my own
> Dart favors on another—
> And those sweet lips (yielding immortal nectar)
> Be gently press'd by any but myself—
> Think, think Francesca, what a cursed thing
> It were beyond expression !

These lines follow the words "Some lines I read the
other day are constantly ringing a peal in my ears"
(COMPLETE edition, Volume v, page 69) ; but they were
specially signed " J "—which might mean " John "—
before he passed on in prose to other matters and
signed " J. Keats." Not having found the passage in
any one else's works since publishing it in 1878, I lately
sought information about it through *The Bookman* ; and
I am now referred by Mr. Arthur Langmead Casserley
to its source, namely Massinger's tragedy *The Duke of
Milan*, Act 1, scene 3, where Sforza, about to go into
battle, tells Marcelia his apprehension of what may
follow on his defeat. Marcelia says—

> 'Tis not in the power
> Of fate to alter me ; for while I am,
> In spite of it, I'm yours.

Sforza replies—

> But should that will
> To be so forced ; Marcelia ; and I live

> To see those eyes I prize above my own
> Dart favours, though compell'd, upon another;
> Or those sweet lips, yielding immortal nectar,
> Be gently touch'd by any but myself;
> Think, think, Marcelia, what a cursed thing
> I were beyond expression.

Keats only left two lines untouched; and, in mitigating the coarseness of Massinger's imagination for his own less indelicate purpose, he also took the liberty of making the situation instead of the sufferer a cursed thing, and thus leaving the lines more characteristic of Keats than of Massinger.

H. B. F.

46 Marlborough Hill, St. John's Wood,
    October, 1906.

Postscript : Midsummer 1914.—Since this edition was published another of Woodhouse's transcript books has been acquired by the Marquess of Crewe, who kindly let me look over it a year or two ago. It furnishes fresh information, and a little more verse of Keats's. Two new pieces and some fragments of *The Castle Builder* from this book have been communicated by Sir Sidney Colvin to *The Times* (Literary Supplement of April 16, 1914). The fragments show that *The Castle Builder* was conceived as a dialogue ; all that is now extant of this project will be found on pp. 298-9 of this volume. Of the two other pieces the better by far is a "little tattle," as Keats would have called it, between Apollo and the Graces, now given at p. 361. The other, "You say you love," follows it on p. 362. Two newly found sonnets, first published in *The Times* of May 18, 1914, are, by the courtesy of the Editor and Dr. Horner, given at p. 288. See also p. lxxix.

TYPE FAC-SIMILE TITLES OF

KEATS'S

THREE BOOKS

The measurements of a single leaf in an uncut copy are as follows:—

$\quad$ *Poems*, 1817--$6\frac{7}{8}$ in. $\times 4\frac{1}{8}$ in.

$\quad$ *Endymion*—$8\frac{11}{16}$ in. $\times 5\frac{5}{8}$ in.

$\quad$ *Lamia, Isabella, &c.*—7 in. $\times 4\frac{3}{16}$ in.

Poems,

BY

JOHN KEATS.

" What more felicity can fall to creature,
" Than to enjoy delight with liberty."

Fate of the Butterfly.—SPENSER.

LONDON:

PRINTED FOR

C. & J. OLLIER, 3, WELBECK STREET,

CAVENDISH SQUARE.

———

1817.

ENDYMION:

A Poetic Romance.

BY JOHN KEATS.

"THE STRETCHED METRE OF AN ANTIQUE SONG."

LONDON:

PRINTED FOR TAYLOR AND HESSEY,

93, FLEET STREET.

1818.

LAMIA,

ISABELLA,

THE EVE OF ST. AGNES,

AND

OTHER POEMS.

BY JOHN KEATS,

AUTHOR OF ENDYMION.

LONDON:

PRINTED FOR TAYLOR AND HESSEY,

FLEET-STREET.

1820.

LIST OF PRINCIPAL WORKS
CONSULTED

THIS List is not meant for a complete Keats bibliography ; but, as it has been necessary to consult a considerable number of books &c., it seems desirable to supplement, by means of such a list, the information given in the Preface as to the sources of this edition. Keats's three volumes published in his life-time, in 1817, 1818, and 1820, do not head the list, as their title-pages immediately precede it, and each volume is fully described in the Introduction. No second edition of the *Poems, Endymion,* or *Lamia, &c.,* was published during the poet's life: hence the sources of "various readings" are either manuscripts or prints occurring in periodical and other works not by Keats.

1. Annals of the Fine Arts, for MDCCCXVI ... London ... Sherwood, Neely, and Jones ... 1817.

2. Annals of the Fine Arts, for MDCCCXVII ... London ... 1818.

3. Annals of the Fine Arts, for MDCCCXVIII ... London ... 1819.

4. Annals of the Fine Arts, for MDCCCXIX ... London ... 1820.

5. Annals of the Fine Arts, for MDCCCXX ... London ... 1820.

These five octavo volumes were edited by James Elmes ; but the ruling spirit and chief contributor to the work was Haydon, although Keats, Wordsworth, Hazlitt, Lamb, and Southey, all figure in its pages. Three numbers appeared in 1816, four each in 1817, 1818, and 1819, and two in 1820,—seventeen in all. The *Nightingale* and *Grecian Urn* odes made their first appearance here ; and the *Elgin Marbles* sonnets were reprinted by Elmes from *The Examiner.* One of Haydon's many fine dissertations, that, namely, on Visconti's mistake as to the action of the Ilissus in the Elgin collection, appeared as an octavo pamphlet in French,—so determined was the learned painter to make his voice heard throughout Europe on this subject.

6. Erreur de Visconti relative a l'Action de la Statue de l'Ilissus dans la collection d'Elgin, au Museum Britannique Par B. R. Haydon, Peintre d'Histoire. Londres: Imprimé par Bulmer et Cie. Cleveland-Row, St. James's. 1819.

7. Foliage; or Poems original and translated, by Leigh Hunt. ... London ... Ollier ... 1818 [one volume foolscap 8vo.].

> The copy consulted (*penes me*) was Keats's. It is inscribed on the title-page, in Hunt's writing, "John Keats from his affectionate friend the Author."

8. The Literary Pocket-Book; or, Companion for the Lover of Nature and Art. 1819. (*To be continued annually.*) London: ... Ollier, Vere-Street, ... (where communications will be received.) ... [1818].

9. The Literary Pocket-Book ... 1820 ... London [1819].

10. The Literary Pocket-Book ... 1821 ... London [1820].

11. The Literary Pocket-Book ... 1822 ... London [1821].

12. The Literary Pocket-Book ... 1823 ... London [1822].

13. Adonais An Elegy on the Death of John Keats by Percy B. Shelley...Pisa with the Types of Didot MDCCCXXI. [quarto pamphlet].

14. The Indicator By Leigh Hunt....London:...Appleyard ... 1822 [two volumes, 8vo.].

> In the number for May 10th 1820, page 248, appeared for the first time, signed "Caviare," *La Belle Dame sans Mercy.*

15. Lord Byron and Some of his Contemporaries; with Recollections of the Author's Life, and of his Visit to Italy. By Leigh Hunt ... London ... Colburn ... 1828 [one volume, quarto].

16. Lord Byron and Some of his Contemporaries ... Second Edition. In two volumes [8vo.] ... London ... Colburn ... 1828.

17. Adonais. An Elegy on the Death of John Keats, Author of Endymion, Hyperion, etc. by Percy B. ... Shelley. Cambridge...Gee & Bridges...MDCCCXXIX. [8vo. pamphlet].

18. The Poetical Works of Coleridge, Shelley, and Keats. Complete in one volume [royal 8vo.]. Paris ... Galignani ... 1829.

19. Leigh Hunt's London Journal. To Assist the Inquiring, Animate the Struggling, and Sympathize with All.... London ... Knight ... 1834 and 1835 [two volumes, folio].

20. Smith's Standard Library. The Poetical Works of John Keats. London ... MDCCCXL [one volume, royal 8vo.].

21. The Poetical Works of John Keats. London ... Smith ... MDCCCXLI [one volume, foolscap 8vo.].

22. The Philosophy of Mystery. By Walter Cooper Dendy, Fellow and Honorary Librarian of the Medical Society of London : Senior Surgeon to the Royal Infirmary for Children, &c., &c. London ... Longmans ... 1841 [one volume, 8vo.].

23. Imagination and Fancy; or Selections from the English Poets, illustrative of those First Requisites of their Art; with Markings of the best Passages, Critical Notices of the Writings, and an Essay in Answer to the Question, "What is Poetry?" By Leigh Hunt ... London ... Smith, Elder and Co. ... 1844 [one volume, crown 8vo.].

24. Imagination and Fancy ... Third Edition ... 1852.

25. The Poetical Works of John Keats. A New Edition. London ... Moxon ... MDCCCXLVII.

> This little pocket edition (folding in twelves) is dated 1846 on the printed wrapper.

26. The Life of Percy Bysshe Shelley. By Thomas Medwin. In Two Volumes [crown 8vo.] ... London ... Newby ... 1847.

> The copy used (*penes me*) is profusely corrected and annotated by Medwin, and is described by him as "corrected for a new edition just about to appear"; but it has certainly not been handled as "copy" by a printer; and I am unable to ascertain that any such edition as was thus prepared by the author ever really appeared.

27. Life, Letters, and Literary Remains, of John Keats. Edited by Richard Monckton Milnes. In Two Volumes [foolscap 8vo.] ... London ... Moxon ... 1848.

> The particular copy used in preparing the Library edition was one in Sir Charles Dilke's collection, largely annotated in manuscript by his grandfather, Charles Wentworth Dilke, the friend of Keats. As Sir Charles allowed me to copy the whole of the notes, I have been able to refer to them again whenever necessary in preparing subsequent editions.

28. The Autobiography of Leigh Hunt; with Reminiscences of Friends and Contemporaries ... In Three Volumes [crown 8vo.] ... London: Smith, Elder and Co. ... 1850.

29. The Autobiography of Leigh Hunt ... A New Edition, Revised by the Author; with further Revision, and an Introduction, by his Eldest Son [Thornton Hunt] ... London: Smith, Elder and Co. ... MDCCCLX [one volume, crown 8vo.].

30. The Poetical Works of John Keats. A new Edition. London ... Moxon ... 1851 [one volume, foolscap 8vo.].

31. Life of Benjamin Robert Haydon, Historical Painter, from his Autobiography and Journals. Edited and Compiled by Tom Taylor ... In Three Volumes [crown 8vo.] ... London ... Longmans ... 1853.

32. Life of Benjamin Robert Haydon ... By Tom Taylor ... Second Edition...in three Volumes [with additions]...London ... Longmans ... 1853.

33. The Poetical Works of John Keats. With a Memoir by Richard Monckton Milnes. London ... Moxon ... 1854 [one volume, foolscap 8vo.].

34. The Correspondence of Leigh Hunt. Edited by his Eldest Son...In Two volumes [crown 8vo.]...London...Smith, Elder & Co. ... MDCCCLXII.

35. Essays and Poems. Selected from the Literary Remains of F. Hinde, M.A., Oxon. Liverpool: Gilbert G. Walmsley ... 1864.

> This little post 8vo. volume contains a notable appreciation of Keats's Life and Works, said to have been read before the Liverpool Philomathic Society in 1862.

36. The Poetical Works of John Keats. With a Memoir by Richard Monckton Milnes. A New Edition. London ... Moxon ... 1863 [one volume, foolscap 8vo.].

37. The Poetical Works of John Keats. With a Memoir, by Lord Houghton. A new, revised, and enlarged edition. London ... Moxon ... 1865 [one volume, foolscap 8vo.].

38. The Poetical Works of John Keats. With a Memoir by the Right Hon. Lord Houghton. Illustrated by ... George Scharf... London ... Moxon ... 1866 [one volume, 8vo., first published in a very handsome form in 1854].

39. The Life and Letters of John Keats. By the Right Hon. Lord Houghton. A new Edition. London ... Moxon ... 1867 [one volume, crown 8vo.].

40. On the Study of Celtic Literature. By Matthew Arnold, Professor of Poetry in the University of Oxford. London: Smith, Elder and Co. ... 1867 [one volume, 8vo.].

41. The Poetical Works of John Keats. Edited with a Critical Memoir, by William Michael Rossetti. Illustrated by Thomas Seccombe. London ... Moxon [no date, one volume, post 8vo., "Moxon's Popular Poets"].

42. Wordsworth, Shelley, Keats, and other Essays. By David Masson, M.A., LL.D., Professor of Rhetoric and English Literature in the University of Edinburgh. London: Macmillan and Co., 1874 [one volume, post 8vo.].

43. The Papers of a Critic. Selected from the Writings of the Late Charles Wentworth Dilke. With a Biographical Sketch by his Grandson, Sir Charles Wentworth Dilke, Bart., M.P. ... In Two Volumes [8vo.] ... London ... Murray ... 1875.

44. Benjamin Robert Haydon: Correspondence and Table-Talk. With a Memoir by his Son, Frederic Wordsworth Haydon. With Facsimile Illustrations from his Journals. In Two Volumes [8vo.] ... London: Chatto and Windus...1876.

45. The Poetical Works of John Keats. Chronologically arranged and edited, with a Memoir by Lord Houghton, D.C.L., Hon. Fellow of Trin. Coll. Cambridge. London: George Bell and Sons ... 1876. [Aldine edition, one volume, foolscap 8vo.]

46. Bryan Waller Procter (Barry Cornwall). An Autobiographical Fragment and Biographical Notes, with Personal Sketches of Contemporaries, Unpublished Lyrics, and Letters of Literary Friends. London: George Bell and Sons ... 1877 [edited by Coventry Patmore, one volume, 8vo.].

47. Clarendon Press Series Keats Hyperion, Book I Edited with Notes [by] W. T. Arnold, B. A. ... Oxford ... MDCCCLXXVIII [pamphlet, crown 8vo.].

48. Recollections of Writers. By Charles and Mary Cowden Clarke ... London: Sampson Low ... 1878 [one volume, crown 8vo.].

49. Letters of John Keats to Fanny Brawne Written in the Years MDCCCXIX and MDCCCXX and now given from the Original Manuscripts with Introduction and Notes by Harry Buxton Forman ... London ... Reeves & Turner ... MDCCCLXXVIII [one volume, foolscap 8vo.].

50. Lives of Famous Poets. By William Michael Rossetti. A Companion Volume to the Series Moxon's Popular Poets. London ... Moxon ... 1878 [one volume, crown 8vo.].

51. The Poetical Works of John Keats. Chronologically arranged and edited, with a Memoir, by Lord Houghton … Second [Aldine] Edition … 1879.

52. The Works of Percy Bysshe Shelley in Verse and Prose now first brought together with Many Pieces not before published Edited with Prefaces Notes and Appendices by Harry Buxton Forman in Eight Volumes [demy 8vo.] … London Reeves and Turner … 1880.

53. John Keats A Study By F. M. Owen … London C. Kegan Paul & Co. … 1880 [one volume, crown 8vo.].

54. The English Poets Selections with Critical Introductions by various Writers and a General Introduction by Matthew Arnold edited by Thomas Humphry Ward, M.A. London Macmillan and Co. 1880 [four volumes, crown 8vo.].

> The fourth volume, "The Nineteenth Century: Wordsworth to Dobell," includes, of course, a selection from Keats's works. This is preceded by an Essay from the pen of Matthew Arnold.

55. English Literature by the Rev. Stopford Brooke, M.A. London: Macmillan and Co. 1880 [one volume, medium 8vo.].

> This book was originally issued as a "Primer of English Literature"—which title it bears as a "dropped head" above Chapter I.

56. The Poetical Works and Other Writings of John Keats now first brought together including Poems and numerous Letters not before published Edited with Notes and Appendices by Harry Buxton Forman in Four Volumes [demy 8vo.] … London Reeves & Turner … 1883.

> This was the first attempt to collect and set out the whole of Keats's Writings. The volumes contained, in addition to all the Writings of Keats known at that time, everything judged of importance from the numerous earlier works cited in the present list, except, of course, Lord Houghton's Memoirs, which were, and are still, accessible in his own editions of Keats, which have circulated very widely. Keats's letters in this first Library edition numbered 196,—157 to his family and friends and 39 to Fanny Brawne.

57. The Letters of John Keats edited by Jno. Gilmer Speed … New-York Dodd, Mead & Company 1883 [one volume, medium 8vo.].

58. The Poems of John Keats with the Annotations of Lord Houghton and a Memoir by Jno. Gilmer Speed... New York Dodd, Mead & Company 1883 [two volumes, medium 8vo.].

> These three handsome volumes, issued together, have half-titles worded " The Letters and Poems of John Keats. In Three Volumes." There are 15 letters to his brothers, 62 to his friends, and 37 to Fanny Brawne, 114 in all. Whatever is new is very inaccurately printed ; and the arrangement of the Poetry does not correctly represent Lord Houghton's editions.

59. The Poetical Works of John Keats given from his own Editions and other Authentic Sources and Collated with many Manuscripts Edited by Harry Buxton Forman London Reeves & Turner... 1884 [one volume, crown 8vo.].

> This is an unannotated edition in large type, with a collection of Cancelled Passages from "Endymion" at the end, full subject index, and index of first lines.

60. The Poetical Works of John Keats edited by William T. Arnold. London Kegan Paul, Trench, & Co. ... MDCCCLXXXIIII [one volume, crown 8vo.].

> This edition is of course incomplete ; but it has a valuable introduction and contains most of Keats's best poetry. The editor treated in a full and systematic way the subject of the sources of Keats's diction,—a subject on which Woodhouse began while Keats was still alive, as shown in the notes to the Library edition. Mr. Arnold added a good deal to what Woodhouse and others had done in this way.

61. The Poetical Works of John Keats Reprinted from the Original Editions with Notes by Francis T. Palgrave London Macmillan and Co. 1884 [A Selection in one volume of the " Golden Treasury " Series, pott 8vo.].

62. The Asclepiad. A Book of Original Research and Observation ... By Benjamin Ward Richardson, M.D., F.R.S. ... published quarterly ... London. April 1884 [octavo].

> This contains an important article entitled " An Esculapian Poet—John Keats."

63. The Life of Percy Bysshe Shelley by Edward Dowden LL.D. ... In Two Volumes [demy 8vo.] ... London ... Kegan Paul, Trench and Co. ... 1886.

64. Keats by Sidney Colvin London: Macmillan and Co. ... 1887 [one volume of Mr. Morley's " English Men of Letters " Series, crown 8vo.].

65. Life of John Keats by William Michael Rossetti. London Walter Scott ... 1887 [one volume, medium 8vo.].

66. The Poetical Works and other Writings of John Keats edited with Notes and Appendices by H Buxton Forman In Four Volumes [demy 8vo.] Reissue with Additions and Corrections ... London Reeves & Turner ... 1889.

67. Letters of John Keats to Fanny Brawne with Introduction and Notes by H Buxton Forman Second Edition Revised and Enlarged London Reeves & Turner ... 1889.

68. Poetry and Prose by John Keats A Book of Fresh Verses and New Readings—Essays and Letters lately found—and Passages formerly suppressed Edited by H Buxton Forman and forming a Supplement to the Library edition of Keats's Works London Reeves & Turner ... 1890 [one volume, demy 8vo.].

> This volume, designed to put those who owned the Library edition of 1883 in the same position as those who owned the Reissue of 1889, contained also some little material special to itself.

69. Letters of John Keats to his Family and Friends Edited by Sidney Colvin London Macmillan and Co. ... 1891 [one volume, large foolscap 8vo.].

> This edition, which does not include the Letters to Fanny Brawne, contains 164 letters in all. The poetry inserted by Keats in the originals is given in full, though in a type smaller than that used for the body of the Letters. The editor has added valuable notes.

70. The Life and Letters of Joseph Severn by William Sharp ... London Sampson Low ... 1892 [one volume, royal 8vo.].

71. The Poetical Works of Percy Bysshe Shelley Edited with a Memoir by H. Buxton Forman In Five Volumes... London George Bell & Sons...1892.

72. Excursions in Criticism Being some Prose Recreations of a Rhymer By William Watson London:...Mathews &... Lane ... MDCCCXCIII.

73. John Keats A Critical Essay by Robert Bridges Privately Printed MDCCCXCV [one volume, post 8vo.].

74. Keats' Jugend und Jugendgedichte. Von J. Hoops. Sonderabdruck aus Englische Studien XXI. Band, 2. Heft 1895 [Leipzig, 8vo. pamphlet.].

75. The Letters of John Keats Complete revised edition with a Portrait not published in previous editions and twenty-four contemporary views of places visited by Keats. Edited by H Buxton Forman London Reeves & Turner... 1895 [one volume, crown 8vo.].

> This edition contains every letter of Keats known to be extant at the time, including those to Fanny Brawne, which take their place in order of date among the rest, not as a separate group. There are 214 letters in all : and these are given with the transcribed poetry in full, set in the same large type as the body of the letters, for easy reference, their textual value being considerable.

76. Literary Anecdotes of the Nineteenth Century : Contributions towards a Literary History of the Period Volume II. Edited by W. Robertson Nicoll, M.A., LL.D., and Thomas T. Wise London : Hodder & Stoughton ... MDCCCXCVI.

> In an article about Keats appear the "nonsense sonnet" at page 291 of this edition and a fac-simile of the manuscript of the sonnet to Miss Wylie.

77. The Poetical Works of John Keats ... Edited by H. Buxton Forman ... Sixth Edition with Seven Portraits and Ten other Illustrations London...Reeves and Turner...1898.

> This is a new edition of No. 59, illustrated and brought up to date. The seventh edition is a reprint of it.

78. Keats' Hyperion Mit Einleitung herausgegeben von Johannes Hoops ... Berlin Verlag von Emil Felber 1899 [one volume, crown 8vo.].

> This little book is No. 3 in a series, namely the "Englische Textbibliothek Herausgegeben von Johannes Hoops a. o. Professor an der Universität von Heidelberg."

79. The Complete Works of John Keats in Five Volumes ...Edited by H. Buxton Forman...Gowans & Gray Glasgow... 1900-1901 Agent for London R. Brimley Johnson...[foolscap 8vo.].

> In this edition the Library editions of 1883 and 1889 were brought up to date, new material being published and all manuscript Sources discovered in the interim being used. The collations and notes variorum are as minute and literal as those of the Library editions ; but the appended matter, not quite so voluminous, is scattered through the volumes beneath or between the poems, letters, &c.; a memoir is prefixed to the poetry ; and a series of brief biographical notes on Keats's relations, friends, and correspondents stands before the letters.

80. Poems By John Keats with an Introduction By Laurence Binyon and Notes by John Masefield With a Frontispiece from the Life Mask London Methuen & Co. 36 Essex Street W.C. MDCCCCIII [one volume, 16mo.].

81. The Monthly Review No. 30. Mar. 1903. London: John Murray.

> Contains an article by Professor Colvin on the Nightingale ode with fac-simile of manuscript.

82. Illustrated Catalogue of Unique Grangerized Books Rare MSS. of Keats Original Drawings ... On Sale by Henry Sotheran & Co. ... London ... 1904.

83. Hyperion A Facsimile of Keats's Autograph Manuscript with a Transliteration of the Manuscript of The Fall of Hyperion a Dream with Introductions and Notes by Ernest de Sélincourt Oxford At the Clarendon Press 1905.

> This large folio volume is very valuable from a critical point of view. The "Transliteration" is a printed text literally given, not from Keats's manuscript but from a copy made by two of Richard Woodhouse's clerks: the original has not yet been found.

84. The Poems of John Keats edited with an Introduction and Notes by E. de Sélincourt with a frontispiece in photogravure Methuen and Co. ... London [1905].

> The introductions and notes are particularly valuable and interesting. Mr. de Sélincourt goes much more exhaustively into the sources of Keats's language than even the late Mr. William Thomas Arnold did.

85. The Bookman Keats Double Number [for October 1906] London: Hodder & Stoughton, Warwick Square, E.C.

> This contains, among other original material relating to Keats, mechanical reproductions of the Sonnet to Spenser, the Sonnet beginning "The day is gone," and the newly discovered passage of *The Eve of St. Mark.*

86. The Poetical Works of John Keats edited with an Introduction and Textual Notes by H. Buxton Forman, C.B. Oxford At The Clarendon Press MCMVI [one volume.].

> "The Oxford Keats" as originally issued in demy 8vo. has on the title-page a reduced fac-simile of a tracing by Keats of a Grecian Urn, a photogravure from an oil painting of Keats by Severn in the Houghton-Crewe Collection, W. B. Scott's etching of the death-bed portrait, Haydon's life-mask as in the present edition, and a two-page fac-simile of the leaf of *The Eve of St. Mark* discovered in 1906.

87. Keats-Shelley Memorial Exhibition & Concert. Stafford House, St. James's, S.W. Wednesday, 20th March, 1907. By Kind Permission of the Duke and Duchess of Sutherland. Catalogue of Relics, Portraits, Manuscripts, and other interesting articles connected with John Keats and Percy Bysshe Shelley with the names of the owners who have kindly placed them for this occasion at the disposal of the Committee of the Keats-Shelley Memorial at Rome.

> The second part of this quarto pamphlet is a program and book of words. The work was supervised by Professor (now Sir) Sidney Colvin.

88. Joseph and his Brethren a Dramatic Poem by Charles Wells with an Introduction by Algernon Charles Swinburne and a Note on Rossetti and Charles Wells by Theodore Watts-Dunton Henry Frowde Oxford University Press London, New York, Toronto and Melbourne [a volume of "The World's Classics," 1908].

89. John Keats Unpublished Poem To His Sister Fanny April 1818 Printed for Members only The Bibliophile Society 1909. [489 copies on vellum, being the whole issue.]

> The text is printed, with an Introduction by C. E. Hurd, in black letter, and is followed by a fac-simile of the MS.—obviously the composition and handwriting of George Keats with one or two trifling amendments by John. Its inclusion here is purely cautionary.

90. Lucien Wolff Agrégé de l'Université Docteur és Lettres John Keats sa Vie et son Œuvre (1795–1821) Paris Hachette & Cie· Éditeurs Boulevard Saint-Germain [1910].

> This royal octavo volume of 680 pages is a careful and elaborate study of the subject, which no student of Keats can afford to neglect, any more than the author could to ignore the Oxford Keats, a glance or two at which would have led him to modify his pages (439 *et seq.*) devoted to *The Eve of St. Mark*.

91. Bulletin of the Keats-Shelley Memorial Rome Edited by Sir Rennell Rodd and H. Nelson Gay London—Macmillan & Co., Ltd. New York—The Macmillan Co. 1910 [No. 1].

> A handsome quarto recording the foundation of the institution, the installation in the Piazza di Spagna, and the books, documents, &c. there collected.

92. Letters of Edward John Trelawny Edited with a brief Introduction and Notes by H. Buxton Forman C.B. Henry Frowde Oxford University Press ... 1910 [one volume, demy 8vo.].

93. Poetry & Life Series. Keats & his Poetry by William Henry Hudson Staff-Lecturer in Literature to the University Extension Board of the University of London ... London : George G. Harrap & Company 9 Portsmouth Street Kingsway W.C. MCMXI.

94. Catalogue of Valuable Books from the libraries of the Right Hon. Sir Charles Wentworth Dilke Bart., M.P., Deceased ... (Including Keats' [*sic*] Own Copy of His "Endymion," with his shorter poems added in MS. in His own Hand, and other First Editions of the same) ... Which will be sold by Auction by Messrs. Christie, Manson & Woods ... May 9, 1911.

> The other Keats lots included a pocket Milton profusely annotated by Mr. Dilke, described as annotated by Keats, and Mr. Dilke's copy of the Life, Letters &c. (No. 27) annotated by him in MS. This last was sold ; but the other two were withdrawn because pronounced by competent authority to be Dilke relics, not Keats relics. See *The Daily News* for 30 March, 5 May, and 9 May, 1911, and *The Athenæum* for June 3and 17, 1911.

95. Catalogue of the Famous Library of Printed Books, Illuminated Manuscripts [&c.] ... collected by Henry Huth, ... The Autograph Letters ... which will be sold by Auction by Messrs. Sotheby, Wilkinson & Hodge ... 12th of June, 1911, and following day.

> Keats was represented by a quarto letter to Taylor about the printing of *Endymion*, with long list of *Errata*. The catalogue contains a fac-simile of the *Errata* page. The letter is fully described and dealt with in *The Athenæum* for June 17, 1911.

96. Illustrated Handbook to the Dilke Collection of Keats Relics preserved at the Central Public Library, Hampstead ... Finchley Road, London, N.W. [October, 1911, a pamphlet compiled by the Librarian, Mr. Doubleday.]

97. Hampstead and Highgate Express and Hampstead Garden Suburb and Golders Green News, October 7, 1911.

> Contains an account of the opening of the Dilke

Collection to the public and parts of an inaugural address by H. Buxton Forman,— Sir William Robertson Nicoll in the Chair.

98. Keats, Shelley and Shakespeare. Studies and Essays in English Literature. By S. J. Mary Suddard, L.L.A., Fellow Univ. Gall. Cambridge: at the University Press. 1912.

Helpful and suggestive to students of Keats's mental and artistic growth, and truly notable as the work of a girl of seventeen to twenty, who died at twenty-one.

99. Catalogue of Valuable & Rare Books and...Manuscripts ...which will be Sold by Auction by Messrs. Sotheby, Wilkinson & Hodge...28th of March, 1912, and following day.

Lot 365 was the Woodhouse book of transcripts referred to (*post*) under No. 105. In the transcript of the *Sonnet to Sleep* the variant "dewy charities" is amended in Keats's handwriting by the substitution of "lulling" for "dewy."

100. The Athenæum, No. 4406, April 6, 1912. Breams Buildings, London, E.C.

Gives an account of a fragment of the draft of *The Pot of Basil* preserved at Welbeck Abbey. See page 201.

101. Souvenir of the Keats-Shelley Memorial Matinées at the Haymarket Theatre ... Tuesday, June 25th, and Friday, June 28th, 1912 ... arranged and organised by Mr. Frederick Harrison, who has given the use of the ... Theatre for the two performances.

A quarto program with full particulars, illustrations including photogravure portraits of Shelley and Keats, a foreword by William Watson, and a cover designed by Baron Arild Rosenkrantz.

102. The Bookman Keats-Shelley Memorlai Souvenir London Hodder & Stoughton Warwick Square E.C. [June 1912].

This is chiefly an album of ingatherings, literary and pictorial. The numerous portraits of patrons and performers concerned in the Haymarket Matinées include those of H.R.H. Princess Louise Duchess of Argyll, the Marchioness of Crewe, Miss Ellen Terry, and Miss Ina Pelly. The literary contributions include a beautiful essay by William Watson on Shelley as a Poet and a Causerie by H. Buxton Forman entitled "Shelley and Keats in the Twentieth Century."

103. The Bookman an Illustrated Magazine of Literature & Life Dodd, Mead & Company New York [February 1913].

Contains an illustrated article by Louis A. Holman on

the recovered portrait of Keats in Haydon's Entry of
Christ into Jerusalem (supposed to have been burnt).

104. The Life of Percy Bysshe Shelley By Thomas Medwin
A New Edition ... With an Introduction and Commentary by
H. Buxton Forman, C.B. Humphrey Milford Oxford
University Press ... 1913 [one volume, demy 8vo.]. See *ante*,
No. 26.

105. Twelfth Year Book 1913 The Bibliophile Society
Printed for Members only Boston MCMXIII.

> Contains an essay "Concerning the Friend who sent
> Keats some Roses" by H. Buxton Forman, with collo-
> type fac-simile of the manuscript of Keats's Sonnet to
> Charles Wells.

106. Bulletin and Review of the Keats-Shelley Memorial
Rome edited by Sir Rennell Rodd and H. Nelson Gay
London—Macmillan & Co. Ltd. New York—The Macmillan
Co. 1913 [No. 2].

> Shows the satisfactory progress of the Memorial,
> gives details of interest by the editors concerning the
> Protestant Burial Ground, an account by Mr. R. Underwood
> Johnson of books once owned by Keats, and photo-
> graphic fac-similes of the actual drawing made by
> Severn at Keats's death-bed and of two fragments of an
> autograph draft of *Lamia*, showing one abortive reading
> of no importance.

107. The Times Literary Supplement. No. 639...April 16,
1914. ... Keats and his Friends. Unpublished Poems and
Letters. (By Sir Sidney Colvin.)

> See postscript to Introduction.

108. The Keats Letters Papers and other Relics forming
the Dilke Bequest in the Hampstead Public Library, repro-
duced in fifty-eight collotype facsimiles, edited with full
transcriptions and notes, and an account of the portraits of
Keats, by George C. Williamson, Litt.D., together with fore-
words by Theodore Watts-Dunton, an Introduction by
H. Buxton Forman, C.B., and fourteen portraits of Keats.
London : John Lane, The Bodley Head New York : John
Lane Company Toronto : Bell and Cockburn MCMXIV
[310 copies only, for England and America.]

> The Introduction is in the main an adaptation of the
> Inaugural Address delivered at Hampstead. See *ante*,
> No. 97.

109. The Times.   May 18, 1914.   New Sonnets by Keats.

110. The Times Literary Supplement.   May 21, 1914. John Keats.   Recent Additions to our Knowledge.   A Critical Note.   By Ernest de Sélincourt.

> Both No. 109 and No. 110 show by photographic reproduction how Keats filled a page of the fly-leaf of John Hamilton Reynolds's copy of the Poems (1817, see p. lxv) by writing out the two unpublished sonnets now first included in any edition of Keats's Poetical Works (page 288).   The book has lain *perdu* for years, and was recently found by Dr. E. Horner, who obliged the world of letters by placing his find at the disposal of *The Times*.   I have pleasure in thanking Dr. Horner himself, the Editor of *The Times*, and the Editor of the Literary Supplement, for the courtesy shown me in regard to the reproduction of the sonnets in this edition.

111. The Isle of Wight County Press, June 13 and 20, 1914.

> Deals with the recent identification of Keats's lodgings at Carisbrooke.

CHRONOLOGY OF PRINCIPAL EVENTS
COMPOSITIONS, AND PUBLICATIONS

1795. John Keats's birth in Finsbury, October 31.

1797. Birth of his brother George, Spring.

1798. Birth of his brother Thomas, November 18.

1803. Birth of his sister, June 3.

1804. Death of his father, April 16.

1807. Death of his mother.

1803-9. Is educated at Mr. Clarke's school, Enfield.
     Begins translating THE ÆNEID.

1809. Apprenticed to Thomas Hammond, Surgeon.
     Finishes translating THE ÆNEID.

1812. Writes IMITATION OF SPENSER.
     Rupture with Hammond.

1813. Introduced to Severn.

1815. Writes ODE and HYMN TO APOLLO.
     Writes EPISTLE TO GEORGE FELTON MATHEW, November.

1816. First published poem appears in *The Examiner*, May 5.
     Addresses a sonnet to Charles Wells, June.
     Writes the Chapman's Homer Sonnet.
     Writes EPISTLE TO GEORGE KEATS, August.
     Writes EPISTLE TO CHARLES COWDEN CLARKE, September.
     Introduced to Haydon, November.
     Contemplates the subject of ENDYMION and writes "I stood tip-toe upon a little hill."

1817. First volume of POEMS published, early.
     ENDYMION begun, Spring.
     Stays in the Isle of Wight, April, and Margate, May.
     Visits Benjamin Bailey at Oxford, September.
     Stays at Leatherhead, November.
     Draft of ENDYMION finished at Burford Bridge, November 28.
     Sees Kean's return to the public and criticizes it in *The Champion*, December.

1817-18. Winters at Hampstead.

1818. Book I of ENDYMION sent to press, January.
Seeing "a good deal" of Wordsworth, January.
Joins his brothers at Teignmouth, March.
Revision of ENDYMION finished, March.
ENDYMION published, April.
ISABELLA, OR THE POT OF BASIL, finished by April 27.
FRAGMENT OF AN ODE TO MAIA written, May 1.
Returns to Hampstead, May.
Departure of George Keats and his bride for America, June.
Visits the Lakes with Brown, June.
Scotch tour with Brown, July and August.
A flying visit to Ireland, July.
A violent cold caught in the Isle of Mull, July.
"Cockney School" attack in *Blackwood's Magazine* published, August.
Returns to Hampstead, August.
Return of sore throat, September.
Attack in *The Quarterly Review* published, September.
At Well Walk, Hampstead, September to December.
First meeting with Fanny Brawne, October or November.
Thomas Keats dies and John moves to Wentworth Place to live with Brown, December.
Sore throat again, December.

1818-19. HYPERION begun, Winter.

1819. Stays at Chichester and Bedhampton, January.
THE EVE OF ST. AGNES written, January.
Returns to Wentworth Place, February.
Persistent sore throat, February.
ODE TO PSYCHE written, April.
Probably engaged to Fanny Brawne, April.
LA BELLE DAME SANS MERCI written, April–May.
ODE TO A NIGHTINGALE composed, May.
Throat still sore in June and July.
Visits the Isle of Wight with James Rice, July.
ODE TO A NIGHTINGALE published, July.
Writes LAMIA, Part I, and OTHO THE GREAT, Act I, July.
Removes with Brown to Winchester, August.
OTHO THE GREAT finished, HYPERION continued, August.

1819. Flying visit to London and return to Winchester, September.

To AUTUMN composed, HYPERION abandoned, LAMIA finished, THE EVE OF ST. AGNES revised, September.

Resolves to work for periodicals, September.

Returns to Hampstead to winter, October.

Leaves off animal food, October.

Throat in a threatening state again, December.

1820. ODE ON A GRECIAN URN published, January.

Fatal illness commences, February 3.

Keats and Brown finally part at Gravesend, May 7.

LA BELLE DAME SANS MERCI published in *The Indicator*, May 10.

Fragment of THE CAP AND BELLS written, June (?).

LAMIA, ISABELLA &c. published, first week in July.

Stays at Kentish Town near and with Hunt, June–July.

Fresh attack of blood-spitting, June 22.

Returns to Wentworth Place to be nursed by Mrs. and Miss Brawne, August.

Sails for Italy with Severn, September.

His last Sonnet, written on board ship.

Writes his last letter from Rome, November.

1821. His death, February 23, and burial near the tomb of Caius Cestius, February 26.

HAYDON'S LIFE-MASK OF KEATS PLACED IN THE
POSITION OF SEVERN'S DRAWING FORMING
THE FRONTISPIECE TO THIS EDITION

POEMS

PUBLISHED IN 1817.

DEDICATION.

TO LEIGH HUNT, ESQ.

GLORY and loveliness have pass'd away;
    For if we wander out in early morn,
    No wreathed incense do we see upborne
Into the east, to meet the smiling day:
No crowd of nymphs soft voic'd and young, and gay,
    In woven baskets bringing ears of corn,
    Roses, and pinks, and violets, to adorn
The shrine of Flora in her early May.
But there are left delights as high as these,
    And I shall ever bless my destiny,
That in a time, when under pleasant trees
    Pan is no longer sought, I feel a free,
A leafy luxury, seeing I could please
    With these poor offerings, a man like thee.

POEMS

"Places of nestling green for Poets made."
Story of Rimini.

I STOOD tip-toe upon a little hill,
The air was cooling, and so very still,
That the sweet buds which with a modest pride
Pull droopingly, in slanting curve aside,
Their scantly leav'd, and finely tapering stems,
Had not yet lost those starry diadems
Caught from the early sobbing of the morn.
The clouds were pure and white as flocks new shorn,
And fresh from the clear brook ; sweetly they slept
On the blue fields of heaven, and then there crept
A little noiseless noise among the leaves,   11
Born of the very sigh that silence heaves :
For not the faintest motion could be seen
Of all the shades that slanted o'er the green.
There was wide wand'ring for the greediest eye,
To peer about upon variety ;
Far round the horizon's crystal air to skim,
And trace the dwindled edgings of its brim ;
To picture out the quaint, and curious bending
Of a fresh woodland alley, never ending ;   20
Or by the bowery clefts, and leafy shelves,
Guess where the jaunty streams refresh themselves.
I gazed awhile, and felt as light, and free
As though the fanning wings of Mercury
Had play'd upon my heels : I was light-hearted,
And many pleasures to my vision started ;
So I straightway began to pluck a posey
Of luxuries bright, milky, soft and rosy.

A bush of May flowers with the bees about them ;
Ah, sure no tasteful nook would be without them ;
And let a lush labernum oversweep them,   31
And let long grass grow round the roots to keep them
Moist, cool and green ; and shade the violets,
That they may bind the moss in leafy nets.

A filbert hedge with wild briar overtwined,
And clumps of woodbine taking the soft wind
Upon their summer thrones ; there too should be
The frequent chequer of a youngling tree,
That with a score of light green brethren shoots
From the quaint mossiness of aged roots :   40
Round which is heard a spring-head of clear waters
Babbling so wildly of its lovely daughters
The spreading blue-bells : it may haply mourn
That such fair clusters should be rudely torn
From their fresh beds, and scattered thoughtlessly
By infant hands, left on the path to die.

Open afresh your round of starry folds,
Ye ardent marigolds !
Dry up the moisture from your golden lids,
For great Apollo bids   50
That in these days your praises should be sung
On many harps, which he has lately strung ;
And when again your dewiness he kisses,
Tell him, I have you in my world of blisses :
So haply when I rove in some far vale,
His mighty voice may come upon the gale.

Here are sweet peas, on tip-toe for a flight :
With wings of gentle flush o'er delicate white,
And taper fingers catching at all things,
To bind them all about with tiny rings.   60

Linger awhile upon some bending planks
That lean against a streamlet's rushy banks,
And watch intently Nature's gentle doings :
They will be found softer than ring-dove's cooings.
How silent comes the water round that bend ;
Not the minutest whisper does it send
To the o'erhanging sallows : blades of grass
Slowly across the chequer'd shadows pass.

61-67 *Lord Houghton records the following alternative reading :*
    Linger awhile among some bending planks
    That lean against a streamlet's daisied banks,
    And watch intently Nature's gentle doings:
    That will be found as soft as ringdoves' cooings.
    The inward ear will hear her and be blest,
    And tingle with a joy too light for rest.

Why, you might read two sonnets, ere they reach
To where the hurrying freshnesses aye preach   70
A natural sermon o'er their pebbly beds ;
Where swarms of minnows show their little heads,
Staying their wavy bodies 'gainst the streams,
To taste the luxury of sunny beams
Temper'd with coolness. How they ever wrestle
With their own sweet delight, and ever nestle
Their silver bellies on the pebbly sand.
If you but scantily hold out the hand,
That very instant not one will remain ;
But turn your eye, and they are there again.   80
The ripples seem right glad to reach those cresses,
And cool themselves among the em'rald tresses ;
The while they cool themselves, they freshness give,
And moisture, that the bowery green may live :
So keeping up an interchange of favours,
Like good men in the truth of their behaviours.
Sometimes goldfinches one by one will drop
From low hung branches ; little space they stop ;
But sip, and twitter, and their feathers sleek ;
Then off at once, as in a wanton freak :   90
Or perhaps, to show their black, and golden wings,
Pausing upon their yellow flutterings.
Were I in such a place, I sure should pray
That naught less sweet, might call my thoughts away,
Than the soft rustle of a maiden's gown
Fanning away the dandelion's down ;
Than the light music of her nimble toes
Patting against the sorrel as she goes.
How she would start, and blush, thus to be caught
Playing in all her innocence of thought.   100
O let me lead her gently o'er the brook,
Watch her half-smiling lips, and downward look ;
O let me for one moment touch her wrist ;
Let me one moment to her breathing list ;
And as she leaves me may she often turn
Her fair eyes looking through her locks auburne.
What next ? A tuft of evening primroses,
O'er which the mind may hover till it dozes ;
O'er which it well might take a pleasant sleep,
But that 'tis ever startled by the leap   110

Of buds into ripe flowers ; or by the flitting
Of diverse moths, that aye their rest are quitting;
Or by the moon lifting her silver rim
Above a cloud, and with a gradual swim
Coming into the blue with all her light.
O Maker of sweet poets, dear delight
Of this fair world, and all its gentle livers ;
Spangler of clouds, halo of crystal rivers,
Mingler with leaves, and dew and tumbling streams,
Closer of lovely eyes to lovely dreams,   120
Lover of loneliness, and wandering,
Of upcast eye, and tender pondering !
Thee must I praise above all other glories
That smile us on to tell delightful stories.
For what has made the sage or poet write
But the fair paradise of Nature's light ?
In the calm grandeur of a sober line,
We see the waving of the mountain pine ;
And when a tale is beautifully staid,
We feel the safety of a hawthorn glade :   130
When it is moving on luxurious wings,
The soul is lost in pleasant smotherings :
Fair dewy roses brush against our faces,
And flowering laurels spring from diamond vases ;
O'er head we see the jasmine and sweet briar,
And bloomy grapes laughing from green attire ;
While at our feet, the voice of crystal bubbles
Charms us at once away from all our troubles :
So that we feel uplifted from the world,
Walking upon the white clouds wreath'd and curl'd.
So felt he, who first told, how Psyche went   141
On the smooth wind to realms of wonderment ;
What Psyche felt, and Love, when their full lips
First touch'd ; what amorous, and fondling nips
They gave each other's cheeks ; with all their sighs,
And how they kist each other's tremulous eyes :
The silver lamp,—the ravishment,—the wonder—

115, 116 *Lord Houghton records the following variation :*
        Floating through space with ever-living eye,
        The crowned queen of ocean and the sky.
    144 what . . . nips] What fondleing and amorous nips *MS.*
but marked for transposition.

The darkness,—loneliness,—the fearful thunder ;
Their woes gone by, and both to heaven upflown,
To bow for gratitude before Jove's throne.   150
So did he feel, who pull'd the boughs aside,
That we might look into a forest wide,
To catch a glimpse of Fauns, and Dryades
Coming with softest rustle through the trees ;
And garlands woven of flowers wild, and sweet,
Upheld on ivory wrists, or sporting feet :
Telling us how fair, trembling Syrinx fled
Arcadian Pan, with such a fearful dread.
Poor nymph,—poor Pan,—how he did weep to find,
Nought but a lovely sighing of the wind   160
Along the reedy stream ; a half-heard strain,
Full of sweet desolation—balmy pain.

What first inspired a bard of old to sing
Narcissus pining o'er the untainted spring ?
In some delicious ramble, he had found
A little space, with boughs all woven round ;
And in the midst of all, a clearer pool
Than e'er reflected in its pleasant cool,
The blue sky here, and there, serenely peeping
Through tendril wreaths fantastically creeping.   170
And on the bank a lonely flower he spied,
A meek and forlorn flower, with naught of pride,
Drooping its beauty o'er the watery clearness,
To woo its own sad image into nearness :
Deaf to light Zephyrus it would not move ;
But still would seem to droop, to pine, to love.
So while the poet stood in this sweet spot,
Some fainter gleamings o'er his fancy shot ;
Nor was it long ere he had told the tale
Of young Narcissus, and sad Echo's bale.   180

Where had he been, from whose warm head out-flew
That sweetest of all songs, that ever new,
That aye refreshing, pure deliciousness,
Coming ever to bless
The wanderer by moonlight ? to him bringing
Shapes from the invisible world, unearthly singing
From out the middle air, from flowery nests,

And from the pillowy silkiness that rests
Full in the speculation of the stars.
Ah! surely he had burst our mortal bars;   190
Into some wond'rous region he had gone,
To search for thee, divine Endymion!

He was a Poet, sure a lover too,
Who stood on Latmus' top, what time there blew
Soft breezes from the myrtle vale below;
And brought in faintness solemn, sweet, and slow
A hymn from Dian's temple; while upswelling,
The incense went to her own starry dwelling.
But though her face was clear as infant's eyes,
Though she stood smiling o'er the sacrifice,   200
The Poet wept at her so piteous fate,
Wept that such beauty should be desolate:
So in fine wrath some golden sounds he won,
And gave meek Cynthia her Endymion.

Queen of the wide air; thou most lovely queen
Of all the brightness that mine eyes have seen!
As thou exceedest all things in thy shine,
So every tale, does this sweet tale of thine.
O for three words of honey, that I might
Tell but one wonder of thy bridal night!   210

Where distant ships do seem to show their keels,
Phoebus awhile delay'd his mighty wheels,
And turn'd to smile upon thy bashful eyes,
Ere he his unseen pomp would solemnize.
The evening weather was so bright, and clear,
That men of health were of unusual cheer;
Stepping like Homer at the trumpet's call,
Or young Apollo on the pedestal:
And lovely women were as fair and warm,
As Venus looking sideways in alarm.   220
The breezes were ethereal, and pure,
And crept through half-closed lattices to cure
The languid sick; it cool'd their fever'd sleep,
And soothed them into slumbers full and deep.
Soon they awoke clear eyed: nor burnt with thirsting,
Nor with hot fingers, nor with temples bursting:
And springing up, they met the wond'ring sight

Of their dear friends, nigh foolish with delight;
Who feel their arms, and breasts, and kiss and stare,
And on their placid foreheads part the hair.   230
Young men, and maidens at each other gaz'd
With hands held back, and motionless, amaz'd
To see the brightness in each other's eyes;
And so they stood, fill'd with a sweet surprise,
Until their tongues were loos'd in poesy.
Therefore no lover did of anguish die:
But the soft numbers, in that moment spoken,
Made silken ties, that never may be broken.
Cynthia! I cannot tell the greater blisses,
That follow'd thine, and thy dear shepherd's kisses: 240
Was there a poet born?—but now no more,
My wand'ring spirit must no further soar.—

SPECIMEN OF AN INDUCTION TO A POEM

Lo! I must tell a tale of chivalry;
For large white plumes are dancing in mine eye.
Not like the formal crest of latter days:
But bending in a thousand graceful ways;
So graceful, that it seems no mortal hand,
Or e'en the touch of Archimago's wand,
Could charm them into such an attitude.
We must think rather, that in playful mood,
Some mountain breeze had turn'd its chief delight,
To show this wonder of its gentle might.   10
Lo! I must tell a tale of chivalry;
For while I muse, the lance points slantingly
Athwart the morning air: some lady sweet,
Who cannot feel for cold her tender feet,
From the worn top of some old battlement
Hails it with tears, her stout defender sent:
And from her own pure self no joy dissembling,
Wraps round her ample robe with happy trembling.
Sometimes, when the good Knight his rest would take,
It is reflected, clearly, in a lake,   20
With the young ashen boughs, 'gainst which it rests,
And th' half seen mossiness of linnets' nests.

1 *Namely Calidore.*

*B 3

Ah! shall I ever tell its cruelty,
When the fire flashes from a warrior's eye,
And his tremendous hand is grasping it,
And his dark brow for very wrath is knit?
Or when his spirit, with more calm intent,
Leaps to the honors of a tournament,
And makes the gazers round about the ring
Stare at the grandeur of the ballancing?   30
No, no! this is far off:—then how shall I
Revive the dying tones of minstrelsy,
Which linger yet about long gothic arches,
In dark green ivy, and among wild larches?
How sing the splendour of the revelries,
When butts of wine are drunk off to the lees?
And that bright lance, against the fretted wall,
Beneath the shade of stately banneral,
Is slung with shining cuirass, sword, and shield?
Where ye may see a spur in bloody field.   40
Light-footed damsels move with gentle paces
Round the wide hall, and show their happy faces;
Or stand in courtly talk by fives and sevens:
Like those fair stars that twinkle in the heavens.
Yet must I tell a tale of chivalry:
Or wherefore comes that steed so proudly by?
Wherefore more proudly does the gentle knight,
Rein in the swelling of his ample might?

Spenser! thy brows are arched, open, kind,
And come like a clear sun-rise to my mind;   50
And always does my heart with pleasure dance,
When I think on thy noble countenance:
Where never yet was aught more earthly seen
Than the pure freshness of thy laurels green.
Therefore, great bard, I not so fearfully
Call on thy gentle spirit to hover nigh
My daring steps: or if thy tender care,
Thus startled unaware,
Be jealous that the foot of other wight
Should madly follow that bright path of light   60

46 knight *for* steed, *Poems 1817, but* steed *in a copy corrected by*
Keats.

Trac'd by thy lov'd Libertas ; he will speak,
And tell thee that my prayer is very meek ;
That I will follow with due reverence,
And start with awe at mine own strange pretence.
Him thou wilt hear ; so I will rest in hope
To see wide plains, fair trees and lawny slope :
The morn, the eve, the light, the shade, the flowers ;
Clear streams, smooth lakes, and overlooking towers.

CALIDORE

A FRAGMENT

YOUNG Calidore is paddling o'er the lake ;
His healthful spirit eager and awake
To feel the beauty of a silent eve,
Which seem'd full loth this happy world to leave ;
The light dwelt o'er the scene so lingeringly.
He bares his forehead to the cool blue sky,
And smiles at the far clearness all around,
Until his heart is well nigh over wound,
And turns for calmness to the pleasant green
Of easy slopes, and shadowy trees that lean   10
So elegantly o'er the waters' brim
And show their blossoms trim.
Scarce can his clear and nimble eye-sight follow
The freaks, and dartings of the black-wing'd swallow,
Delighting much, to see it half at rest,
Dip so refreshingly its wings, and breast
'Gainst the smooth surface, and to mark anon,
The widening circles into nothing gone.

And now the sharp keel of his little boat
Comes up with ripple, and with easy float,   20
And glides into a bed of water lillies :
Broad leav'd are they and their white canopies
Are upward turn'd to catch the heavens' dew.
Near to a little island's point they grew ;
Whence Calidore might have the goodliest view
Of this sweet spot of earth. The bowery shore
Went off in gentle windings to the hoar

61 Libertas *means* Leigh Hunt.

And light blue mountains: but no breathing man
With a warm heart, and eye prepared to scan
Nature's clear beauty, could pass lightly by   30
Objects that look'd out so invitingly
On either side. These, gentle Calidore
Greeted, as he had known them long before.

The sidelong view of swelling leafiness,
Which the glad setting sun, in gold doth dress;
Whence ever, and anon the jay outsprings,
And scales upon the beauty of its wings.
The lonely turret, shatter'd, and outworn,
Stands venerably proud; too proud to mourn
Its long lost grandeur: fir trees grow around,   40
Aye dropping their hard fruit upon the ground.

The little chapel with the cross above
Upholding wreaths of ivy; the white dove,
That on the window spreads his feathers light,
And seems from purple clouds to wing its flight.
Green tufted islands casting their soft shades
Across the lake; sequester'd leafy glades,
That through the dimness of their twilight show
Large dock leaves, spiral foxgloves, or the glow
Of the wild cat's eyes, or the silvery stems   50
Of delicate birch trees, or long grass which hems
A little brook. The youth had long been viewing
These pleasant things, and heaven was bedewing
The mountain flowers, when his glad senses caught
A trumpet's silver voice. Ah! it was fraught
With many joys for him: the warder's ken
Had found white coursers prancing in the glen:
Friends very dear to him he soon will see;
So pushes off his boat most eagerly,
And soon upon the lake he skims along,   60
Deaf to the nightingale's first under-song;
Nor minds he the white swans that dream so sweetly:
His spirit flies before him so completely.

And now he turns a jutting point of land,

28 But sure no breathing man *Tom Keats's MS.*
40, 41 Its long lost grandeur. Laburnums grow around
          And bow their golden honors to the ground.
                                        Tom Keats's MS.

Whence may be seen the castle gloomy, and grand:
Nor will a bee buzz round two swelling peaches,
Before the point of his light shallop reaches
Those marble steps that through the water dip:
Now over them he goes with hasty trip,
And scarcely stays to ope the folding doors: 70
Anon he leaps along the oaken floors
Of halls and corridors.
Delicious sounds! those little bright-eyed things
That float about the air on azure wings,
Had been less heartfelt by him than the clang
Of clattering hoofs; into the court he sprang,
Just as two noble steeds, and palfreys twain,
Were slanting out their necks with loosened rein;
While from beneath the threat'ning portcullis
They brought their happy burthens. What a kiss,   80
What gentle squeeze he gave each lady's hand!
How tremblingly their delicate ankles spann'd!
Into how sweet a trance his soul was gone,
While whisperings of affection
Made him delay to let their tender feet
Come to the earth; with an incline so sweet
From their low palfreys o'er his neck they bent:
And whether there were tears of languishment,
Or that the evening dew had pearl'd their tresses
He feels a moisture on his cheek, and blesses   90
With lips that tremble, and with glistening eye,
All the soft luxury
That nestled in his arms. A dimpled hand,
Fair as some wonder out of fairy land,
Hung from his shoulder like the drooping flowers
Of whitest Cassia, fresh from summer showers:
And this he fondled with his happy cheek
As if for joy he would no further seek;
When the kind voice of good Sir Clerimond
Came to his ear, like something from beyond   100
His present being; so he gently drew
His warm arms, thrilling now with pulses new,
From their sweet thrall, and forward meekly bending,
Thank'd heaven that his joy was never ending;

103 meekly *Tom Keats's MS.* : gently *1817*.

While 'gainst his forehead he devoutly press'd
A hand heaven made to succour the distress'd;
A hand that from the world's bleak promontory
Had lifted Calidore for deeds of Glory.

Amid the pages, and the torches' glare,
There stood a knight, patting the flowing hair   110
Of his proud horse's mane: he was withal
A man of elegance, and stature tall:
So that the waving of his plumes would be
High as the berries of a wild ash tree,
Or as the winged cap of Mercury.
His armour was so dexterously wrought
In shape, that sure no living man had thought
It hard, and heavy steel: but that indeed
It was some glorious form, some splendid weed,
In which a spirit new come from the skies   120
Might live, and show itself to human eyes.
'Tis the far-fam'd, the brave Sir Gondibert,
Said the good man to Calidore alert;
While the young warrior with a step of grace
Came up,—a courtly smile upon his face,
And mailed hand held out, ready to greet
The large-eyed wonder, and ambitious heat
Of the aspiring boy; who as he led
Those smiling ladies, often turn'd his head
To admire the visor arch'd so gracefully   130
Over a knightly brow; while they went by
The lamps that from the high roof'd hall were pendent,
And gave the steel a shining quite transcendent.

Soon in a pleasant chamber they are seated;
The sweet-lipp'd ladies have already greeted
All the green leaves that round the window clamber,
To show their purple stars, and bells of amber.
Sir Gondibert has doff'd his shining steel,
Gladdening in the free, and airy feel
Of a light mantle; and while Clerimond   140
Is looking round about him with a fond,
And placid eye, young Calidore is burning
To hear of knightly deeds, and gallant spurning

139 free and easy *Tom Keats's MS.*

Of all unworthiness; and how the strong of arm
Kept off dismay, and terror, and alarm
From lovely woman: while brimful of this,
He gave each damsel's hand so warm a kiss,
And had such manly ardour in his eye,
That each at other look'd half staringly;
And then their features started into smiles   150
Sweet as blue heavens o'er enchanted isles.

Softly the breezes from the forest came,
Softly they blew aside the taper's flame;
Clear was the song from Philomel's far bower;
Grateful the incense from the lime-tree flower;
Mysterious, wild, the far heard trumpet's tone;
Lovely the moon in ether, all alone:
Sweet too the converse of these happy mortals,
As that of busy spirits when the portals
Are closing in the west; or that soft humming   160
We hear around when Hesperus is coming.
Sweet be their sleep. * * * * * * * * *

TO SOME LADIES

What though while the wonders of nature exploring,
    I cannot your light, mazy footsteps attend;
Nor listen to accents, that almost adoring,
    Bless Cynthia's face, the enthusiast's friend:

Yet over the steep, whence the mountain stream rushes,
    With you, kindest friends, in idea I muse;
Mark the clear tumbling crystal, its passionate gushes,
    In spray that the wild flower kindly bedews.

Why linger you so, the wild labyrinth strolling?
    Why breathless, unable your bliss to declare?   10
Ah! you list to the nightingale's tender condoling,
    Responsive to sylphs, in the moon-beamy air.

'Tis morn, and the flowers with dew are yet drooping,
    I see you are treading the verge of the sea:
And now! ah, I see it—you just now are stooping
    To pick up the keep-sake intended for me.

Title] To the Misses M—— *MS.*
6 muse *MS.:* rove *Poems 1817.*
8 In . . . flower *MS.:* Its . . . flowers *Poems 1817.*

If a cherub, on pinions of silver descending,
   Had brought me a gem from the fret-work of heaven ;
And smiles, with his star-cheering voice sweetly blending,
   The blessings of Tighe had melodiously given; 20

It had not created a warmer emotion
   Than the present, fair nymphs, I was blest with from
      you,
Than the shell, from the bright golden sands of the ocean
   Which the emerald waves at your feet gladly threw.

For, indeed, 'tis a sweet and peculiar pleasure
   (And blissful is he who such happiness finds),
To possess but a span of the hour of leisure,
   In elegant, pure, and aerial minds.

ON RECEIVING A CURIOUS SHELL, AND A COPY OF VERSES,

FROM THE SAME LADIES

HAST thou from the caves of Golconda, a gem
   Pure as the ice-drop that froze on the mountain ?
Bright as the humming-bird's green diadem,
   When it flutters in sun-beams that shine through
      a fountain ?

Hast thou a goblet for dark sparkling wine ?
   That goblet right heavy, and massy, and gold ?
And splendidly mark'd with the story divine
   Of Armida the fair, and Rinaldo the bold ?

Hast thou a steed with a mane richly flowing ?
   Hast thou a sword that thine enemy's smart is ?
Hast thou a trumpet rich melodies blowing ?   11
   And wear'st thou the shield of the fam'd Britomartis ?

Title] *In Tom Keats's MS*. On receiving a curious shell and
a copy of verses ; *but in George Keats's MS*. Written on receiving
a copy of Tom Moore's 'Golden Chain,' and a most beautiful
Dome-shaped shell from a Lady.

What is it that hangs from thy shoulder, so brave,
  Embroider'd with many a spring peering flower?
Is it a scarf that thy fair lady gave?
  And hastest thou now to that fair lady's bower?

Ah! courteous Sir Knight, with large joy thou art
    crown'd;
  Full many the glories that brighten thy youth!
I will tell thee my blisses, which richly abound
  In magical powers to bless, and to sooth.   20

On this scroll thou seest written in characters fair
  A sun-beamy tale of a wreath, and a chain;
And, warrior, it nurtures the property rare
  Of charming my mind from the trammels of pain.

This canopy mark: 'tis the work of a fay;
  Beneath its rich shade did King Oberon languish,
When lovely Titania was far, far away,
  And cruelly left him to sorrow, and anguish.

There, oft would he bring from his soft sighing lute
  Wild strains to which, spell-bound, the nightin-
      gales listen'd;   30
The wondering spirits of heaven were mute,
  And tears 'mong the dewdrops of morning oft glisten'd.

In this little dome, all those melodies strange,
  Soft, plaintive, and melting, for ever will sigh;
Nor e'er will the notes from their tenderness change;
  Nor e'er will the music of Oberon die.

So, when I am in a voluptuous vein,
  I pillow my head on the sweets of the rose,
And list to the tale of the wreath, and the chain,
  Till its echoes depart; then I sink to repose.   40

Adieu, valiant Eric! with joy thou art crown'd;
  Full many the glories that brighten thy youth,
I too have my blisses, which richly abound
  In magical powers, to bless and to sooth.

TO * * * *

[Georgiana Augusta Wylie, afterwards
Mrs. George Keats]

Hadst thou liv'd in days of old,
O what wonders had been told
Of thy lively countenance,
And thy humid eyes that dance
In the midst of their own brightness ;
In the very fane of lightness.
Over which thine eyebrows, leaning,
Picture out each lovely meaning :
In a dainty bend they lie,
Like to streaks across the sky,   10
Or the feathers from a crow,
Fallen on a bed of snow.
Of thy dark hair that extends
Into many graceful bends :
As the leaves of Hellebore
Turn to whence they sprung before
And behind each ample curl
Peeps the richness of a pearl.
Downward too flows many a tress
With a glossy waviness ;   20
Full, and round like globes that rise
From the censer to the skies

3 *Richard Woodhouse records in his Keats Commonplace Book that
this poem was altered from a copy of verses written by K. at the request
of his brother George, and by the latter sent as a valentine to Georgiana
Wylie. This valentine, after line 2, read :—*

Of thy lively dimpled face
And thy footsteps full of grace :
Of thy hair's luxurious darkling,
Of thine eyes' expressive sparkling.
And thy voice's swelling rapture,
Taking hearts a ready capture.
Oh ! if thou hadst breathed then,
Thou hadst made the Muses ten.

Then came lines 37 to 68 as in the text, and lastly,

Ah me ! whither shall I flee ?
Thou hast metamorphosed me.
Do not let me sigh and pine,
Prythee be my valentine.

14 Feby. 1816.

Through sunny air. Add too, the sweetness
Of thy honey'd voice ; the neatness
Of thine ankle lightly turn'd :
With those beauties, scarce discern'd,
Kept with such sweet privacy,
That they seldom meet the eye
Of the little loves that fly
Round about with eager pry.   30
Saving when, with freshening lave,
Thou dipp'st them in the taintless wave ;
Like twin water lillies, born
In the coolness of the morn.
O, if thou hadst breathed then,
Now the Muses had been ten.
Couldst thou wish for lineage higher
Than twin sister of Thalia ?
At least for ever, evermore,
Will I call the Graces four.   40

Hadst thou liv'd when chivalry
Lifted up her lance on high,
Tell me what thou wouldst have been ?
Ah ! I see the silver sheen
Of thy broider'd, floating vest
Cov'ring half thine ivory breast ;
Which, O heavens ! I should see,
But that cruel destiny
Has placed a golden cuirass there ;
Keeping secret what is fair.   50
Like sunbeams in a cloudlet nested
Thy locks in knightly casque are rested :
O'er which bend four milky plumes
Like the gentle lilly's blooms
Springing from a costly vase.
See with what a stately pace
Comes thine alabaster steed ;
Servant of heroic deed !
O'er his loins, his trappings glow
Like the northern lights on snow.   60
Mount his back ! thy sword unsheath !
Sign of the enchanter's death ;
Bane of every wicked spell ;

Silencer of dragon's yell.
Alas! thou this wilt never do:
Thou art an enchantress too,
And wilt surely never spill
Blood of those whose eyes can kill.

TO HOPE

WHEN by my solitary hearth I sit,
  And hateful thoughts enwrap my soul in gloom;
When no fair dreams before my 'mind's eye' flit,
  And the bare heath of life presents no bloom;
    Sweet Hope, ethereal balm upon me shed,
    And wave thy silver pinions o'er my head.

Whene'er I wander, at the fall of night,
  Where woven boughs shut out the moon's bright ray,
Should sad Despondency my musings fright,
  And frown, to drive fair Cheerfulness away,   10
    Peep with the moon-beams through the leafy roof,
    And keep that fiend Despondence far aloof.

Should Disappointment, parent of Despair,
  Strive for her son to seize my careless heart;
When, like a cloud, he sits upon the air,
  Preparing on his spell-bound prey to dart:
    Chace him away, sweet Hope, with visage bright,
    And fright him as the morning frightens night!

Whene'er the fate of those I hold most dear
  Tells to my fearful breast a tale of sorrow,   20
O bright-eyed Hope, my morbid fancy cheer;
  Let me awhile thy sweetest comforts borrow:
    Thy heaven-born radiance around me shed,
    And wave thy silver pinions o'er my head!

Should e'er unhappy love my bosom pain,
  From cruel parents, or relentless fair;
O let me think it is not quite in vain
  To sigh out sonnets to the midnight air!
    Sweet Hope, ethereal balm upon me shed,
    And wave thy silver pinions o'er my head!   30

In the long vista of the years to roll,
  Let me not see our country's honour fade :
O let me see our land retain her soul,
  Her pride, her freedom; and not freedom's shade.
    From thy bright eyes unusual brightness shed—
    Beneath thy pinions canopy my head !

Let me not see the patriot's high bequest,
  Great liberty ! how great in plain attire !
With the base purple of a court oppress'd,
  Bowing her head, and ready to expire :   40
    But let me see thee stoop from heaven on wings
    That fill the skies with silver glitterings !

And as, in sparkling majesty, a star
  Gilds the bright summit of some gloomy cloud ;
Brightening the half veil'd face of heaven afar :
  So, when dark thoughts my boding spirit shroud,
    Sweet Hope, celestial influence round me shed,
    Waving thy silver pinions o'er my head.

February, 1815.

IMITATION OF SPENSER

* * * * * *

Now Morning from her orient chamber came,
And her first footsteps touch'd a verdant hill ;
Crowning its lawny crest with amber flame,
Silv'ring the untainted gushes of its rill ;
Which, pure from mossy beds, did down distill,
And after parting beds of simple flowers,
By many streams a little lake did fill,
Which round its marge reflected woven bowers,
And, in its middle space, a sky that never lowers.

There the king-fisher saw his plumage bright   10
Vieing with fish of brilliant dye below ;
Whose silken fins, and golden scales' light
Cast upward, through the waves, a ruby glow :

12 golden scalès light *Tom Keats's MS.*

There saw the swan his neck of arched snow,
And oar'd himself along with majesty ;
Sparkled his jetty eyes ; his feet did show
Beneath the waves like Afric's ebony,
And on his back a fay reclined voluptuously.

Ah ! could I tell the wonders of an isle
That in that fairest lake had placed been,   20
I could e'en Dido of her grief beguile ;
Or rob from aged Lear his bitter teen :
For sure so fair a place was never seen,
Of all that ever charm'd romantic eye :
It seem'd an emerald in the silver sheen
Of the bright waters ; or as when on high,
Through clouds of fleecy white, laughs the cœrulean sky.

And all around it dipp'd luxuriously
Slopings of verdure through the glossy tide,
Which, as it were in gentle amity,   30
Rippled delighted up the flowery side ;
As if to glean the ruddy tears, it tried,
Which fell profusely from the rose-tree stem !
Haply it was the workings of its pride,
In strife to throw upon the shore a gem
Outvieing all the buds in Flora's diadem.

* * * * * * *

[EDMONTON.]

WOMAN ! when I behold thee flippant, vain,
   Inconstant, childish, proud, and full of fancies ;
   Without that modest softening that enhances
The downcast eye, repentant of the pain
That its mild light creates to heal again :
   E'en then, elate, my spirit leaps, and prances,
   E'en then my soul with exultation dances
For that to love, so long, I've dormant lain :
But when I see thee meek, and kind, and tender,
   Heavens ! how desperately do I adore   10

29 glossy *1817* : glassy *Tom Keats's MS.*

Thy winning graces;—to be thy defender
  I hotly burn—to be a Calidore—
A very Red Cross Knight—a stout Leander—
  Might I be loved by thee like these of yore.

Light feet, dark violet eyes, and parted hair;
  Soft dimpled hands, white neck, and creamy breast,
  Are things on which the dazzled senses rest
Till the fond, fixed eyes, forget they stare.
From such fine pictures, heavens! I cannot dare
  To turn my admiration, though unpossess'd   20
  They be of what is worthy,—though not drest
In lovely modesty, and virtues rare.
Yet these I leave as thoughtless as a lark;
  These lures I straight forget,—e'en ere I dine,
Or thrice my palate moisten: but when I mark
  Such charms with mild intelligences shine,
My ear is open like a greedy shark,
  To catch the tunings of a voice divine.

Ah! who can e'er forget so fair a being?
  Who can forget her half retiring sweets?   30
  God! she is like a milk-white lamb that bleats
For man's protection. Surely the All-seeing,
Who joys to see us with his gifts agreeing,
  Will never give him pinions, who intreats
  Such innocence to ruin,—who vilely cheats
A dove-like bosom. In truth there is no freeing
One's thoughts from such a beauty; when I hear
  A lay that once I saw her hand awake,
Her form seems floating palpable, and near;
  Had I e'er seen her from an arbour take   40
A dewy flower, oft would that hand appear,
  And o'er my eyes the trembling moisture shake.

EPISTLES.

TO GEORGE FELTON MATHEW

SWEET are the pleasures that to verse belong,
And doubly sweet a brotherhood in song;
Nor can remembrance, Mathew! bring to view
A fate more pleasing, a delight more true
Than that in which the brother Poets joy'd,
Who with combined powers, their wit employ'd
To raise a trophy to the drama's muses.
The thought of this great partnership diffuses
Over the genius loving heart, a feeling
Of all that's high, and great, and good, and healing.

Too partial friend! fain would I follow thee   11
Past each horizon of fine poesy;
Fain would I echo back each pleasant note
As o'er Sicilian seas, clear anthems float
'Mong the light skimming gondolas far parted,
Just when the sun his farewell beam has darted:
But 'tis impossible; far different cares
Beckon me sternly from soft 'Lydian airs,'
And hold my faculties so long in thrall,
That I am oft in doubt whether at all   20
I shall again see Phœbus in the morning:
Or flush'd Aurora in the roseate dawning!
Or a white Naiad in a rippling stream;
Or a rapt seraph in a moonlight beam;
Or again witness what with thee I've seen,
The dew by fairy feet swept from the green,
After a night of some quaint jubilee
Which every elf and fay had come to see:
When bright processions took their airy march
Beneath the curved moon's triumphal arch.   30

*This and the two other Epistles form a separate section of the 1817
volume, with a half-title bearing the following motto from Browne's
'Britannia's Pastorals' :—*
        " Among the rest a shepheard (though but young
        "Yet hartned to his pipe) with all the skill
        " His few yeeres could, began to fit his quill."

But might I now each passing moment give
To the coy muse, with me she would not live
In this dark city, nor would condescend
'Mid contradictions her delights to lend.
Should e'er the fine-eyed maid to me be kind,
Ah! surely it must be whene'er I find
Some flowery spot, sequester'd, wild, romantic,
That often must have seen a poet frantic;
Where oaks, that erst the Druid knew, are growing,
And flowers, the glory of one day, are blowing;   40
Where the dark-leav'd laburnum's drooping clusters
Reflect athwart the stream their yellow lustres,
And intertwined the cassia's arms unite,
With its own drooping buds, but very white.
Where on one side are covert branches hung,
'Mong which the nightingales have always sung
In leafy quiet: where to pry, aloof,
Atween the pillars of the sylvan roof,
Would be to find where violet beds were nestling,
And where the bee with cowslip bells was wrestling.
There must be too a ruin dark, and gloomy,   51
To say 'joy not too much in all that's bloomy.'

Yet this is vain—O Mathew lend thy aid
To find a place where I may greet the maid—
Where we may soft humanity put on,
And sit, and rhyme and think on Chatterton;
And that warm-hearted Shakspeare sent to meet him
Four laurell'd spirits, heaven-ward to intreat him.
With reverence would we speak of all the sages   59
Who have left streaks of light athwart their ages:
And thou shouldst moralize on Milton's blindness,
And mourn the fearful dearth of human kindness
To those who strove with the bright golden wing
Of genius, to flap away each sting
Thrown by the pitiless world. We next could tell
Of those who in the cause of freedom fell;
Of our own Alfred, of Helvetian Tell;
Of him whose name to ev'ry heart's a solace,
High-minded and unbending William Wallace.
While to the rugged north our musing turns   70
We well might drop a tear for him, and Burns.

Felton ! without incitements such as these,
How vain for me the niggard Muse to tease :
For thee, she will thy every dwelling grace,
And make ' a sun-shine in a shady place : '
For thou wast once a flowret blooming wild,
Close to the source, bright, pure, and undefil'd,
Whence gush the streams of song : in happy hour
Came chaste Diana from her shady bower,
Just as the sun was from the east uprising ;   80
And, as for him some gift she was devising,
Beheld thee, pluck'd thee, cast thee in the stream
To meet her glorious brother's greeting beam.
I marvel much that thou hast never told
How, from a flower, into a fish of gold
Apollo chang'd thee ; how thou next didst seem
A black-eyed swan upon the widening stream ;
And when thou first didst in that mirror trace
The placid features of a human face :
That thou hast never told thy travels strange,   90
And all the wonders of the mazy range
O'er pebbly crystal, and o'er golden sands ;
Kissing thy daily food from Naiad's pearly hands.

   November, 1815.

TO MY BROTHER GEORGE

FULL many a dreary hour have I past,
My brain bewilder'd, and my mind o'ercast
With heaviness ; in seasons when I've thought
No spherey strains by me could e'er be caught
From the blue dome, though I to dimness gaze
On the far depth where sheeted lightning plays ;
Or, on the wavy grass outstretch'd supinely,
Pry 'mong the stars, to strive to think divinely :
That I should never hear Apollo's song,
Though feathery clouds were floating all along   10
The purple west, and, two bright streaks between,
The golden lyre itself were dimly seen :
That the still murmur of the honey bee
Would never teach a rural song to me :

That the bright glance from beauty's eyelids slanting
Would never make a lay of mine enchanting,
Or warm my breast with ardour to unfold
Some tale of love and arms in time of old.

But there are times, when those that love the bay,
Fly from all sorrowing far, far away ;   20
A sudden glow comes on them, naught they see
In water, earth, or air, but poesy.
It has been said, dear George, and true I hold it,
(For knightly Spenser to Libertas told it,)
That when a Poet is in such a trance,
In air he sees white coursers paw, and prance,
Bestridden of gay knights, in gay apparel,
Who at each other tilt in playful quarrel,
And what we, ignorantly, sheet-lightning call,
Is the swift opening of their wide portal,   30
When the bright warder blows his trumpet clear,
Whose tones reach naught on earth but Poet's ear.
When these enchanted portals open wide,
And through the light the horsemen swiftly glide,
The Poet's eye can reach those golden halls,
And view the glory of their festivals :
Their ladies fair, that in the distance seem
Fit for the silv'ring of a seraph's dream ;
Their rich brimm'd goblets, that incessant run
Like the bright spots that move about the sun ;   40
And, when upheld, the wine from each bright jar
Pours with the lustre of a falling star.
Yet further off, are dimly seen their bowers,
Of which, no mortal eye can reach the flowers ;
And 'tis right just, for well Apollo knows
'Twould make the Poet quarrel with the rose.
All that's reveal'd from that far seat of blisses,
Is, the clear fountains' interchanging kisses,
As gracefully descending, light and thin,
Like silver streaks across a dolphin's fin,   50
When he upswimmeth from the coral caves,
And sports with half his tail above the waves.

These wonders strange he sees, and many more,
Whose head is pregnant with poetic lore.

24 Libertas = Leigh Hunt. *See page* 11.

Should he upon an evening ramble fare
With forehead to the soothing breezes bare,
Would he naught see but the dark, silent blue
With all its diamonds trembling through and through?
Or the coy moon, when in the waviness
Of whitest clouds she does her beauty dress,   60
And staidly paces higher up, and higher,
Like a sweet nun in holy-day attire?
Ah, yes! much more would start into his sight—
The revelries, and mysteries of night:
And should I ever see them, I will tell you
Such tales as needs must with amazement spell you.

These are the living pleasures of the bard:
But richer far posterity's award.
What does he murmur with his latest breath,   69
While his proud eye looks through the film of death?
'What though I leave this dull, and earthly mould,
Yet shall my spirit lofty converse hold
With after times.—The patriot shall feel
My stern alarum, and unsheath his steel;
Or, in the senate thunder out my numbers
To startle princes from their easy slumbers.
The sage will mingle with each moral theme
My happy thoughts sententious; he will teem
With lofty periods when my verses fire him,
And then I'll stoop from heaven to inspire him.   80
Lays have I left of such a dear delight
That maids will sing them on their bridal night.
Gay villagers, upon a morn of May,
When they have tired their gentle limbs with play,
And form'd a snowy circle on the grass,
And plac'd in midst of all that lovely lass
Who chosen is their queen,—with her fine head
Crowned with flowers purple, white, and red:
For there the lilly, and the musk-rose, sighing,
Are emblems true of hapless lovers dying: 90
Between her breasts, that never yet felt trouble,
A bunch of violets full blown, and double,
Serenely sleep:—she from a casket takes
A little book,—and then a joy awakes
About each youthful heart,—with stifled cries,

And rubbing of white hands, and sparkling eyes :
For she's to read a tale of hopes, and fears ;
One that I foster'd in my youthful years :
The pearls, that on each glist'ning circlet sleep,
Gush ever and anon with silent creep,   100
Lured by the innocent dimples.   To sweet rest
Shall the dear babe, upon its mother's breast,
Be lull'd with songs of mine.   Fair world, adieu !
Thy dales, and hills, are fading from my view :
Swiftly I mount, upon wide spreading pinions,
Far from the narrow bounds of thy dominions.
Full joy I feel, while thus I cleave the air,
That my soft verse will charm thy daughters fair,
And warm thy sons !' Ah, my dear friend and brother,
Could I, at once, my mad ambition smother,   110
For tasting joys like these, sure I should be
Happier, and dearer to society.
At times, 'tis true, I've felt relief from pain
When some bright thought has darted through my brain :
Through all that day I've felt a greater pleasure
Than if I'd brought to light a hidden treasure.
As to my sonnets, though none else should heed them,
I feel delighted, still, that you should read them.
Of late, too, I have had much calm enjoyment,   119
Stretch'd on the grass at my best lov'd employment
Of scribbling lines for you.   These things I thought
While, in my face, the freshest breeze I caught.
E'en now I'm pillow'd on a bed of flowers
That crowns a lofty clift, which proudly towers
Above the ocean-waves.   The stalks, and blades,
Chequer my tablet with their quivering shades.
On one side is a field of drooping oats,
Through which the poppies show their scarlet coats ;
So pert and useless, that they bring to mind
The scarlet coats that pester human-kind.   130
And on the other side, outspread, is seen
Ocean's blue mantle streak'd with purple, and green.
Now 'tis I see a canvass'd ship, and now
Mark the bright silver curling round her prow.
I see the lark down-dropping to his nest,
And the broad winged sea-gull never at rest ;
For when no more he spreads his feathers free,

His breast is dancing on the restless sea.
Now I direct my eyes into the west,
Which at this moment is in sunbeams drest: 140
Why westward turn? 'Twas but to say adieu!
'Twas but to kiss my hand, dear George, to you!

    [MARGATE] *August* 1816.

TO CHARLES COWDEN CLARKE

OFT have you seen a swan superbly frowning,
And with proud breast his own white shadow crowning;
He slants his neck beneath the waters bright
So silently, it seems a beam of light
Come from the galaxy: anon he sports,—
With outspread wings the Naiad Zephyr courts,
Or ruffles all the surface of the lake
In striving from its crystal face to take
Some diamond water drops, and them to treasure
In milky nest, and sip them off at leisure.   10
But not a moment can he there insure them,
Nor to such downy rest can he allure them;
For down they rush as though they would be free,
And drop like hours into eternity.
Just like that bird am I in loss of time,
Whene'er I venture on the stream of rhyme;
With shatter'd boat, oar snapt, and canvass rent
I slowly sail, scarce knowing my intent;
Still scooping up the water with my fingers,
In which a trembling diamond never lingers.   20
By this, friend Charles, you may full plainly see
Why I have never penn'd a line to thee:
Because my thoughts were never free, and clear,
And little fit to please a classic ear;
Because my wine was of too poor a savour
For one whose palate gladdens in the flavour
Of sparkling Helicon:—small good it were
To take him to a desert rude, and bare,
Who had on Baiæ's shore reclin'd at ease,
While Tasso's page was floating in a breeze   30
That gave soft music from Armida's bowers,
Mingled with fragrance from her rarest flowers:

Small good to one who had by Mulla's stream
Fondled the maidens with the breasts of cream ;
Who had beheld Belphœbe in a brook,
And lovely Una in a leafy nook,
And Archimago leaning o'er his book:
Who had of all that's sweet tasted, and seen,
From silv'ry ripple, up to beauty's queen ;
From the sequester'd haunts of gay Titania,   40
To the blue dwelling of divine Urania :
One, who, of late, had ta'en sweet forest walks
With him who elegantly chats, and talks—
The wrong'd Libertas,—who has told you stories
Of laurel chaplets, and Apollo's glories ;
Of troops chivalrous prancing through a city,
And tearful ladies made for love, and pity :
With many else which I have never known.
Thus have I thought ; and days on days have flown
Slowly, or rapidly—unwilling still   50
For you to try my dull, unlearned quill.
Nor should I now, but that I've known you long ;
That you first taught me all the sweets of song :
The grand, the sweet, the terse, the free, the fine ;
What swell'd with pathos, and what right divine :
Spenserian vowels that elope with ease,
And float along like birds o'er summer seas ;
Miltonian storms, and more, Miltonian tenderness ;
Michael in arms, and more, meek Eve's fair slenderness.
Who read for me the sonnet swelling loudly   60
Up to its climax and then dying proudly ?
Who found for me the grandeur of the ode,
Growing, like Atlas, stronger from its load ?
Who let me taste that more than cordial dram,
The sharp, the rapier-pointed epigram ?
Show'd me that epic was of all the king,
Round, vast, and spanning all like Saturn's ring ?
You too upheld the veil from Clio's beauty,
And pointed out the patriot's stern duty ;
The might of Alfred, and the shaft of Tell ;   70
The hand of Brutus, that so grandly fell
Upon a tyrant's head. Ah ! had I never seen,

44 Libertas = Leigh Hunt. *See pages* 11 *and* 27.

Or known your kindness, what might I have been?
What my enjoyments in my youthful years,
Bereft of all that now my life endears?
And can I e'er these benefits forget?
And can I e'er repay the friendly debt?
No, doubly no;—yet should these rhymings please,
I shall roll on the grass with two-fold ease:
For I have long time been my fancy feeding   80
With hopes that you would one day think the reading
Of my rough verses not an hour misspent;
Should it e'er be so, what a rich content!
Some weeks have pass'd since last I saw the spires
In lucent Thames reflected:—warm desires
To see the sun o'erpeep the eastern dimness,
And morning shadows streaking into slimness
Across the lawny fields, and pebbly water;
To mark the time as they grow broad, and shorter;
To feel the air that plays about the hills,   90
And sips its freshness from the little rills;
To see high, golden corn wave in the light
When Cynthia smiles upon a summer's night,
And peers among the cloudlets jet and white,
As though she were reclining in a bed
Of bean blossoms, in heaven freshly shed.
No sooner had I stepp'd into these pleasures
Than I began to think of rhymes and measures:
The air that floated by me seem'd to say
"Write! thou wilt never have a better day."   100
And so I did. When many lines I'd written,
Though with their grace I was not oversmitten,
Yet, as my hand was warm, I thought I'd better
Trust to my feelings, and write you a letter.
Such an attempt required an inspiration
Of a peculiar sort,—a consummation;—
Which, had I felt, these scribblings might have been
Verses from which the soul would never wean:
But many days have passed since last my heart
Was warm'd luxuriously by divine Mozart;   110
By Arne delighted, or by Handel madden'd;
Or by the song of Erin pierc'd and sadden'd:
What time you were before the music sitting,
And the rich notes to each sensation fitting.

Since I have walk'd with you through shady lanes
That freshly terminate in open plains,
And revel'd in a chat that ceased not
When at night-fall among your books we got:
No, nor when supper came, nor after that,—
Nor when reluctantly I took my hat ;   120
No, nor till cordially you shook my hand
Mid-way between our homes :—your accents bland
Still sounded in my ears, when I no more
Could hear your footsteps touch the grav'ly floor.
Sometimes I lost them, and then found again ;
You chang'd the footpath for the grassy plain.
In those still moments I have wish'd you joys
That well you know to honour :—" Life's very toys
" With him," said I, " will take a pleasant charm ;
" It cannot be that aught will work him harm." 130
These thoughts now come o'er me with all their might:—
Again I shake your hand,—friend Charles, good night.

  September, 1816.

SONNETS

I

TO MY BROTHER GEORGE

MANY the wonders I this day have seen :
  The sun, when first he kist away the tears
  That fill'd the eyes of morn ;—the laurell'd peers
Who from the feathery gold of evening lean ;—
The ocean with its vastness, its blue green,
  Its ships, its rocks, its caves, its hopes, its fears,—
  Its voice mysterious, which whoso hears
Must think on what will be, and what has been.
E'en now, dear George, while this for you I write,
  Cynthia is from her silken curtains peeping   10
So scantly, that it seems her bridal night,
  And she her half-discover'd revels keeping.
But what, without the social thought of thee,
Would be the wonders of the sky and sea?

II

TO * * * * * *

HAD I a man's fair form, then might my sighs
  Be echoed swiftly through that ivory shell
  Thine ear, and find thy gentle heart ; so well
Would passion arm me for the enterprize :
But ah! I am no knight whose foeman dies ;
  No cuirass glistens on my bosom's swell ;
  I am no happy shepherd of the dell
Whose lips have trembled with a maiden's eyes.
Yet must I dote upon thee,—call thee sweet,
  Sweeter by far than Hybla's honied roses   10
    When steep'd in dew rich to intoxication.
Ah! I will taste that dew, for me 'tis meet,
  And when the moon her pallid face discloses,
    I'll gather some by spells, and incantation.

III

WRITTEN ON THE DAY THAT MR. LEIGH HUNT LEFT PRISON

WHAT though, for showing truth to flatter'd state,
  Kind Hunt was shut in prison, yet has he,
  In his immortal spirit, been as free
As the sky-searching lark, and as elate.
Minion of grandeur! think you he did wait?
  Think you he naught but prison walls did see,
  Till, so unwilling, thou unturn'dst the key?
Ah, no! far happier, nobler was his fate!
In Spenser's halls he stray'd, and bowers fair,
  Culling enchanted flowers; and he flew   10
With daring Milton through the fields of air:
  To regions of his own his genius true
Took happy flights. Who shall his fame impair
  When thou art dead, and all thy wretched crew?

IV

How many bards gild the lapses of time!
  A few of them have ever been the food
  Of my delighted fancy,—I could brood
Over their beauties, earthly, or sublime:
And often, when I sit me down to rhyme,
  These will in throngs before my mind intrude:
  But no confusion, no disturbance rude
Do they occasion; 'tis a pleasing chime.
So the unnumber'd sounds that evening store;   9
The songs of birds—the whisp'ring of the leaves—
  The voice of waters—the great bell that heaves
With solemn sound,—and thousand others more,
  That distance of recognizance bereaves,
Make pleasing music, and not wild uproar.

V

TO A FRIEND WHO SENT ME SOME ROSES

As late I rambled in the happy fields,
  What time the sky-lark shakes the tremulous dew
  From his lush clover covert ;—when anew
Adventurous knights take up their dinted shields :
I saw the sweetest flower wild nature yields,
  A fresh-blown musk-rose ; 'twas the first that threw
  Its sweets upon the summer : graceful it grew
As is the wand that queen Titania wields.
And, as I feasted on its fragrancy,
  I thought the garden-rose it far excell'd :   10
But when, O Wells ! thy roses came to me
  My sense with their deliciousness was spell'd :
Soft voices had they, that with tender plea
  Whisper'd of peace, and truth, and friendliness
    unquell'd.

[*June* 29, 1816.]

VI

TO G. A. W.

[Georgiana Augusta Wylie.]

Nymph of the downward smile and sidelong glance,
  In what diviner moments of the day
  Art thou most lovely ?—when gone far astray
Into the labyrinths of sweet utterance,
Or when serenely wand'ring in a trance
  Of sober thought?—or when starting away
  With careless robe to meet the morning ray
Thou spar'st the flowers in thy mazy dance?
Haply 'tis when thy ruby lips part sweetly,
  And so remain, because thou listenest :   10
But thou to please wert nurtured so completely
  That I can never tell what mood is best.
I shall as soon pronounce which Grace more neatly
  Trips it before Apollo than the rest.

V. Title] To Charles Wells on receiving a bunch of roses.
Tom Keats's MS.
14 Whispered of truth, Humanity and Friendliness un-
quell'd. *Tom Keats's MS.*

VII

O SOLITUDE! if I must with thee dwell,
  Let it not be among the jumbled heap
  Of murky buildings; climb with me the steep,—
Nature's observatory—whence the dell,
Its flowery slopes, its river's crystal swell,
  May seem a span; let me thy vigils keep
  'Mongst boughs pavillion'd, where the deer's swift leap
Startles the wild bee from the fox-glove bell.
But though I'll gladly trace these scenes with thee,
  Yet the sweet converse of an innocent mind,   10
  Whose words are images of thoughts refin'd,
Is my soul's pleasure; and it sure must be
  Almost the highest bliss of human-kind,
When to thy haunts two kindred spirits flee.

VIII

TO MY BROTHERS

SMALL, busy flames play through the fresh laid coals,
  And their faint cracklings o'er our silence creep
  Like whispers of the household gods that keep
A gentle empire o'er fraternal souls.
And while, for rhymes, I search around the poles,
  Your eyes are fix'd, as in poetic sleep,
  Upon the lore so voluble and deep,
That aye at fall of night our care condoles.
This is your birth-day Tom, and I rejoice
  That thus it passes smoothly, quietly.   10
Many such eves of gently whisp'ring noise
  May we together pass, and calmly try
What are this world's true joys,—ere the great voice,
  From its fair face, shall bid our spirits fly.

November 18, 1816.

VII. 9, 10.
Ah! fain would I frequent such scenes with thee;
  But the sweet converse of an innocent mind. *Examiner.*
VIII. Title] Written to his brother Tom on his Birthday.
Tom Keats's MS.

IX

KEEN, fitful gusts are whisp'ring here and there
　Among the bushes half leafless, and dry ;
　The stars look very cold about the sky,
And I have many miles on foot to fare.
Yet feel I little of the cool bleak air,
　Or of the dead leaves rustling drearily,
　Or of those silver lamps that burn on high,
Or of the distance from home's pleasant lair :
For I am brimfull of the friendliness
　That in a little cottage I have found ;　　　　10
Of fair-hair'd Milton's eloquent distress,
　And all his love for gentle Lycid drown'd ;
Of lovely Laura in her light green dress,
　And faithful Petrarch gloriously crown'd.

X

To one who has been long in city pent,
　'Tis very sweet to look into the fair
　And open face of heaven,—to breathe a prayer
Full in the smile of the blue firmament.
Who is more happy, when, with heart's content,
　Fatigued he sinks into some pleasant lair
　Of wavy grass, and reads a debonair
And gentle tale of love and languishment ?
Returning home at evening, with an ear
　Catching the notes of Philomel,—an eye　　　10
Watching the sailing cloudlet's bright career,
　He mourns that day so soon has glided by :
E'en like the passage of an angel's tear
　That falls through the clear ether silently.

IX. *Clarke records that this sonnet was written on the occasion of Keats's first becoming acquainted with Leigh Hunt at the Cottage in the Vale of Health, Hampstead.*
X. Written in the Fields—June 1816.　*George Keats's MS.*

XI

ON FIRST LOOKING INTO CHAPMAN'S HOMER

Much have I travell'd in the realms of gold,
  And many goodly states and kingdoms seen;
  Round many western islands have I been
Which bards in fealty to Apollo hold.
Oft of one wide expanse had I been told
  That deep-brow'd Homer ruled as his demesne;
  Yet did I never breathe its pure serene
Till I heard Chapman speak out loud and bold:
Then felt I like some watcher of the skies
  When a new planet swims into his ken;   10
Or like stout Cortez when with eagle eyes
  He star'd at the Pacific—and all his men
Look'd at each other with a wild surmise—
  Silent, upon a peak in Darien.

. XII

ON LEAVING SOME FRIENDS AT AN EARLY HOUR

Give me a golden pen, and let me lean
  On heap'd up flowers, in regions clear, and far;
  Bring me a tablet whiter than a star,
Or hand of hymning angel, when 'tis seen
The silver strings of heavenly harp atween:
  And let there glide by many a pearly car,
  Pink robes, and wavy hair, and diamond jar,
And half discovered wings, and glances keen.
The while let music wander round my ears,
  And as it reaches each delicious ending,   10
Let me write down a line of glorious tone,
And full of many wonders of the spheres:
  For what a height my spirit is contending!
  'Tis not content so soon to be alone.

XIII

ADDRESSED TO HAYDON

HIGHMINDEDNESS, a jealousy for good,
    A loving-kindness for the great man's fame,
    Dwells here and there with people of no name,
In noisome alley, and in pathless wood :
And where we think the truth least understood,
    Oft may be found a 'singleness of aim,'
    That ought to frighten into hooded shame
A money-mong'ring, pitiable brood.
How glorious this affection for the cause
    Of stedfast genius, toiling gallantly !   10
What when a stout unbending champion awes
    Envy, and Malice to their native sty ?
Unnumber'd souls breathe out a still applause,
    Proud to behold him in his country's eye.

XIV

ADDRESSED TO THE SAME

GREAT spirits now on earth are sojourning ;
    He of the cloud, the cataract, the lake,
    Who on Helvellyn's summit, wide awake,
Catches his freshness from Archangel's wing :
He of the rose, the violet, the spring,
    The social smile, the chain for Freedom's sake :
    And lo !—whose stedfastness would never take
A meaner sound than Raphael's whispering.
And other spirits there are standing apart
    Upon the forehead of the age to come ;   10
These, these will give the world another heart,
    And other pulses. Hear ye not the hum
Of mighty workings ?——
    Listen awhile ye nations, and be dumb.

XV

ON THE GRASSHOPPER AND CRICKET

The poetry of earth is never dead:
  When all the birds are faint with the hot sun,
  And hide in cooling trees, a voice will run
From hedge to hedge about the new-mown mead;
That is the Grasshopper's—he takes the lead
  In summer luxury,—he has never done
  With his delights; for when tired out with fun
He rests at ease beneath some pleasant weed.
The poetry of earth is ceasing never:
  On a lone winter evening, when the frost   10
  Has wrought a silence, from the stove there shrills
The Cricket's song, in warmth increasing ever,
  And seems to one in drowsiness half lost,
    The Grasshopper's among some grassy hills.

December 30, 1816.

XVI

TO KOSCIUSKO

Good Kosciusko, thy great name alone
  Is a full harvest whence to reap high feeling;
  It comes upon us like the glorious pealing
Of the wide spheres—an everlasting tone.
And now it tells me, that in worlds unknown,
  The names of heroes, burst from clouds concealing,
  And change to harmonies, for ever stealing
Through cloudless blue, and round each silver throne.
It tells me too, that on a happy day,
  When some good spirit walks upon the earth, 10
  Thy name with Alfred's, and the great of yore
Gently commingling, gives tremendous birth
To a loud hymn, that sounds far, far away
  To where the great God lives for evermore.

[*December*, 1816.]

XVI. 7. changed *Poems 1817; but* change *is authorized by Woodhouse.*

*C 3

XVII

Happy is England! I could be content
    To see no other verdure than its own;
    To feel no other breezes than are blown
Through its tall woods with high romances blent:
Yet do I sometimes feel a languishment
    For skies Italian, and an inward groan
    To sit upon an Alp as on a throne,
And half forget what world or worldling meant.
Happy is England, sweet her artless daughters;
    Enough their simple loveliness for me,   10
        Enough their whitest arms in silence clinging:
    Yet do I often warmly burn to see
        Beauties of deeper glance, and hear their singing,
And float with them about the summer waters.

SLEEP AND POETRY

"As I lay in my bed slepe full unmete
"Was unto me, but why that I ne might
"Rest I ne wist, for there n'as erthly wight
"[As I suppose] had more of hertis ese
"Than I, for I n'ad sicknesse nor disese."
                                        CHAUCER.

WHAT is more gentle than a wind in summer?
What is more soothing than the pretty hummer
That stays one moment in an open flower,
And buzzes cheerily from bower to bower?
What is more tranquil than a musk-rose blowing
In a green island, far from all men's knowing?
More healthful than the leafiness of dales?
More secret than a nest of nightingales?
More serene than Cordelia's countenance?
More full of visions than a high romance?   10
What, but thee Sleep? Soft closer of our eyes!
Low murmurer of tender lullabies!
Light hoverer around our happy pillows!
Wreather of poppy buds, and weeping willows!
Silent entangler of a beauty's tresses!
Most happy listener! when the morning blesses
Thee for enlivening all the cheerful eyes
That glance so brightly at the new sun-rise.

But what is higher beyond thought than thee?
Fresher than berries of a mountain tree?   20
More strange, more beautiful, more smooth, more regal,
Than wings of swans, than doves, than dim-seen eagle?
What is it? And to what shall I compare it?
It has a glory, and naught else can share it:
The thought thereof is awful, sweet, and holy,
Chasing away all worldliness and folly;
Coming sometimes like fearful claps of thunder,
Or the low rumblings earth's regions under;
And sometimes like a gentle whispering
Of all the secrets of some wond'rous thing   30

That breathes about us in the vacant air;
So that we look around with prying stare,
Perhaps to see shapes of light, aerial limning,
And catch soft floatings from a faint-heard hymning;
To see the laurel wreath, on high suspended,
That is to crown our name when life is ended.
Sometimes it gives a glory to the voice,
And from the heart up-springs, rejoice! rejoice!
Sounds which will reach the Framer of all things,
And die away in ardent mutterings.   40

No one who once the glorious sun has seen,
And all the clouds, and felt his bosom clean
For his great Maker's presence, but must know
What 'tis I mean, and feel his being glow:
Therefore no insult will I give his spirit,
By telling what he sees from native merit.

O Poesy! for thee I hold my pen
That am not yet a glorious denizen
Of thy wide heaven—Should I rather kneel
Upon some mountain-top until I feel   50
A glowing splendour round about me hung,
And echo back the voice of thine own tongue?
O Poesy! for thee I grasp my pen
That am not yet a glorious denizen
Of thy wide heaven; yet, to my ardent prayer,
Yield from thy sanctuary some clear air,
Smooth'd for intoxication by the breath
Of flowering bays, that I may die a death
Of luxury, and my young spirit follow
The morning sun-beams to the great Apollo   60
Like a fresh sacrifice; or, if I can bear
The o'erwhelming sweets, 'twill bring to me the fair
Visions of all places: a bowery nook
Will be elysium—an eternal book
Whence I may copy many a lovely saying
About the leaves, and flowers—about the playing
Of nymphs in woods, and fountains; and the shade
Keeping a silence round a sleeping maid;
And many a verse from so strange influence

That we must ever wonder how, and whence   70
It came. Also imaginings will hover
Round my fire-side, and haply there discover
Vistas of solemn beauty, where I'd wander
In happy silence, like the clear Meander
Through its lone vales ; and where I found a spot
Of awfuller shade, or an enchanted grot,
Or a green hill o'erspread with chequer'd dress
Of flowers, and fearful from its loveliness,
Write on my tablets all that was permitted,
All that was for our human senses fitted,   80
Then the events of this wide world I'd seize
Like a strong giant, and my spirit teaze
Till at its shoulders it should proudly see
Wings to find out an immortality.

Stop and consider ! life is but a day ;
A fragile dew-drop on its perilous way
From a tree's summit ; a poor Indian's sleep
While his boat hastens to the monstrous steep
Of Montmorenci. Why so sad a moan ?
Life is the rose's hope while yet unblown ;   90
The reading of an ever-changing tale ;
The light uplifting of a maiden's veil ;
A pigeon tumbling in clear summer air ;
A laughing school-boy, without grief or care,
Riding the springy branches of an elm.

O for ten years, that I may overwhelm
Myself in poesy ; so I may do the deed
That my own soul has to itself decreed.
Then will I pass the countries that I see
In long perspective, and continually   100
Taste their pure fountains. First the realm I'll pass
Of Flora, and old Pan : sleep in the grass,
Feed upon apples red, and strawberries,
And choose each pleasure that my fancy sees ;
Catch the white-handed nymphs in shady places,
To woo sweet kisses from averted faces,—
Play with their fingers, touch their shoulders white
Into a pretty shrinking with a bite

74 meander *with a small* m *Poems 1817.*

As hard as lips can make it : till agreed,
A lovely tale of human life we'll read.   110
And one will teach a tame dove how it best
May fan the cool air gently o'er my rest ;
Another, bending o'er her nimble tread,
Will set a green robe floating round her head,
And still will dance with ever varied ease,
Smiling upon the flowers and the trees :
Another will entice me on, and on
Through almond blossoms and rich cinnamon ;
Till in the bosom of a leafy world
We rest in silence, like two gems upcurl'd   120
In the recesses of a pearly shell.

And can I ever bid these joys farewell ?
Yes, I must pass them for a nobler life,
Where I may find the agonies, the strife
Of human hearts : for lo ! I see afar,
O'ersailing the blue cragginess, a car
And steeds with streamy manes—the charioteer
Looks out upon the winds with glorious fear :
And now the numerous tramplings quiver lightly
Along a huge cloud's ridge ; and now with sprightly
Wheel downward come they into fresher skies,   131
Tipt round with silver from the sun's bright eyes.
Still downward with capacious whirl they glide ;
And now I see them on the green-hill's side
In breezy rest among the nodding stalks.
The charioteer with wond'rous gesture talks
To the trees and mountains ; and there soon appear
Shapes of delight, of mystery, and fear,
Passing along before a dusky space
Made by some mighty oaks : as they would chase   140
Some ever-fleeting music on they sweep.
Lo ! how they murmur, laugh, and smile, and weep :
Some with upholden hand and mouth severe ;
Some with their faces muffled to the ear
Between their arms ; some, clear in youthful bloom,
Go glad and smilingly athwart the gloom ;
Some looking back, and some with upward gaze ;
Yes, thousands in a thousand different ways
Flit onward—now a lovely wreath of girls

Dancing their sleek hair into tangled curls ;   150
And now broad wings. Most awfully intent
The driver of those steeds is forward bent,
And seems to listen : O that I might know
All that he writes with such a hurrying glow.

The visions all are fled—the car is fled
Into the light of heaven, and in their stead
A sense of real things comes doubly strong,
And, like a muddy stream, would bear along
My soul to nothingness : but I will strive
Against all doubtings, and will keep alive   160
The thought of that same chariot, and the strange
Journey it went.

     Is there so small a range
In the present strength of manhood, that the high
Imagination cannot freely fly
As she was wont of old ? prepare her steeds,
Paw up against the light, and do strange deeds
Upon the clouds ? Has she not shown us all ?
From the clear space of ether, to the small
Breath of new buds unfolding ? From the meaning
Of Jove's large eye-brow, to the tender greening 170
Of April meadows ? Here her altar shone,
E'en in this isle ; and who could paragon
The fervid choir that lifted up a noise
Of harmony, to where it aye will poise
Its mighty self of convoluting sound,
Huge as a planet, and like that roll round,
Eternally around a dizzy void ?
Ay, in those days the Muses were nigh cloy'd
With honors ; nor had any other care
Than to sing out and sooth their wavy hair.   180

Could all this be forgotten ? Yes, a schism
Nurtured by foppery and barbarism,
Made great Apollo blush for this his land.
Men were thought wise who could not understand
His glories : with a puling infant's force
They sway'd about upon a rocking horse,
And thought it Pegasus. Ah dismal soul'd !

181 scism *Poems 1817.*

The winds of heaven blew, the ocean roll'd
Its gathering waves—ye felt it not. The blue
Bared its eternal bosom, and the dew   190
Of summer nights collected still to make
The morning precious : beauty was awake!
Why were ye not awake ? But ye were dead
To things ye knew not of,—were closely wed
To musty laws lined out with wretched rule
And compass vile : so that ye taught a school
Of dolts to smooth, inlay, and clip, and fit,
Till, like the certain wands of Jacob's wit,
Their verses tallied. Easy was the task :
A thousand handicraftsmen wore the mask   200
Of Poesy. Ill-fated, impious race!
That blasphemed the bright Lyrist to his face,
And did not know it,—no, they went about,
Holding a poor, decrepid standard out
Mark'd with most flimsy mottos, and in large
The name of one Boileau!

                              O ye whose charge
It is to hover round our pleasant hills!
Whose congregated majesty so fills
My boundly reverence, that I cannot trace
Your hallowed names, in this unholy place,   210
So near those common folk ; did not their shames
Affright you? Did our old lamenting Thames
Delight you? Did ye never cluster round
Delicious Avon, with a mournful sound,
And weep? Or did ye wholly bid adieu
To regions where no more the laurel grew ?
Or did ye stay to give a welcoming
To some lone spirits who could proudly sing
Their youth away, and die? 'Twas even so :
But let me think away those times of woe :   220
Now 'tis a fairer season ; ye have breathed
Rich benedictions o'er us ; ye have wreathed
Fresh garlands : for sweet music has been heard
In many places ;—some has been upstirr'd
From out its crystal dwelling in a lake,
By a swan's ebon bill ; from a thick brake,
Nested and quiet in a valley mild,

Bubbles a pipe; fine sounds are floating wild
About the earth: happy are ye and glad. 229

These things are doubtless: yet in truth we've had
Strange thunders from the potency of song;
Mingled indeed with what is sweet and strong,
From majesty: but in clear truth the themes
Are ugly clubs, the Poets' Polyphemes
Disturbing the grand sea. A drainless shower
Of light is poesy; 'tis the supreme of power;
'Tis might half slumb'ring on its own right arm.
The very archings of her eye-lids charm
A thousand willing agents to obey,
And still she governs with the mildest sway: 240
But strength alone though of the Muses born
Is like a fallen angel: trees uptorn,
Darkness, and worms, and shrouds, and sepulchres
Delight it; for it feeds upon the burrs,
And thorns of life; forgetting the great end
Of poesy, that it should be a friend
To sooth the cares, and lift the thoughts of man.

Yet I rejoice: a myrtle fairer than
E'er grew in Paphos, from the bitter weeds
Lifts its sweet head into the air, and feeds 250
A silent space with ever sprouting green.
All tenderest birds there find a pleasant screen,
Creep through the shade with jaunty fluttering,
Nibble the little cupped flowers and sing.
Then let us clear away the choking thorns
From round its gentle stem; let the young fawns,
Yeaned in after times, when we are flown,
Find a fresh sward beneath it, overgrown
With simple flowers: let there nothing be
More boisterous than a lover's bended knee; 260
Nought more ungentle than the placid look
Of one who leans upon a closed book;
Nought more untranquil than the grassy slopes
Between two hills. All hail delightful hopes!
As she was wont, th' imagination
Into most lovely labyrinths will be gone,
And they shall be accounted poet kings

Who simply tell the most heart-easing things.
O may these joys be ripe before I die.

Will not some say that I presumptuously   270
Have spoken? that from hastening disgrace
'Twere better far to hide my foolish face?
That whining boyhood should with reverence bow
Ere the dread thunderbolt could reach? How!
If I do hide myself, it sure shall be
In the very fane, the light of Poesy:
If I do fall, at least I will be laid
Beneath the silence of a poplar shade;
And over me the grass shall be smooth shaven;
And there shall be a kind memorial graven.   280
But off Despondence! miserable bane!
They should not know thee, who athirst to gain
A noble end, are thirsty every hour.
What though I am not wealthy in the dower
Of spanning wisdom; though I do not know
The shiftings of the mighty winds that blow
Hither and thither all the changing thoughts
Of man: though no great minist'ring reason sorts
Out the dark mysteries of human souls
To clear conceiving: yet there ever rolls   290
A vast idea before me, and I glean
Therefrom my liberty; thence too I've seen
The end and aim of Poesy. 'Tis clear
As anything most true; as that the year
Is made of the four seasons—manifest
As a large cross, some old cathedral's crest,
Lifted to the white clouds. Therefore should I
Be but the essence of deformity,
A coward, did my very eye-lids wink
At speaking out what I have dared to think.   300
Ah! rather let me like a madman run
Over some precipice; let the hot sun
Melt my Dedalian wings, and drive me down
Convuls'd and headlong! Stay! an inward frown
Of conscience bids me be more calm awhile.
An ocean dim, sprinkled with many an isle,
Spreads awfully before me. How much toil!
How many days! what desperate turmoil!

Ere I can have explored its widenesses.
Ah, what a task! upon my bended knees,   310
I could unsay those—no, impossible!
Impossible!

        For sweet relief I'll dwell
On humbler thoughts, and let this strange assay
Begun in gentleness die so away.
E'en now all tumult from my bosom fades:
I turn full hearted to the friendly aids
That smooth the path of honour; brotherhood,
And friendliness the nurse of mutual good.
The hearty grasp that sends a pleasant sonnet
Into the brain ere one can think upon it;   320
The silence when some rhymes are coming out;
And when they're come, the very pleasant rout:
The message certain to be done to-morrow.
'Tis perhaps as well that it should be to borrow
Some precious book from out its snug retreat,
To cluster round it when we next shall meet.
Scarce can I scribble on; for lovely airs
Are fluttering round the room like doves in pairs;
Many delights of that glad day recalling,
When first my senses caught their tender falling.   330
And with these airs come forms of elegance
Stooping their shoulders o'er a horse's prance,
Careless, and grand—fingers soft and round
Parting luxuriant curls;—and the swift bound
Of Bacchus from his chariot, when his eye
Made Ariadne's cheek look blushingly.
Thus I remember all the pleasant flow
Of words at opening a portfolio.

Things such as these are ever harbingers
To trains of peaceful images: the stirs   340
Of a swan's neck unseen among the rushes:
A linnet starting all about the bushes:
A butterfly, with golden wings broad parted,
Nestling a rose, convuls'd as though it smarted
With over pleasure—many, many more,
Might I indulge at large in all my store
Of luxuries: yet I must not forget
Sleep, quiet with his poppy coronet:

For what there may be worthy in these rhymes
I partly owe to him: and thus, the chimes   350
Of friendly voices had just given place
To as sweet a silence, when I 'gan retrace
The pleasant day, upon a couch at ease.
It was a poet's house who keeps the keys
Of pleasure's temple. Round about were hung
The glorious features of the bards who sung
In other ages—cold and sacred busts
Smiled at each other. Happy he who trusts
To clear Futurity his darling fame!
Then there were fauns and satyrs taking aim   360
At swelling apples with a frisky leap
And reaching fingers, 'mid a luscious heap
Of vine-leaves. Then there rose to view a fane
Of liny marble, and thereto a train
Of nymphs approaching fairly o'er the sward:
One, loveliest, holding her white hand toward
The dazzling sun-rise: two sisters sweet
Bending their graceful figures till they meet
Over the trippings of a little child:
And some are hearing, eagerly, the wild   370
Thrilling liquidity of dewy piping.
See, in another picture, nymphs are wiping
Cherishingly Diana's timorous limbs;—
A fold of lawny mantle dabbling swims
At the bath's edge, and keeps a gentle motion
With the subsiding crystal: as when ocean
Heaves calmly its broad swelling smoothness o'er
Its rocky marge, and balances once more
The patient weeds; that now unshent by foam
Feel all about their undulating home.   380

Sappho's meek head was there half smiling down
At nothing; just as though the earnest frown
Of over thinking had that moment gone
From off her brow, and left her all alone.

Great Alfred's too, with anxious, pitying eyes,
As if he always listened to the sighs
Of the goaded world; and Kosciusko's worn
By horrid suffrance—mightily forlorn.

Petrarch, outstepping from the shady green,
Starts at the sight of Laura; nor can wean   390
His eyes from her sweet face. Most happy they!
For over them was seen a free display
Of out-spread wings, and from between them shone
The face of Poesy: from off her throne
She overlook'd things that I scarce could tell.
The very sense of where I was might well
Keep Sleep aloof: but more than that there came
Thought after thought to nourish up the flame
Within my breast; so that the morning light
Surprised me even from a sleepless night;   400
And up I rose refresh'd, and glad, and gay,
Resolving to begin that very day
These lines; and howsoever they be done,
I leave them as a father does his son.

ENDYMION:

A POETIC ROMANCE.

INSCRIBED

TO THE MEMORY

OF

THOMAS CHATTERTON.

1818.

PREFACE

KNOWING within myself the manner in which this Poem has been produced, it is not without a feeling of regret that I make it public.

What manner I mean, will be quite clear to the reader, who must soon perceive great inexperience, immaturity, and every error denoting a feverish attempt, rather than a deed accomplished. The two first books, and indeed the two last, I feel sensible are not of such completion as to warrant their passing the press; nor should they if I thought a year's castigation would do them any good;—it will not: the foundations are too sandy. It is just that this youngster should die away: a sad thought for me, if I had not some hope that while it is dwindling I may be plotting, and fitting myself for verses fit to live.

This may be speaking too presumptuously, and may deserve a punishment: but no feeling man will be forward to inflict it: he will leave me alone, with the conviction that there is not a fiercer hell than the failure in a great object. This is not written with the least atom of purpose to forestall criticisms of course, but from the desire I have to conciliate men who are competent to look, and who do look with a zealous eye, to the honour of English literature.

The imagination of a boy is healthy, and the mature imagination of a man is healthy; but there is a space of life between, in which the soul is in a ferment, the character undecided, the way of life uncertain, the ambition thick-sighted: thence proceeds mawkishness, and all the thousand bitters which those men I speak of must necessarily taste in going over the following pages.

I hope I have not in too late a day touched the beautiful mythology of Greece, and dulled its brightness: for I wish to try once more [1], before I bid it farewell.

TEIGNMOUTH, *April* 10, 1818.

---

[1] *Woodhouse notes*—This alluded to his then intention of writing a poem on the fall of Hyperion. He commenced this poem : but, thanks to the critics who fell foul of *this* work, he discontinued it. The fragment was published in 1820.

ENDYMION

BOOK I

A THING of beauty is a joy for ever:
Its loveliness increases; it will never
Pass into nothingness; but still will keep
A bower quiet for us, and a sleep
Full of sweet dreams, and health, and quiet breathing.
Therefore, on every morrow, are we wreathing
A flowery band to bind us to the earth,
Spite of despondence, of the inhuman dearth
Of noble natures, of the gloomy days,
Of all the unhealthy and o'er-darkened ways   10
Made for our searching: yes, in spite of all,
Some shape of beauty moves away the pall
From our dark spirits. Such the sun, the moon,
Trees old, and young, sprouting a shady boon
For simple sheep; and such are daffodils
With the green world they live in; and clear rills
That for themselves a cooling covert make
'Gainst the hot season; the mid forest brake,
Rich with a sprinkling of fair musk-rose blooms:
And such too is the grandeur of the dooms   20
We have imagined for the mighty dead;
All lovely tales that we have heard or read:

1 *The manuscript shows no variation in the opening line; but the
late Sir Benjamin Ward Richardson told me that Mr. Henry Stephens of
Finchley, who was a fellow student in medicine with Keats, and lived in
the same rooms with him for a time, recollected an earlier first line.
Keats is said to have written in some rough draft of his intended opening*

    A thing of beauty is a constant joy:

*Stephens, on hearing this, pronounced it 'a fine line, but wanting
something.' Keats pondered it over, and at length broke out with an
inspired 'I have it,' and set down the household word that now stands at
the head of the poem.*

13 *Instead of line 13 there were originally three lines in the manuscript:*

  From our dark Spirits, and before us dances
  Like glitter on the points of Arthur's Lances.
    Of these bright powers are the Sun, and Moon . . .

An endless fountain of immortal drink,
Pouring unto us from the heaven's brink.

Nor do we merely feel these essences
For one short hour; no, even as the trees
That whisper round a temple become soon
Dear as the temple's self, so does the moon,
The passion poesy, glories infinite,
Haunt us till they become a cheering light   30
Unto our souls, and bound to us so fast,
That, whether there be shine, or gloom o'ercast,
They always must be with us, or we die.

Therefore, 'tis with full happiness that I
Will trace the story of Endymion.
The very music of the name has gone
Into my being, and each pleasant scene
Is growing fresh before me as the green
Of our own vallies: so I will begin
Now while I cannot hear the city's din;   40
Now while the early budders are just new,
And run in mazes of the youngest hue
About old forests; while the willow trails
Its delicate amber; and the dairy pails
Bring home increase of milk. And, as the year
Grows lush in juicy stalks, I'll smoothly steer
My little boat, for many quiet hours,
With streams that deepen freshly into bowers.
Many and many a verse I hope to write,
Before the daisies, vermeil rimm'd and white,   50
Hide in deep herbage; and ere yet the bees
Hum about globes of clover and sweet peas,
I must be near the middle of my story.
O may no wintry season, bare and hoary,
See it half finish'd: but let Autumn bold,
With universal tinge of sober gold,
Be all about me when I make an end.
And now at once, adventuresome, I send
My herald thought into a wilderness:
There let its trumpet blow, and quickly dress   60
My uncertain path with green, that I may speed
Easily onward, thorough flowers and weed.

  Upon the sides of Latmos was outspread
A mighty forest; for the moist earth fed
So plenteously all weed-hidden roots
Into o'er-hanging boughs, and precious fruits.
And it had gloomy shades, sequestered deep,
Where no man went; and if from shepherd's keep
A lamb stray'd far a-down those inmost glens,
Never again saw he the happy pens   70
Whither his brethren, bleating with content,
Over the hills at every nightfall went.
Among the shepherds, 'twas believed ever,
That not one fleecy lamb which thus did sever
From the white flock, but pass'd unworried
By angry wolf, or pard with prying head,
Until it came to some unfooted plains
Where fed the herds of Pan: aye great his gains
Who thus one lamb did lose. Paths there were many,
Winding through palmy fern, and rushes fenny,   80
And ivy banks; all leading pleasantly
To a wide lawn, whence one could only see
Stems thronging all around between the swell
Of turf and slanting branches: who could tell
The freshness of the space of heaven above,
Edg'd round with dark tree tops? through which a dove
Would often beat its wings, and often too
A little cloud would move across the blue.

  Full in the middle of this pleasantness
There stood a marble altar, with a tress   90
Of flowers budded newly; and the dew
Had taken fairy phantasies to strew
Daisies upon the sacred sward last eve,
And so the dawned light in pomp receive.
For 'twas the morn: Apollo's upward fire
Made every eastern cloud a silvery pyre
Of brightness so unsullied, that therein
A melancholy spirit well might win
Oblivion, and melt out his essence fine
Into the winds: rain-scented eglantine   100
Gave temperate sweets to that well-wooing sun;
The lark was lost in him; cold springs had run
To warm their chilliest bubbles in the grass;

Man's voice was on the mountains ; and the mass
Of nature's lives and wonders puls'd tenfold,
To feel this sun-rise and its glories old.

  Now while the silent workings of the dawn
Were busiest, into that self-same lawn
All suddenly, with joyful cries, there sped
A troop of little children garlanded ;   110
Who gathering round the altar, seem'd to pry
Earnestly round as wishing to espy
Some folk of holiday : nor had they waited
For many moments, ere their ears were sated
With a faint breath of music, which ev'n then
Fill'd out its voice, and died away again.
Within a little space again it gave
Its airy swellings, with a gentle wave,
To light-hung leaves, in smoothest echoes breaking
Through copse-clad vallies,—ere their death, o'ertaking
The surgy murmurs of the lonely sea.   121

  And now, as deep into the wood as we
Might mark a lynx's eye, there glimmered light
Fair faces and a rush of garments white,
Plainer and plainer showing, till at last
Into the widest alley they all past,
Making directly for the woodland altar.
O kindly muse ! let not my weak tongue faulter
In telling of this goodly company,
Of their old piety, and of their glee :   130
But let a portion of ethereal dew
Fall on my head, and presently unmew
My soul ; that I may dare, in wayfaring,
To stammer where old Chaucer us'd to sing.

  Leading the way, young damsels danced along,
Bearing the burden of a shepherd song ;
Each having a white wicker over brimm'd
With April's tender younglings : next, well trimm'd,
A crowd of shepherds with as sunburnt looks
As may be read of in Arcadian books ;   140
Such as sat listening round Apollo's pipe,
When the great deity, for earth too ripe,

    115 e'en *MS.*   125 showing *MS.* : shewing *1818.*

Let his divinity o'erflowing die
In music, through the vales of Thessaly :
Some idly trail'd their sheep-hooks on the ground,
And some kept up a shrilly mellow sound
With ebon-tipped flutes: close after these,
Now coming from beneath the forest trees,
A venerable priest full soberly,
Begirt with ministring looks : alway his eye   150
Stedfast upon the matted turf he kept,
And after him his sacred vestments swept.
From his right hand there swung a vase, milk-white,
Of mingled wine, out-sparkling generous light ;
And in his left he held a basket full
Of all sweet herbs that searching eye could cull :
Wild thyme, and valley-lillies whiter still
Than Leda's love, and cresses from the rill.
His aged head, crowned with beechen wreath,
Seem'd like a poll of ivy in the teeth   160
Of winter hoar.   Then came another crowd
Of shepherds, lifting in due time aloud
Their share of the ditty.   After them appear'd,
Up-followed by a multitude that rear'd
Their voices to the clouds, a fair wrought car,
Easily rolling so as scarce to mar
The freedom of three steeds of dapple brown :
Who stood therein did seem of great renown
Among the throng.   His youth was fully blown,
Showing like Ganymede to manhood grown ;   170
And, for those simple times, his garments were
A chieftain king's : beneath his breast, half bare,
Was hung a silver bugle, and between
His nervy knees there lay a boar-spear keen.
A smile was on his countenance ; he seem'd,
To common lookers on, like one who dream'd
Of idleness in groves Elysian :
But there were some who feelingly could scan
A lurking trouble in his nether lip,
And see that oftentimes the reins would slip   180
Through his forgotten hands : then would they sigh,
And think of yellow leaves, of owlets' cry,

153 From his right hand there swung a milk-white vase
      Of mingled wines, outsparkling like the Stars—*MS.*

Of logs piled solemnly.—Ah, well-a-day,
Why should our young Endymion pine away ɪ

   Soon the assembly, in a circle rang'd,
Stood silent round the shrine : each look was chang'd
To sudden veneration : women meek
Beckon'd their sons to silence ; while each cheek
Of virgin bloom paled gently for slight fear.
Endymion too, without a forest peer,   190
Stood, wan, and pale, and with an awed face,
Among his brothers of the mountain chace.
In midst of all, the venerable priest
Eyed them with joy from greatest to the least,
And, after lifting up his aged hands,
Thus spake he : 'Men of Latmos ! shepherd bands !
Whose care it is to guard a thousand flocks :
Whether descended from beneath the rocks
That overtop your mountains ; whether come
From vallies where the pipe is never dumb ;   200
Or from your swelling downs, where sweet air stirs
Blue hare-bells lightly, and where prickly furze
Buds lavish gold ; or ye, whose precious charge
Nibble their fill at ocean's very marge,
Whose mellow reeds are touch'd with sounds forlorn
By the dim echoes of old Triton's horn :
Mothers and wives ! who day by day prepare
The scrip, with needments, for the mountain air ;
And all ye gentle girls who foster up
Udderless lambs, and in a little cup   210
Will put choice honey for a favoured youth :
Yea, every one attend ! for in good truth
Our vows are wanting to our great god Pan.
Are not our lowing heifers sleeker than
Night-swollen mushrooms ? Are not our wide plains
Speckled with countless fleeces ? Have not rains
Green'd over April's lap ? No howling sad
Sickens our fearful ewes ; and we have had
Great bounty from Endymion our lord.
The earth is glad : the merry lark has pour'd   220
His early song against yon breezy sky,
That spreads so clear o'er our solemnity.'

   Thus ending, on the shrine he heap'd a spire

Of teeming sweets, enkindling sacred fire ;
Anon he stain'd the thick and spongy sod
With wine, in honour of the shepherd-god.
Now while the earth was drinking it, and while
Bay leaves were crackling in the fragrant pile,
And gummy frankincense was sparkling bright
'Neath smothering parsley, and a hazy light   230
Spread greyly eastward, thus a chorus sang:

"O thou, whose mighty palace roof doth hang
From jagged trunks, and overshadoweth
Eternal whispers, glooms, the birth, life, death
Of unseen flowers in heavy peacefulness ;
Who lov'st to see the hamadryads dress
Their ruffled locks where meeting hazels darken ;
And through whole solemn hours dost sit, and hearken
The dreary melody of bedded reeds—
In desolate places, where dank moisture breeds   240
The pipy hemlock to strange overgrowth ;
Bethinking thee, how melancholy loth
Thou wast to lose fair Syrinx—do thou now,
By thy love's milky brow !
By all the trembling mazes that she ran,
Hear us, great Pan !

"O thou, for whose soul-soothing quiet, turtles
Passion their voices cooingly 'mong myrtles,
What time thou wanderest at eventide
Through sunny meadows, that outskirt the side   250
Of thine enmossed realms : O thou, to whom
Broad leaved fig trees even now foredoom
Their ripen'd fruitage ; yellow girted bees
Their golden honeycombs ; our village leas
Their fairest blossom'd beans and poppied corn ;
The chuckling linnet its five young unborn,
To sing for thee ; low creeping strawberries
Their summer coolness ; pent up butterflies
Their freckled wings ; yea, the fresh budding year
All its completions—be quickly near,   260
By every wind that nods the mountain pine,
O forester divine !

"Thou, to whom every faun and satyr flies
263 fawn *MS. and 1818.*

For willing service; whether to surprise
The squatted hare while in half sleeping fit;
Or upward ragged precipices flit
To save poor lambkins from the eagle's maw;
Or by mysterious enticement draw
Bewildered shepherds to their path again;
Or to tread breathless round the frothy main,   270
And gather up all fancifullest shells
For thee to tumble into Naiads' cells,
And, being hidden, laugh at their out-peeping;
Or to delight thee with fantastic leaping,
The while they pelt each other on the crown
With silvery oak apples, and fir cones brown—
By all the echoes that about thee ring,
Hear us, O satyr king!

    "O Hearkener to the loud clapping shears
While ever and anon to his shorn peers   280
A ram goes bleating: Winder of the horn,
When snouted wild-boars routing tender corn
Anger our huntsmen: Breather round our farms,
To keep off mildews, and all weather harms:
Strange ministrant of undescribed sounds,
That come a swooning over hollow grounds,
And wither drearily on barren moors:
Dread opener of the mysterious doors
Leading to universal knowledge—see,
Great son of Dryope,   290
The many that are come to pay their vows
With leaves about their brows!

    " Be still the unimaginable lodge
For solitary thinkings; such as dodge
Conception to the very bourne of heaven,
Then leave the naked brain: be still the leaven,
That spreading in this dull and clodded earth
Gives it a touch ethereal—a new birth:
Be still a symbol of immensity;
A firmament reflected in a sea;   300
An element filling the space between;
An unknown—but no more: we humbly screen

283 Huntsmen *MS.* : huntsman *1818.*
293 *The quotation marks here are supplied from the corrected copy.*

With uplift hands our foreheads, lowly bending,
And giving out a shout most heaven rending,
Conjure thee to receive our humble Pæan,
Upon thy Mount Lycean!"

   Even while they brought the burden to a close,
A shout from the whole multitude arose,
That lingered in the air like dying rolls
Of abrupt thunder, when Ionian shoals   310
Of dolphins bob their noses through the brine.
Meantime, on shady levels, mossy fine,
Young companies nimbly began dancing
To the swift treble pipe, and humming string.
Aye, those fair living forms swam heavenly
To tunes forgotten—out of memory:
Fair creatures! whose young children's children bred
Thermopylæ its heroes—not yet dead,
But in old marbles ever beautiful.
High genitors, unconscious did they cull   320
Time's sweet first-fruits—they danc'd to weariness,
And then in quiet circles did they press
The hillock turf, and caught the latter end
Of some strange history, potent to send
A young mind from its bodily tenement.
Or they might watch the quoit-pitchers, intent
On either side; pitying the sad death
Of Hyacinthus, when the cruel breath
Of Zephyr slew him,—Zephyr penitent,
Who now, ere Phœbus mounts the firmament,   330
Fondles the flower amid the sobbing rain.
The archers too, upon a wider plain,
Beside the feathery whizzing of the shaft,
And the dull twanging bowstring, and the raft
Branch down sweeping from a tall ash top,
Call'd up a thousand thoughts to envelope
Those who would watch. Perhaps, the trembling knee
And frantic gape of lonely Niobe,
Poor, lonely Niobe! when her lovely young
Were dead and gone, and her caressing tongue   340
Lay a lost thing upon her paly lip,
And very, very deadliness did nip
Her motherly cheeks. Arous'd from this sad mood

KEATS   * D

By one, who at a distance loud halloo'd,
Uplifting his strong bow into the air,
Many might after brighter visions stare :
After the Argonauts, in blind amaze
Tossing about on Neptune's restless ways,
Until, from the horizon's vaulted side,
There shot a golden splendour far and wide,   350
Spangling those million poutings of the brine
With quivering ore : 'twas even an awful shine
From the exaltation of Apollo's bow ;
A heavenly beacon in their dreary woe.
Who thus were ripe for high contemplating,
Might turn their steps towards the sober ring
Where sat Endymion and the aged priest
'Mong shepherds gone in eld, whose looks increas'd
The silvery setting of their mortal star.
There they discours'd upon the fragile bar   360
That keeps us from our homes ethereal ;
And what our duties there : to nightly call
Vesper, the beauty-crest of summer weather ;
To summon all the downiest clouds together
For the sun's purple couch ; to emulate
In ministring the potent rule of fate
With speed of fire-tail'd exhalations ;
To tint her pallid cheek with bloom, who cons
Sweet poesy by moonlight : besides these,
A world of other unguess'd offices.   370
Anon they wander'd, by divine converse,
Into Elysium ; vieing to rehearse
Each one his own anticipated bliss.
One felt heart-certain that he could not miss
His quick gone love, among fair blossom'd boughs,
Where every zephyr-sigh pouts, and endows
Her lips with music for the welcoming.
Another wish'd, mid that eternal spring,
To meet his rosy child, with feathery sails,
Sweeping, eye-earnestly, through almond vales :   380
Who, suddenly, should stoop through the smooth wind,
And with the balmiest leaves his temples bind ;
And, ever after, through those regions be

368 pretty cheek, *with* pallid *and* waning *as marginal alternatives.*
MS.

His messenger, his little Mercury.
Some were athirst in soul to see again
Their fellow huntsmen o'er the wide champaign
In times long past ; to sit with them, and talk
Of all the chances in their earthly walk ;
Comparing, joyfully, their plenteous stores
Of happiness, to when upon the moors,   390
Benighted, close they huddled from the cold,
And shar'd their famish'd scrips. Thus all out-told
Their fond imaginations,—saving him
Whose eyelids curtain'd up their jewels dim,
Endymion : yet hourly had he striven
To hide the cankering venom, that had riven
His fainting recollections. Now indeed
His senses had swoon'd off : he did not heed
The sudden silence, or the whispers low,
Or the old eyes dissolving at his woe,   400
Or anxious calls, or close of trembling palms,
Or maiden's sigh, that grief itself embalms :
But in the self-same fixed trance he kept,
Like one who on the earth had never stept.
Aye, even as dead-still as a marble man,
Frozen in that old tale Arabian.

Who whispers him so pantingly and close ?
Peona, his sweet sister : of all those,
His friends, the dearest. Hushing signs she made,
And breath'd a sister's sorrow to persuade   410
A yielding up, a cradling on her care.
Her eloquence did breathe away the curse :

406 Frozen] Sitting *MS.*, *cancelled.*
407-12 Now happily, there sitting on the grass
    Was fair Peona, a most tender Lass,
    And his sweet sister ; who, uprising, went
    With stifled sobs, and o'er his shoulder leant.
    Putting her trembling hand against his cheek
    She said : 'My dear Endymion, let us seek
    A pleasant bower where thou may'st rest apart,
    And ease in slumber thine afflicted heart :
    Come my own dearest brother : these our friends
    Will joy in thinking thou dost sleep where bends
    Our freshening River through yon birchen grove :
    Do come now !' Could he gainsay her who strove,
    So soothingly, to breathe away a Curse ? *MS.*

She led him, like some midnight spirit nurse
Of happy changes in emphatic dreams,
Along a path between two little streams,—
Guarding his forehead, with her round elbow,
From low-grown branches, and his footsteps slow
From stumbling over stumps and hillocks small;
Until they came to where these streamlets fall,
With mingled bubblings and a gentle rush,　　　　420
Into a river, clear, brimful, and flush
With crystal mocking of the trees and sky.
A little shallop, floating there hard by,
Pointed its beak over the fringed bank;
And soon it lightly dipt, and rose, and sank,
And dipt again, with the young couple's weight,—
Peona guiding, through the water straight,
Towards a bowery island opposite;
Which gaining presently, she steered light
Into a shady, fresh, and ripply cove,　　　　　430
Where nested was an arbour, overwove
By many a summer's silent fingering;
To whose cool bosom she was used to bring
Her playmates, with their needle broidery,
And minstrel memories of times gone by.

　So she was gently glad to see him laid
Under her favourite bower's quiet shade,
On her own couch, new made of flower leaves,
Dried carefully on the cooler side of sheaves
When last the sun his autumn tresses shook,　　440

438–42 On her own couch, new made of flower leaves,
　　　Dry'd carefully on the cooler side of sheaves
　　　When last the Harvesters rich armfuls took.
　　　She tied a little bucket to a Crook,
　　　Ran some swift paces to a dark wells side,
　　　And in a sighing-time return'd, supplied
　　　With spar cold water; in which she did squeeze
　　　A snowy napkin, and upon her knees
　　　Began to cherish her poor Brother's face;
　　　Damping refreshfully his forehead's space,
　　　His eyes, his Lips: then in a cupped shell
　　　She brought him ruby wine; then let him smell,
　　　Time after time, a precious amulet,
　　　Which seldom took she from its cabinet.
　　　Thus was he quieted to slumbrous rest: MS.

And the tann'd harvesters rich armfuls took.
Soon was he quieted to slumbrous rest:
But, ere it crept upon him, he had prest
Peona's busy hand against his lips,
And still, a sleeping, held her finger-tips
In tender pressure. And as a willow keeps
A patient watch over the stream that creeps
Windingly by it, so the quiet maid
Held her in peace: so that a whispering blade
Of grass, a wailful gnat, a bee bustling   450
Down in the blue-bells, or a wren light rustling
Among sere leaves and twigs, might all be heard.

O magic sleep! O comfortable bird,
That broodest o'er the troubled sea of the mind
Till it is hush'd and smooth! O unconfin'd
Restraint! imprisoned liberty! great key
To golden palaces, strange minstrelsy,
Fountains grotesque, new trees, bespangled caves,
Echoing grottos, full of tumbling waves
And moonlight; aye, to all the mazy world   460
Of silvery enchantment!—who, upfurl'd
Beneath thy drowsy wing a triple hour,
But renovates and lives?—Thus, in the bower,
Endymion was calm'd to life again.
Opening his eyelids with a healthier brain,
He said: "I feel this thine endearing love
All through my bosom: thou art as a dove
Trembling its closed eyes and sleeked wings
About me; and the pearliest dew not brings
Such morning incense from the fields of May,   470
As do those brighter drops that twinkling stray
From those kind eyes,—the very home and haunt
Of sisterly affection. Can I want

466 A cheerfuller resignment, and a smile
    For his fair Sister flowing like the Nile
    Through all the channels of her piety,
    He said: ' Dear Maid, may I this moment die,
    If I feel not this thine endearing Love . . . *MS.*
470 From woodbine hedges such a morning feel,
    As do those brighter drops, that twinkling steal
    Through those pressed lashes, from the blossom'd
    plant . . . *MS.*

Aught else, aught nearer heaven, than such tears?
Yet dry them up, in bidding hence all fears
That, any longer, I will pass my days
Alone and sad. No, I will once more raise
My voice upon the mountain-heights; once more
Make my horn parley from their foreheads hoar:
Again my trooping hounds their tongues shall loll   480
Around the breathed boar: again I'll poll
The fair-grown yew tree, for a chosen bow:
And, when the pleasant sun is getting low,
Again I'll linger in a sloping mead
To hear the speckled thrushes, and see feed
Our idle sheep. So be thou cheered sweet,
And, if thy lute is here, softly intreat
My soul to keep in its resolved course."

Hereat Peona, in their silver source,
Shut her pure sorrow drops with glad exclaim,   490
And took a lute, from which there pulsing came
A lively prelude, fashioning the way
In which her voice should wander. 'Twas a lay
More subtle cadenced, more forest wild
Than Dryope's lone lulling of her child;
And nothing since has floated in the air
So mournful strange. Surely some influence rare
Went, spiritual, through the damsel's hand;
For still, with Delphic emphasis, she spann'd
The quick invisible strings, even though she saw   500
Endymion's spirit melt away and thaw
Before the deep intoxication.
But soon she came, with sudden burst, upon
Her self-possession—swung the lute aside,
And earnestly said: "Brother, 'tis vain to hide
That thou dost know of things mysterious,
Immortal, starry; such alone could thus
Weigh down thy nature. Hast thou sinn'd in aught
Offensive to the heavenly powers? Caught

494-5 More forest-wild, more subtle-cadenced
    Than can be told by mortal: even wed
    The fainting tenors of a thousand shells
    To a million whisperings of Lilly bells;
    And mingle too the Nightingale's complain
    Caught in its hundredth echo; 'twould be vain: ... MS.

A Paphian dove upon a message sent? 510
Thy deathful bow against some deer-herd bent
Sacred to Dian? Haply, thou hast seen
Her naked limbs among the alders green;
And that, alas! is death. No, I can trace
Something more high perplexing in thy face!"

Endymion look'd at her, and press'd her hand,
And said, "Art thou so pale, who wast so bland
And merry in our meadows? How is this?
Tell me thine ailment: tell me all amiss!—
Ah! thou hast been unhappy at the change 520
Wrought suddenly in me. What indeed more strange?
Or more complete to overwhelm surmise?
Ambition is so sluggard: 'tis no prize,
That toiling years would put within my grasp,
That I have sighed for: with so deadly gasp
No man e'er panted for a mortal love.
So all have set my heavier grief above
These things which happen. Rightly have they done:
I, who still saw the horizontal sun
Heave his broad shoulder o'er the edge of the world,
Out-facing Lucifer, and then had hurl'd 531
My spear aloft, as signal for the chace—
I, who, for very sport of heart, would race
With my own steed from Araby; pluck down
A vulture from his towery perching; frown
A lion into growling, loth retire—
To lose, at once, all my toil-breeding fire,
And sink thus low! but I will ease my breast
Of secret grief, here in this bowery nest.

"This river does not see the naked sky, 540
Till it begins to progress silverly
Around the western border of the wood,
Whence, from a certain spot, its winding flood
Seems at the distance like a crescent moon:
And in that nook, the very pride of June,
Had I been used to pass my weary eves;
The rather for the sun unwilling leaves
So dear a picture of his sovereign power,
And I could witness his most kingly hour,

When he doth tighten up the golden reins,   550
And paces leisurely down amber plains
His snorting four. Now when his chariot last
Its beams against the zodiac-lion cast,
There blossom'd suddenly a magic bed
Of sacred ditamy, and poppies red:
At which I wondered greatly, knowing well
That but one night had wrought this flowery spell;
And, sitting down close by, began to muse
What it might mean. Perhaps, thought I, Morpheus,
In passing here, his owlet pinions shook;   560
Or, it may be, ere matron Night uptook
Her ebon urn, young Mercury, by stealth,
Had dipt his rod in it: such garland wealth
Came not by common growth. Thus on I thought,
Until my head was dizzy and distraught.
Moreover, through the dancing poppies stole
A breeze, most softly lulling to my soul;
And shaping visions all about my sight
Of colours, wings, and bursts of spangly light;
The which became more strange, and strange, and dim,
And then were gulph'd in a tumultuous swim: 571
And then I fell asleep. Ah, can I tell
The enchantment that afterwards befel?
Yet it was but a dream: yet such a dream
That never tongue, although it overteem
With mellow utterance, like a cavern spring,
Could figure out and to conception bring
All I beheld and felt. Methought I lay
Watching the zenith, where the milky way
Among the stars in virgin splendour pours;   580
And travelling my eye, until the doors
Of heaven appear'd to open for my flight,
I became loth and fearful to alight
From such high soaring by a downward glance:
So kept me stedfast in that airy trance,
Spreading imaginary pinions wide.
When, presently, the stars began to glide,
And faint away, before my eager view:
At which I sigh'd that I could not pursue,

550 tighten *MS.*: lighten *1818.*

And dropt my vision to the horizon's verge ; 590
And lo ! from opening clouds, I saw emerge
The loveliest moon, that ever silver'd o'er
A shell for Neptune's goblet : she did soar
So passionately bright, my dazzled soul
Commingling with her argent spheres did roll
Through clear and cloudy, even when she went
At last into a dark and vapoury tent—
Whereat, methought, the lidless-eyed train
Of planets all were in the blue again.
To commune with those orbs, once more I rais'd 600
My sight right upward : but it was quite dazed
By a bright something, sailing down apace,
Making me quickly veil my eyes and face :
Again I look'd, and, O ye deities,
Who from Olympus watch our destinies !
Whence that completed form of all completeness ?
Whence came that high perfection of all sweetness ?
Speak, stubborn earth, and tell me where, O where
Hast thou a symbol of her golden hair ?
Not oat-sheaves drooping in the western sun ; 610
Not—thy soft hand, fair sister ! let me shun
Such follying before thee—yet she had,
Indeed, locks bright enough to make me mad ;
And they were simply gordian'd up and braided,
Leaving, in naked comeliness, unshaded,
Her pearl round ears, white neck, and orbed brow ;
The which were blended in, I know not how,
With such a paradise of lips and eyes,
Blush-tinted cheeks, half smiles, and faintest sighs,
That, when I think thereon, my spirit clings 620
And plays about its fancy, till the stings
Of human neighbourhood envenom all.
Unto what awful power shall I call ?
To what high fane ?—Ah ! see her hovering feet,
More bluely vein'd, more soft, more whitely sweet
Than those of sea-born Venus, when she rose
From out her cradle shell. The wind out-blows
Her scarf into a fluttering pavillion ;
'Tis blue, and over-spangled with a million
Of little eyes, as though thou wert to shed, 630
Over the darkest, lushest blue-bell bed.

Handfuls of daisies."—"Endymion, how strange!
Dream within dream!"—"She took an airy range,
And then, towards me, like a very maid,
Came blushing, waning, willing, and afraid,
And press'd me by the hand: Ah! 'twas too much;
Methought I fainted at the charmed touch,
Yet held my recollection, even as one
Who dives three fathoms where the waters run
Gurgling in beds of coral: for anon,   640
I felt upmounted in that region
Where falling stars dart their artillery forth,
And eagles struggle with the buffeting north
That ballances the heavy meteor-stone;—
Felt too, I was not fearful, nor alone,
But lapp'd and lull'd along the dangerous sky.
Soon, as it seem'd, we left our journeying high,
And straightway into frightful eddies swoop'd;
Such as aye muster where grey time has scoop'd
Huge dens and caverns in a mountain's side: 650
There hollow sounds arous'd me, and I sigh'd
To faint once more by looking on my bliss—
I was distracted; madly did I kiss
The wooing arms which held me, and did give
My eyes at once to death: but 'twas to live,
To take in draughts of life from the gold fount
Of kind and passionate looks; to count, and count
The moments, by some greedy help that seem'd
A second self, that each might be redeem'd
And plunder'd of its load of blessedness.   660
Ah, desperate mortal! I e'en dar'd to press
Her very cheek against my crowned lip,
And, at that moment, felt my body dip
Into a warmer air: a moment more,
Our feet were soft in flowers. There was store
Of newest joys upon that alp. Sometimes
A scent of violets, and blossoming limes,
Loiter'd around us; then of honey cells,
Made delicate from all white-flower bells;
And once, above the edges of our nest,   670
An arch face peep'd,—an Oread as I guess'd.

649 aye MS.: ay 1818.
661 e'en MS.: ev'n 1818.

"Why did I dream that sleep o'er-power'd me
In midst of all this heaven? Why not see,
Far off, the shadows of his pinions dark,
And stare them from me? But no, like a spark
That needs must die, although its little beam
Reflects upon a diamond, my sweet dream
Fell into nothing—into stupid sleep.
And so it was, until a gentle creep,
A careful moving caught my waking ears,   630
And up I started: Ah! my sighs, my tears,
My clenched hands;—for lo! the poppies hung
Dew-dabbled on their stalks, the ouzel sung
A heavy ditty, and the sullen day
Had chidden herald Hesperus away,
With leaden looks: the solitary breeze
Bluster'd, and slept, and its wild self did teaze
With wayward melancholy; and I thought,
Mark me, Peona! that sometimes it brought
Faint fare-thee-wells, and sigh-shrilled adieus!—   690
Away I wander'd—all the pleasant hues
Of heaven and earth had faded: deepest shades
Were deepest dungeons; heaths and sunny glades
Were full of pestilent light; our taintless rills
Seem'd sooty, and o'er-spread with upturn'd gills
Of dying fish; the vermeil rose had blown
In frightful scarlet, and its thorns out-grown
Like spiked aloe. If an innocent bird
Before my heedless footsteps stirr'd, and stirr'd
In little journeys, I beheld in it   700
A disguis'd demon, missioned to knit
My soul with under darkness; to entice
My stumblings down some monstrous precipice:
Therefore I eager followed, and did curse
The disappointment. Time, that aged nurse,
Rock'd me to patience. Now, thank gentle heaven!
These things, with all their comfortings, are given
To my down-sunken hours, and with thee,
Sweet sister, help to stem the ebbing sea
Of weary life."

                Thus ended he, and both   710
Sat silent: for the maid was very loth
To answer; feeling well that breathed words

Would all be lost, unheard, and vain as swords
Against the enchased crocodile, or leaps
Of grasshoppers against the sun. She weeps,
And wonders; struggles to devise some blame;
To put on such a look as would say, *Shame
On this poor weakness!* but, for all her strife,
She could as soon have crush'd away the life   719
From a sick dove. At length, to break the pause,
She said with trembling chance: "Is this the cause?
This all? Yet it is strange, and sad, alas!
That one who through this middle earth should pass
Most like a sojourning demi-god, and leave
His name upon the harp-string, should achieve
No higher bard than simple maidenhood,
Singing alone, and fearfully,—how the blood
Left his young cheek; and how he used to stray
He knew not where; and how he would say, *nay,*
If any said 'twas love: and yet 'twas love;   730
What could it be but love? How a ring-dove
Let fall a sprig of yew tree in his path;
And how he died: and then, that love doth scathe,
The gentle heart, as northern blasts do roses;
And then the ballad of his sad life closes
With sighs, and an alas!—Endymion!
Be rather in the trumpet's mouth,—anon
Among the winds at large—that all may hearken!
Although, before the crystal heavens darken,
I watch and dote upon the silver lakes   740
Pictur'd in western cloudiness, that takes
The semblance of gold rocks and bright gold sands,
Islands, and creeks, and amber-fretted strands
With horses prancing o'er them, palaces
And towers of amethyst,—would I so teaze
My pleasant days, because I could not mount
Into those regions? The Morphean fount
Of that fine element that visions, dreams,
And fitful whims of sleep are made of, streams
Into its airy channels with so subtle,   750
So thin a breathing, not the spider's shuttle,
Circled a million times within the space

741 Pictur'd in] Pight among *and* Pight amid *MS., rejected.*

Of a swallow's nest-door, could delay a trace,
A tinting of its quality : how light
Must dreams themselves be ; seeing they're more slight
Than the mere nothing that engenders them !
Then wherefore sully the entrusted gem
Of high and noble life with thoughts so sick ?
Why pierce high-fronted honour to the quick
For nothing but a dream ? " Hereat the youth   760
Look'd up : a conflicting of shame and ruth
Was in his plaited brow : yet, his eyelids
Widened a little, as when Zephyr bids
A little breeze to creep between the fans
Of careless butterflies : amid his pains
He seem'd to taste a drop of manna-dew,
Full palatable ; and a colour grew
Upon his cheek, while thus he lifeful spake.

    "Peona ! ever have I long'd to slake
My thirst for the world's praises : nothing base,   770
No merely slumberous phantasm, could unlace
The stubborn canvas for my voyage prepar'd—
Though now 'tis tatter'd ; leaving my bark bar'd
And sullenly drifting : yet my higher hope
Is of too wide, too rainbow-large a scope,
To fret at myriads of earthly wrecks.
Wherein lies happiness ? In that which becks
Our ready minds to fellowship divine,
A fellowship with essence ; till we shine,
Full alchemiz'd, and free of space. Behold   780
The clear religion of heaven ! Fold
A rose leaf round thy finger's taperness,
And soothe thy lips : hist, when the airy stress
Of music's kiss impregnates the free winds,
And with a sympathetic touch unbinds
Æolian magic from their lucid wombs :
Then old songs waken from enclouded tombs ;
Old ditties sigh above their father's grave ;
Ghosts of melodious prophecyings rave
Round every spot where trod Apollo's foot ;   790
Bronze clarions awake, and faintly bruit,
Where long ago a giant battle was ;

762 pleated *MS.*   790 where *MS.* : were *1813.*

And, from the turf, a lullaby doth pass
In every place where infant Orpheus slept.
Feel we these things?—that moment have we stept
Into a sort of oneness, and our state
Is like a floating spirit's. But there are
Richer entanglements, enthralments far
More self-destroying, leading, by degrees,
To the chief intensity: the crown of these   800
Is made of love and friendship, and sits high
Upon the forehead of humanity.
All its more ponderous and bulky worth
Is friendship, whence there ever issues forth
A steady splendour; but at the tip-top,
There hangs by unseen film, an orbed drop
Of light, and that is love: its influence,
Thrown in our eyes, genders a novel sense,
At which we start and fret; till in the end,
Melting into its radiance, we blend,   810
Mingle, and so become a part of it,—
Nor with aught else can our souls interknit
So wingedly: when we combine therewith,
Life's self is nourish'd by its proper pith,
And we are nurtured like a pelican brood.
Aye, so delicious is the unsating food,
That men, who might have tower'd in the van
Of all the congregated world, to fan
And winnow from the coming step of time
All chaff of custom, wipe away all slime   820
Left by men-slugs and human serpentry,
Have been content to let occasion die,
Whilst they did sleep in love's elysium.
And, truly, I would rather be struck dumb,
Than speak against this ardent listlessness:
For I have ever thought that it might bless
The world with benefits unknowingly;
As does the nightingale, upperched high,
And cloister'd among cool and bunched leaves—
She sings but to her love, nor e'er conceives   830
How tiptoe Night holds back her dark-grey hood.
Just so may love, although 'tis understood
The mere commingling of passionate breath,
Produce more than our searching witnesseth:

What I know not: but who, of men, can tell
That flowers would bloom, or that green fruit would swell
To melting pulp, that fish would have bright mail,
The earth its dower of river, wood, and vale,
The meadows runnels, runnels pebble-stones,
The seed its harvest, or the lute its tones,   840
Tones ravishment, or ravishment its sweet
If human souls did never kiss and greet?

"Now, if this earthly love has power to make
Men's being mortal, immortal; to shake
Ambition from their memories, and brim
Their measure of content: what merest whim,
Seems all this poor endeavour after fame,
To one, who keeps within his stedfast aim
A love immortal, an immortal too.
Look not so wilder'd; for these things are true, 850
And never can be born of atomies
That buzz about our slumbers, like brain-flies,
Leaving us fancy-sick. No, no, I'm sure,
My restless spirit never could endure
To brood so long upon one luxury,
Unless it did, though fearfully, espy
A hope beyond the shadow of a dream.
My sayings will the less obscured seem,
When I have told thee how my waking sight
Has made me scruple whether that same night 860
Was pass'd in dreaming. Hearken, sweet Peona!
Beyond the matron-temple of Latona,
Which we should see but for these darkening boughs,
Lies a deep hollow, from whose ragged brows
Bushes and trees do lean all round athwart
And meet so nearly, that with wings outraught,
And spreaded tail, a vulture could not glide
Past them, but he must brush on every side.
Some moulder'd steps lead into this cool cell,
Far as the slabbed margin of a well,   870
Whose patient level peeps its crystal eye
Right upward, through the bushes, to the sky.
Oft have I brought thee flowers, on their stalks set
Like vestal primroses, but dark velvet
Edges them round, and they have golden pits:

'Twas there I got them, from the gaps and slits
In a mossy stone, that sometimes was my seat,
When all above was faint with mid-day heat.
And there in strife no burning thoughts to heed,
I'd bubble up the water through a reed;   880
So reaching back to boy-hood: make me ships
Of moulted feathers, touchwood, alder chips,
With leaves stuck in them; and the Neptune be
Of their petty ocean. Oftener, heavily,
When love-lorn hours had left me less a child,
I sat contemplating the figures wild
Of o'er-head clouds melting the mirror through.
Upon a day, while thus I watch'd, by flew
A cloudy Cupid, with his bow and quiver;
So plainly character'd, no breeze would shiver   890
The happy chance: so happy, I was fain
To follow it upon the open plain,
And, therefore, was just going; when, behold!
A wonder, fair as any I have told—
The same bright face I tasted in my sleep,
Smiling in the clear well. My heart did leap
Through the cool depth.—It moved as if to flee—
I started up, when lo! refreshfully,
There came upon my face in plenteous showers   899
Dew-drops, and dewy buds, and leaves, and flowers,
Wrapping all objects from my smothered sight,
Bathing my spirit in a new delight.
Aye, such a breathless honey-feel of bliss
Alone preserved me from the drear abyss
Of death, for the fair form had gone again.
Pleasure is oft a visitant; but pain
Clings cruelly to us, like the gnawing sloth
On the deer's tender haunches: late, and loth,
'Tis scar'd away by slow returning pleasure.
How sickening, how dark the dreadful leisure   910
Of weary days, made deeper exquisite,
By a fore-knowledge of unslumbrous night!
Like sorrow came upon me, heavier still,
Than when I wander'd from the poppy hill:
And a whole age of lingering moments crept
Sluggishly by, ere more contentment swept
Away at once the deadly yellow spleen.

Yes, thrice have I this fair enchantment seen ;
Once more been tortured with renewed life.
When last the wintry gusts gave over strife   920
With the conquering sun of spring, and left the skies
Warm and serene, but yet with moistened eyes
In pity of the shatter'd infant buds,—
That time thou didst adorn, with amber studs,
My hunting cap, because I laugh'd and smil'd,
Chatted with thee, and many days exil'd
All torment from my breast ;—'twas even then,
Straying about, yet, coop'd up in the den
Of helpless discontent,—hurling my lance
From place to place, and following at chance,   930
At last, by hap, through some young trees it struck,
And, plashing among bedded pebbles, stuck
In the middle of a brook,—whose silver ramble
Down twenty little falls, through reeds and bramble,
Tracing along, it brought me to a cave,
Whence it ran brightly forth, and white did lave
The nether sides of mossy stones and rock,—
'Mong which it gurgled blythe adieus, to mock
Its own sweet grief at parting.   Overhead,   939
Hung a lush screen of drooping weeds, and spread
Thick, as to curtain up some wood-nymph's home.
"Ah ! impious mortal, whither do I roam ? "
Said I, low voic'd : "Ah, whither ! 'Tis the grot
"Of Proserpine, when Hell, obscure and hot,
"Doth her resign ; and where her tender hands
"She dabbles, on the cool and sluicy sands :
"Or 'tis the cell of Echo, where she sits,
"And babbles thorough silence, till her wits
"Are gone in tender madness, and anon,
"Faints into sleep, with many a dying tone   950
"Of sadness.   O that she would take my vows,
"And breathe them sighingly among the boughs,
"To sue her gentle ears for whose fair head,
"Daily, I pluck sweet flowerets from their bed,
"And weave them dyingly—send honey-whispers
"Round every leaf, that all those gentle lispers
"May sigh my love unto her pitying !

933 I' th' *MS.*
940 screne *MS.* : scene *1818* : screen *1818 corrected.*

"O charitable Echo! hear, and sing
"This ditty to her!—tell her"—so I stay'd
My foolish tongue, and listening, half afraid,   960
Stood stupefied with my own empty folly,
And blushing for the freaks of melancholy.
Salt tears were coming, when I heard my name
Most fondly lipp'd, and then these accents came:
"Endymion! the cave is secreter
"Than the isle of Delos. Echo hence shall stir
"No sighs but sigh-warm kisses, or light noise
"Of thy combing hand, the while it travelling cloys
"And trembles through my labyrinthine hair."
At that oppress'd I hurried in.—Ah! where   970
Are those swift moments? Whither are they fled?
I'll smile no more, Peona; nor will wed
Sorrow the way to death; but patiently
Bear up against it: so farewell, sad sigh;
And come instead demurest meditation,
To occupy me wholly, and to fashion
My pilgrimage for the world's dusky brink.
No more will I count over, link by link,
My chain of grief: no longer strive to find
A half-forgetfulness in mountain wind   980
Blustering about my ears: aye, thou shalt see,
Dearest of sisters, what my life shall be;
What a calm round of hours shall make my days.
There is a paly flame of hope that plays
Where'er I look: but yet, I'll say 'tis naught—
And here I bid it die. Have not I caught,
Already, a more healthy countenance?
By this the sun is setting; we may chance
Meet some of our near-dwellers with my car."

This said, he rose, faint-smiling like a star   990
Through autumn mists, and took Peona's hand:
They stept into the boat, and launch'd from land.

BOOK II

O SOVEREIGN power of love! O grief! O balm!
All records, saving thine, come cool, and calm,
And shadowy, through the mist of passed years:
For others, good or bad, hatred and tears
Have become indolent; but touching thine,
One sigh doth echo, one poor sob doth pine,
One kiss brings honey-dew from buried days.
The woes of Troy, towers smothering o'er their blaze,
Stiff-holden shields, far-piercing spears, keen blades,
Struggling, and blood, and shrieks—all dimly fades
Into some backward corner of the brain;   11
Yet, in our very souls, we feel amain
The close of Troilus and Cressid sweet.
Hence, pageant history! hence, gilded cheat!
Swart planet in the universe of deeds!
Wide sea, that one continuous murmur breeds
Along the pebbled shore of memory!
Many old rotten-timber'd boats there be
Upon thy vaporous bosom, magnified
To goodly vessels; many a sail of pride,   20
And golden keel'd, is left unlaunch'd and dry.
But wherefore this? What care, though owl did fly
About the great Athenian admiral's mast?
What care, though striding Alexander past
The Indus with his Macedonian numbers?
Though old Ulysses tortured from his slumbers
The glutted Cyclops, what care?—Juliet leaning
Amid her window-flowers,—sighing,—weaning
Tenderly her fancy from its maiden snow,
Doth more avail than these: the silver flow   30
Of Hero's tears, the swoon of Imogen,

13–14 The close of Troilus and Cressida.
Hence pageant history! away proud star. *Draft.*

31 *The reference is of course not to the story of Hero and Leander,
but to the tears of Hero in* Much Ado about Nothing, *shed when she
was falsely accused; and Imogen must, equally of course, be Shakespeare's
heroine in* Cymbeline, *though she is not the only Imogen of fiction who
has swooned. For Pastorella see* Faerie Queene, *Book* VI, *Canto* ii,
stanza 1 *et seq.*

Fair Pastorella in the bandit's den,
Are things to brood on with more ardency
Than the death-day of empires. Fearfully
Must such conviction come upon his head,
Who, thus far, discontent, has dared to tread,
Without one muse's smile, or kind behest,
The path of love and poesy. But rest,
In chaffing restlessness, is yet more drear
Than to be crush'd, in striving to uprear   40
Love's standard on the battlements of song.
So once more days and nights aid me along,
Like legion'd soldiers.

              Brain-sick shepherd prince,
What promise hast thou faithful guarded since
The day of sacrifice? Or, have new sorrows
Come with the constant dawn upon thy morrows?
Alas! 'tis his old grief. For many days,
Has he been wandering in uncertain ways:
Through wilderness, and woods of mossed oaks;
Counting his woe-worn minutes, by the strokes   50
Of the lone woodcutter; and listening still,
Hour after hour, to each lush-leav'd rill.
Now he is sitting by a shady spring,
And elbow-deep with feverous fingering
Stems the upbursting cold: a wild rose tree
Pavillions him in bloom, and he doth see
A bud which snares his fancy: lo! but now
He plucks it, dips its stalk in the water: how!
It swells, it buds, it flowers beneath his sight;
And, in the middle, there is softly pight   60
A golden butterfly; upon whose wings
There must be surely character'd strange things,
For with wide eye he wonders, and smiles oft.

   Lightly this little herald flew aloft,
Follow'd by glad Endymion's clasped hands:
Onward it flies. From languor's sullen bands
His limbs are loos'd, and eager, on he hies

38-9 *The draft affords here a curious comment on the precise value
of the word* rest *as employed on this occasion. What was originally
written was* To rest In chaffing discontent.

Dazzled to trace it in the sunny skies.
It seem'd he flew, the way so easy was;
And like a new-born spirit did he pass   70
Through the green evening quiet in the sun,
O'er many a heath, through many a woodland dun,
Through buried paths, where sleepy twilight dreams
The summer time away. One track unseams
A wooded cleft, and, far away, the blue
Of ocean fades upon him; then, anew,
He sinks adown a solitary glen,
Where there was never sound of mortal men,
Saving, perhaps, some snow-light cadences
Melting to silence, when upon the breeze   80
Some holy bark let forth an anthem sweet,
To cheer itself to Delphi. Still his feet
Went swift beneath the merry-winged guide,
Until it reach'd a splashing fountain's side
That, near a cavern's mouth, for ever pour'd
Unto the temperate air: then high it soar'd,
And, downward, suddenly began to dip,
As if, athirst with so much toil, 'twould sip
The crystal spout-head: so it did, with touch
Most delicate, as though afraid to smutch   90
Even with mealy gold the waters clear.
But, at that very touch, to disappear
So fairy-quick, was strange! Bewildered,
Endymion sought around, and shook each bed
Of covert flowers in vain; and then he flung
Himself along the grass. What gentle tongue,
What whisperer disturb'd his gloomy rest?
It was a nymph uprisen to the breast
In the fountain's pebbly margin, and she stood
'Mong lillies, like the youngest of the brood.   100
To him her dripping hand she softly kist,
And anxiously began to plait and twist
Her ringlets round her fingers, saying: "Youth!
Too long, alas, hast thou starv'd on the ruth,
The bitterness of love: too long indeed,
Seeing thou art so gentle. Could I weed
Thy soul of care, by heavens, I would offer
All the bright riches of my crystal coffer
To Amphitrite; all my clear-eyed fish,

Golden, or rainbow-sided, or purplish,   110
Vermilion-tail'd, or finn'd with silvery gauze ;
Yea, or my veined pebble-floor, that draws
A virgin light to the deep ; my grotto-sands
Tawny and gold, ooz'd slowly from far lands
By my diligent springs ; my level lillies, shells,
My charming rod, my potent river spells ;
Yes, every thing, even to the pearly cup
Meander gave me,—for I bubbled up
To fainting creatures in a desert wild.
But woe is me, I am but as a child   120
To gladden thee ; and all I dare to say,
Is, that I pity thee ; that on this day
I've been thy guide ; that thou must wander far
In other regions, past the scanty bar
To mortal steps, before thou cans't be ta'en
From every wasting sigh, from every pain,
Into the gentle bosom of thy love.
Why it is thus, one knows in heaven above :
But, a poor Naiad, I guess not. Farewell !
I have a ditty for my hollow cell."   130

   Hereat, she vanished from Endymion's gaze,
Who brooded o'er the water in amaze :
The dashing fount pour'd on, and where its pool
Lay, half asleep, in grass and rushes cool,
Quick waterflies and gnats were sporting still,
And fish were dimpling, as if good nor ill
Had fallen out that hour. The wanderer,
Holding his forehead, to keep off the burr
Of smothering fancies, patiently sat down ;
And, while beneath the evening's sleepy frown   140
Glow-worms began to trim their starry lamps,
Thus breath'd he to himself : "Whoso encamps
To take a fancied city of delight,

131-4 Hereat, she vanish'd from the listener's gaze,
      Whose soul kept o'er the water in amaze ;
      The dashing fall pour'd on, and where the pool
      Crept smoothly by fresh grass and rushes cool,...
                                Draft.

143 *The manner in which the rhyme to this line was lost appears from
the draft, where the passage originally stood thus :*

O what a wretch is he ! and when 'tis his,
After long toil and travelling, to miss
The kernel of his hopes, how more than vile :
Yet, for him there's refreshment even in toil ;
Another city doth he set about,
Free from the smallest pebble-bead of doubt
That he will seize on trickling honey-combs :   150
Alas, he finds them dry ; and then he foams,
And onward to another city speeds.
But this is human life : the war, the deeds,
The disappointment, the anxiety,
Imagination's struggles, far and nigh,
All human ; bearing in themselves this good,
That they are still the air, the subtle food,
To make us feel existence, and to show
How quiet death is.   Where soil is men grow,
Whether to weeds or flowers ; but for me,   160
There is no depth to strike in : I can see
Naught earthly worth my compassing ; so stand
Upon a misty, jutting head of land—
Alone ? No, no ; and by the Orphean lute,
When mad Eurydice is listening to't ;
I'd rather stand upon this misty peak,
With not a thing to sigh for, or to seek,
But the soft shadow of my thrice-seen love,
Than be—I care not what.   O meekest dove
Of heaven ! O Cynthia, ten-times bright and fair !
From thy blue throne, now filling all the air,   171
Glance but one little beam of temper'd light
Into my bosom, that the dreadful might
And tyranny of love be somewhat scar'd !
Yet do not so, sweet queen ; one torment spar'd,
Would give a pang to jealous misery,
Worse than the torment's self : but rather tie
Large wings upon my shoulders, and point out

Whoso encamps
His soul to take a city of delight
O what a wretch is he : 'tis in his sight...

Then 'tis in his sight *was struck out in favour of* and when 'tis his ;
*but nothing was done, in transcribing for the press, to remedy the defect
thus produced.*

149 pebble-bead *MS. and 1818 corrected :* pebble-head *1818.*

My love's far dwelling. Though the playful rout
Of Cupids shun thee, too divine art thou,   180
Too keen in beauty, for thy silver prow
Not to have dipp'd in love's most gentle stream.
O be propitious, nor severely deem
My madness impious; for, by all the stars
That tend thy bidding, I do think the bars
That kept my spirit in are burst—that I
Am sailing with thee through the dizzy sky!
How beautiful thou art! The world how deep!
How tremulous-dazzlingly the wheels sweep
Around their axle! Then these gleaming reins, 190
How lithe! When this thy chariot attains
Its airy goal, haply some bower veils
Those twilight eyes? Those eyes!—my spirit fails—
Dear goddess, help! or the wide-gaping air
Will gulph me—help!"—At this with madden'd
          stare,
And lifted hands, and trembling lips he stood;
Like old Deucalion mountain'd o'er the flood,
Or blind Orion hungry for the morn.
And, but from the deep cavern there was borne
A voice, he had been froze to senseless stone;   200
Nor sigh of his, nor plaint, nor passion'd moan
Had more been heard. Thus swell'd it forth: "Descend,
Young mountaineer! descend where alleys bend
Into the sparry hollows of the world!
Oft hast thou seen bolts of the thunder hurl'd
As from thy threshold; day by day hast been
A little lower than the chilly sheen
Of icy pinnacles, and dipp'dst thine arms
Into the deadening ether that still charms
Their marble being: now, as deep profound   210
As those are high, descend! He ne'er is crown'd
With immortality, who fears to follow
Where airy voices lead: so through the hollow,
The silent mysteries of earth, descend!"

He heard but the last words, nor could contend
One moment in reflection: for he fled

198 dawn *Draft*.   199 borne *1818*: born *Draft*.

Into the fearful deep, to hide his head
From the clear moon, the trees, and coming madness.

'Twas far too strange, and wonderful for sadness ;
Sharpening, by degrees, his appetite   220
To dive into the deepest.   Dark, nor light,
The region ; nor bright, nor sombre wholly,
But mingled up ; a gleaming melancholy ;
A dusky empire and its diadems ;
One faint eternal eventide of gems.
Aye, millions sparkled on a vein of gold,
Along whose track the prince quick footsteps told,
With all its lines abrupt and angular :
Out-shooting sometimes, like a meteor-star,
Through a vast antre ; then the metal woof,   230
Like Vulcan's rainbow, with some monstrous roof
Curves hugely : now, far in the deep abyss,
It seems an angry lightning, and doth hiss
Fancy into belief : anon it leads
Through winding passages, where sameness breeds
Vexing conceptions of some sudden change ;
Whether to silver grots, or giant range
Of sapphire columns, or fantastic bridge
Athwart a flood of crystal.   On a ridge
Now fareth he, that o'er the vast beneath   240
Towers like an ocean-cliff, and whence he seeth
A hundred waterfalls, whose voices come
But as the murmuring surge.   Chilly and numb
His bosom grew, when first he, far away
Descried an orbed diamond, set to fray
Old darkness from his throne : 'twas like the sun
Uprisen o'er chaos : and with such a stun
Came the amazement, that, absorb'd in it,
He saw not fiercer wonders—past the wit
Of any spirit to tell, but one of those   250
Who, when this planet's sphering time doth close,
Will be its high remembrancers : who they ?

227-30 Whose track the venturous Latmian follows bold
        Thro' all its lines abrupt and angular :
        And sometimes like a shooting meteor star
        Past a vast antre's gloom. *Draft.*

The mighty ones who have made eternal day
For Greece and England. While astonishment
With deep-drawn sighs was quieting, he went
Into a marble gallery, passing through
A mimic temple, so complete and true
In sacred custom, that he well nigh fear'd
To search it inwards; whence far off appear'd,
Through a long pillar'd vista, a fair shrine,   260
And just beyond, on light tiptoe divine,
A quiver'd Dian. Stepping awfully,
The youth approach'd; oft turning his veil'd eye
Down sidelong aisles, and into niches old.
And when, more near against the marble cold
He had touch'd his forehead, he began to thread
All courts and passages, where silence dead
Rous'd by his whispering footsteps murmured faint:
And long he travers'd to and fro, to acquaint
Himself with every mystery, and awe;   270
Till, weary, he sat down before the maw
Of a wide outlet, fathomless and dim,
To wild uncertainty and shadows grim.
There, when new wonders ceas'd to float before,
And thoughts of self came on, how crude and sore
The journey homeward to habitual self!
A mad-pursuing of the fog-born elf,
Whose flitting lantern, through rude nettle-briar,
Cheats us into a swamp, into a fire,
Into the bosom of a hated thing.   280

   What misery most drowningly doth sing
In lone Endymion's ear, now he has raught

   253-4 The mighty ones who've shone athwart the day
            Of Greece and England. *Draft.*
   261-3 Thro' a long vist' of columns a fair shrine
            And just beyond lightly diminished
            A Dian quiver'd tiptoe, crescented— *Draft.*
   278 Whose flitting Lantern, through rude nettle-beds,
            Cheats us into a bog,—cuttings and shreds
            Of old Vexations plaited to a rope
            Wherewith to haul us from the sight of hope,
            And bind us to our earthly baiting-ring. *Draft.*
*The grotesque imagery reminds us, in its rude vigour, that Keats had
actually witnessed, and forcibly described to Clarke, a bear-baiting.*
   282 raught *MS. :* caught *1818.*

The goal of consciousness? Ah, 'tis the thought,
The deadly feel of solitude: for lo!
He cannot see the heavens, nor the flow
Of rivers, nor hill-flowers running wild
In pink and purple chequer, nor, up-pil'd,
The cloudy rack slow journeying in the west,
Like herded elephants; nor felt, nor prest
Cool grass, nor tasted the fresh slumberous air; 290
But far from such companionship to wear
An unknown time, surcharg'd with grief, away,
Was now his lot. And must he patient stay,
Tracing fantastic figures with his spear?
"No!" exclaim'd he, "why should I tarry here?"
No! loudly echoed times innumerable.
At which he straightway started, and 'gan tell
His paces back into the temple's chief;
Warming and glowing strong in the belief
Of help from Dian: so that when again   300
He caught her airy form, thus did he plain,
Moving more near the while: "O Haunter chaste
Of river sides, and woods, and heathy waste,
Where with thy silver bow and arrows keen
Art thou now forested? O woodland Queen,
What smoothest air thy smoother forehead woos?
Where dost thou listen to the wide halloos
Of thy disparted nymphs? Through what dark tree
Glimmers thy crescent? Wheresoe'er it be,
'Tis in the breath of heaven: thou dost taste   310
Freedom as none can taste it, nor dost waste
Thy loveliness in dismal elements;
But, finding in our green earth sweet contents,
There livest blissfully. Ah, if to thee
It feels Elysian, how rich to me,
An exil'd mortal, sounds its pleasant name!
Within my breast there lives a choking flame—

290 the free sleepy air. *Draft.*
301   thus gan he plain,
     Pacing towards the while. *Draft.*
Moving towards the while. *MS.*
304 Where now with silver bow and arrows keen
     Art thou in covert hid? *Draft.*
313 in *1818:* on *MS.*

O let me cool 't the zephyr-boughs among!
A homeward fever parches up my tongue—
O let me slake it at the running springs!   320
Upon my ear a noisy nothing rings—
O let me once more hear the linnet's note!
Before mine eyes thick films and shadows float—
O let me 'noint them with the heaven's light!
Dost thou now lave thy feet and ankles white?
O think how sweet to me the freshening sluice!
Dost thou now please thy thirst with berry-juice?
O think how this dry palate would rejoice!
If in soft slumber thou dost hear my voice,
O think how I should love a bed of flowers!—   330
Young goddess! let me see my native bowers!
Deliver me from this rapacious deep!"

Thus ending loudly, as he would o'erleap
His destiny, alert he stood: but when
Obstinate silence came heavily again,
Feeling about for its old couch of space
And airy cradle, lowly bow'd his face
Desponding, o'er the marble floor's cold thrill.
But 'twas not long; for, sweeter than the rill
To its old channel, or a swollen tide   340
To margin sallows, were the leaves he spied,
And flowers, and wreaths, and ready myrtle crowns
Up heaping through the slab: refreshment drowns
Itself, and strives its own delights to hide—
Nor in one spot alone; the floral pride

318 *In the finished manuscript,* cool't *for* cool it : *otherwise the line is really written as the first edition gives it—*

    O let me cool it among the zephyr-boughs!

But it seems absolutely certain that among *was meant to be at the end, to rhyme with* tongue,—*an assurance made doubly sure by the fact that the line was originally written in the draft—*

    O let me cool't among the waving boughs!

and marked for transposition of among *to the end. Thus Keats clearly in copying the line altered* waving *to* zephyr *but forgot the transposition.*
   327 cherry-juice. *Draft.*
   332 Lift me, oh lift me from this horrid deep ! *Draft.*
   340 To its cool channel, the o'erswollen tide... *Draft.* cold channel *MS.* : old channel *1818.*
   343-4 Upswelling through the slab ; refreshment drowns
     Itself, lush tumbling down on every side : *Draft.*

In a long whispering birth enchanted grew
Before his footsteps; as when heav'd anew
Old ocean rolls a lengthened wave to the shore,
Down whose green back the short-liv'd foam, all hoar,
Bursts gradual, with a wayward indolence.   350

    Increasing still in heart, and pleasant sense,
Upon his fairy journey on he hastes;
So anxious for the end, he scarcely wastes
One moment with his hand among the sweets:
Onward he goes—he stops—his bosom beats
As plainly in his ear, as the faint charm
Of which the throbs were born. This still alarm,
This sleepy music, forc'd him walk tiptoe:
For it came more softly than the east could blow
Arion's magic to the Atlantic isles;   360
Or than the west, made jealous by the smiles
Of thron'd Apollo, could breathe back the lyre
To seas Ionian and Tyrian.

    O did he ever live, that lonely man,
Who lov'd—and music slew not? 'Tis the pest
Of love, that fairest joys give most unrest;
That things of delicate and tenderest worth
Are swallow'd all, and made a seared dearth,
By one consuming flame: it doth immerse
And suffocate true blessings in a curse.   370
Half-happy, by comparison of bliss,
Is miserable. 'Twas even so with this
Dew-dropping melody, in the Carian's ear;
First heaven, then hell, and then forgotten clear,
Vanish'd in elemental passion.

353 wastes *1818 :* waits *MS.*
363 *The draft supplies the history of the loss of a rhyme to this line.*
The passage was left thus :
        To seas Ionian and Tyrian.   Dire
        Was the love lorn despair to which it wrought
        Endymion—for dire is the bare thought
        That among lovers things of tenderest worth
        Are swallow'd all, and made a blank—a dearth
        By one devouring flame : and far far worse
        Blessing to them become a heavy curse
        Half happy till comparisons of bliss
        To misery lead them. 'Twas even so with this...

And down some swart abysm he had gone,
Had not a heavenly guide benignant led
To where thick myrtle branches, 'gainst his head
Brushing, awakened : then the sounds again
Went noiseless as a passing noontide rain   380
Over a bower, where little space he stood ;
For as the sunset peeps into a wood
So saw he panting light, and towards it went
Through winding alleys ; and lo, wonderment !
Upon soft verdure saw, one here, one there,
Cupids a slumbering on their pinions fair.

After a thousand mazes overgone,
At last, with sudden step, he came upon
A chamber, myrtle wall'd, embowered high,
Full of light, incense, tender minstrelsy,   390
And more of beautiful and strange beside :
For on a silken couch of rosy pride,
In midst of all, there lay a sleeping youth
Of fondest beauty ; fonder, in fair sooth,
Than sighs could fathom, or contentment reach :
And coverlids gold-tinted like the peach,
Or ripe October's faded marigolds,
Fell sleek about him in a thousand folds—
Not hiding up an Apollonian curve
Of neck and shoulder, nor the tenting swerve   400
Of knee from knee, nor ankles pointing light ;
But rather, giving them to the filled sight
Officiously.   Sideway his face repos'd
On one white arm, and tenderly unclos'd,
By tenderest pressure, a faint damask mouth
To slumbery pout ; just as the morning south
Disparts a dew-lipp'd rose. Above his head,
Four lilly stalks did their white honours wed
To make a coronal ; and round him grew

379–83   Brushing awaken'd him : the sounds again
          Came softly as a gentle evening rain,
          Around a bower, where he stay'd harkening
          And through whose tufted shrubby darkening
          Bright starry glimmers came, towards which he
             went... *Draft.*
396–7   And draperies mellow-tinted like the peach,
          Or lady peas entwined with marigolds. *Draft.*

All tendrils green, of every bloom and hue,   410
Together intertwin'd and trammel'd fresh :
The vine of glossy sprout ; the ivy mesh,
Shading its Ethiop berries ; and woodbine,
Of velvet leaves and bugle-blooms divine ;
Convolvulus in streaked vases flush ;
The creeper, mellowing for an autumn blush ;
And virgin's bower, trailing airily ;
With others of the sisterhood. Hard by,
Stood serene Cupids watching silently.
One, kneeling to a lyre, touch'd the strings,   420
Muffling to death the pathos with his wings ;
And, ever and anon, uprose to look
At the youth's slumber ; while another took
A willow-bough, distilling odorous dew,
And shook it on his hair ; another flew
In through the woven roof, and fluttering-wise
Rain'd violets upon his sleeping eyes.

At these enchantments, and yet many more,
The breathless Latmian wonder'd o'er and o'er ;
Until, impatient in embarrassment,   430
He forthright pass'd, and lightly treading went
To that same feather'd lyrist, who straightway,
Smiling, thus whisper'd : "Though from upper day
Thou art a wanderer, and thy presence here
Might seem unholy, be of happy cheer !
For 'tis the nicest touch of human honour,
When some ethereal and high-favouring donor
Presents immortal bowers to mortal sense ;
As now 'tis done to thee, Endymion. Hence
Was I in no wise startled. So recline   440
Upon these living flowers. Here is wine,

---

410 All tendril green, of pleasant lush and hue. *Draft.*
414 With all its honey bugle tufts divine. *Draft.*
416 The creeper, blushing deep at Autumn's blush. *Draft.*
419 Stood Cupids holding o'er an upward gaze
    Each a slim wand tipt with a silver blaze
    Each one a silver torch... *Draft.*
424 A myrtle-bough. *Draft.*
429 The mortal Latmian. *Draft.*
436 the highest reach of human honor. *Draft.*

Alive with sparkles—never, I aver,
Since Ariadne was a vintager,
So cool a purple: taste these juicy pears,
Sent me by sad Vertumnus, when his fears
Were high about Pomona: here is cream,
Deepening to richness from a snowy gleam;
Sweeter than that nurse Amalthea skimm'd
For the boy Jupiter: and here, undimm'd
By any touch, a bunch of blooming plums   450
Ready to melt between an infant's gums:
And here is manna pick'd from Syrian trees,
In starlight, by the three Hesperides.
Feast on, and meanwhile I will let thee know
Of all these things around us." He did so,
Still brooding o'er the cadence of his lyre;
And thus: "I need not any hearing tire
By telling how the sea-born goddess pin'd
For a mortal youth, and how she strove to bind
Him all in all unto her doting self.   460
Who would not be so prison'd? but, fond elf,
He was content to let her amorous plea
Faint through his careless arms; content to see
An unseiz'd heaven dying at his feet;
Content, O fool! to make a cold retreat,
When on the pleasant grass such love, lovelorn,
Lay sorrowing; when every tear was born
Of diverse passion; when her lips and eyes
Were clos'd in sullen moisture, and quick sighs
Came vex'd and pettish through her nostrils small.
Hush! no exclaim—yet, justly mightst thou call
Curses upon his head.—I was half glad,   472
But my poor mistress went distract and mad,
When the boar tusk'd him: so away she flew
To Jove's high throne, and by her plainings drew

442   Sparkling up diamonds. *Draft.*
448   Even sweet as that which Amalthea skimm'd. *Draft.*
456-7 Keeping a ravishing cadence with his lyre.
       And thus it was "I'll not thy knowing tire... *Draft.*
461-4 Who would not be so bound, but, foolish elf,
       He was content to let Divinity
       Slip through his careless arms—content to see
       An unseized heaven sighing at his feet; *Draft.*
474 tusk'd *1818:* tush'd *MS.*

Immortal tear-drops down the thunderer's beard ;
Whereon, it was decreed he should be rear'd
Each summer time to life. Lo ! this is he,
That same Adonis, safe in the privacy
Of this still region all his winter-sleep.   480
Aye, sleep ; for when our love-sick queen did weep
Over his waned corse, the tremulous shower
Heal'd up the wound, and, with a balmy power,
Medicined death to a lengthened drowsiness :
The which she fills with visions, and doth dress
In all this quiet luxury ; and hath set
Us young immortals, without any let,
To watch his slumber through. 'Tis well nigh pass'd,
Even to a moment's filling up, and fast
She scuds with summer breezes, to pant through   490
The first long kiss, warm firstling, to renew
Embower'd sports in Cytherea's isle.
Look ! how those winged listeners all this while
Stand anxious : see ! behold !"—This clamant word
Broke through the careful silence ; for they heard
A rustling noise of leaves, and out there flutter'd
Pigeons and doves : Adonis something mutter'd
The while one hand, that erst upon his thigh
Lay dormant, mov'd convuls'd and gradually
Up to his forehead. Then there was a hum   500
Of sudden voices, echoing, " Come ! come !
Arise ! awake ! Clear summer has forth walk'd
Unto the clover-sward, and she has talk'd
Full soothingly to every nested finch :
Rise, Cupids ! or we'll give the blue-bell pinch
To your dimpled arms. Once more sweet life begin ! "
At this, from every side they hurried in,
Rubbing their sleepy eyes with lazy wrists,
And doubling over head their little fists
In backward yawns. But all were soon alive :   510

479 in the *1818* : i' the *MS*.
482 Over this paly corse, the crystal shower... *Draft*.
501 Of sudden voices, echoing out, " Come ! come ! *Draft*.
504 *The draft reads* Most *for* Full.
505 Cupids awake ! or black and blue we'll pinch
    Your dimpled arms—for lo ! your Queen, your Queen.
                                                    Draft.

For as delicious wine doth, sparkling, dive
In nectar'd clouds and curls through water fair,
So from the arbour roof down swell'd an air
Odorous and enlivening ; making all
To laugh, and play, and sing, and loudly call
For their sweet queen : when lo ! the wreathed green
Disparted, and far upward could be seen
Blue heaven, and a silver car, air-borne,
Whose silent wheels, fresh wet from clouds of morn,
Spun off a drizzling dew,—which falling chill   520
On soft Adonis' shoulders, made him still
Nestle and turn uneasily about.
Soon were the white doves plain, with neck stretch'd out,
And silken traces lighten'd in descent ;
And soon, returning from love's banishment,
Queen Venus leaning downward open arm'd :
Her shadow fell upon his breast, and charm'd
A tumult to his heart, and a new life
Into his eyes. Ah, miserable strife,
But for her comforting ! unhappy sight,   530
But meeting her blue orbs ! Who, who can write
Of these first minutes ? The unchariest muse
To embracements warm as theirs makes coy excuse.

O it has ruffled every spirit there,
Saving Love's self, who stands superb to share

525 *The finished manuscript reads* next *instead of* soon.
526 Queen Venus bending downward, so o'ertaken,
    So suffering sweet, so blushing mad, so shaken
    That the wild warmth prob'd the young sleeper's heart
    Enchantingly ; and with a sudden start
    His trembling arms were out in instant time
    To catch his fainting love.—O foolish rhyme
    What mighty power is in thee that so often
    Thou strivest rugged syllables to soften
    Even to the telling of a sweet like this.
    Away ! let them embrace alone ! that kiss
    Was far too rich for thee to talk upon.
    Poor wretch ! mind not those sobs and sighs ! begone !
    Speak not one atom of thy paltry stuff,
    That they are met is poetry enough.
        O this has ruffled every spirit there, ... *Draft.*
These lines are struck out of the draft, where their place is not supplied ;
but the finished copy corresponds with the printed text.
    535 Love's *MS. :* love's *1818.*

The general gladness : awfully he stands ;
A sovereign quell is in his waving hands ;
No sight can bear the lightning of his bow ;
His quiver is mysterious, none can know   539
What themselves think of it ; from forth his eyes
There darts strange light of varied hues and dies :
A scowl is sometimes on his brow, but who
Look full upon it feel anon the blue
Of his fair eyes run liquid through their souls.
Endymion feels it, and no more controls
The burning prayer within him ; so, bent low,
He had begun a plaining of his woe.
But Venus, bending forward, said : "My child,
Favour this gentle youth ; his days are wild
With love—he—but alas ! too well I see   550
Thou know'st the deepness of his misery.
Ah, smile not so, my son : I tell thee true,
That when through heavy hours I used to rue
The endless sleep of this new-born Adon',
This stranger aye I pitied. For upon
A dreary morning once I fled away
Into the breezy clouds, to weep and pray
For this my love : for vexing Mars had teaz'd
Me even to tears : thence, when a little eas'd,
Down-looking, vacant, through a hazy wood,   560
I saw this youth as he despairing stood :
Those same dark curls blown vagrant in the wind ;
Those same full fringed lids a constant blind
Over his sullen eyes : I saw him throw
Himself on wither'd leaves, even as though
Death had come sudden ; for no jot he mov'd,
Yet mutter'd wildly. I could hear he lov'd
Some fair immortal, and that his embrace
Had zoned her through the night. There is no trace
Of this in heaven : I have mark'd each cheek,   570
And find it is the vainest thing to seek ;
And that of all things 'tis kept secretest.
Endymion ! one day thou wilt be blest :

538 His bow no sight can bear for lightning so. *MS.*
541 dies *MS. :* dyes *1818.*
552 sweet boy ! *Draft.*   554 mad-brain'd *Draft.*

So still obey the guiding hand that fends
Thee safely through these wonders for sweet ends.
'Tis a concealment needful in extreme ;
And if I guess'd not so, the sunny beam
Thou shouldst mount up to with me. Now adieu !
Here must we leave thee."—At these words upflew
The impatient doves, uprose the floating car,   580
Up went the hum celestial. High afar
The Latmian saw them minish into naught ;
And, when all were clear vanish'd, still he caught
A vivid lightning from that dreadful bow.
When all was darkened, with Ætnean throe
The earth clos'd—gave a solitary moan—
And left him once again in twilight lone.

He did not rave, he did not stare aghast,
For all those visions were o'ergone, and past,
And he in loneliness : he felt assur'd   590
Of happy times, when all he had endur'd
Would seem a feather to the mighty prize.
So, with unusual gladness, on he hies
Through caves, and palaces of mottled ore,
Gold dome, and crystal wall, and turquois floor,
Black polish'd porticos of awful shade,
And, at the last, a diamond balustrade,
Leading afar past wild magnificence,
Spiral through ruggedest loopholes, and thence
Stretching across a void, then guiding o'er   600
Enormous chasms, where, all foam and roar,
Streams subterranean teaze their granite beds ;
Then heighten'd just above the silvery heads
Of a thousand fountains, so that he could dash
The waters with his spear ; but at the splash,
Done heedlessly, those spouting columns rose
Sudden a poplar's height, and 'gan to enclose
His diamond path with fretwork, streaming round

584–5 Anon and ever gleams from that dread bow.
          One lightning more—then with Œtnœan throe... *Draft.*
œtnean *MS. :* Etnean *1818.*
    597–8 Then diamond steps and ruby balustrade
          Leading to fierce and wild magnificence... *Draft.*
    606 He playfully made *Draft.*
    608 His mid-air path with fretwork, quivering round *Draft.*

Alive, and dazzling cool, and with a sound,
Haply, like dolphin tumults, when sweet shells 610
Welcome the float of Thetis. Long he dwells
On this delight ; for, every minute's space,
The streams with changed magic interlace :
Sometimes like delicatest lattices,
Cover'd with crystal vines ; then weeping trees.
Moving about as in a gentle wind,
Which, in a wink, to watery gauze refin'd,
Pour'd into shapes of curtain'd canopies,
Spangled, and rich with liquid broideries
Of flowers, peacocks, swans, and naiads fair. 620
Swifter than lightning went these wonders rare ;
And then the water, into stubborn streams
Collecting, mimick'd the wrought oaken beams,
Pillars, and frieze, and high fantastic roof,
Of those dusk places in times far aloof
Cathedrals call'd. He bade a loth farewell
To these founts Protean, passing gulph, and dell,
And torrent, and ten thousand jutting shapes,
Half seen through deepest gloom, and griesly gapes,
Blackening on every side, and overhead 630
A vaulted dome like Heaven's, far bespread
With starlight gems : aye, all so huge and strange,
The solitary felt a hurried change
Working within him into something dreary,—
Vex'd like a morning eagle, lost, and weary,
And purblind amid foggy, midnight wolds.
But he revives at once : for who beholds
New sudden things, nor casts his mental slough ?
Forth from a rugged arch, in the dusk below,
Came mother Cybele ! alone—alone— 640
In sombre chariot ; dark foldings thrown
About her majesty, and front death-pale,

615-16 O'erspread with crystal vines ; then weeping peas,
    Waving about *Draft.*
642-7 About her majesty, and her pale brow
    With turrets crown'd, which forward heavily bow
    Weighing her chin to the breast. Four lions draw
    The wheels in sluggish time—each toothed maw
    Shut patiently—eyes hid in tawny veils—
    Drooping about their paws, and nervy tails
    Cowering their tufted brushes to the dust. *Draft.*

With turrets crown'd. Four maned lions hale
The sluggish wheels ; solemn their toothed maws,
Their surly eyes brow-hidden, heavy paws
Uplifted drowsily, and nervy tails
Cowering their tawny brushes. Silent sails
This shadowy queen athwart, and faints away
In another gloomy arch.

                      Wherefore delay,
Young traveller, in such a mournful place ?   650
Art thou wayworn, or canst not further trace
The diamond path ? And does it indeed end
Abrupt in middle air ? Yet earthward bend
Thy forehead, and to Jupiter cloud-borne
Call ardently ! He was indeed wayworn ;
Abrupt, in middle air, his way was lost ;
To cloud-borne Jove he bowed, and there crost
Towards him a large eagle, 'twixt whose wings,
Without one impious word, himself he flings,
Committed to the darkness and the gloom :   660
Down, down, uncertain to what pleasant doom,
Swift as a fathoming plummet down he fell
Through unknown things ; till exhaled asphodel,
And rose, with spicy fannings interbreath'd,
Came swelling forth where little caves were wreath'd
So thick with leaves and mosses, that they seem'd
Large honey-combs of green, and freshly teem'd
With airs delicious. In the greenest nook
The eagle landed him, and farewell took.

It was a jasmine bower, all bestrown   670
With golden moss. His every sense had grown

657-62 To cloudborne Jove he bent : and there was tost
          Into his grasping hands a silken cord
          At which without a single impious word
          He swung upon it off into the gloom.
          Down, down, uncertain to what pleasant doom,
          Dropt like a fathoming plummet, down he fell...*Draft*.
668-71 With airs delicious. Long he hung about
          Before his nice enjoyment could pick out
          The resting place : but at the last he swung
          Into the greenest cell of all—among
          Dark leaved jasmine : star flower'd and bestrown
          With golden moss. *Draft*.

Ethereal for pleasure; 'bove his head
Flew a delight half-graspable; his tread
Was Hesperean; to his capable ears
Silence was music from the holy spheres;
A dewy luxury was in his eyes;
The little flowers felt his pleasant sighs
And stirr'd them faintly. Verdant cave and cell
He wander'd through, oft wondering at such swell
Of sudden exaltation : but, "Alas!"   680
Said he, "will all this gush of feeling pass
Away in solitude? And must they wane,
Like melodies upon a sandy plain,
Without an echo? Then shall I be left
So sad, so melancholy, so bereft!
Yet still I feel immortal! O my love,
My breath of life, where art thou? High above,
Dancing before the morning gates of heaven?
Or keeping watch among those starry seven,
Old Atlas' children? Art a maid of the waters, 690
One of shell-winding Triton's bright-hair'd daughters?
Or art, impossible! a nymph of Dian's,
Weaving a coronal of tender scions
For very idleness? Where'er thou art,
Methinks it now is at my will to start
Into thine arms; to scare Aurora's train,
And snatch thee from the morning; o'er the main
To scud like a wild bird, and take thee off
From thy sea-foamy cradle; or to doff
Thy shepherd vest, and woo thee mid fresh leaves. 700
No, no, too eagerly my soul deceives
Its powerless self: I know this cannot be.
O let me then by some sweet dreaming flee
To her entrancements: hither sleep awhile!
Hither most gentle sleep! and soothing foil
For some few hours the coming solitude."

Thus spake he, and that moment felt endued
With power to dream deliciously; so wound

679 He wandered through, with still encreasing swell...*Draft*.
697 And snatch thee from among them; to attain
    The starry hights and find thee ere a breath... *Draft*.
706 *The draft reads* With thy quick magic *for* For some few hours.

Through a dim passage, searching till he found
The smoothest mossy bed and deepest, where   710
He threw himself, and just into the air
Stretching his indolent arms, he took, O bliss!
A naked waist: "Fair Cupid, whence is this?"
A well-known voice sigh'd, "Sweetest, here am I!"
At which soft ravishment, with doting cry
They trembled to each other.—Helicon!
O fountain'd hill! Old Homer's Helicon!
That thou wouldst spout a little streamlet o'er
These sorry pages; then the verse would soar
And sing above this gentle pair, like lark   720
Over his nested young: but all is dark
Around thine aged top, and thy clear fount
Exhales in mists to heaven. Aye, the count
Of mighty Poets is made up; the scroll
Is folded by the Muses; the bright roll
Is in Apollo's hand: our dazed eyes
Have seen a new tinge in the western skies:
The world has done its duty. Yet, oh yet,
Although the sun of poesy is set,
These lovers did embrace, and we must weep   730
That there is no old power left to steep
A quill immortal in their joyous tears.
Long time ere silence did their anxious fears
Question that thus it was; long time they lay
Fondling and kissing every doubt away;
Long time ere soft caressing sobs began
To mellow into words, and then there ran
Two bubbling springs of talk from their sweet lips.
"O known Unknown! from whom my being sips
Such darling essence, wherefore may I not   740
Be ever in these arms? in this sweet spot
Pillow my chin for ever? ever press
These toying hands and kiss their smooth excess?
Why not for ever and for ever feel
That breath about my eyes? Ah, thou wilt steal
Away from me again, indeed, indeed—
Thou wilt be gone away, and wilt not heed

713 Fair Cupid *1818*: Good heavens! *Draft.*
715 Doting *MS.*: doating *1818.*

My lonely madness. Speak, delicious fair!
Is—is it to be so? No! Who will dare
To pluck thee from me? And, of thine own will,   750
Full well I feel thou wouldst not leave me. Still
Let me entwine thee surer, surer—now
How can we part? Elysium! who art thou?
Who, that thou canst not be for ever here,
Or lift me with thee to some starry sphere?
Enchantress! tell me by this soft embrace,
By the most soft completion of thy face,
Those lips, O slippery blisses, twinkling eyes,
And by these tenderest, milky sovereignties—
These tenderest, and by the nectar-wine,   760
The passion"————"O dov'd Ida the divine!
Endymion! dearest! Ah, unhappy me!
His soul will 'scape us—O felicity!
How he does love me! His poor temples beat
To the very tune of love—how sweet, sweet, sweet.
Revive, dear youth, or I shall faint and die;
Revive, or these soft hours will hurry by
In tranced dulness; speak, and let that spell
Affright this lethargy! I cannot quell
Its heavy pressure, and will press at least   770
My lips to thine, that they may richly feast
Until we taste the life of love again.
What! dost thou move? dost kiss? O bliss! O pain!
I love thee, youth, more than I can conceive;
And so long absence from thee doth bereave
My soul of any rest: yet must I hence:
Yet, can I not to starry eminence
Uplift thee; nor for very shame can own
Myself to thee: Ah, dearest, do not groan
Or thou wilt force me from this secrecy,   780
And I must blush in heaven. O that I
Had done 't already; that the dreadful smiles
At my lost brightness, my impassion'd wiles,

748 delicious fair! *1818 corrected :* my kindest fair! *MS. and
1818.*
  756-7 Enchantress! tell me by this mad embrace,
            By the moist languor of thy breathing face... *Draft.*
  760-1 These tenderest—and by the breath—the love
            The passion—nectar—Heaven!"——"Jove above! *Draft.*
  782 done 't *1818 corrected :* done it *1818 :* do n't *MS.*

*E 3

Had waned from Olympus' solemn height,
And from all serious Gods; that our delight
Was quite forgotten, save of us alone!
And wherefore so ashamed? 'Tis but to atone
For endless pleasure, by some coward blushes:
Yet must I be a coward!—Horror rushes
Too palpable before me—the sad look   790
Of Jove—Minerva's start—no bosom shook
With awe of purity—no Cupid pinion
In reverence vailed—my crystalline dominion
Half lost, and all old hymns made nullity!
But what is this to love? O I could fly
With thee into the ken of heavenly powers,
So thou wouldst thus, for many sequent hours,
Press me so sweetly. Now I swear at once
That I am wise, that Pallas is a dunce—
Perhaps her love like mine is but unknown—   800
O I do think that I have been alone
In chastity: yes, Pallas has been sighing,
While every eve saw me my hair uptying
With fingers cool as aspen leaves. Sweet love,
I was as vague as solitary dove,
Nor knew that nests were built. Now a soft kiss—
Aye, by that kiss, I vow an endless bliss,
An immortality of passion's thine:
Ere long I will exalt thee to the shine
Of heaven ambrosial; and we will shade   810
Ourselves whole summers by a river glade;
And I will tell thee stories of the sky,
And breathe thee whispers of its minstrelsy.
My happy love will overwing all bounds!
O let me melt into thee; let the sounds
Of our close voices marry at their birth;
Let us entwine hoveringly—O dearth
Of human words! roughness of mortal speech!

789 Honour *1818 text:* Horror *1818 errata.*
793 veiled *1818:* vailed *MS.*
800 Does Pallas self not love? she must—she must! *Draft.*
815–27   let the sounds
      Of both our voices marry at their birth;
      Let us entwine inextricably—O dearth
      Of mortal words! I'll teach thee other speech;

Lispings empyrean will I sometime teach
Thine honied tongue—lute-breathings, which I gasp
To have thee understand, now while I clasp 821
Thee thus, and weep for fondness—I am pain'd,
Endymion: woe! woe! is grief contain'd
In the very deeps of pleasure, my sole life?"—
Hereat, with many sobs, her gentle strife
Melted into a languor. He return'd
Entranced vows and tears.

                 Ye who have yearn'd
With too much passion, will here stay and pity,
For the mere sake of truth; as 'tis a ditty
Not of these days, but long ago 'twas told 830
By a cavern wind unto a forest old;
And then the forest told it in a dream
To a sleeping lake, whose cool and level gleam
A poet caught as he was journeying
To Phœbus' shrine; and in it he did fling
His weary limbs, bathing an hour's space,
And after, straight in that inspired place
He sang the story up into the air,
Giving it universal freedom. There
Has it been ever sounding for those ears 840
Whose tips are glowing hot. The legend cheers
Yon centinel stars; and he who listens to it
Must surely be self-doom'd or he will rue it:
For quenchless burnings come upon the heart,
Made fiercer by a fear lest any part
Should be engulphed in the eddying wind.
As much as here is penn'd doth always find
A resting place, thus much comes clear and plain;

Lispings immortal will I sometime teach
Thine honied tongue—Gold-breathings, which I gasp
To have thee understand, now while I clasp
Thee thus, and shed these $\begin{Bmatrix} \text{tears} \\ \text{drops} \end{Bmatrix}$ —I am pain'd,
Endymion. There is a grief contain'd
In the very shrine of pleasure, O my life!"
Hereat with fainting sobs her gentle strife
Died into passive languor—he return'd
No answer, saving tears. *Draft.*

Anon the strange voice is upon the wane—
And 'tis but echo'd from departing sound,   850
That the fair visitant at last unwound
Her gentle limbs, and left the youth asleep.—
Thus the tradition of the gusty deep.

   Now turn we to our former chroniclers.—
Endymion awoke, that grief of hers
Sweet paining on his ear: he sickly guess'd
How lone he was once more, and sadly press'd
His empty arms together, hung his head,
And most forlorn upon that widow'd bed
Sat silently. Love's madness he had known: 860
Often with more than tortured lion's groan
Moanings had burst from him; but now that rage
Had pass'd away: no longer did he wage
A rough-voic'd war against the dooming stars.
No, he had felt too much for such harsh jars:
The lyre of his soul Æolian tun'd
Forgot all violence, and but commun'd
With melancholy thought: O he had swoon'd
Drunken from pleasure's nipple; and his love
Henceforth was dove-like.—Loth was he to move   870
From the imprinted couch, and when he did,
'Twas with slow, languid paces, and face hid
In muffling hands. So temper'd, out he stray'd
Half seeing visions that might have dismay'd
Alecto's serpents; ravishments more keen
Than Hermes' pipe, when anxious he did lean
Over eclipsing eyes: and at the last
It was a sounding grotto, vaulted, vast,
O'er studded with a thousand, thousand pearls,
And crimson mouthed shells with stubborn curls,   880
Of every shape and size, even to the bulk
In which whales arbour close, to brood and sulk
Against an endless storm. Moreover too,

849-50 But after the strange voice is on the wane—
     And 'tis but guess'd from the departing sound, *Draft.*
866 Œolian *MS.:* Eolian *1818.*
870-1   Scarcely could he move
From the dear couch. *Draft.*
880 And shells outswelling their faint tinged curls. *Draft.*

Fish-semblances, of green and azure hue,
Ready to snort their streams. In this cool wonder
Endymion sat down, and 'gan to ponder
On all his life: his youth, up to the day
When 'mid acclaim, and feasts, and garlands gay,
He stept upon his shepherd throne: the look
Of his white palace in wild forest nook,   890
And all the revels he had lorded there:
Each tender maiden whom he once thought fair,
With every friend and fellow-woodlander—
Pass'd like a dream before him. Then the spur
Of the old bards to mighty deeds: his plans
To nurse the golden age 'mong shepherd clans:
That wondrous night: the great Pan-festival:
His sister's sorrow; and his wanderings all,
Until into the earth's deep maw he rush'd:
Then all its buried magic, till it flush'd   900
High with excessive love. "And now," thought he,
"How long must I remain in jeopardy
Of blank amazements that amaze no more?
Now I have tasted her sweet soul to the core
All other depths are shallow: essences,
Once spiritual, are like muddy lees,
Meant but to fertilize my earthly root,
And make my branches lift a golden fruit
Into the bloom of heaven: other light,
Though it be quick and sharp enough to blight   910
The Olympian eagle's vision, is dark,
Dark as the parentage of chaos. Hark!
My silent thoughts are echoing from these shells;
Or they are but the ghosts, the dying swells
Of noises far away?—list!"—Hereupon
He kept an anxious ear. The humming tone
Came louder, and behold, there as he lay,
On either side outgush'd, with misty spray,
A copious spring; and both together dash'd
Swift, mad, fantastic round the rocks, and lash'd   920
Among the conchs and shells of the lofty grot,
Leaving a trickling dew. At last they shot
Down from the ceiling's height, pouring a noise

914 Or they are subtlest and dying swells *Draft.*

As of some breathless racers whose hopes poize
Upon the last few steps, and with spent force
Along the ground they took a winding course.
Endymion follow'd—for it seem'd that one
Ever pursued, the other strove to shun—
Follow'd their languid mazes, till well nigh
He had left thinking of the mystery,—   930
And was now rapt in tender hoverings
Over the vanish'd bliss. Ah! what is it sings
His dream away? What melodies are these?
They sound as through the whispering of trees,
Not native in such barren vaults. Give ear!

  " O Arethusa, peerless nymph! why fear
Such tenderness as mine? Great Dian, why,
Why didst thou hear her prayer? O that I
Were rippling round her dainty fairness now,
Circling about her waist, and striving how   940
To entice her to a dive! then stealing in
Between her luscious lips and eyelids thin.
O that her shining hair· was in the sun;
And I distilling from it thence to run
In amorous rillets down her shrinking form!
To linger on her lilly shoulders, warm
Between her kissing breasts, and every charm
Touch raptur'd!—See how painfully I flow:
Fair maid, be pitiful to my great woe.
Stay, stay thy weary course, and let me lead,   950
A happy wooer, to the flowery mead
Where all that beauty snar'd me."—"Cruel god,
Desist! or my offended mistress' nod
Will stagnate all thy fountains:—teaze me not
With syren words—Ah, have I really got
Such power to madden thee? And is it true—
Away, away, or I shall dearly rue
My very thoughts: in mercy then away,
Kindest Alpheus, for should I obey
My own dear will, 'twould be a deadly bane.   960
O, Oread-Queen! would that thou hadst a pain

  960–75 "Cruel god . . . cruel thing." *All one speech MS. and
1818 corrected:* "O, Oread-Queen . . . criminal" *separated as if
spoken by Alpheus 1818.*

Like this of mine, then would I fearless turn
And be a criminal. Alas, I burn,
I shudder—gentle river, get thee hence.
Alpheus! thou enchanter! every sense
Of mine was once made perfect in these woods.
Fresh breezes, bowery lawns, and innocent floods,
Ripe fruits, and lonely couch, contentment gave;
But ever since I heedlessly did lave
In thy deceitful stream, a panting glow   970
Grew strong within me: wherefore serve me so,
And call it love? Alas, 'twas cruelty.
Not once more did I close my happy eye
Amid the thrushes' song. Away! Avaunt!
O 'twas a cruel thing."—"Now thou dost taunt
So softly, Arethusa, that I think
If thou wast playing on my shady brink,
Thou wouldst bathe once again. Innocent maid!
Stifle thine heart no more; nor be afraid
Of angry powers: there are deities   980
Will shade us with their wings. Those fitful sighs
'Tis almost death to hear: O let me pour
A dewy balm upon them!—fear no more,
Sweet Arethusa! Dian's self must feel
Sometime these very pangs. Dear maiden, steal
Blushing into my soul, and let us fly
These dreary caverns for the open sky.
I will delight thee all my winding course,
From the green sea up to my hidden source
About Arcadian forests; and will show   990
The channels where my coolest waters flow
Through mossy rocks; where, 'mid exuberant green,
I roam in pleasant darkness, more unseen
Than Saturn in his exile; where I brim
Round flowery islands, and take thence a skim
Of mealy sweets, which myriads of bees
Buzz from their honey'd wings: and thou shouldst please
Thyself to choose the richest, where we might
Be incense-pillow'd every summer night.

973 eye *Draft* : eyes *MS. and 1818*.
974 thrushes' *Draft:* Thrushes *MS.* : thrush's *1818*.
985 Some time *MS.*: Sometimes *1818*.

Doff all sad fears, thou white deliciousness,   1000
And let us be thus comforted; unless
Thou couldst rejoice to see my hopeless stream
Hurry distracted from Sol's temperate beam,
And pour to death along some hungry sands."—
"What can I do, Alpheus? Dian stands
Severe before me: persecuting fate!
Unhappy Arethusa! thou wast late
A huntress free in"—At this, sudden fell
Those two sad streams adown a fearful dell.
The Latmian listen'd, but he heard no more,   1010
Save echo, faint repeating o'er and o'er
The name of Arethusa. On the verge
Of that dark gulph he wept, and said: "I urge
Thee, gentle Goddess of my pilgrimage,
By our eternal hopes, to soothe, to assuage,
If thou art powerful, these lovers' pains;
And make them happy in some happy plains."

He turn'd—there was a whelming sound—he stept,
There was a cooler light; and so he kept
Towards it by a sandy path, and lo!   1020
More suddenly than doth a moment go,
The visions of the earth were gone and fled—
He saw the giant sea above his head.

BOOK III

THERE are who lord it o'er their fellow-men
With most prevailing tinsel: who unpen
Their baaing vanities, to browse away
The comfortable green and juicy hay
From human pastures; or, O torturing fact!
Who, through an idiot blink, will see unpack'd
Fire-branded foxes to sear up and singe
Our gold and ripe-ear'd hopes. With not one tinge
Of sanctuary splendour, not a sight
Able to face an owl's, they still are dight   10

1016 Lovers *MS. and 1818*.
1017 *no turned commas 1818*.

By the blear-eyed nations in empurpled vests,
And crowns, and turbans. With unladen breasts,
Save of blown self-applause, they proudly mount
To their spirit's perch, their being's high account,
Their tiptop nothings, their dull skies, their thrones—
Amid the fierce intoxicating tones
Of trumpets, shoutings, and belabour'd drums,
And sudden cannon. Ah! how all this hums,
In wakeful ears, like uproar past and gone—
Like thunder clouds that spake to Babylon,   20
And set those old Chaldeans to their tasks.—
Are then regalities all gilded masks?
No, there are throned seats unscalable
But by a patient wing, a constant spell,
Or by ethereal things that, unconfin'd,
Can make a ladder of the eternal wind,
And poize about in cloudy thunder-tents
To watch the abysm-birth of elements.
Aye, 'bove the withering of old-lipp'd Fate
A thousand Powers keep religious state,   30
In water, fiery realm, and airy bourne;
And, silent as a consecrated urn,
Hold sphery sessions for a season due.
Yet few of these far majesties, ah, few!
Have bared their operations to this globe—
Few, who with gorgeous pageantry enrobe
Our piece of heaven—whose benevolence
Shakes hand with our own Ceres; every sense
Filling with spiritual sweets to plenitude,
As bees gorge full their cells. And, by the feud   40
'Twixt Nothing and Creation, I here swear,
Eterne Apollo! that thy Sister fair
Is of all these the gentlier-mightiest.
When thy gold breath is misting in the west,
She unobserved steals unto her throne,
And there she sits most meek and most alone;
As if she had not pomp subservient;

21-3 And set these old Chaldeans to their work.—
    Are then all regal things so gone, so murk?
    No there are other thrones to mount. *Draft.*
31-2 In the several vastnesses of air and fire;
    And silent, as a corpse upon a pyre. *Draft.*

As if thine eye, high Poet! was not bent
Towards her with the Muses in thine heart;
As if the ministring stars kept not apart,   50
Waiting for silver-footed messages.
O Moon! the oldest shades 'mong oldest trees
Feel palpitations when thou lookest in:
O Moon! old boughs lisp forth a holier din
The while they feel thine airy fellowship.
Thou dost bless every where, with silver lip
Kissing dead things to life. The sleeping kine,
Couch'd in thy brightness, dream of fields divine:
Innumerable mountains rise, and rise,
Ambitious for the hallowing of thine eyes;   60
And yet thy benediction passeth not
One obscure hiding-place, one little spot
Where pleasure may be sent: the nested wren
Has thy fair face within its tranquil ken,
And from beneath a sheltering ivy leaf
Takes glimpses of thee; thou art a relief
To the poor patient oyster, where it sleeps
Within its pearly house.—The mighty deeps,
The monstrous sea is thine—the myriad sea!
O Moon! far-spooming Ocean bows to thee,   70
And Tellus feels his forehead's cumbrous load.

   Cynthia! where art thou now? What far abode
Of green or silvery bower doth enshrine
Such utmost beauty? Alas, thou dost pine
For one as sorrowful: thy cheek is pale
For one whose cheek is pale: thou dost bewail
His tears, who weeps for thee. Where dost thou sigh?
Ah! surely that light peeps from Vesper's eye,
Or what a thing is love! 'Tis She, but lo!
How chang'd, how full of ache, how gone in woe!
She dies at the thinnest cloud; her loveliness   81
Is wan on Neptune's blue: yet there's a stress
Of love-spangles, just off yon cape of trees,
Dancing upon the waves, as if to please
The curly foam with amorous influence.

71 his *MS. 1818 erratum and 1818 corrected :* her *1818 text.*
77–8   Where art thou Ah
   Surely that light is from the Evening star... *Draft.*

O, not so idle : for down-glancing thence
She fathoms eddies, and runs wild about
O'erwhelming water-courses ; scaring out
The thorny sharks from hiding-holes, and fright'ning
Their savage eyes with unaccustom'd lightning.   90
Where will the splendour be content to reach ?
O love ! how potent hast thou been to teach
Strange journeyings ! Wherever beauty dwells,
In gulph or aerie, mountains or deep dells,
In light, in gloom, in star or blazing sun,
Thou pointest out the way, and straight 'tis won.
Amid his toil thou gav'st Leander breath ;
Thou leddest Orpheus through the gleams of death ;
Thou madest Pluto bear thin element ;
And now, O winged Chieftain ! thou hast sent   100
A moon-beam to the deep, deep water-world,
To find Endymion.

              On gold sand impearl'd
With lilly shells, and pebbles milky white,
Poor Cynthia greeted him, and sooth'd her light
Against his pallid face : he felt the charm
To breathlessness, and suddenly a warm
Of his heart's blood : 'twas very sweet ; he stay'd
His wandering steps, and half-entranced laid
His head upon a tuft of straggling weeds,
To taste the gentle moon, and freshening beads,   110
Lash'd from the crystal roof by fishes' tails.
And so he kept, until the rosy veils
Mantling the east, by Aurora's peering hand
Were lifted from the water's breast, and fann'd
Into sweet air ; and sober'd morning came
Meekly through billows :—when like taper-flame
Left sudden by a dallying breath of air,
He rose in silence, and once more 'gan fare
Along his fated way.

              Far had he roam'd,
With nothing save the hollow vast, that foam'd,   120
Above, around, and at his feet ; save things
More dead than Morpheus' imaginings :
Old rusted anchors, helmets, breast-plates large

Of gone sea-warriors; brazen beaks and targe;
Rudders that for a hundred years had lost
The sway of human hand; gold vase emboss'd
With long-forgotten story, and wherein
No reveller had ever dipp'd a chin
But those of Saturn's vintage; mouldering scrolls,
Writ in the tongue of heaven, by those souls   130
Who first were on the earth; and sculptures rude
In ponderous stone, developing the mood
Of ancient Nox;—then skeletons of man,
Of beast, behemoth, and leviathan,
And elephant, and eagle, and huge jaw
Of nameless monster. A cold leaden awe
These secrets struck into him; and unless
Dian had chaced away that heaviness,
He might have died: but now, with cheered feel,
He onward kept; wooing these thoughts to steal   140
About the labyrinth in his soul of love.

"What is there in thee, Moon! that thou shouldst
    move
My heart so potently? When yet a child
I oft have dried my tears when thou hast smil'd.
Thou seem'dst my sister: hand in hand we went
From eve to morn across the firmament.
No apples would I gather from the tree,
Till thou hadst cool'd their cheeks deliciously:
No tumbling water ever spake romance,
But when my eyes with thine thereon could dance:
No woods were green enough, no bower divine,   151
Until thou liftedst up thine eyelids fine:
In sowing time ne'er would I dibble take,
Or drop a seed, till thou wast wide awake;
And, in the summer tide of blossoming,
No one but thee hath heard me blythly sing
And mesh my dewy flowers all the night.
No melody was like a passing spright
If it went not to solemnize thy reign.
Yes, in my boyhood, every joy and pain   160
By thee were fashion'd to the self-same end;
And as I grew in years, still didst thou blend

156 blythly *MS.* : blithly *1818.*

With all my ardours : thou wast the deep glen ;
Thou wast the mountain-top—the sage's pen—
The poet's harp—the voice of friends—the sun ;
Thou wast the river—thou wast glory won ;
Thou wast my clarion's blast—thou wast my steed—
My goblet full of wine—my topmost deed :—
Thou wast the charm of women, lovely Moon !
O what a wild and harmonized tune   170
My spirit struck from all the beautiful !
On some bright essence could I lean, and lull
Myself to immortality : I prest
Nature's soft pillow in a wakeful rest.
But, gentle Orb ! there came a nearer bliss—
My strange love came—Felicity's abyss !
She came, and thou didst fade, and fade away—
Yet not entirely ; no, thy starry sway
Has been an under-passion to this hour.
Now I begin to feel thine orby power   180
Is coming fresh upon me : O be kind,
Keep back thine influence, and do not blind
My sovereign vision.—Dearest love, forgive
That I can think away from thee and live !—
Pardon me, airy planet, that I prize
One thought beyond thine argent luxuries !
How far beyond ! " At this a surpris'd start
Frosted the springing verdure of his heart ;
For as he lifted up his eyes to swear
How his own goddess was past all things fair,   190
He saw far in the concave green of the sea
An old man sitting calm and peacefully.
Upon a weeded rock this old man sat,
And his white hair was awful, and a mat
Of weeds were cold beneath his cold thin feet ;
And, ample as the largest winding-sheet,
A cloak of blue wrapp'd up his aged bones,
O'erwrought with symbols by the deepest groans
Of ambitious magic : every ocean-form
Was woven in with black distinctness ; storm,   200
And calm, and whispering, and hideous roar,
Quicksand, and whirlpool, and deserted shore,

201 *line restored from Draft : wanting in MS. and 1818.*

Were emblem'd in the woof; with every shape
That skims, or dives, or sleeps, 'twixt cape and cape.
The gulphing whale was like a dot in the spell,
Yet look upon it, and 'twould size and swell
To its huge self; and the minutest fish
Would pass the very hardest gazer's wish,
And show his little eye's anatomy.
Then there was pictur'd the regality   210
Of Neptune; and the sea nymphs round his state,
In beauteous vassalage, look up and wait.
Beside this old man lay a pearly wand,
And in his lap a book, the which he conn'd
So stedfastly, that the new denizen
Had time to keep him in amazed ken,
To mark these shadowings, and stand in awe.

The old man rais'd his hoary head and saw
The wilder'd stranger—seeming not to see,
His features were so lifeless. Suddenly   220
He woke as from a trance; his snow-white brows
Went arching up, and like two magic ploughs
Furrow'd deep wrinkles in his forehead large,
Which kept as fixedly as rocky marge,
Till round his wither'd lips had gone a smile.
Then up he rose, like one whose tedious toil
Had watch'd for years in forlorn hermitage,
Who had not from mid-life to utmost age
Eas'd in one accent his o'er-burden'd soul,
Even to the trees. He rose: he grasp'd his stole,
With convuls'd clenches waving it abroad,   231
And in a voice of solemn joy, that aw'd
Echo into oblivion, he said:—

"Thou art the man! Now shall I lay my head
In peace upon my watery pillow: now
Sleep will come smoothly to my weary brow.
O Jove! I shall be young again, be young!
O shell-borne Neptune, I am pierc'd and stung
With new-born life! What shall I do? Where go,
When I have cast this serpent-skin of woe?—   240
I'll swim to the syrens, and one moment listen
Their melodies, and see their long hair glisten;

Anon upon that giant's arm I'll be,
That writhes about the roots of Sicily:
To northern seas I'll in a twinkling sail,
And mount upon the snortings of a whale
To some black cloud; thence down I'll madly sweep
On forked lightning, to the deepest deep,
Where through some sucking pool I will be hurl'd
With rapture to the other side of the world!   250
O, I am full of gladness! Sisters three,
I bow full hearted to your old decree!
Yes, every god be thank'd, and power benign,
For I no more shall wither, droop, and pine.
Thou art the man!" Endymion started back
Dismay'd; and, like a wretch from whom the rack
Tortures hot breath, and speech of agony,
Mutter'd: "What lonely death am I to die
In this cold region? Will he let me freeze,
And float my brittle limbs o'er polar seas?   260
Or will he touch me with his searing hand,
And leave a black memorial on the sand?
Or tear me piece-meal with a bony saw,
And keep me as a chosen food to draw
His magian fish through hated fire and flame?
O misery of hell! resistless, tame,
Am I to be burnt up? No, I will shout,
Until the gods through heaven's blue look out!—
O Tartarus! but some few days agone
Her soft arms were entwining me, and on   270
Her voice I hung like fruit among green leaves:
Her lips were all my own, and—ah, ripe sheaves
Of happiness! ye on the stubble droop,
But never may be garner'd. I must stoop
My head, and kiss death's foot. Love! love, farewell!
Is there no hope from thee? This horrid spell
Would melt at thy sweet breath.—By Dian's hind
Feeding from her white fingers, on the wind
I see thy streaming hair! and now, by Pan,
I care not for this old mysterious man!"   280

He spake, and walking to that aged form,
Look'd high defiance. Lo! his heart 'gan warm
With pity, for the grey-hair'd creature wept.

Had he then wrong'd a heart where sorrow kept?
Had he, though blindly contumelious, brought
Rheum to kind eyes, a sting to humane thought,
Convulsion to a mouth of many years?
He had in truth; and he was ripe for tears.
The penitent shower fell, as down he knelt
Before that care-worn sage, who trembling felt   290
About his large dark locks, and faultering spake:

"Arise, good youth, for sacred Phœbus' sake!
I know thine inmost bosom, and I feel
A very brother's yearning for thee steal
Into mine own: for why? thou openest
The prison gates that have so long opprest
My weary watching. Though thou know'st it not,
Thou art commission'd to this fated spot
For great enfranchisement. O weep no more;
I am a friend to love, to loves of yore: 300
Aye, hadst thou never lov'd an unknown power,
I had been grieving at this joyous hour.
But even now most miserable old,
I saw thee, and my blood no longer cold
Gave mighty pulses: in this tottering case
Grew a new heart, which at this moment plays
As dancingly as thine. Be not afraid,
For thou shalt hear this secret all display'd,
Now as we speed towards our joyous task."

So saying, this young soul in age's mask   310
Went forward with the Carian side by side:
Resuming quickly thus; while ocean's tide
Hung swollen at their backs, and jewel'd sands
Took silently their foot-prints.

                    "My soul stands
Now past the midway from mortality,
And so I can prepare without a sigh
To tell thee briefly all my joy and pain.
I was a fisher once, upon this main,
And my boat danc'd in every creek and bay;

286 humane *MS.*: human *1818.*

Rough billows were my home by night and day,—
The sea-gulls not more constant; for I had   321
No housing from the storm and tempests mad,
But hollow rocks,—and they were palaces
Of silent happiness, of slumberous ease:
Long years of misery have told me so.
Aye, thus it was one thousand years ago.
One thousand years!—Is it then possible
To look so plainly through them? to dispel
A thousand years with backward glance sublime?
To breathe away as 'twere all scummy slime   330
From off a crystal pool, to see its deep,
And one's own image from the bottom peep?
Yes: now I am no longer wretched thrall,
My long captivity and moanings all
Are but a slime, a thin-pervading scum,
The which I breathe away, and thronging come
Like things of yesterday my youthful pleasures.

"I touch'd no lute, I sang not, trod no measures:
I was a lonely youth on desert shores.
My sports were lonely, 'mid continuous roars,   340
And craggy isles, and sea-mew's plaintive cry
Plaining discrepant between sea and sky.
Dolphins were still my playmates; shapes unseen
Would let me feel their scales of gold and green,
Nor be my desolation; and, full oft,
When a dread waterspout had rear'd aloft
Its hungry hugeness, seeming ready ripe
To burst with hoarsest thunderings, and wipe
My life away like a vast sponge of fate,
Some friendly monster, pitying my sad state,   350
Has dived to its foundations, gulph'd it down,
And left me tossing safely. But the crown
Of all my life was utmost quietude:
More did I love to lie in cavern rude,
Keeping in wait whole days for Neptune's voice,
And if it came at last, hark, and rejoice!
There blush'd no summer eve but I would steer
My skiff along green shelving coasts, to hear

329 At one glance back the mistiness of time? *Draft.*

The shepherd's pipe come clear from aery steep,
Mingled with ceaseless bleatings of his sheep: 360
And never was a day of summer shine,
But I beheld its birth upon the brine:
For I would watch all night to see unfold
Heaven's gates, and Æthon snort his morning gold
Wide o'er the swelling streams: and constantly
At brim of day-tide, on some grassy lea,
My nets would be spread out, and I at rest.
The poor folk of the sea-country I blest
With daily boon of fish most delicate:
They knew not whence this bounty, and elate   370
Would strew sweet flowers on a sterile beach.

"Why was I not contented? Wherefore reach
At things which, but for thee, O Latmian!
Had been my dreary death? Fool! I began
To feel distemper'd longings: to desire
The utmost privilege that ocean's sire
Could grant in benediction: to be free
Of all his kingdom. Long in misery
I wasted, ere in one extremest fit
I plung'd for life or death. To interknit   380
One's senses with so dense a breathing stuff
Might seem a work of pain; so not enough
Can I admire how crystal-smooth it felt,
And buoyant round my limbs. At first I dwelt
Whole days and days in sheer astonishment;
Forgetful utterly of self-intent;
Moving but with the mighty ebb and flow.
Then, like a new fledg'd bird that first doth show
His spreaded feathers to the morrow chill,
I tried in fear the pinions of my will.   390
'Twas freedom! and at once I visited
The ceaseless wonders of this ocean-bed.
No need to tell thee of them, for I see
That thou hast been a witness—it must be—
For these I know thou canst not feel a drouth,
By the melancholy corners of that mouth.
So I will in my story straightway pass

395 For such a drink thou canst not feel a drouth,... *Draft.*

To more immediate matter. Woe, alas!
That love should be my bane! Ah, Scylla fair!
Why did poor Glaucus ever—ever dare   400
To sue thee to his heart? Kind stranger-youth!
I lov'd her to the very white of truth,
And she would not conceive it. Timid thing!
She fled me swift as sea-bird on the wing,
Round every isle, and point, and promontory,
From where large Hercules wound up his story
Far as Egyptian Nile. My passion grew
The more, the more I saw her dainty hue
Gleam delicately through the azure clear:
Until 'twas too fierce agony to bear;   410
And in that agony, across my grief
It flash'd, that Circe might find some relief—
Cruel enchantress! So above the water
I rear'd my head, and look'd for Phœbus' daughter.
Æœa's isle was wondering at the moon:—
It seem'd to whirl around me, and a swoon
Left me dead-drifting to that fatal power.

"When I awoke, 'twas in a twilight bower;
Just when the light of morn, with hum of bees,
Stole through its verdurous matting of fresh trees.
How sweet, and sweeter! for I heard a lyre,   421
And over it a sighing voice expire.
It ceased—I caught light footsteps; and anon
The fairest face that morn e'er look'd upon
Push'd through a screen of roses. Starry Jove!
With tears, and smiles, and honey-words she wove
A net whose thraldom was more bliss than all
The range of flower'd Elysium. Thus did fall
The dew of her rich speech: "Ah! Art awake?
"O let me hear thee speak, for Cupid's sake!   430
"I am so oppress'd with joy! Why, I have shed
"An urn of tears, as though thou wert cold dead;
"And now I find thee living, I will pour
"From these devoted eyes their silver store,
"Until exhausted of the latest drop,
"So it will pleasure thee, and force thee stop

430-43 *Turned commas before each line, 1818 corrected: not in 1818.*

"Here, that I too may live: but if beyond
"Such cool and sorrowful offerings, thou art fond
"Of soothing warmth, of dalliance supreme;
"If thou art ripe to taste a long love dream;   440
"If smiles, if dimples, tongues for ardour mute,
"Hang in thy vision like a tempting fruit,
"O let me pluck it for thee." Thus she link'd
Her charming syllables, till indistinct
Their music came to my o'er-sweeten'd soul;
And then she hover'd over me, and stole
So near, that if no nearer it had been
This furrow'd visage thou hadst never seen.

"Young man of Latmos! thus particular
Am I, that thou may'st plainly see how far   450
This fierce temptation went: and thou may'st not
Exclaim, How then, was Scylla quite forgot?

"Who could resist? Who in this universe?
She did so breathe ambrosia; so immerse
My fine existence in a golden clime.
She took me like a child of suckling time,
And cradled me in roses. Thus condemn'd,
The current of my former life was stemm'd,
And to this arbitrary queen of sense
I bow'd a tranced vassal: nor would thence   460
Have mov'd, even though Amphion's harp had woo'd
Me back to Scylla o'er the billows rude.
For as Apollo each eve doth devise
A new appareling for western skies;
So every eve, nay every spendthrift hour
Shed balmy consciousness within that bower.
And I was free of haunts umbrageous;
Could wander in the mazy forest-house
Of squirrels, foxes shy, and antler'd deer,
And birds from coverts innermost and drear   470
Warbling for very joy mellifluous sorrow—
To me new born delights!

445-7   Their music came to my o'ersweeten'd sense
       And then I felt a hovering influence
       A breathing on my forehead. *Draft.*
466   Shed nectarous Influence within that bower. *Draft.*

"Now let me borrow,
For moments few, a temperament as stern
As Pluto's sceptre, that my words not burn
These uttering lips, while I in calm speech tell
How specious heaven was changed to real hell.

"One morn she left me sleeping: half awake
I sought for her smooth arms and lips, to slake
My greedy thirst with nectarous camel-draughts;
But she was gone. Whereat the barbed shafts   480
Of disappointment stuck in me so sore,
That out I ran and search'd the forest o'er.
Wandering about in pine and cedar gloom
Damp awe assail'd me; for there 'gan to boom
A sound of moan, an agony of sound,
Sepulchral from the distance all around.
Then came a conquering earth-thunder, and rumbled
That fierce complain to silence: while I stumbled
Down a precipitous path, as if impell'd.
I came to a dark valley.—Groanings swell'd   490
Poisonous about my ears, and louder grew,
The nearer I approach'd a flame's gaunt blue,
That glar'd before me through a thorny brake.
This fire, like the eye of gordian snake,
Bewitch'd me towards; and I soon was near
A sight too fearful for the feel of fear:
In thicket hid I curs'd the haggard scene—
The banquet of my arms, my arbour queen,
Seated upon an uptorn forest root;
And all around her shapes, wizard and brute,   500
Laughing, and wailing, groveling, serpenting,
Showing tooth, tusk, and venom-bag, and sting!
O such deformities! Old Charon's self,
Should he give up awhile his penny pelf,
And take a dream 'mong rushes Stygian,
It could not be so phantasied. Fierce, wan,
And tyrannizing was the lady's look,
As over them a gnarled staff she shook.
Oft-times upon the sudden she laugh'd out,
And from a basket emptied to the rout   510

495 Drew me towards it; *Draft.*

Clusters of grapes, the which they raven'd quick
And roar'd for more; with many a hungry lick
About their shaggy jaws. Avenging, slow,
Anon she took a branch of mistletoe,
And emptied on't a black dull-gurgling phial:
Groan'd one and all, as if some piercing trial
Was sharpening for their pitiable bones.
She lifted up the charm: appealing groans
From their poor breasts went sueing to her ear
In vain; remorseless as an infant's bier   520
She whisk'd against their eyes the sooty oil.
Whereat was heard a noise of painful toil,
Increasing gradual to a tempest rage,
Shrieks, yells, and groans of torture-pilgrimage;
Until their grieved bodies 'gan to bloat
And puff from the tail's end to stifled throat:
Then was appalling silence: then a sight
More wildering than all that hoarse affright;
For the whole herd, as by a whirlwind writhen,
Went through the dismal air like one huge Python
Antagonizing Boreas,—and so vanish'd.   531
Yet there was not a breath of wind: she banish'd
These phantoms with a nod. Lo! from the dark
Came waggish fauns, and nymphs, and satyrs stark,
With dancing and loud revelry,—and went
Swifter than centaurs after rapine bent.—
Sighing an elephant appear'd and bow'd
Before the fierce witch, speaking thus aloud
In human accent: "Potent goddess! chief
"Of pains resistless! make my being brief,   540
"Or let me from this heavy prison fly:
"Or give me to the air, or let me die!
"I sue not for my happy crown again;
"I sue not for my phalanx on the plain;
"I sue not for my lone, my widow'd wife;
"I sue not for my ruddy drops of life,
"My children fair, my lovely girls and boys!

540-54 *Turned commas before each line, MS. : not in 1818.*
545-8 I sue not for my lonely, my dear wife,
    I sue not for my hearts blood drops of life,
    My sweetest babes, my lovely girls and boys,
    Ah, likely they are dead—I pass these joys... *Draft.*

"I will forget them; I will pass these joys;
"Ask nought so heavenward, so too—too high:
"Only I pray, as fairest boon, to die, 550
"Or be deliver'd from this cumbrous flesh,
"From this gross, detestable, filthy mesh,
"And merely given to the cold bleak air.
"Have mercy, Goddess! Circe, feel my prayer!"

"That curst magician's name fell icy numb
Upon my wild conjecturing: truth had come
Naked and sabre-like against my heart.
I saw a fury whetting a death-dart;
And my slain spirit, overwrought with fright,
Fainted away in that dark lair of night. 560
Think, my deliverer, how desolate
My waking must have been! disgust, and hate,
And terrors manifold divided me
A spoil amongst them. I prepar'd to flee
Into the dungeon core of that wild wood:
I fled three days—when lo! before me stood
Glaring the angry witch. O Dis, even now,
A clammy dew is beading on my brow,
At mere remembering her pale laugh, and curse.
"Ha! ha! Sir Dainty! there must be a nurse 570
"Made of rose leaves and thistledown, express,
"To cradle thee my sweet, and lull thee: yes,
"I am too flinty-hard for thy nice touch:
"My tenderest squeeze is but a giant's clutch.
"So, fairy-thing, it shall have lullabies
"Unheard of yet: and it shall still its cries
"Upon some breast more lilly-feminine.
"Oh, no—it shall not pine, and pine, and pine
"More than one pretty, trifling thousand years;
"And then 'twere pity, but fate's gentle shears 580
"Cut short its immortality. Sea-flirt!

554   Have mercy goddess! feel oh feel my prayer.
        Pity great Circe!"—Nor sight nor syllable
        Saw I or heard I more of this sick spell. *Draft.*
   570–600 *Turned commas before each line, MS. and 1818 corrected, not
in 1818.*
581–3   Great Jove
        What fury of the three could harm this dove
        Dear youth! see how I weep, hear how I sigh... *Draft.*

"Young dove of the waters! truly I'll not hurt
"One hair of thine: see how I weep and sigh,
"That our heart-broken parting is so nigh.
"And must we part? Ah, yes, it must be so.
"Yet ere thou leavest me in utter woe,
"Let me sob over thee my last adieus,
"And speak a blessing: Mark me! Thou hast thews
"Immortal, for thou art of heavenly race:
"But such a love is mine, that here I chace   590
"Eternally away from thee all bloom
"Of youth, and destine thee towards a tomb.
"Hence shalt thou quickly to the watery vast;
"And there, ere many days be overpast,
"Disabled age shall seize thee; and even then
"Thou shalt not go the way of aged men;
"But live and wither, cripple and still breathe
"Ten hundred years: which gone, I then bequeath
"Thy fragile bones to unknown burial.
"Adieu, sweet love, adieu!"—As shot stars fall,
She fled ere I could groan for mercy. Stung   601
And poison'd was my spirit: despair sung
A war-song of defiance 'gainst all hell.
A hand was at my shoulder to compel
My sullen steps; another 'fore my eyes
Moved on with pointed finger. In this guise
Enforced, at the last by ocean's foam
I found me; by my fresh, my native home.
Its tempering coolness, to my life akin,
Came salutary as I waded in;   610
And, with a blind voluptuous rage, I gave
Battle to the swollen billow-ridge, and drave
Large froth before me, while there yet remain'd
Hale strength, nor from my bones all marrow drain'd.

   "Young lover, I must weep—such hellish spite
With dry cheek who can tell? While thus my might
Proving upon this element, dismay'd,
Upon a dead thing's face my hand I laid;
I look'd—'twas Scylla! Cursed, cursed Circe!
O vulture-witch, hast never heard of mercy?   620
Could not thy harshest vengeance be content,

621 Was not thine harshest Avengeance content, _MS._

But thou must nip this tender innocent
Because I lov'd her?— Cold, O cold indeed
Were her fair limbs, and like a common weed
The sea-swell took her hair.   Dead as she was
I clung about her waist, nor ceas'd to pass
Fleet as an arrow through unfathom'd brine,
Until there shone a fabric crystalline,
Ribb'd and inlaid with coral, pebble, and pearl.
Headlong I darted ; at one eager swirl   630
Gain'd its bright portal, enter'd, and behold !
'Twas vast, and desolate, and icy-cold ;
And all around—But wherefore this to thee
Who in few minutes more thyself shalt see ?—
I left poor Scylla in a niche and fled.
My fever'd parchings up, my scathing dread
Met palsy half way : soon these limbs became
Gaunt, wither'd, sapless, feeble, cramp'd, and lame.

" Now let me pass a cruel, cruel space,
Without one hope, without one faintest trace   640
Of mitigation, or redeeming bubble
Of colour'd phantasy ; for I fear 'twould trouble
Thy brain to loss of reason : and next tell
How a restoring chance came down to quell
One half of the witch in me.

                              " On a day,
Sitting upon a rock above the spray,
I saw grow up from the horizon's brink
A gallant vessel : soon she seem'd to sink
Away from me again, as though her course
Had been resum'd in spite of hindering force—   650
So vanish'd : and not long, before arose
Dark clouds, and muttering of winds morose.
Old Æolus would stifle his mad spleen,
But could not : therefore all the billows green
Toss'd up the silver spume against the clouds.
The tempest came : I saw that vessel's shrouds

626 I clung about her waist and dived nor ceas'd to pass...
                                                        Draft.
653 Œolus *MS. :* Eolus *1818.*

KEATS   *   F

In perilous bustle; while upon the deck
Stood trembling creatures. I beheld the wreck;
The final gulphing; the poor struggling souls:
I heard their cries amid loud thunder-rolls.   660
O they had all been sav'd but crazed eld
Annull'd my vigorous cravings: and thus quell'd
And curb'd, think on't, O Latmian! did I sit
Writhing with pity, and a cursing fit
Against that hell-born Circe. The crew had gone,
By one and one, to pale oblivion;
And I was gazing on the surges prone,
With many a scalding tear and many a groan,
When at my feet emerg'd an old man's hand,
Grasping this scroll, and this same slender wand. 670
I knelt with pain—reach'd out my hand—had grasp'd
These treasures—touch'd the knuckles—they un-
          clasp'd—
I caught a finger: but the downward weight
O'erpowered me—it sank. Then 'gan abate
The storm, and through chill aguish gloom outburst
The comfortable sun. I was athirst
To search the book, and in the warming air
Parted its dripping leaves with eager care.
Strange matters did it treat of, and drew on
My soul page after page, till well-nigh won   680
Into forgetfulness; when, stupefied,
I read these words, and read again, and tried
My eyes against the heavens, and read again.
O what a load of misery and pain
Each Atlas-line bore off!—a shine of hope
Came gold around me, cheering me to cope
Strenuous with hellish tyranny. Attend!
For thou hast brought their promise to an end.

   "In the wide sea there lives a forlorn wretch,
Doom'd with enfeebled carcase to outstretch   690
His loath'd existence through ten centuries,
And then to die alone. Who can devise
A total opposition? No one. So

685-6   sweet rays of hope
       Glanc'd round me cheering me at once to cope... _Draft._

One million times ocean must ebb and flow,
And he oppressed.   Yet he shall not die,
These things accomplish'd :—If he utterly
Scans all the depths of magic, and expounds
The meanings of all motions, shapes and sounds ;
If he explores all forms and substances
Straight homeward to their symbol-essences ;   700
He shall not die.   Moreover, and in chief,
He must pursue this task of joy and grief
Most piously ;—all lovers tempest-tost,
And in the savage overwhelming lost,
He shall deposit side by side, until
Time's creeping shall the dreary space fulfil :
Which done, and all these labours ripened,
A youth, by heavenly power lov'd and led,
Shall stand before him ; whom he shall direct
How to consummate all.   The youth elect   710
Must do the thing, or both will be destroy'd."—

" Then," cried the young Endymion, overjoy'd,
" We are twin brothers in this destiny !
Say, I intreat thee, what achievement high
Is, in this restless world, for me reserv'd.
What ! if from thee my wandering feet had swerv'd,
Had we both perish'd ?"—" Look !" the sage replied,
" Dost thou not mark a gleaming through the tide,
Of diverse brilliances ?   'tis the edifice
I told thee of, where lovely Scylla lies ;   720
And where I have enshrined piously
All lovers, whom fell storms have doom'd to die
Throughout my bondage."   Thus discoursing, on
They went till unobscur'd the porches shone ;
Which hurryingly they gain'd, and enter'd straight.
Sure never since king Neptune held his state
Was seen such wonder underneath the stars.
Turn to some level plain where haughty Mars
Has legion'd all his battle ; and behold
How every soldier, with firm foot, doth hold   730
His even breast : see, many steeled squares,
And rigid ranks of iron—whence who dares
One step ?   Imagine further, line by line,

719 diverse *MS.* : divers *1818.*

These warrior thousands on the field supine:—
So in that crystal place, in silent rows,
Poor lovers lay at rest from joys and woes.—
The stranger from the mountains, breathless, trac'd
Such thousands of shut eyes in order plac'd;
Such ranges of white feet, and patient lips
All ruddy,—for here death no blossom nips.   740
He mark'd their brows and foreheads; saw their hair
Put sleekly on one side with nicest care:
And each one's gentle wrists, with reverence,
Put cross-wise to its heart.

                            "Let us commence,"
Whisper'd the guide, stuttering with joy, "even now."
He spake, and, trembling like an aspen-bough,
Began to tear his scroll in pieces small,
Uttering the while some mumblings funeral.
He tore it into pieces small as snow
That drifts unfeather'd when bleak northerns blow;
And having done it, took his dark blue cloak   751
And bound it round Endymion: then struck
His wand against the empty air times nine.—
"What more there is to do, young man, is thine:
But first a little patience; first undo
This tangled thread, and wind it to a clue.
Ah, gentle! 'tis as weak as spider's skein;
And shouldst thou break it—What, is it done so clean?
A power overshadows thee! O, brave!
The spite of hell is tumbling to its grave.   760
Here is a shell; 'tis pearly blank to me,
Nor mark'd with any sign or charactery—
Canst thou read aught? O read for pity's sake!
Olympus! we are safe! Now, Carian, break
This wand against yon lyre on the pedestal."

     'Twas done: and straight with sudden swell and fall
Sweet music breath'd her soul away, and sigh'd
A lullaby to silence.—"Youth! now strew
These minced leaves on me, and passing through

    744-5 *No turned commas after* commence *or before* even *MS. and
1818.*
    752 struck *MS. :* stroke *1818.*

Those files of dead, scatter the same around,   770
And thou wilt see the issue."—'Mid the sound
Of flutes and viols, ravishing his heart,
Endymion from Glaucus stood apart,
And scatter'd in his face some fragments light.
How lightning-swift the change! a youthful wight
Smiling beneath a coral diadem,
Out-sparkling sudden like an upturn'd gem,
Appear'd, and, stepping to a beauteous corse,
Kneel'd down beside it, and with tenderest force
Press'd its cold hand, and wept,—and Scylla sigh'd!
Endymion, with quick hand, the charm applied—   781
The nymph arose: he left them to their joy,
And onward went upon his high employ,
Showering those powerful fragments on the dead.
And, as he pass'd, each lifted up his head,
As doth a flower at Apollo's touch.
Death felt it to his inwards: 'twas too much:
Death fell a weeping in his charnel-house.
The Latmian persever'd along, and thus
All were re-animated. There arose   790
A noise of harmony, pulses and throes
Of gladness in the air—while many, who
Had died in mutual arms devout and true,
Sprang to each other madly; and the rest
Felt a high certainty of being blest.
They gaz'd upon Endymion. Enchantment
Grew drunken, and would have its head and bent.
Delicious symphonies, like airy flowers,
Budded, and swell'd, and, full-blown, shed full showers
Of light, soft, unseen leaves of sounds divine.   800
The two deliverers tasted a pure wine
Of happiness, from fairy-press ooz'd out.
Speechless they eyed each other, and about
The fair assembly wander'd to and fro,
Distracted with the richest overflow
Of joy that ever pour'd from heaven.

                              ——"Away!"
Shouted the new born god; "Follow, and pay
Our piety to Neptunus supreme!"—

802 Of happiness, not from earthly grapes press'd out. *Draft.*

Then Scylla, blushing sweetly from her dream,
They led on first, bent to her meek surprise,   810
Through portal columns of a giant size,
Into the vaulted, boundless emerald.
Joyous all follow'd as the leader call'd,
Down marble steps; pouring as easily
As hour-glass sand,—and fast, as you might see
Swallows obeying the south summer's call,
Or swans upon a gentle waterfall.

    Thus went that beautiful multitude, nor far,
Ere from among some rocks of glittering spar.
Just within ken, they saw descending thick   820
Another multitude. Whereat more quick
Moved either host. On a wide sand they met,
And of those numbers every eye was wet;
For each their old love found. A murmuring rose,
Like what was never heard in all the throes
Of wind and waters: 'tis past human wit
To tell; 'tis dizziness to think of it.

    This mighty consummation made, the host
Mov'd on for many a league; and gain'd, and lost
Huge sea-marks; vanward swelling in array,   830
And from the rear diminishing away,—
Till a faint dawn surpris'd them. Glaucus cried,
"Behold! behold, the palace of his pride!
God Neptune's palaces!" With noise increas'd,
They shoulder'd on towards that brightening east.
At every onward step proud domes arose
In prospect,—diamond gleams, and golden glows
Of amber 'gainst their faces levelling.
Joyous, and many as the leaves in spring,
Still onward; still the splendour gradual swell'd.   840

        811 Though *MS. and 1818.*
        832-40 Till a faint dawning bloom'd—and Glaucus cried,
            "Behold! behold, the palace of his pride!
            Of God Neptunus pride." With hum increased
            The host moved on towards that brightening east.
            And as it moved along proud domes arose
            In prospect,—diamond gleams, and golden glows
            Of amber levelling against their faces.
            With expectation high, and hurried paces
            Still onward; *Draft.*

Rich opal domes were seen, on high upheld
By jasper pillars, letting through their shafts
A blush of coral. Copious wonder-draughts
Each gazer drank; and deeper drank more near:
For what poor mortals fragment up, as mere
As marble was there lavish, to the vast
Of one fair palace, that far far surpass'd,
Even for common bulk, those olden three,
Memphis, and Babylon, and Nineveh.

As large, as bright, as colour'd as the bow   850
Of Iris, when unfading it doth show
Beyond a silvery shower, was the arch
Through which this Paphian army took its march,
Into the outer courts of Neptune's state:
Whence could be seen, direct, a golden gate,
To which the leaders sped; but not half raught
Ere it burst open swift as fairy thought,
And made those dazzled thousands veil their eyes
Like callow eagles at the first sunrise.
Soon with an eagle nativeness their gaze   860
Ripe from hue-golden swoons took all the blaze,
And then, behold! large Neptune on his throne
Of emerald deep: yet not exalt alone;
At his right hand stood winged Love, and on
His left sat smiling Beauty's paragon.

Far as the mariner on highest mast
Can see all round upon the calmed vast,
So wide was Neptune's hall: and as the blue
Doth vault the waters, so the waters drew
Their doming curtains, high, magnificent,   870
Aw'd from the throne aloof;—and when storm-rent
Disclos'd the thunder-gloomings in Jove's air;
But sooth'd as now, flash'd sudden everywhere,
Noiseless, sub-marine cloudlets, glittering
Death to a human eye: for there did spring
From natural west, and east, and south, and north,
A light as of four sunsets, blazing forth

864–5 At his right hand stood winged Love, elate
    And on his left Love's fairest mother sate. *Draft.*

A gold-green zenith 'bove the Sea-God's head.
Of lucid depth the floor, and far outspread
As breezeless lake, on which the slim canoe   880
Of feather'd Indian darts about, as through
The delicatest air: air verily,
But for the portraiture of clouds and sky:
This palace floor breath-air,—but for the amaze
Of deep-seen wonders motionless,—and blaze
Of the dome pomp, reflected in extremes,
Globing a golden sphere.

                 They stood in dreams
Till Triton blew his horn. The palace rang;
The Nereids danc'd; the Syrens faintly sang;
And the great Sea-King bow'd his dripping head.   890
Then Love took wing, and from his pinions shed
On all the multitude a nectarous dew.
The ooze-born Goddess beckoned and drew
Fair Scylla and her guides to conference;
And when they reach'd the throned eminence
She kist the sea-nymph's cheek,—who sat her down
A toying with the doves. Then,—"Mighty crown
And sceptre of this kingdom!" Venus said,
"Thy vows were on a time to Nais paid:
Behold!"— Two copious tear-drops instant fell   900
From the God's large eyes; he smil'd delectable,
And over Glaucus held his blessing hands.—
"Endymion! Ah! still wandering in the bands
Of love? Now this is cruel. Since the hour
I met thee in earth's bosom, all my power
Have I put forth to serve thee. What, not yet
Escap'd from dull mortality's harsh net?
A little patience, youth! 'twill not be long,
Or I am skilless quite: an idle tongue,
A humid eye, and steps luxurious,   910
Where these are new and strange, are ominous.
Aye, I have seen these signs in one of heaven,
When others were all blind: and were I given
To utter secrets, haply I might say
Some pleasant words:—but Love will have his day.
So wait awhile expectant. Pr'ythee soon,
Even in the passing of thine honey-moon,

Visit thou my Cythera: thou wilt find
Cupid well-natured, my Adonis kind;
And pray persuade with thee—Ah, I have done,
All blisses be upon thee, my sweet son!"—   921
Thus the fair goddess: While Endymion
Knelt to receive those accents halcyon.

Meantime a glorious revelry began
Before the Water-Monarch. Nectar ran
In courteous fountains to all cups outreach'd;
And plunder'd vines, teeming exhaustless, pleach'd
New growth about each shell and pendent lyre;
The which, in disentangling for their fire,
Pull'd down fresh foliage and coverture   930
For dainty toying. Cupid, empire-sure,
Flutter'd and laugh'd, and oft-times through the throng
Made a delighted way. Then dance, and song,
And garlanding grew wild; and pleasure reign'd.
In harmless tendril they each other chain'd,
And strove who should be smother'd deepest in
Fresh crush of leaves.

                    O 'tis a very sin
For one so weak to venture his poor verse
In such a place as this. O do not curse,
High Muses! let him hurry to the ending.   940

All suddenly were silent. A soft blending
Of dulcet instruments came charmingly;
And then a hymn.

                "KING of the stormy sea!
Brother of Jove, and co-inheritor
Of elements! Eternally before
Thee the waves awful bow. Fast, stubborn rock,
At thy fear'd trident shrinking, doth unlock
Its deep foundations, hissing into foam.
All mountain-rivers, lost in the wide home
Of thy capacious bosom, ever flow.   950

918 Visit thou my Cithera *Draft:* Visit my Cytherea *MS. and 1818.*
949-50 *Punctuated from Draft and MS.:* 1818 places a comma after lost and none after bosom.

F 3

Thou frownest, and old Æolus thy foe
Skulks to his cavern, 'mid the gruff complaint
Of all his rebel tempests. Dark clouds faint
When, from thy diadem, a silver gleam
Slants over blue dominion. Thy bright team
Gulphs in the morning light, and scuds along
To bring thee nearer to that golden song
Apollo singeth, while his chariot
Waits at the doors of heaven. Thou art not
For scenes like this: an empire stern hast thou; 960
And it hath furrow'd that large front: yet now,
As newly come of heaven, dost thou sit
To blend and interknit
Subdued majesty with this glad time.
O shell-borne King sublime!
We lay our hearts before thee evermore—
We sing, and we adore!

     " Breathe softly, flutes;
Be tender of your strings, ye soothing lutes;
Nor be the trumpet heard! O vain, O vain;   970
Not flowers budding in an April rain,
Nor breath of sleeping dove, nor river's flow,—
No, nor the Æolian twang of Love's own bow,
Can mingle music fit for the soft ear
Of goddess Cytherea!
Yet deign, white Queen of Beauty, thy fair eyes
On our souls' sacrifice.

     " Bright-winged Child!
Who has another care when thou hast smil'd?
Unfortunates on earth, we see at last   980
All death-shadows, and glooms that overcast
Our spirits, fann'd away by thy light pinions.
O sweetest essence! sweetest of all minions!
God of warm pulses, and dishevell'd hair,
And panting bosoms bare!
Dear unseen light in darkness! eclipser
Of light in light! delicious poisoner!

     954-6 When thy bright diadem a silver gleam
               O'er blue dominion starts. Thy finny team
               Snorts in the morning light, and sends along... *Draft.*

Thy venom'd goblet will we quaff until
We fill—we fill!
And by thy Mother's lips————"

                  Was heard no more   990
For clamour, when the golden palace door
Opened again, and from without, in shone
A new magnificence. On oozy throne
Smooth-moving came Oceanus the old,
To take a latest glimpse at his sheep-fold,
Before he went into his quiet cave
To muse for ever—Then a lucid wave,
Scoop'd from its trembling sisters of mid-sea,
Afloat, and pillowing up the majesty
Of Doris, and the Ægean seer, her spouse—   1000
Next, on a dolphin, clad in laurel boughs,
Theban Amphion leaning on his lute:
His fingers went across it—All were mute
To gaze on Amphitrite, queen of pearls,
And Thetis pearly too.—

                 The palace whirls
Around giddy Endymion; seeing he
Was there far strayed from mortality.
He could not bear it—shut his eyes in vain;
Imagination gave a dizzier pain.
"O I shall die! sweet Venus, be my stay!   1010
Where is my lovely mistress? Well-away!
I die—I hear her voice—I feel my wing—"
At Neptune's feet he sank. A sudden ring
Of Nereids were about him, in kind strife
To usher back his spirit into life:
But still he slept. At last they interwove
Their cradling arms, and purpos'd to convey
Towards a crystal bower far away.

Lo! while slow carried through the pitying crowd,

1007 Was there, a stray lamb from mortality. *Draft.*
1012 I die—love calls me hence"—thus muttering... *Draft.*
1016-18 They gave him nectar—shed bright drops, and strove
           Long time in vain. At last they interwove
           Their cradling arms, and carefully conveyed
           His body towards a quiet bowery shade. *Draft.*

To his inward senses these words spake aloud;　1020
Written in star-light on the dark above:
Dearest Endymion! my entire love!
How have I dwelt in fear of fate: 'tis done —
Immortal bliss for me too hast thou won.
Arise then! for the hen-dove shall not hatch
Her ready eggs, before I'll kissing snatch
Thee into endless heaven. Awake! awake!

　　The youth at once arose: a placid lake
Came quiet to his eyes; and forest green,
Cooler than all the wonders he had seen,　　1030
Lull'd with its simple song his fluttering breast.
How happy once again in grassy nest!

BOOK IV

MUSE of my native land! loftiest Muse!
O first-born on the mountains! by the hues
Of heaven on the spiritual air begot:
Long didst thou sit alone in northern grot,
While yet our England was a wolfish den;
Before our forests heard the talk of men;
Before the first of Druids was a child;—
Long didst thou sit amid our regions wild
Rapt in a deep prophetic solitude.
There came an eastern voice of solemn mood:—　　10
Yet wast thou patient. Then sang forth the Nine,
Apollo's garland:—yet didst thou divine
Such home-bred glory, that they cry'd in vain,
"Come hither, Sister of the Island!" Plain
Spake fair Ausonia; and once more she spake
A higher summons:—still didst thou betake
Thee to thy native hopes. O thou hast won
A full accomplishment! The thing is done,
Which undone, these our latter days had risen
On barren souls. Great Muse, thou know'st what prison,

10 an eastern voice *1818:* an hebrew voice *MS.*
14 from the Island *Draft.*
16 In self surpassing summons *Draft.*

Of flesh and bone, curbs, and confines, and frets 21
Our spirit's wings: despondency besets
Our pillows ; and the fresh to-morrow morn
Seems to give forth its light in very scorn
Of our dull, uninspired, snail-paced lives.
Long have I said, how happy he who shrives
To thee ! But then I thought on poets gone,
And could not pray :—nor could I now—so on
I move to the end in lowliness of heart.——

"Ah, woe is me ! that I should fondly part   30
From my dear native land ! Ah, foolish maid !
Glad was the hour, when, with thee, myriads bade
Adieu to Ganges and their pleasant fields !
To one so friendless the clear freshet yields
A bitter coolness ; the ripe grape is sour :
Yet I would have, great gods ! but one short hour
Of native air—let me but die at home."

Endymion to heaven's airy dome
Was offering up a hecatomb of vows,
When these words reach'd him. Whereupon he bows
His head through thorny-green entanglement   41
Of underwood, and to the sound is bent,
Anxious as hind towards her hidden fawn.

"Is no one near to help me ? No fair dawn
Of life from charitable voice ? No sweet saying
To set my dull and sadden'd spirit playing?
No hand to toy with mine ? No lips so sweet
That I may worship them ? No eyelids meet
To twinkle on my bosom ? No one dies
Before me, till from these enslaving eyes   50
Redemption sparkles !—I am sad and lost."

34 Where no friends are, the very freshet yields *Draft.*
36 Then take my life, great Gods ! for one short hour *Draft.*
49-54 To twinkle on my bosom ! false ! 'twas false
They said how beautiful I was ! who calls
Me now divine ? Who now kneels down and dies
Before me till from these enslaving eyes
Redemption sparkles. Ah me how sad I am !

Thou, Carian lord, hadst better have been tost
Into a whirlpool.   Vanish into air,
Warm mountaineer! for canst thou only bear
A woman's sigh alone and in distress?
See not her charms!   Is Phœbe passionless?
Phœbe is fairer far—O gaze no more:—
Yet if thou wilt behold all beauty's store,
Behold her panting in the forest grass!
Do not those curls of glossy jet surpass   60
For tenderness the arms so idly lain
Amongst them?   Feelest not a kindred pain,
To see such lovely eyes in swimming search
After some warm delight, that seems to perch
Dovelike in the dim cell lying beyond
Their upper lids?—Hist!

                     "O for Hermes' wand,
To touch this flower into human shape!
That woodland Hyacinthus could escape
From his green prison, and here kneeling down
Call me his queen, his second life's fair crown!   70
Ah me, how I could love!—My soul doth melt
For the unhappy youth—Love! I have felt
So faint a kindness, such a meek surrender
To what my own full thoughts had made too tender,
That but for tears my life had fled away!—
Ye deaf and senseless minutes of the day,
And thou, old forest, hold ye this for true,
There is no lightning, no authentic dew
But in the eye of love: there's not a sound,
Melodious howsoever, can confound   80
The heavens and earth in one to such a death
As doth the voice of love: there's not a breath
Will mingle kindly with the meadow air,

         Of all the poisons sent to make us mad
         Of all death's overwhelmings"—Stay Beware
         Young Mountaineer! *Draft.*
55 A woman's sigh in the luxury of distress? *Draft.*
72-3 After some beauteous youth—Who, who hath felt
         So warm a faintness, such a meek surrender *Draft.*
76-7 Sweet shadow, be distinct awhile and stay
         While I speak to thee—trust me it is true... *Draft.*

Till it has panted round, and stolen a share
Of passion from the heart ! "—

       Upon a bough
He leant, wretched. He surely cannot now
Thirst for another love : O impious,
That he can ever dream upon it thus !—
Thought he, "Why am I not as are the dead,
Since to a woe like this I have been led   90
Through the dark earth, and through the wondrous sea?
Goddess ! I love thee not the less : from thee
By Juno's smile I turn not—no, no, no—
While the great waters are at ebb and flow.—
I have a triple soul ! O fond pretence—
For both, for both my love is so immense,
I feel my heart is cut for them in twain."

And so he groan'd, as one by beauty slain.
The lady's heart beat quick, and he could see
Her gentle bosom heave tumultuously.   100
He sprang from his green covert: there she lay,
Sweet as a muskrose upon new-made hay ;
With all her limbs on tremble, and her eyes
Shut softly up alive. To speak he tries.
"Fair damsel, pity me ! forgive that I
Thus violate thy bower's sanctity !
O pardon me, for I am full of grief—
Grief born of thee, young angel ! fairest thief !

85-7 Of passion from the heart—Where love is not
  Only is solitude—poor shadow ! what
  I say thou hearest not ! away begone
  And leave me prythee with my grief alone !"
  The Latmian lean'd his arm upon a bough,
  A wretched mortal : what can he do now ?
  Must he another Love ? O impious... *Draft.*
94-5 While the fair moon gives light, or rivers flow
  My adoration of thee is yet pure
  As infants prattling. How is this—why sure
  I have a tripple soul ! *Draft.*
97 for them in twain. *MS. :* in twain for them. *1818.*
104-5 Shut softly up alive—Ye harmonies
  Ye tranced visions—ye flights ideal
  Nothing are ye to life so dainty real
  O Lady pity me ! *Draft.*

Who stolen hast away the wings wherewith
I was to top the heavens. Dear maid, sith   110
Thou art my executioner, and I feel
Loving and hatred, misery and weal,
Will in a few short hours be nothing to me,
And all my story that much passion slew me ;
Do smile upon the evening of my days :
And, for my tortur'd brain begins to craze,
Be thou my nurse ; and let me understand
How dying I shall kiss that lilly hand.—
Dost weep for me ? Then should I be content.
Scowl on, ye fates ! until the firmament   120
Outblackens Erebus, and the full-cavern'd earth
Crumbles into itself. By the cloud girth
Of Jove, those tears have given me a thirst
To meet oblivion."—As her heart would burst
The maiden sobb'd awhile, and then replied :
"Why must such desolation betide
As that thou speak'st of ? Are not these green nooks
Empty of all misfortune ? Do the brooks
Utter a gorgon voice ? Does yonder thrush,
Schooling its half-fledg'd little ones to brush   130
About the dewy forest, whisper tales ?—
Speak not of grief, young stranger, or cold snails
Will slime the rose to night. Though if thou wilt,
Methinks 'twould be a guilt—a very guilt—
Not to companion thee, and sigh away
The light—the dusk—the dark—till break of day ! "
" Dear lady," said Endymion, " 'tis past :

127 speakst *MS. :* speakest *1818.*
137-45 Canst thou do so ? Is there no balm, no cure
      Could not a beckoning Hebe soon allure
      Thee into Paradise ? What sorrowing
      So weighs thee down what utmost woe could bring
      This madness—Sit thee down by me, and ease
      Thine heart in whispers—haply by degrees
      I may find out some soothing medicine."—
      "Dear Lady," said Endymion, "I pine
      I die—the tender accents thou hast spoken
      Have finish'd all—my heart is lost and broken.
      That I may pass in patience still speak :
      Let me have music dying, and I seek
      No more delight—I bid adieu to all.
      Didst thou not after other climates call

I love thee! and my days can never last.
That I may pass in patience still speak:
Let me have music dying, and I seek   140
No more delight—I bid adieu to all.
Didst thou not after other climates call,
And murmur about Indian streams?"—Then she,
Sitting beneath the midmost forest tree,
For pity sang this roundelay————

      "O Sorrow,
      Why dost borrow
The natural hue of health, from vermeil lips?—
      To give maiden blushes
      To the white rose bushes?   150
Or is't thy dewy hand the daisy tips?

      "O Sorrow,
      Why dost borrow
The lustrous passion from a falcon-eye?—
      To give the glow-worm light?
      Or, on a moonless night,
To tinge, on syren shores, the salt sea-spry?

      "O Sorrow,
      Why dost borrow
The mellow ditties from a mourning tongue?—   160
      To give at evening pale
      Unto the nightingale,
That thou mayst listen the cold dews among?

      "O Sorrow,
      Why dost borrow
Heart's lightness from the merriment of May?—
      A lover would not tread
      A cowslip on the head,
Though he should dance from eve till peep of day—
      Nor any drooping flower   170
      Held sacred for thy bower,
Wherever he may sport himself and play.

    And murmur about Indian streams—now, now—
    I listen, it may save me—O my vow—
    Let me have music dying!" The ladye
    Sitting beneath the midmost forest tree
    With tears of pity sang this roundelay— *Draft.*

"To Sorrow,
    I bade good-morrow,
And thought to leave her far away behind;
    But cheerly, cheerly,
    She loves me dearly;
She is so constant to me, and so kind:
    I would deceive her
    And so leave her,   180
But ah! she is so constant and so kind.

"Beneath my palm trees, by the river side,
I sat a weeping: in the whole world wide
There was no one to ask me why I wept,—
    And so I kept
Brimming the water-lilly cups with tears
    Cold as my fears.

"Beneath my palm trees, by the river side,
I sat a weeping: what enamour'd bride,
Cheated by shadowy wooer from the clouds,   190
    But hides and shrouds
Beneath dark palm trees by a river side?

"And as I sat, over the light blue hills
There came a noise of revellers: the rills
Into the wide stream came of purple hue—
    'Twas Bacchus and his crew!
The earnest trumpet spake, and silver thrills
From kissing cymbals made a merry din—
    'Twas Bacchus and his kin!
Like to a moving vintage down they came,   200
Crown'd with green leaves, and faces all on flame;
All madly dancing through the pleasant valley,
    To scare thee, Melancholy!
O then, O then, thou wast a simple name!
And I forgot thee, as the berried holly
By shepherds is forgotten, when, in June,
Tall chesnuts keep away the sun and moon:—
    I rush'd into the folly!

"Within his car, aloft, young Bacchus stood,
Trifling his ivy-dart, in dancing mood,   210
    With sidelong laughing;

And little rills of crimson wine imbrued
His plump white arms, and shoulders, enough white
     For Venus' pearly bite:
And near him rode Silenus on his ass,
Pelted with flowers as he on did pass
     Tipsily quaffing.

" Whence came ye, merry Damsels ! whence came ye !
So many, and so many, and such glee ?
Why have ye left your bowers desolate,   220
     Your lutes, and gentler fate ?—
' We follow Bacchus ! Bacchus on the wing,
     A conquering !
Bacchus, young Bacchus ! good or ill betide,
We dance before him thorough kingdoms wide :—
Come hither, lady fair, and joined be
     To our wild minstrelsy ! '

" Whence came ye, jolly Satyrs ! whence came ye !
So many, and so many, and such glee ?
Why have ye left your forest haunts, why left   230
     Your nuts in oak-tree cleft ?—
' For wine, for wine we left our kernel tree ;
For wine we left our heath, and yellow brooms,
     And cold mushrooms ;
For wine we follow Bacchus through the earth ;
Great God of breathless cups and chirping mirth !—
Come hither, lady fair, and joined be
     To our mad minstrelsy ! '

" Over wide streams and mountains great we went,
And, save when Bacchus kept his ivy tent,   240
Onward the tiger and the leopard pants,
     With Asian elephants :
Onward these myriads—with song and dance,
With zebras striped, and sleek Arabians' prance,
Web-footed alligators, crocodiles,
Bearing upon their scaly backs, in files,
Plump infant laughers mimicking the coil
Of seamen, and stout galley-rowers' toil :
With toying oars and silken sails they glide,
     Nor care for wind and tide.   250

232 kernel tree *1818 :* forest meat *Draft.*

"Mounted on panthers' furs and lions' manes,
From rear to van they scour about the plains;
A three days' journey in a moment done:
And always, at the rising of the sun,
About the wilds they hunt with spear and horn,
     On spleenful unicorn.

"I saw Osirian Egypt kneel adown
     Before the vine-wreath crown!
I saw parch'd Abyssinia rouse and sing
     To the silver cymbals' ring!   260
I saw the whelming vintage hotly pierce
     Old Tartary the fierce!
The kings of Inde their jewel-sceptres vail,
And from their treasures scatter pearled hail;
Great Brahma from his mystic heaven groans,
     And all his priesthood moans;
Before young Bacchus' eye-wink turning pale.—
Into these regions came I following him,
Sick hearted, weary—so I took a whim
To stray away into these forests drear   270
     Alone, without a peer:
And I have told thee all thou mayest hear.

     "Young stranger!
     I've been a ranger
In search of pleasure throughout every clime:
     Alas, 'tis not for me!
     Bewitch'd I sure must be,
To lose in grieving all my maiden prime.

     "Come then, Sorrow!
     Sweetest Sorrow!   280
Like an own babe I nurse thee on my breast:
     I thought to leave thee
     And deceive thee,
But now of all the world I love thee best.

     "There is not one,
     No, no, not one
But thee to comfort a poor lonely maid;
     Thou art her mother,
     And her brother,
Her playmate, and her wooer in the shade."   290

O what a sigh she gave in finishing,
And look, quite dead to every worldly thing!
Endymion could not speak, but gazed on her;
And listened to the wind that now did stir
About the crisped oaks full drearily,
Yet with as sweet a softness as might be
Remember'd from its velvet summer song.
At last he said: "Poor lady, how thus long
Have I been able to endure that voice?
Fair Melody! kind Syren! I've no choice;   300
I must be thy sad servant evermore:
I cannot choose but kneel here and adore.
Alas, I must not think—by Phœbe, no!
Let me not think, soft Angel! shall it be so?
Say, beautifullest, shall I never think?
O thou could'st foster me beyond the brink
Of recollection! make my watchful care
Close up its bloodshot eyes, nor see despair!
Do gently murder half my soul, and I
Shall feel the other half so utterly!—   310
I'm giddy at that cheek so fair and smooth;
O let it blush so ever! let it soothe
My madness! let it mantle rosy-warm
With the tinge of love, panting in safe alarm.—
This cannot be thy hand, and yet it is;
And this is sure thine other softling—this
Thine own fair bosom, and I am so near!
Wilt fall asleep? O let me sip that tear!
And whisper one sweet word that I may know
This is this world—sweet dewy blossom!"—*Woe!* 320
Woe! Woe to that Endymion! Where is he?—
Even these words went echoing dismally
Through the wide forest—a most fearful tone,
Like one repenting in his latest moan;
And while it died away a shade pass'd by,
As of a thunder cloud. When arrows fly
Through the thick branches, poor ring-doves sleek forth
Their timid necks and tremble; so these both
Leant to each other trembling, and sat so
Waiting for some destruction—when lo,   330
Foot-feather'd Mercury appear'd sublime
Beyond the tall tree tops; and in less time

Than shoots the slanted hail-storm, down he dropt
Towards the ground ; but rested not, nor stopt
One moment from his home : only the sward
He with his wand light touch'd, and heavenward
Swifter than sight was gone—even before
The teeming earth a sudden witness bore
Of his swift magic. Diving swans appear
Above the crystal circlings white and clear ;   340
And catch the cheated eye in wide surprise,
How they can dive in sight and unseen rise—
So from the turf outsprang two steeds jet-black,
Each with large dark blue wings upon his back.
The youth of Caria plac'd the lovely dame
On one, and felt himself in spleen to tame
The other's fierceness. Through the air they flew,
High as the eagles. Like two drops of dew
Exhal'd to Phœbus' lips, away they are gone,
Far from the earth away—unseen, alone,   350
Among cool clouds and winds, but that the free,
The buoyant life of song can floating be
Above their heads, and follow them untir'd.—
Muse of my native land, am I inspir'd ?
This is the giddy air, and I must spread
Wide pinions to keep here ; nor do I dread
Or height, or depth, or width, or any chance
Precipitous : I have beneath my glance
Those towering horses and their mournful freight.
Could I thus sail, and see, and thus await   360
Fearless for power of thought, without thine aid ?—

There is a sleepy dusk, an odorous shade
From some approaching wonder, and behold
Those winged steeds, with snorting nostrils bold
Snuff at its faint extreme, and seem to tire,
Dying to embers from their native fire !

There curl'd a purple mist around them ; soon,
It seem'd as when around the pale new moon
Sad Zephyr droops the clouds like weeping willow :
'Twas Sleep slow journeying with head on pillow.   370

341 wide surprise *Draft and MS. :* wild surprise *1818.*
366 Seeming but embers to their former fire. *Draft.*

For the first time, since he came nigh dead born
From the old womb of night, his cave forlorn
Had he left more forlorn; for the first time,
He felt aloof the day and morning's prime—
Because into his depth Cimmerian
There came a dream, showing how a young man,
Ere a lean bat could plump its wintery skin,
Would at high Jove's empyreal footstool win
An immortality, and how espouse
Jove's daughter, and be reckon'd of his house.   380
Now was he slumbering towards heaven's gate,
That he might at the threshold one hour wait
To hear the marriage melodies, and then
Sink downward to his dusky cave again.
His litter of smooth semilucent mist,
Diversely ting'd with rose and amethyst,
Puzzled those eyes that for the centre sought;
And scarcely for one moment could be caught
His sluggish form reposing motionless.
Those two on winged steeds, with all the stress 390
Of vision search'd for him, as one would look
Athwart the sallows of a river nook
To catch a glance at silver-throated eels,—
Or from old Skiddaw's top, when fog conceals
His rugged forehead in a mantle pale,
With an eye-guess towards some pleasant vale
Descry a favourite hamlet faint and far.

These raven horses, though they foster'd are
Of earth's splenetic fire, dully drop
Their full-vein'd ears, nostrils blood wide, and stop; 400
Upon the spiritless mist have they outspread
Their ample feathers, are in slumber dead,—
And on those pinions, level in mid air,
Endymion sleepeth and the lady fair.
Slowly they sail, slowly as icy isle
Upon a calm sea drifting: and meanwhile
The mournful wanderer dreams. Behold! he walks
On heaven's pavement; brotherly he talks
To divine powers: from his hand full fain
Juno's proud birds are pecking pearly grain: 410
He tries the nerve of Phœbus' golden bow,

And asketh where the golden apples grow:
Upon his arm he braces Pallas' shield,
And strives in vain to unsettle and wield
A Jovian thunderbolt: arch Hebe brings
A full-brimm'd goblet, dances lightly, sings
And tantalizes long; at last he drinks,
And lost in pleasure at her feet he sinks,
Touching with dazzled lips her starlight hand.
He blows a bugle,—an ethereal band   420
Are visible above: the Seasons four,—
Green-kyrtled Spring, flush Summer, golden store
In Autumn's sickle, Winter frosty hoar,
Join dance with shadowy Hours; while still the blast,
In swells unmitigated, still doth last
To sway their floating morris. "Whose is this?
Whose bugle?" he inquires; they smile—"O Dis!
Why is this mortal here? Dost thou not know
Its mistress' lips? Not thou?—'Tis Dian's: lo!
She rises crescented!" He looks, 'tis she,   430
His very goddess: good-bye earth, and sea,
And air, and pains, and care, and suffering;
Good-bye to all but love! Then doth he spring
Towards her, and awakes—and, strange, o'erhead,
Of those same fragrant exhalations bred,
Beheld awake his very dream: the gods
Stood smiling; merry Hebe laughs and nods;
And Phœbe bends towards him crescented.
O state perplexing! On the pinion bed,
Too well awake, he feels the panting side   440
Of his delicious lady. He who died
For soaring too audacious in the sun,
When that same treacherous wax began to run,

418 With pleasure at her knees he swoons and sinks, *Draft.*

429–30 *In both manuscripts the preceding line stands rhymeless, and* these *two stand thus—*

    Its Mistress' Lips? Not thou? Ah, Ah, Ah, Ah!
    'Tis Dian's, here she comes, look out afar,

so that by compression two very noticeable flaws were remedied.

442–4 Because in sunshine treacherous wax would melt,
    Even at the fatal melting thereof, felt
    Not more tongue-tied than did Endymion. *Draft.*

443 When *MS.:* Where *1818.*

Felt not more tongue-tied than Endymion.
His heart leapt up as to its rightful throne,
To that fair shadow'd passion puls'd its way—
Ah, what perplexity! Ah, well a day!
So fond, so beauteous was his bed-fellow,
He could not help but kiss her: then he grew
Awhile forgetful of all beauty save   450
Young Phœbe's, golden hair'd; and so 'gan crave
Forgiveness: yet he turn'd once more to look
At the sweet sleeper,—all his soul was shook,—
She press'd his hand in slumber; so once more
He could not help but kiss her and adore.
At this the shadow wept, melting away.
The Latmian started up: "Bright goddess, stay!
Search my most hidden breast! By truth's own tongue,
I have no dædale heart: why is it wrung
To desperation? Is there nought for me,   460
Upon the bourne of bliss, but misery?"

These words awoke the stranger of dark tresses:
Her dawning love-look rapt Endymion blesses
With 'haviour soft. Sleep yawn'd from underneath.
"Thou swan of Ganges, let us no more breathe
This murky phantasm! thou contented seem'st
Pillow'd in lovely idleness, nor dream'st
What horrors may discomfort thee and me.
Ah, shouldst thou die from my heart-treachery!—
Yet did she merely weep—her gentle soul   470
Hath no revenge in it: as it is whole
In tenderness, would I were whole in love!
Can I prize thee, fair maid, all price above,
Even when I feel as true as innocence?
I do, I do.—What is this soul then? Whence
Came it? It does not seem my own, and I
Have no self-passion or identity.
Some fearful end must be: where, where is it?
By Nemesis, I see my spirit flit
Alone about the dark—Forgive me, sweet: 480
Shall we away?" He rous'd the steeds: they beat
Their wings chivalrous into the clear air,
Leaving old Sleep within his vapoury lair.

The good-night blush of eve was waning slow,

And Vesper, risen star, began to throe
In the dusk heavens silverly, when they
Thus sprang direct towards the Galaxy.
Nor did speed hinder converse soft and strange—
Eternal oaths and vows they interchange,
In such wise, in such temper, so aloof   490
Up in the winds, beneath a starry roof,
So witless of their doom, that verily
'Tis well nigh past man's search their hearts to see;
Whether they wept, or laugh'd, or griev'd, or toy'd—
Most like with joy gone mad, with sorrow cloy'd.

   Full facing their swift flight, from ebon streak,
The moon put forth a little diamond peak,
No bigger than an unobserved star,
Or tiny point of fairy scymetar;
Bright signal that she only stoop'd to tie   500
Her silver sandals, ere deliciously
She bow'd into the heavens her timid head.
Slowly she rose, as though she would have fled,
While to his lady meek the Carian turn'd,
To mark if her dark eyes had yet discern'd
This beauty in its birth—Despair! despair!
He saw her body fading gaunt and spare
In the cold moonshine. Straight he seiz'd her wrist;
It melted from his grasp: her hand he kiss'd,
And, horror! kiss'd his own—he was alone.   510
Her steed a little higher soar'd, and then
Dropt hawkwise to the earth.

                              There lies a den,
Beyond the seeming confines of the space
Made for the soul to wander in and trace
Its own existence, of remotest glooms.
Dark regions are around it, where the tombs
Of buried griefs the spirit sees, but scarce
One hour doth linger weeping, for the pierce
Of new-born woe it feels more inly smart:
And in these regions many a venom'd dart   520
At random flies; they are the proper home
Of every ill: the man is yet to come
Who hath not journeyed in this native hell.
But few have ever felt how calm and well

Sleep may be had in that deep den of all.
There anguish does not sting; nor pleasure pall:
Woe-hurricanes beat ever at the gate,
Yet all is still within and desolate.
Beset with plainful gusts, within ye hear
No sound so loud as when on curtain'd bier 　　530
The death-watch tick is stifled. Enter none
Who strive therefore: on the sudden it is won.
Just when the sufferer begins to burn,
Then it is free to him; and from an urn,
Still fed by melting ice, he takes a draught—
Young Semele such richness never quaft
In her maternal longing! Happy gloom!
Dark Paradise! where pale becomes the bloom
Of health by due; where silence dreariest
Is most articulate; where hopes infest; 　　540
Where those eyes are the brightest far that keep
Their lids shut longest in a dreamless sleep.
O happy spirit-home! O wondrous soul!
Pregnant with such a den to save the whole
In thine own depth. Hail, gentle Carian!
For, never since thy griefs and woes began,
Hast thou felt so content: a grievous feud
Hath led thee to this Cave of Quietude.
Aye, his lull'd soul was there, although upborne
With dangerous speed: and so he did not mourn
Because he knew not whither he was going. 　　551
So happy was he, not the aerial blowing
Of trumpets at clear parley from the east
Could rouse from that fine relish, that high feast.
They stung the feather'd horse: with fierce alarm
He flapp'd towards the sound. Alas, no charm
Could lift Endymion's head, or he had view'd
A skyey mask, a pinion'd multitude,—

534 This den is free to him *Draft.*
539 The rightful tinge of health *Draft.*
546 griefs and joys *Draft.*
548 led *Draft and MS.: let 1818.*
554 Could rouse { him from that } inward feast—and yet to
　　　　　　{ 　　from 　　} hear't
　　'Twas like a gift of Prophecy—alert
　　The feather'd horse he snorted with alarm
　　And towards it flapp'd away—Alas no charm... *Draft.*

And silvery was its passing: voices sweet
Warbling the while as if to lull and greet   560
The wanderer in his path. Thus warbled they,
While past the vision went in bright array.

"Who, who from Dian's feast would be away?
For all the golden bowers of the day
Are empty left? Who, who away would be
From Cynthia's wedding and festivity?
Not Hesperus: lo! upon his silver wings
He leans away for highest heaven and sings,
Snapping his lucid fingers merrily!—
Ah, Zephyrus! art here, and Flora too!   570
Ye tender bibbers of the rain and dew,
Young playmates of the rose and daffodil,
Be careful, ere ye enter in, to fill
              Your baskets high
With fennel green, and balm, and golden pines,
Savory, latter-mint, and columbines,
Cool parsley, basil sweet, and sunny thyme;
Yea, every flower and leaf of every clime,
All gather'd in the dewy morning: hie
              Away! fly, fly!—   580
Crystalline brother of the belt of heaven,
Aquarius! to whom king Jove has given
Two liquid pulse streams 'stead of feather'd wings,
Two fan-like fountains,—thine illuminings
              For Dian play:
Dissolve the frozen purity of air;
Let thy white shoulders silvery and bare
Show cold through watery pinions; make more bright
The Star-Queen's crescent on her marriage night:

563 Who, who would absent be from Dian's feast
        For all the golden chambers of the East
        Are empty left? Who, who away would be
        From Cynthia's wedding and festivity?
              Who, who would be? *Draft*.
569 *The draft has two additional lines after this one,*
              He stay behind—he glad of lazy plea?
                Not he! not he!
573 Mind ere ye enter in to oppress and fill... *Draft*.
577 Cool parsley, dripping cresses, sunny thyme... *Draft*.
589 Night-Queen's *Draft*.

Warm as a dove's nest among summer trees,
And warm with dew at ooze from living blood!
Whither didst melt? Ah, what of that!—all good
We'll talk about—no more of dreaming.—Now,
Where shall our dwelling be? Under the brow   670
Of some steep mossy hill, where ivy dun
Would hide us up, although spring leaves were none;
And where dark yew trees, as we rustle through,
Will drop their scarlet berry cups of dew?
O thou wouldst joy to live in such a place;
Dusk for our loves, yet light enough to grace
Those gentle limbs on mossy bed reclin'd:
For by one step the blue sky shouldst thou find,
And by another, in deep dell below,
See, through the trees, a little river go   680
All in its mid-day gold and glimmering.
Honey from out the gnarled hive I'll bring,
And apples, wan with sweetness, gather thee,—
Cresses that grow where no man may them see,
And sorrel untorn by the dew-claw'd stag:
Pipes will I fashion of the syrinx flag,
That thou mayst always know whither I roam,
When it shall please thee in our quiet home
To listen and think of love. Still let me speak;
Still let me dive into the joy I seek,—   690
For yet the past doth prison me. The rill,
Thou haply mayst delight in, will I fill
With fairy fishes from the mountain tarn,
And thou shalt feed them from the squirrel's barn.
Its bottom will I strew with amber shells,
And pebbles blue from deep enchanted wells.
Its sides I'll plant with dew-sweet eglantine,
And honeysuckles full of clear bee-wine.
I will entice this crystal rill to trace
Love's silver name upon the meadow's face.   700
I'll kneel to Vesta, for a flame of fire;
And to god Phœbus, for a golden lyre;
To Empress Dian, for a hunting spear;

700 *After this line there is a couplet in the MS., which does not
appear in the printed book :*—
    And by it shalt thou sit and sing, hey nonny!
    While doves coo to thee for a little honey.

To Vesper, for a taper silver-clear,
That I may see thy beauty through the night;
To Flora, and a nightingale shall light
Tame on thy finger; to the River-gods,
And they shall bring thee taper fishing-rods
Of gold, and lines of Naiads' long bright tress.
Heaven shield thee for thine utter loveliness!   710
Thy mossy footstool shall the altar be
'Fore which I'll bend, bending, dear love, to thee:
Those lips shall be my Delphos, and shall speak
Laws to my footsteps, colour to my cheek,
Trembling or stedfastness to this same voice,
And of three sweetest pleasurings the choice:
And that affectionate light, those diamond things,
Those eyes, those passions, those supreme pearl springs,
Shall be my grief, or twinkle me to pleasure.
Say, is not bliss within our perfect seisure?   720
O that I could not doubt!"

                              The mountaineer
Thus strove by fancies vain and crude to clear
His briar'd path to some tranquillity.
It gave bright gladness to his lady's eye,
And yet the tears she wept were tears of sorrow;
Answering thus, just as the golden morrow
Beam'd upward from the vallies of the east:
"O that the flutter of this heart had ceas'd,
Or the sweet name of love had pass'd away.
Young feather'd tyrant! by a swift decay   730
Wilt thou devote this body to the earth:
And I do think that at my very birth
I lisp'd thy blooming titles inwardly;
For at the first, first dawn and thought of thee,
With uplift hands I blest the stars of heaven.
Art thou not cruel? Ever have I striven
To think thee kind, but ah, it will not do!
When yet a child, I heard that kisses drew
Favour from thee, and so I kisses gave
To the void air, bidding them find out love: 740
But when I came to feel how far above

739 so I kisses gave *margin of MS. and 1818 corrected:* so I gave
gave *MS.:* so I gave and gave *1818.*

All fancy, pride, and fickle maidenhood,
All earthly pleasure, all imagin'd good,
Was the warm tremble of a devout kiss,—
Even then, that moment, at the thought of this,
Fainting I fell into a bed of flowers,
And languish'd there three days. Ye milder powers,
Am I not cruelly wrong'd? Believe, believe
Me, dear Endymion, were I to weave
With my own fancies garlands of sweet life, 750
Thou shouldst be one of all. Ah, bitter strife!
I may not be thy love: I am forbidden—
Indeed I am—thwarted, affrighted, chidden,
By things I trembled at, and gorgon wrath.
Twice hast thou ask'd whither I went: henceforth
Ask me no more! I may not utter it,
Nor may I be thy love. We might commit
Ourselves at once to vengeance; we might die;
We might embrace and die: voluptuous thought!
Enlarge not to my hunger, or I'm caught 760
In trammels of perverse deliciousness.
No, no, that shall not be: thee will I bless,
And bid a long adieu."

The Carian
No word return'd: both lovelorn, silent, wan,
Into the vallies green together went.
Far wandering, they were perforce content
To sit beneath a fair lone beechen tree;
Nor at each other gaz'd, but heavily
Por'd on its hazle cirque of shedded leaves.

Endymion! unhappy! it nigh grieves 770
Me to behold thee thus in last extreme:
Ensky'd ere this, but truly that I deem
Truth the best music in a first-born song.
Thy lute-voic'd brother will I sing ere long,
And thou shalt aid—hast thou not aided me?
Yes, moonlight Emperor! felicity

750-1 My own imaginations to sweet life
Thou would'st o'ertop them all. *Draft.*
769 carpet of shed leaves. *Draft.*
772 That hadst been high ere this, but that I deem... *Draft.*
KEATS * G

Has been thy meed for many thousand years;
Yet often have I, on the brink of tears,
Mourn'd as if yet thou wert a forester;—
Forgetting the old tale.

               He did not stir   780
His eyes from the dead leaves, or one small pulse
Of joy he might have felt. The spirit culls
Unfaded amaranth, when wild it strays
Through the old garden-ground of boyish days.
A little onward ran the very stream
By which he took his first soft poppy dream;
And on the very bark 'gainst which he leant
A crescent he had carv'd, and round it spent
His skill in little stars. The teeming tree
Had swollen and green'd the pious charactery,   790
But not ta'en out. Why, there was not a slope
Up which he had not fear'd the antelope;
And not a tree, beneath whose rooty shade
He had not with his tamed leopards play'd:
Nor could an arrow light, or javelin,
Fly in the air where his had never been—
And yet he knew it not.

               O treachery!
Why does his lady smile, pleasing her eye
With all his sorrowing? He sees her not.
But who so stares on him? His sister sure!   800
Peona of the woods!—Can she endure—
Impossible—how dearly they embrace!
His lady smiles; delight is in her face;
It is no treachery.

            "Dear brother mine!
Endymion, weep not so! Why shouldst thou pine
When all great Latmos so exalt will be?
Thank the great gods, and look not bitterly;
And speak not one pale word, and sigh no more.
Sure I will not believe thou hast such store

    778 mid some foolish tears, *Draft.*

    794 *Woodhouse notes, presumably from the draft, the variation* jessied falcons *for* tamed leopards.

    805 *Woodhouse notes the variation* Dear Endy : weep, *etc., which I should not like to accept literally without seeing the original.*

Of grief, to last thee to my kiss again.   810
Thou surely canst not bear a mind in pain,
Come hand in hand with one so beautiful.
Be happy both of you! for I will pull
The flowers of autumn for your coronals.
Pan's holy priest for young Endymion calls;
And when he is restor'd, thou, fairest dame,
Shalt be our queen. Now, is it not a shame
To see ye thus,—not very, very sad?
Perhaps ye are too happy to be glad:
O feel as if it were a common day;   820
Free-voic'd as one who never was away.
No tongue shall ask, whence come ye? but ye shall
Be gods of your own rest imperial.
Not even I, for one whole month, will pry
Into the hours that have pass'd us by,
Since in my arbour I did sing to thee.
O Hermes! on this very night will be
A hymning up to Cynthia, queen of light;
For the soothsayers old saw yesternight
Good visions in the air,—whence will befal,   830
As say these sages, health perpetual
To shepherds and their flocks; and furthermore,
In Dian's face they read the gentle lore:
Therefore for her these vesper-carols are.
Our friends will all be there from nigh and far.
Many upon thy death have ditties made;
And many, even now, their foreheads shade

811 *At this point Woodhouse gives the following passage, which is
doubtless from the draft:*—

> Were this sweet damsel like a long neck'd crane
> Or an old rocking barn owl half asleep
> Some reason would there be for thee to keep
> So dull-eyed—but thou knowst she's beautiful
> Yes, Yes! and thou dost love her well—I'll pull...

815 *Woodhouse notes here the variation* Great Pan's high priest,
and for the next line—

> This Shepherd Prince restor'd, thou, fairest dame,...

and for line 819 *the following two variants—one expressly and the other
presumably from the draft:*—

> (1) Perhaps ye feel too much joy—too overglad:
> (2) Perhaps ye are too glad—too overglad:

827 Why! hark ye! on this very eve will be... *Draft.*

With cypress, on a day of sacrifice.
New singing for our maids shalt thou devise,
And pluck the sorrow from our huntsmen's brows. 840
Tell me, my lady-queen, how to espouse
This wayward brother to his rightful joys!
His eyes are on thee bent, as thou didst poize
His fate most goddess-like. Help me, I pray,
To lure—Endymion, dear brother, say
What ails thee?" He could bear no more, and so
Bent his soul fiercely like a spiritual bow,
And twang'd it inwardly, and calmly said:
"I would have thee my only friend, sweet maid!
My only visitor! not ignorant though,   850
That those deceptions which for pleasure go
'Mong men, are pleasures real as real may be:
But there are higher ones I may not see,
If impiously an earthly realm I take.
Since I saw thee, I have been wide awake
Night after night, and day by day, until
Of the empyrean I have drunk my fill.
Let it content thee, Sister, seeing me
More happy than betides mortality.
A hermit young, I'll live in mossy cave,   860
Where thou alone shalt come to me, and lave
Thy spirit in the wonders I shall tell.
Through me the shepherd realm shall prosper well;
For to thy tongue will I all health confide.
And, for my sake, let this young maid abide
With thee as a dear sister. Thou alone,
Peona, mayst return to me. I own
This may sound strangely: but when, dearest girl,
Thou seest it for my happiness, no pearl
Will trespass down those cheeks. Companion fair! 870
Wilt be content to dwell with her, to share
This sister's love with me?" Like one resign'd
And bent by circumstance, and thereby blind
In self-commitment, thus that meek unknown:
"Aye, but a buzzing by my ears has flown,
Of jubilee to Dian:—truth I heard?
Well then, I see there is no little bird,

840 cypress for sorrow Draft.
876 heard? MS. and 1818 corrected: heard! 1818.

Tender soever, but is Jove's own care.
Long have I sought for rest, and, unaware,
Behold I find it! so exalted too! 880
So after my own heart! I knew, I knew
There was a place untenanted in it:
In that same void white Chastity shall sit,
And monitor me nightly to lone slumber.
With sanest lips I vow me to the number
Of Dian's sisterhood; and, kind lady,
With thy good help, this very night shall see
My future days to her fane consecrate."

As feels a dreamer what doth most create
His own particular fright, so these three felt: 890
Or like one who, in after ages, knelt
To Lucifer or Baal, when he'd pine
After a little sleep: or when in mine
Far under-ground, a sleeper meets his friends
Who know him not. Each diligently bends
Towards common thoughts and things for very
     fear;
Striving their ghastly malady to cheer,
By thinking it a thing of yes and no,
That housewives talk of. But the spirit-blow
Was struck, and all were dreamers. At the last 900
Endymion said: "Are not our fates all cast?
Why stand we here? Adieu, ye tender pair!
Adieu!" Whereat those maidens, with wild stare,
Walk'd dizzily away. Pained and hot
His eyes went after them, until they got
Near to a cypress grove, whose deadly maw,
In one swift moment, would what then he saw
Engulph for ever. "Stay!" he cried, "ah, stay!
Turn, damsels! hist! one word I have to say.
Sweet Indian, I would see thee once again. 910
It is a thing I dote on: so I'd fain,
Peona, ye should hand in hand repair
Into those holy groves, that silent are
Behind great Dian's temple. I'll be yon,
At vesper's earliest twinkle—they are gone—
But once, once, once again—" At this he press'd
His hands against his face, and then did rest

His head upon a mossy hillock green,
And so remain'd as he a corpse had been
All the long day; save when he scantly lifted   920
His eyes abroad, to see how shadows shifted
With the slow move of time,—sluggish and weary
Until the poplar tops, in journey dreary,
Had reach'd the river's brim. Then up he rose,
And, slowly as that very river flows,
Walk'd towards the temple grove with this lament:
"Why such a golden eve? The breeze is sent
Careful and soft, that not a leaf may fall
Before the serene father of them. all
Bows down his summer head below the west.   930
Now am I of breath, speech, and speed possest,
But at the setting I must bid adieu
To her for the last time. Night will strew
On the damp grass myriads of lingering leaves,
And with them shall I die; nor much it grieves
To die, when summer dies on the cold sward.
Why, I have been a butterfly, a lord
Of flowers, garlands, love-knots, silly posies,
Groves, meadows, melodies, and arbour roses;
My kingdom's at its death, and just it is   940
That I should die with it: so in all this
We miscall grief, bale, sorrow, heartbreak, woe,
What is there to plain of? By Titan's foe
I am but rightly serv'd." So saying, he
Tripp'd lightly on, in sort of deathful glee;
Laughing at the clear stream and setting sun,
As though they jests had been: nor had he done
His laugh at nature's holy countenance,

918–22 His hands upon a pillow of green moss
         And so remained without impatient toss
         All the day long—save when he scantly lifted
         His eyes abroad, to see how shadows shifted,
         And note the weary time.—Ah weary, weary,...*Draft.*
The word hands *in line* 918 *was probably a mere slip.*
  926–7 *Woodhouse gives, presumably from the draft, the couplet :—*
      Walk'd towards the temple grove lamenting "O
  "Why such a golden eve? The breezes blow...
  933 *This line, though possibly corrupt, stands thus in the finished
manuscript and in Keats's edition. Woodhouse does not bring the draft
in evidence. Perhaps* To *should be* Unto.

Until that grove appear'd, as if perchance,
And then his tongue with sober seemlihed   950
Gave utterance as he enter'd: "Ha! I said,
King of the butterflies; but by this gloom,
And by old Rhadamanthus' tongue of doom,
This dusk religion, pomp of solitude,
And the Promethean clay by thief endued,
By old Saturnus' forelock, by his head
Shook with eternal palsy, I did wed
Myself to things of light from infancy;
And thus to be cast out, thus lorn to die,
Is sure enough to make a mortal man   960
Grow impious." So he inwardly began
On things for which no wording can be found;
Deeper and deeper sinking, until drown'd
Beyond the reach of music: for the choir
Of Cynthia he heard not, though rough briar
Nor muffling thicket interpos'd to dull
The vesper hymn, far swollen, soft and full,
Through the dark pillars of those sylvan aisles.
He saw not the two maidens, nor their smiles,
Wan as primroses gather'd at midnight   970
By chilly finger'd spring. "Unhappy wight!
Endymion!" said Peona, "we are here!
What wouldst thou ere we all are laid on bier?"
Then he embrac'd her, and his lady's hand
Press'd, saying: "Sister, I would have command,
If it were heaven's will, on our sad fate."
At which that dark-eyed stranger stood elate
And said, in a new voice, but sweet as love,
To Endymion's amaze: "By Cupid's dove,
And so thou shalt! and by the lilly truth   980
Of my own breast thou shalt, beloved youth!"
And as she spake, into her face there came
Light, as reflected from a silver flame:

949-50 Until he saw that grove, as if perchance,
      And then his soul was changed... *Draft.*
  951 *The inverted commas are closed after* Ha! *in 1818, but not in MS.
or 1818 corrected.*
  974-7 Her brother kiss'd her, and his lady's hand
      Saying, "Sweet sister I would have command,
      If it were heaven's will, on our sad fate."
      Then that dark-tressed stranger stood elate... *Draft.*

Her long black hair swell'd ampler, in display
Full golden ; in her eyes a brighter day
Dawn'd blue and full of love. Aye, he beheld
Phœbe, his passion ! joyous she upheld
Her lucid bow, continuing thus : " Drear, drear
Has our delaying been ; but foolish fear
Withheld me first ; and then decrees of fate ;   990
And then 'twas fit that from this mortal state
Thou shouldst, my love, by some unlook'd for change
Be spiritualiz'd.   Peona, we shall range
These forests, and to thee they safe shall be
As was thy cradle ; hither shalt thou flee
To meet us many a time."   Next Cynthia bright
Peona kiss'd, and bless'd with fair good night :
Her brother kiss'd her too, and knelt adown
Before his goddess, in a blissful swoon.
She gave her fair hands to him, and behold,   1000
Before three swiftest kisses he had told,
They vanish'd far away !—Peona went
Home through the gloomy wood in wonderment.

THE END.

984-6 Her long black hair swell'd ampler, while it turned
      Golden—and her eyes of jet dawned forth a brighter
      day
      Blue—blue—and full of love. *Draft.*

LAMIA,

ISABELLA,

THE EVE OF ST. AGNES,

AND

OTHER POEMS.

1820.

ADVERTISEMENT.

If any apology be thought necessary for the appearance of the unfinished poem of HYPERION, the publishers beg to state that they alone are responsible, as it was printed at their particular request, and contrary to the wish of the author. The poem was intended to have been of equal length with ENDYMION, but the reception given to that work discouraged the author from proceeding.

FLEET STREET, *June* 26, 1820.

LAMIA

PART I

Upon a time, before the faery broods
Drove Nymph and Satyr from the prosperous woods,
Before king Oberon's bright diadem,
Sceptre, and mantle, clasp'd with dewy gem,
Frighted away the Dryads and the Fauns
From rushes green, and brakes, and cowslip'd lawns,
The ever-smitten Hermes empty left
His golden throne, bent warm on amorous theft:
From high Olympus had he stolen light,
On this side of Jove's clouds, to escape the sight   10
Of his great summoner, and made retreat
Into a forest on the shores of Crete.
For somewhere in that sacred island dwelt
A nymph, to whom all hoofed Satyrs knelt;
At whose white feet the languid Tritons poured
Pearls, while on land they wither'd and adored.
Fast by the springs where she to bathe was wont,
And in those meads where sometime she might haunt,
Were strewn rich gifts, unknown to any Muse,
Though Fancy's casket were unlock'd to choose.   20
Ah, what a world of love was at her feet!
So Hermes thought, and a celestial heat
Burnt from his winged heels to either ear,
That from a whiteness, as the lilly clear,
Blush'd into roses 'mid his golden hair,
Fallen in jealous curls about his shoulders bare.

From vale to vale, from wood to wood, he flew,
Breathing upon the flowers his passion new,
And wound with many a river to its head,   29
To find where this sweet nymph prepar'd her secret bed:
In vain; the sweet nymph might nowhere be found,
And so he rested, on the lonely ground,

4 mantle] sandals *MS., cancelled.*
15 And at whose feet *MS., cancelled.*

Pensive, and full of painful jealousies
Of the Wood-Gods, and even the very trees.
There as he stood, he heard a mournful voice,
Such as once heard, in gentle heart, destroys
All pain but pity: thus the lone voice spake:
"When from this wreathed tomb shall I awake!
"When move in a sweet body fit for life,
"And love, and pleasure, and the ruddy strife   40
"Of hearts and lips! Ah, miserable me!"
The God, dove-footed, glided silently
Round bush and tree, soft-brushing, in his speed,
The taller grasses and full-flowering weed,
Until he found a palpitating snake,
Bright, and cirque-couchant in a dusky brake.

She was a gordian shape of dazzling hue,
Vermilion-spotted, golden, green, and blue;
Striped like a zebra, freckled like a pard,
Eyed like a peacock, and all crimson barr'd;   50
And full of silver moons, that, as she breathed,
Dissolv'd, or brighter shone, or interwreathed
Their lustres with the gloomier tapestries—
So rainbow-sided, touch'd with miseries,
She seem'd, at once, some penanced lady elf,
Some demon's mistress, or the demon's self.
Upon her crest she wore a wannish fire
Sprinkled with stars, like Ariadne's tiar:
Her head was serpent, but ah, bitter-sweet!   59
She had a woman's mouth with all its pearls complete:
And for her eyes: what could such eyes do there
But weep, and weep, that they were born so fair?
As Proserpine still weeps for her Sicilian air.
Her throat was serpent, but the words she spake
Came, as through bubbling honey, for Love's sake,
And thus; while Hermes on his pinions lay,
Like a stoop'd falcon ere he takes his prey.

"Fair Hermes, crown'd with feathers, fluttering light,
"I had a splendid dream of thee last night:
"I saw thee sitting, on a throne of gold,   70
"Among the Gods, upon Olympus old,

48 Cerulean-spotted, *MS.*
69 splendid] silver *MS.*

"The only sad one ; for thou didst not hear
"The soft, lute-finger'd Muses chaunting clear,
"Nor even Apollo when he sang alone,
"Deaf to his throbbing throat's long, long melodious
    moan.
"I dreamt I saw thee, robed in purple flakes,
"Break amorous through the clouds, as morning breaks,
"And, swiftly as a bright Phœbean dart,
"Strike for the Cretan isle ; and here thou art !
"Too gentle Hermes, hast thou found the maid ? "
Whereat the star of Lethe not delay'd   81
His rosy eloquence, and thus inquired :
"Thou smooth-lipp'd serpent, surely high inspired !
"Thou beauteous wreath, with melancholy eyes,
"Possess whatever bliss thou canst devise,
"Telling me only where my nymph is fled,—
"Where she doth breathe ! "   "Bright planet, thou
    hast said,"
Return'd the snake, "but seal with oaths, fair God ! "
"I swear," said Hermes, "by my serpent rod,
"And by thine eyes, and by thy starry crown ! "   90
Light flew his earnest words, among the blossoms
    blown.
Then thus again the brilliance feminine :
"Too frail of heart ! for this lost nymph of thine,
"Free as the air, invisibly, she strays
"About these thornless wilds ; her pleasant days
"She tastes unseen ; unseen her nimble feet
"Leave traces in the grass and flowers sweet ;
"From weary tendrils, and bow'd branches green,
"She plucks the fruit unseen, she bathes unseen :
"And by my power is her beauty veil'd   100
"To keep it unaffronted, unassail'd
"By the love-glances of unlovely eyes,
"Of Satyrs, Fauns, and blear'd Silenus' sighs.
"Pale grew her immortality, for woe
"Of all these lovers, and she grieved so
"I took compassion on her, bade her steep
"Her hair in weïrd syrops, that would keep

78 And, swiftly as a mission'd phœbean dart, *MS.*
93 Superb of heart ! *MS.*, *cancelled.*
104 grew] wox *MS.*   106 bade *1820 :* bad *MS.*

"Her loveliness invisible, yet free
"To wander as she loves, in liberty.
"Thou shalt behold her, Hermes, thou alone,   110
"If thou wilt, as thou swearest, grant my boon!"
Then, once again, the charmed God began
An oath, and through the serpent's ears it ran
Warm, tremulous, devout, psalterian.
Ravish'd, she lifted her Circean head,
Blush'd a live damask, and swift-lisping said,
"I was a woman, let me have once more
"A woman's shape, and charming as before.
"I love a youth of Corinth—O the bliss!
"Give me my woman's form, and place me where he is.
"Stoop, Hermes, let me breathe upon thy brow,   121
"And thou shalt see thy sweet nymph even now."
The God on half-shut feathers sank serene,
She breath'd upon his eyes, and swift was seen
Of both the guarded nymph near-smiling on the green.
It was no dream; or say a dream it was,
Real are the dreams of Gods, and smoothly pass
Their pleasures in a long immortal dream.
One warm, flush'd moment, hovering, it might seem
Dash'd by the wood-nymph's beauty, so he burn'd;   130
Then, lighting on the printless verdure, turn'd
To the swoon'd serpent, and with languid arm,
Delicate, put to proof the lythe Caducean charm.
So done, upon the nymph his eyes he bent
Full of adoring tears and blandishment,
And towards her stept: she, like a moon in wane,
Faded before him, cower'd, nor could restrain
Her fearful sobs, self-folding like a flower
That faints into itself at evening hour:
But the God fostering her chilled hand,   140
She felt the warmth, her eyelids open'd bland,
And, like new flowers at morning song of bees,
Bloom'd, and gave up her honey to the lees.

114 Warm, tremulous, devout, bright-ton'd, psalterian. *MS.*
115 Ravish'd she lifted up her circean head, *MS.*
116 Blush'd to live damask, *MS.*
123 sank *1820 :* sunk *MS.*
132 languid] langrous *MS.*
142 And she like flowers... *MS., cancelled.*

Into the green-recessed woods they flew;
Nor grew they pale, as mortal lovers do.

Left to herself, the serpent now began
To change; her elfin blood in madness ran,
Her mouth foam'd, and the grass, therewith besprent,
Wither'd at dew so sweet and virulent;
Her eyes in torture fix'd, and anguish drear,   150
Hot, glaz'd, and wide, with lid-lashes all sear,
Flash'd phosphor and sharp sparks, without one cooling
    tear.
The colours all inflam'd throughout her train,
She writh'd about, convuls'd with scarlet pain:
A deep volcanian yellow took the place
Of all her milder-mooned body's grace;
And, as the lava ravishes the mead,
Spoilt all her silver mail, and golden brede;
Made gloom of all her frecklings, streaks and bars,
Eclips'd her crescents, and lick'd up her stars: 160
So that, in moments few, she was undrest
Of all her sapphires, greens, and amethyst,
And rubious-argent: of all these bereft,
Nothing but pain and ugliness were left.
Still shone her crown; that vanish'd, also she
Melted and disappear'd as suddenly;
And in the air, her new voice luting soft,
Cried, "Lycius! gentle Lycius!"—Borne aloft
With the bright mists about the mountains hoar
These words dissolv'd: Crete's forests heard no more.

Whither fled Lamia, now a lady bright,   171
A full-born beauty new and exquisite?
She fled into that valley they pass o'er
Who go to Corinth from Cenchreas' shore;
And rested at the foot of those wild hills,
The rugged founts of the Peræan rills,

155 volcanian *1820:* vulcanian *MS.*
167–8 And her new voice, soft luting in the air
    Cried "Lycius! gentle Lycius, where, ah where!" *MS.*
173–4 She fled into that valley they must pass
    Who go from Corinth out to Cencreas, *MS.*
176 The rugged paps of little Perea's rills, *MS.*

And of that other ridge whose barren back
Stretches, with all its mist and cloudy rack,
South-westward to Cleone.   There she stood
About a young bird's flutter from a wood,   180
Fair, on a sloping green of mossy tread,
By a clear pool, wherein she passioned
To see herself escap'd from so sore ills,
While her robes flaunted with the daffodils.

'Ah, happy Lycius!—for she was a maid
More beautiful than ever twisted braid,
Or sigh'd, or blush'd, or on spring-flowered lea
Spread a green kirtle to the minstrelsy:
A virgin purest lipp'd, yet in the lore
Of love deep learned to the red heart's core: 190
Not one hour old, yet of sciential brain
To unperplex bliss from its neighbour pain;
Define their pettish limits, and estrange
Their points of contact, and swift counterchange;
Intrigue with the specious chaos, and dispart
Its most ambiguous atoms with sure art;
As though in Cupid's college she had spent
Sweet days a lovely graduate, still unshent,
And kept his rosy terms in idle languishment.

Why this fair creature chose so faerily   200
By the wayside to linger, we shall see;
But first 'tis fit to tell how she could muse
And dream, when in the serpent prison-house,
Of all she list, strange or magnificent:
How, ever, where she will'd, her spirit went;
Whether to faint Elysium, or where
Down through tress-lifting waves the Nereids fair
Wind into Thetis' bower by many a pearly stair;
Or where God Bacchus drains his cups divine,
Stretch'd out, at ease, beneath a glutinous pine; 210
Or where in Pluto's gardens palatine

185 *The manuscript has three lines in place of this one :—*
        Ah! never heard of, delight never known
        Save of one happy mortal! only one,—
        Lycius the happy: for she was a Maid...
192 its *1820 :* her *MS.*
196 Its *1820 :* Their *MS.*

Mulciber's columns gleam in far piazzian line.
And sometimes into cities she would send
Her dream, with feast and rioting to blend;
And once, while among mortals dreaming thus,
She saw the young Corinthian Lycius
Charioting foremost in the envious race,
Like a young Jove with calm uneager face,
And fell into a swooning love of him.
Now on the moth-time of that evening dim   220
He would return that way, as well she knew,
To Corinth from the shore; for freshly blew
The eastern soft wind, and his galley now
Grated the quaystones with her brazen prow
In port Cenchreas, from Egina isle
Fresh anchor'd; whither he had been awhile
To sacrifice to Jove, whose temple there
Waits with high marble doors for blood and incense
　　rare.
Jove heard his vows, and better'd his desire;
For by some freakful chance he made retire   230
From his companions, and set forth to walk,
Perhaps grown wearied of their Corinth talk:
Over the solitary hills he fared,
Thoughtless at first, but ere eve's star appeared
His phantasy was lost, where reason fades,
In the calm'd twilight of Platonic shades.
Lamia beheld him coming, near, more near—
Close to her passing, in indifference drear.
His silent sandals swept the mossy green;
So neighbour'd to him, and yet so unseen   240
She stood: he pass'd, shut up in mysteries,
His mind wrapp'd like his mantle, while her eyes
Follow'd his steps, and her neck regal white
Turn'd—syllabling thus, "Ah, Lycius bright,
"And will you leave me on the hills alone?
"Lycius, look back! and be some pity shown."
He did; not with cold wonder fearingly,
But Orpheus-like at an Eurydice;
For so delicious were the words she sung,

225 In harbour Cencreas, *MS*.
236 Platonic] platonian *MS*.

It seem'd he had lov'd them a whole summer long: 250
And soon his eyes had drunk her beauty up,
Leaving no drop in the bewildering cup,
And still the cup was full,—while he, afraid
Lest she should vanish ere his lip had paid
Due adoration, thus began to adore;
Her soft look growing coy, she saw his chain so sure:
"Leave thee alone! Look back! Ah, Goddess, see
"Whether my eyes can ever turn from thee!
"For pity do not this sad heart belie—
"Even as thou vanishest so shall I die.   260
"Stay! though a Naiad of the rivers, stay!
"To thy far wishes will thy streams obey:
"Stay! though the greenest woods be thy domain,
"Alone they can drink up the morning rain:
"Though a descended Pleiad, will not one
"Of thine harmonious sisters keep in tune
"Thy spheres, and as thy silver proxy shine?
"So sweetly to these ravish'd ears of mine
"Came thy sweet greeting, that if thou shouldst fade
"Thy memory will waste me to a shade:—   270
"For pity do not melt!"—"If I should stay,"
Said Lamia, "here, upon this floor of clay,
"And pain my steps upon these flowers too rough,
"What canst thou say or do of charm enough
"To dull the nice remembrance of my home?
"Thou canst not ask me with thee here to roam
"Over these hills and vales, where no joy is,—
"Empty of immortality and bliss!
"Thou art a scholar, Lycius, and must know
"That finer spirits cannot breathe below   280
"In human climes, and live: Alas! poor youth,
"What taste of purer air hast thou to soothe
"My essence? What serener palaces,
"Where I may all my many senses please,
"And by mysterious sleights a hundred thirsts appease?
"It cannot be—Adieu!" So said, she rose

260 *After this line, the manuscript has an additional one, an Alexandrine*—

        Thou to Elysium gone, here for the vultures I.

272 *In the manuscript the word* here *does not occur in this line.*

Tiptoe with white arms spread. He, sick to lose
The amorous promise of her lone complain,
Swoon'd, murmuring of love, and pale with pain.
The cruel lady, without any show   290
Of sorrow for her tender favourite's woe,
But rather, if her eyes could brighter be,
With brighter eyes and slow amenity,
Put her new lips to his, and gave afresh
The life she had so tangled in her mesh :
And as he from one trance was wakening
Into another, she began to sing,
Happy in beauty, life, and love, and every thing,
A song of love, too sweet for earthly lyres,
While, like held breath, the stars drew in their panting
        fires.   300
And then she whisper'd in such trembling tone,
As those who, safe together met alone
For the first time through many anguish'd days,
Use other speech than looks ; bidding him raise
His drooping head, and clear his soul of doubt,
For that she was a woman, and without
Any more subtle fluid in her veins
Than throbbing blood, and that the self-same pains
Inhabited her frail-strung heart as his.
And next she wonder'd how his eyes could miss 310
Her face so long in Corinth, where, she said,
She dwelt but half retir'd, and there had led
Days happy as the gold coin could invent
Without the aid of love ; yet in content
Till she saw him, as once she pass'd him by,
Where 'gainst a column he lent thoughtfully
At Venus' temple porch, 'mid baskets heap'd
Of amorous herbs and flowers, newly reap'd
Late on that eve, as 'twas the night before
The Adonian feast ; whereof she saw no more,   320
But wept alone those days, for why should she adore ?
Lycius from death awoke into amaze,
To see her still, and singing so sweet lays ;
Then from amaze into delight he fell

287 Tip-toe with white spread arms *and* On tip-toe with
white arms *MS. readings.*
322 Lycius from death woke into an amaze... *MS.*

To hear her whisper woman's lore so well;
And every word she spake entic'd him on
To unperplex'd delight and pleasure known.
Let the mad poets say whate'er they please
Of the sweets of Faeries, Peris, Goddesses,
There is not such a treat among them all,   330
Haunters of cavern, lake, and waterfall,
As a real woman, lineal indeed
From Pyrrha's pebbles or old Adam's seed.
Thus gentle Lamia judg'd, and judg'd aright,
That Lycius could not love in half a fright,
So threw the goddess off, and won his heart
More pleasantly by playing woman's part,
With no more awe than what her beauty gave,
That, while it smote, still guaranteed to save.
Lycius to all made eloquent reply,   340
Marrying to every word a twinborn sigh;
And last, pointing to Corinth, ask'd her sweet,
If 'twas too far that night for her soft feet.
The way was short, for Lamia's eagerness
Made, by a spell, the triple league decrease
To a few paces; not at all surmised
By blinded Lycius, so in her comprized.
They pass'd the city gates, he knew not how,
So noiseless, and he never thought to know.

As men talk in a dream, so Corinth all,   350
Throughout her palaces imperial,
And all her populous streets and temples lewd,
Mutter'd, like tempest in the distance brew'd,
To the wide-spreaded night above her towers.
Men, women, rich and poor, in the cool hours,
Shuffled their sandals o'er the pavement white,
Companion'd or alone; while many a light
Flared, here and there, from wealthy festivals,
And threw their moving shadows on the walls,
Or found them cluster'd in the corniced shade   360
Of some arch'd temple door, or dusky colonnade.

Muffling his face, of greeting friends in fear,
Her fingers he press'd hard, as one came near

363 And pressing hard her fingers, one came near... MS.

With curl'd gray beard, sharp eyes, and smooth bald
    crown,
Slow-stepp'd, and robed in philosophic gown:
Lycius shrank closer, as they met and past,
Into his mantle, adding wings to haste,
While hurried Lamia trembled: "Ah," said he,
"Why do you shudder, love, so ruefully?
"Why does your tender palm dissolve in dew?"—
"I'm wearied," said fair Lamia: "tell me who   371
"Is that old man? I cannot bring to mind
"His features:—Lycius! wherefore did you blind
"Yourself from his quick eyes?" Lycius replied,
"'Tis Apollonius sage, my trusty guide
"And good instructor; but to-night he seems
"The ghost of folly haunting my sweet dreams."

    While yet he spake they had arrived before
A pillar'd porch, with lofty portal door,
Where hung a silver lamp, whose phosphor glow
Reflected in the slabbed steps below,   381
Mild as a star in water; for so new,
And so unsullied was the marble's hue,
So through the crystal polish, liquid fine,
Ran the dark veins, that none but feet divine
Could e'er have touch'd there.   Sounds Æolian
Breath'd from the hinges, as the ample span
Of the wide doors disclos'd a place unknown
Some time to any, but those two alone,
And a few Persian mutes, who that same year   390
Were seen about the markets: none knew where
They could inhabit; the most curious
Were foil'd, who watch'd to trace them to their house:
And but the flitter-winged verse must tell,
For truth's sake, what woe afterwards befel,
'Twould humour many a heart to leave them thus,
Shut from the busy world of more incredulous.

377 *The closing inverted commas, wanting in the first edition, appear
in the manuscript.*
379 A royal-squared lofty portal door, *MS.*
383 marble's *MS. :* marble *1820.*
393 trace] maze *MS.*

PART II

Love in a hut, with water and a crust,
Is—Love, forgive us!—cinders, ashes, dust;
Love in a palace is perhaps at last
More grievous torment than a hermit's fast:—
That is a doubtful tale from faery land,
Hard for the non-elect to understand.
Had Lycius liv'd to hand his story down,
He might have given the moral a fresh frown,
Or clench'd it quite: but too short was their bliss
To breed distrust and hate, that make the soft voice hiss.
Beside, there, nightly, with terrific glare,   11
Love, jealous grown of so complete a pair,
Hover'd and buzz'd his wings, with fearful roar,
Above the lintel of their chamber door,
And down the passage cast a glow upon the floor.

For all this came a ruin: side by side
They were enthroned, in the even tide,
Upon a couch, near to a curtaining
Whose airy texture, from a golden string,
Floated into the room, and let appear   20
Unveil'd the summer heaven, blue and clear,
Betwixt two marble shafts:—there they reposed,
Where use had made it sweet, with eyelids closed,
Saving a tythe which love still open kept,
That they might see each other while they almost slept;
When from the slope side of a suburb hill,
Deafening the swallow's twitter, came a thrill
Of trumpets—Lycius started—the sounds fled,
But left a thought, a buzzing in his head.
For the first time, since first he harbour'd in   30
That purple-lined palace of sweet sin,

29 But left a thought at work in Lycius' head. *Houghton Fragment, cancelled.*
30-3 *The following readings are from the Houghton Fragment :—*
      For the first time since that had been his...
      For the first time since he had harbour'd in
      That { happy Palace...
             { purple-lined Palace...
      For the first time since he soft-harbour'd in

His spirit pass'd beyond its golden bourn
Into the noisy world almost forsworn.
The lady, ever watchful, penetrant,
Saw this with pain, so arguing a want
Of something more, more than her empery
Of joys; and she began to moan and sigh
Because he mused beyond her, knowing well
That but a moment's thought is passion's passing bell.
"Why do you sigh, fair creature?" whisper'd he:
"Why do you think?" return'd she tenderly: 41
"You have deserted me;—where am I now?
"Not in your heart while care weighs on your brow:
"No, no, you have dismiss'd me; and I go
"From your breast houseless: aye, it must be so."
He answer'd, bending to her open eyes,
Where he was mirror'd small in paradise,
"My silver planet, both of eve and morn!
"Why will you plead yourself so sad forlorn,
"While I am striving how to fill my heart   50
"With deeper crimson, and a double smart?
"How to entangle, trammel up and snare
"Your soul in mine, and labyrinth you there
"Like the hid scent in an unbudded rose?
"Aye, a sweet kiss—you see your mighty woes.
"My thoughts! shall I unveil them? Listen then!
"What mortal hath a prize, that other men
"May be confounded and abash'd withal,
"But lets it sometimes pace abroad majestical,
"And triumph, as in thee I should rejoice   60
"Amid the hoarse alarm of Corinth's voice.

That purple-lined palace of sweet sin
Not...
His spirit pass'd beyond its golden bourne
Into the world...
Into { the / a } busy world almost foresworn.

34 The Lady] Lamia, *Houghton Fragment.*
40 creature?] Lamia? *Houghton Fragment.*
45 *In the finished manuscript, this speech has another couplet:*—
Too fond was I believing, fancy fed
In high deliriums, and blossoms never shed!
47 Wherein he saw himself in Paradise—*Houghton Fragment.*
53 Your ... you,] Thy ... thee, *MS.*

"Let my foes choke, and my friends shout afar,
"While through the thronged streets your bridal car
"Wheels round its dazzling spokes."—The lady's cheek
Trembled; she nothing said, but, pale and meek,
Arose and knelt before him, wept a rain
Of sorrows at his words; at last with pain
Beseeching him, the while his hand she wrung,
To change his purpose. He thereat was stung,
Perverse, with stronger fancy to reclaim   70
Her wild and timid nature to his aim:
Besides, for all his love, in self despite,
Against his better self, he took delight
Luxurious in her sorrows, soft and new.
His passion, cruel grown, took on a hue
Fierce and sanguineous as 'twas possible
In one whose brow had no dark veins to swell.
Fine was the mitigated fury, like
Apollo's presence when in act to strike
The serpent—Ha, the serpent! certes, she   80
Was none. She burnt, she lov'd the tyranny,
And, all subdued, consented to the hour

82–105 *In the manuscript, instead of lines 82 to 105, the following
originally stood :—*

> Became herself a flame—'twas worth an age
> Of minor joys to revel in such rage.
> She was persuaded, and she fixt the hour
> When he should make a Bride of his fair Paramour.
> After the hot[t]est day comes languidest
> The colour'd Eve, half-hidden in the west ;
> So they both look'd, so spake, if breathed sound,
> That almost silence is, hath ever found
> Compare with nature's quiet. Which lov'd most,
> Which had the weakest, strongest, heart so lost,
> So ruin'd, wreck'd, destroyed ; for certes they
> Scarcely could tell   they could not guess
> Whether 'twas misery or happiness.
> Spells are but made to break. Whisper'd the Youth
> "Sure some sweet name thou hast; though by my truth
> "I had not ask'd it, ever thinking thee
> "Not mortal but of heavenly progeny,
> "As still I do. Hast any mortal name ?
> "Fit silver appellation for this dazzling frame ?
> "Or friends, or kinsfolks on the citied Earth,
> "To share our marriage feast and nuptial mirth ?"
> "I have no friends," said Lamia "as you list
> "Intreat your many guests." Then all was wist

When to the bridal he should lead his paramour.
Whispering in midnight silence, said the youth,
"Sure some sweet name thou hast, though, by my truth,
"I have not ask'd it, ever thinking thee
"Not mortal, but of heavenly progeny,
"As still I do. Hast any mortal name,
"Fit appellation for this dazzling frame?
"Or friends or kinsfolk on the citied earth,   90
"To share our marriage feast and nuptial mirth?"
"I have no friends," said Lamia, "no, not one;
"My presence in wide Corinth hardly known:

> She fell asleep, and Lycius to the Shade
> Of deep sleep in a moment was betray'd.

The passage beginning at

> After the hottest day comes languidest

occurs also in the Houghton Fragment, and shows some variations, as

> The colour'd eve, half-lidded in the west—

and again ·   for certes they

> Scarcely could tell if this was misery.

In the next line the Houghton Fragment has the cancelled reading, said
then the youth *for* whisper'd the youth, *and a little lower down*
As now I do *stands rejected in favour of* As still I do. *There is also
a further variation of line* 99, *namely*

> Of fit sound for this soft ethereal frame.

Lamia's avowal that she had no friends is followed by several cancellings:—

> "I have no friends" said Lamia as you list
> Seeing it must be...
> Do with your own...
> Intreat your many guests. Then all was was [*sic*] wist
> She fell asleep, and Lycius to the shade
> Of sleep sunk with her { when / dreaming } his fancy stray'd
> Into a dream...
> Of sleep went...
> Of deep sleep in a moment was betray'd.

*Before this was all struck out and remodelled according to the text, Keats
cancelled in the finished manuscript from* as you list, *and wrote in*

> no not one;

> My presence in wide Corinth is unknown;

and the next six lines as in the text, adding—

> With any pleasure on me, summon not
> Old Apollonius. Lycius ignorant what
> Strange thought had led her to an end so blank,

and so on as in the text, lines 103-5.

89-90 *In writing these two lines the second time, Keats inserted the
word* silver *before* appellation, *and put* kinsfolks *again.*

"My parents' bones are in their dusty urns
"Sepulchred, where no kindled incense burns,
"Seeing all their luckless race are dead, save me,
"And I neglect the holy rite for thee.
"Even as you list invite your many guests;
"But if, as now it seems, your vision rests
"With any pleasure on me, do not bid   100
"Old Apollonius—from him keep me hid."
Lycius, perplex'd at words so blind and blank,
Made close inquiry; from whose touch she shrank,
Feigning a sleep; and he to the dull shade
Of deep sleep in a moment was betray'd.

It was the custom then to bring away
The bride from home at blushing shut of day,
Veil'd, in a chariot, heralded along
By strewn flowers, torches, and a marriage song,
With other pageants: but this fair unknown   110
Had not a friend. So being left alone,
(Lycius was gone to summon all his kin)
And knowing surely she could never win
His foolish heart from its mad pompousness,
She set herself, high-thoughted, how to dress
The misery in fit magnificence.
She did so, but 'tis doubtful how and whence
Came, and who were her subtle servitors.
About the halls, and to and from the doors,
There was a noise of wings, till in short space   120
The glowing banquet-room shone with wide-arched
        grace.
A haunting music, sole perhaps and lone
Supportress of the faery-roof, made moan
Throughout, as fearful the whole charm might fade.
Fresh carved cedar, mimicking a glade

122 A haunting music lone perhaps and sole...
                                        Houghton Fragment.
125-30 *There was also some hesitation as to what line* 125 *should be.*
        The carved cedar...
        Sweet cedar carv'd there...
        Fresh Carved Cedar { spread a
                           { mimicking a glade
appear successively.   There is a rejected reading for line 129—
        On either side a forest they...

Of palm and plantain, met from either side,
High in the midst, in honour of the bride:
Two palms and then two plantains, and so on,
From either side their stems branch'd one to one
All down the aisled place ; and beneath all   130
There ran a stream of lamps straight on from wall
    to wall.
So canopied, lay an untasted feast
Teeming with odours.   Lamia, regal drest,
Silently paced about, and as she went,
In pale contented sort of discontent,
Mission'd her viewless servants to enrich
The fretted splendour of each nook and niche.
Between the tree-stems, marbled plain at first,
Came jasper pannels ; then, anon, there burst
Forth creeping imagery of slighter trees,   140
And with the larger wove in small intricacies.
Approving all, she faded at self-will,
And shut the chamber up, close, hush'd and still,
Complete and ready for the revels rude,
When dreadful guests would come to spoil her solitude.

and another of line 130—
    All down the aisled-place—far as the eye could view.
   133 Teeming a perfume *and* Teeming wing'd odours *MS.,*
cancelled.
   134-7 *In the Houghton Fragment, in line* 134 silverly *occurs in place
of* silently ; *line* 135 *is wanting ; and line* 137 *stands as follows*—
    The splendid finish of each nook and niche.
   138 marbled plain] wainscoated *MS., cancelled.*

140 Forth $\begin{Bmatrix} \text{creeping} \\ \text{tenderer} \end{Bmatrix}$ imagery of $\begin{Bmatrix} \text{slighter} \\ \text{smaller} \end{Bmatrix}$ trees.

                                   Houghton Fragment.
   141-4 *In the Houghton Fragment, in line* 141 smallest *is cancelled
in favour of* in small, *and between that and line* 142 *occurs the following
passage :*—
    And so till she was sated—then came down
    Soft ligh[t]ing $\begin{Bmatrix} \text{on her head} \\ \text{o'er her Brows} \end{Bmatrix}$ a brilliant crown
    Wreathed turban- $\begin{Bmatrix} \text{wise} \\ \text{like} \end{Bmatrix}$ of tender wannish fire
    And sprinkled o'er with stars like Ariadne's tiar.
The close of line 144 *shows no fewer than four readings rejected in favour
of* revels rude, *namely* woeful time, woeful day, time of woe, *and*
day of woe, *each of which, preferable in itself to the reading adopted,
must have had to give place on account of the exigencies of rhyme*

The day appear'd, and all the gossip rout.
O senseless Lycius! Madman! wherefore flout
The silent-blessing fate, warm cloister'd hours,
And show to common eyes these secret bowers?
The herd approach'd; each guest, with busy brain,
Arriving at the portal, gaz'd amain,   151
And enter'd marveling: for they knew the street,
Remember'd it from childhood all complete
Without a gap, yet ne'er before had seen
That royal porch, that high-built fair demesne;
So in they hurried all, maz'd, curious and keen:
Save one, who look'd thereon with eye severe,
And with calm-planted steps walk'd in austere;
'Twas Apollonius: something too he laugh'd,
As though some knotty problem, that had daft   160
His patient thought, had now begun to thaw,
And solve and melt:—'twas just as he foresaw.

He met within the murmurous vestibule
His young disciple. "'Tis no common rule,
Lycius," said he, "for uninvited guest
"To force himself upon you, and infest
"With an unbidden presence the bright throng
"Of younger friends; yet must I do this wrong,
"And you forgive me." Lycius blush'd, and led
The old man through the inner doors broad-spread;
With reconciling words and courteous mien   171
Turning into sweet milk the sophist's spleen.

Of wealthy lustre was the banquet-room,
Fill'd with pervading brilliance and perfume:
Before each lucid pannel fuming stood
A censer fed with myrrh and spiced wood,
Each by a sacred tripod held aloft,

146-7 The day came soon and all the gossip-rout
      O senseless Lycius Dolt! Fool! Madman! Lout!
                                        Houghton Fragment.
163-72 *This passage was an afterthought.   The line following* 162
in the manuscript in the first instance was
      Of wealthy Lustre was the Banquet room.
174 Fill'd with light, music, jewels, gold, perfume
                                        MS., cancelled.
177 *The manuscript has* slender *in lieu of* sacred, *and in the next
line* tripple *instead of* slender.

Whose slender feet wide-swerv'd upon the soft
Wool-woofed carpets: fifty wreaths of smoke
From fifty censers their light voyage took   180
To the high roof, still mimick'd as they rose
Along the mirror'd walls by twin-clouds odorous.
Twelve sphered tables, by silk seats insphered,
High as the level of a man's breast rear'd
On libbard's paws, upheld the heavy gold
Of cups and goblets, and the store thrice told
Of Ceres' horn, and, in huge vessels, wine
Come from the gloomy tun with merry shine.
Thus loaded with a feast the tables stood,
Each shrining in the midst the image of a God.   190

When in an antichamber every guest
Had felt the cold full sponge to pleasure press'd,
By minist'ring slaves, upon his hands and feet,
And fragrant oils with ceremony meet
Pour'd on his hair, they all mov'd to the feast
In white robes, and themselves in order placed
Around the silken couches, wondering
Whence all this mighty cost and blaze of wealth
    could spring.

Soft went the music the soft air along,
While fluent Greek a vowel'd undersong   200
Kept up among the guests, discoursing low
At first, for scarcely was the wine at flow ;
But when the happy vintage touch'd their brains,
Louder they talk, and louder come the strains

191 *This passage occurs in the Houghton Fragment with cancellings
thus :—*

> When in an antichamber every guest
> With fragrant oils his...

> When in an antichamber every guest
> Tended by ministering slaves his...

> When in an antichamber every guest
> Had $\left\{ \begin{matrix} \text{felt} \\ \text{had} \end{matrix} \right\}$ the cold full sponge to pleasure press'd.

195–6 *In the Houghton Fragment occurs the rejected reading,*
>   they all to banquet came
> In white robes hymeneal.

203 the happy] Sicilian *MS., cancelled.*

Of powerful instruments :—the gorgeous dyes,
The space, the splendour of the draperies,
The roof of awful richness, nectarous cheer,
Beautiful slaves, and Lamia's self, appear,
Now, when the wine has done its rosy deed,
And every soul from human trammels freed,   210
No more so strange ; for merry wine, sweet wine,
Will make Elysian shades not too fair, too divine.
Soon was God Bacchus at meridian height ;
Flush'd were their cheeks, and bright eyes double
        bright:
Garlands of every green, and every scent
From vales deflower'd, or forest-trees branch-rent,
In baskets of bright osier'd gold were brought
High as the handles heap'd, to suit the thought
Of every guest ; that each, as he did please,
Might fancy-fit his brows, silk-pillow'd at his ease.   220

    What wreath for Lamia ?   What for Lycius ?
What for the sage, old Apollonius ?
Upon her aching forehead be there hung
The leaves of willow and of adder's tongue ;
And for the youth, quick, let us strip for him
The thyrsus, that his watching eyes may swim
Into forgetfulness ; and, for the sage,
Let spear-grass and the spiteful thistle wage
War on his temples. Do not all charms fly
At the mere touch of cold philosophy ?   230
There was an awful rainbow once in heaven :
We know her woof, her texture ; she is given
In the dull catalogue of common things.
Philosophy will clip an Angel's wings,
Conquer all mysteries by rule and line,
Empty the haunted air, and gnomed mine—
Unweave a rainbow, as it erewhile made
The tender-person'd Lamia melt into a shade.

    218-9 High as the handles heap'd, of every sort
            Of fragrant wreath, that each as he did please...
                                        MS., cancelled.

    237 *Cancelled readings of the manuscript*, Destroy *for* Unweave. *and*
    once *for* erewhile.

By her glad Lycius sitting, in chief place,
Scarce saw in all the room another face,   240
Till, checking his love trance, a cup he took
Full brimm'd, and opposite sent forth a look
'Cross the broad table, to beseech a glance
From his old teacher's wrinkled countenance,
And pledge him. The bald-head philosopher
Had fix'd his eye, without a twinkle or stir
Full on the alarmed beauty of the bride,
Brow-beating her fair form, and troubling her sweet
    pride.
Lycius then press'd her hand, with devout touch,
As pale it lay upon the rosy couch: 250
'Twas icy, and the cold ran through his veins;
Then sudden it grew hot, and all the pains
Of an unnatural heat shot to his heart.
" Lamia, what means this ? Wherefore dost thou start ?
" Know'st thou that man ? " Poor Lamia answer'd not.
He gaz'd into her eyes, and not a jot
Own'd they the lovelorn piteous appeal :
More, more he gaz'd : his human senses reel :
Some hungry spell that loveliness absorbs ;
There was no recognition in those orbs.   260
" Lamia ! " he cried—and no soft-toned reply.
The many heard, and the loud revelry
Grew hush ; the stately music no more breathes ;
The myrtle sicken'd in a thousand wreaths.
By faint degrees, voice, lute, and pleasure ceased ;
A deadly silence step by step increased,
Until it seem'd a horrid presence there,
And not a man but felt the terror in his hair.
" Lamia ! " he shriek'd ; and nothing but the shriek
With its sad echo did the silence break.   270
" Begone, foul dream ! " he cried, gazing again
In the bride's face, where now no azure vein
Wander'd on fair-spaced temples ; no soft bloom
Misted the cheek ; no passion to illume

239 her] whom *MS*.
246-7 Had got his eye, without a twinkle or stir,
    Fix'd on the alarmed Beauty of his Bride. *MS*.
254-5   Wherefore dost so start ?
    Dost know that **Man** ? *MS*.

The deep-recessed vision:—all was blight ;
Lamia, no longer fair, there sat a deadly white.
" Shut, shut those juggling eyes, thou ruthless man!
" Turn them aside, wretch ! or the righteous ban
" Of all the Gods, whose dreadful images
" Here represent their shadowy presences,   280
" May pierce them on the sudden with the thorn
" Of painful blindness ; leaving thee forlorn,
" In trembling dotage to the feeblest fright
" Of conscience, for their long offended might,
" For all thine impious proud-heart sophistries,
" Unlawful magic, and enticing lies.
" Corinthians ! look upon that grey-beard wretch !
" Mark how, possess'd, his lashless eyelids stretch
" Around his demon eyes ! Corinthians, see !
" My sweet bride withers at their potency."   290
" Fool !" said the sophist, in an under-tone
Gruff with contempt ; which a death-nighing moan
From Lycius answer'd, as heart-struck and lost,
He sank supine beside the aching ghost.
" Fool ! Fool !" repeated he, while his eyes still
Relented not, nor mov'd ; " from every ill
" Of life have I preserv'd thee to this day,
" And shall I see thee made a serpent's prey ?"
Then Lamia breath'd death breath ; the sophist's eye,
Like a sharp spear, went through her utterly,   300
Keen, cruel, perceant, stinging : she, as well
As her weak hand could any meaning tell,
Motion'd him to be silent ; vainly so,
He look'd and look'd again a level—No !
" A serpent !" echoed he ; no sooner said,
Than with a frightful scream she vanished :
And Lycius' arms were empty of delight,
As were his limbs of life, from that same night.
On the high couch he lay !—his friends came round—

293-4 From Lycius answer'd, as he sunk supine
        Upon the couch where Lamia's beauties pine. *MS.*
296   " from every ill
        That youth might suffer have I shielded thee
        Up to this very hour, and shall I see
        Thee married to a Serpent? Pray you Mark,
        Corinthians ! A Serpent, plain and stark !" *MS.*

Supported him—no pulse, or breath they found, 310
And, in its marriage robe, the heavy body wound.

311 *The following extract is appended in Keats's edition as a note to
the last line :—*

"Philostratus, in his fourth book *de Vita Apollonii,* hath a
memorable instance in this kind, which I may not omit, of
one Menippus Lycius, a young man twenty-five years of age,
that going betwixt Cenchreas and Corinth, met such a phantasm
in the habit of a fair gentlewoman, which, taking him by the
hand, carried him home to her house, in the suburbs of Corinth,
and told him she was a Phœnician by birth, and if he would
tarry with her, he should hear her sing and play, and drink
such wine as never any drank, and no man should molest him ;
but she, being fair and lovely, would live and die with him,
that was fair and lovely to behold. The young man, a philosopher, otherwise staid and discreet, able to moderate his
passions, though not this of love, tarried with her a while to
his great content, and at last married her, to whose wedding,
amongst other guests, came Apollonius ; who, by some probable
conjectures, found her out to be a serpent, a lamia ; and that
all her furniture was, like Tantalus' gold, described by Homer,
no substance but mere illusions. When she saw herself descried,
she wept, and desired Apollonius to be silent, but he would not
be moved, and thereupon she, plate, house, and all that was in
it, vanished in an instant : many thousands took notice of this
fact, for it was done in the midst of Greece."

Burton's 'Anatomy of Melancholy,' *Part* 3. *Sect.* 2.
Memb. 1. *Subs.* 1.

ISABELLA;

THE POT OF BASIL.

A Story from Boccaccio.

I.

FAIR Isabel, poor simple Isabel!
  Lorenzo, a young palmer in Love's eye!
They could not in the self-same mansion dwell
  Without some stir of heart, some malady;
They could not sit at meals but feel how well
  It soothed each to be the other by;
They could not, sure, beneath the same roof sleep
But to each other dream, and nightly weep.

II.

With every morn their love grew tenderer,
  With every eve deeper and tenderer still;
He might not in house, field, or garden stir,
  But her full shape would all his seeing fill;
And his continual voice was pleasanter
  To her, than noise of trees or hidden rill;
Her lute-string gave an echo of his name,
She spoilt her half-done broidery with the same.

III.

He knew whose gentle hand was at the latch
  Before the door had given her to his eyes;
And from her chamber-window he would catch
  Her beauty farther than the falcon spies;
And constant as her vespers would he watch,
  Because her face was turn'd to the same skies;
And with sick longing all the night outwear,
To hear her morning-step upon the stair.

II 6 noise] sigh *Holograph.*

IV.

A whole long month of May in this sad plight
  Made their cheeks paler by the break of June:
"To-morrow will I bow to my delight,
  "To-morrow will I ask my lady's boon."—
"O may I never see another night,
  "Lorenzo, if thy lips breathe not love's tune."—
So spake they to their pillows; but, alas,
Honeyless days and days did he let pass;

V.

Until sweet Isabella's untouch'd cheek
  Fell sick within the rose's just domain,
Fell thin as a young mother's, who doth seek
  By every lull to cool her infant's pain:
"How ill she is," said he, "I may not speak,
  "And yet I will, and tell my love all plain:
"If looks speak love-laws, I will drink her tears,
"And at the least 'twill startle off her cares."

VI.

So said he one fair morning, and all day
  His heart beat awfully against his side;
And to his heart he inwardly did pray
  For power to speak; but still the ruddy tide
Stifled his voice, and puls'd resolve away—
  Fever'd his high conceit of such a bride,
Yet brought him to the meekness of a child:
Alas! when passion is both meek and wild!

VII.

So once more he had wak'd and anguished
  A dreary night of love and misery,
If Isabel's quick eye had not been wed
  To every symbol on his forehead high;
She saw it waxing very pale and dead,
  And straight all flush'd; so, lisped tenderly,

IV 6 Lorenzo, if thy tongue speak not love's tune. *Holograph.*
VI *Opposite the close of this stanza, in the Woodhouse transcript,*
Keats has written in pencil Stop this as you please.
VII *The word* said *stands cancelled before* lisped (line 6) *in the*
holograph, in which, as in the transcript, the stanza closes with a different

" Lorenzo !"—here she ceas'd her timid quest,
But in her tone and look he read the rest.

VIII.

" O Isabella, I can half perceive
  " That I may speak my grief into thine ear ;
" If thou didst ever anything believe,
  " Believe how I love thee, believe how near
" My soul is to its doom : I would not grieve
  " Thy hand by unwelcome pressing, would not fear
" Thine eyes by gazing ; but I cannot live
" Another night, and not my passion shrive.

IX.

" Love ! thou art leading me from wintry cold,
  " Lady ! thou leadest me to summer clime,
" And I must taste the blossoms that unfold
  " In its ripe warmth this gracious morning time."
So said, his erewhile timid lips grew bold,
  And poesied with hers in dewy rhyme :
Great bliss was with them, and great happiness
Grew, like a lusty flower in June's caress.

*couplet from that of the text and is followed by a stanza ultimately rejected :
here are the ten cancelled lines*—

    " Lorenzo, I would clip my ringlet hair
  To make thee laugh again and debonnair."
    "Then should I be," said he, "full deified ;
    And yet I would not have it, clip it not :
  For, lady, I do love it where 'tis tied
    About the neck I dote on, and that spot
  That anxious dimple it doth take a pride
    To play about—Aye lady, I have got
  Its shadow in my heart and every sweet
  Its mistress owns there summed all complete.

*In another handwriting, on the blank page opposite this passage in the
holograph, stand the verses*—

    Lorenzo in the twilight Morn was wont
    To rouse the clamorous Kennel to the Hunt ;

    And then his cheek inherited the Ray
    Of the outpouring Sun ; and ere the Horn
  Could call the Hunters to the Chace away
    His voice more softly woke me : Many a Morn
  From sweetest Dreams it drew me to a Day
    More sweet ; but now Lorenzo holds in scorn
  His Health ; and all those bygone Joys are Dreams
  To me—to him, I mean—so chang'd he seems.

X.

Parting they seem'd to tread upon the air,
  Twin roses by the zephyr blown apart
Only to meet again more close, and share
  The inward fragrance of each other's heart.
She, to her chamber gone, a ditty fair
  Sang, of delicious love and honey'd dart;
He with light steps went up a western hill,
And bade the sun farewell, and joy'd his fill.

XI.

All close they met again, before the dusk
  Had taken from the stars its pleasant veil,
All close they met, all eves, before the dusk
  Had taken from the stars its pleasant veil,
Close in a bower of hyacinth and musk,
  Unknown of any, free from whispering tale.
Ah! better had it been for ever so,
Than idle ears should pleasure in their woe.

XII.

Were they unhappy then?—It cannot be—
  Too many tears for lovers have been shed,
Too many sighs give we to them in fee,
  Too much of pity after they are dead,
Too many doleful stories do we see,
  Whose matter in bright gold were best be read;
Except in such a page where Theseus' spouse
Over the pathless waves towards him bows.

XIII.

But, for the general award of love,
  The little sweet doth kill much bitterness;
Though Dido silent is in under-grove,
  And Isabella's was a great distress,
Though young Lorenzo in warm Indian clove
  Was not embalm'd, this truth is not the less—
Even bees, the little almsmen of spring-bowers,
Know there is richest juice in poison-flowers.

XIV.

With her two brothers this fair lady dwelt,
  Enriched from ancestral merchandize,

And for them many a weary hand did swelt
  In torched mines and noisy factories,
And many once proud-quiver'd loins did melt
  In blood from stinging whip;—with hollow eyes
Many all day in dazzling river stood,
To take the rich-ored driftings of the flood.

XV.

For them the Ceylon diver held his breath,
  And went all naked to the hungry shark;
For them his ears gush'd blood; for them in death
  The seal on the cold ice with piteous bark
Lay full of darts; for them alone did seethe
  A thousand men in troubles wide and dark:
Half-ignorant, they turn'd an easy wheel,
That set sharp racks at work, to pinch and peel.

XVI.

Why were they proud? Because their marble founts
  Gush'd with more pride than do a wretch's tears?—
Why were they proud? Because fair orange-mounts
  Were of more soft ascent than lazar stairs?—
Why were they proud? Because red-lin'd accounts
  Were richer than the songs of Grecian years?—
Why were they proud? again we ask aloud,
Why in the name of Glory were they proud?

XVII.

Yet were these Florentines as self-retired
  In hungry pride and gainful cowardice,
As two close Hebrews in that land inspired,
  Paled in and vineyarded from beggar-spies;
The hawks of ship-mast forests—the untired
  And pannier'd mules for ducats and old lies—
Quick cat's-paws on the generous stray-away,—
Great wits in Spanish, Tuscan, and Malay.

XIV 5 proud-quiver'd *1820: no MS. authority for hyphen.*
XVII *This stanza is followed in the holograph by a cancelled one—*
    Two young Orlandos far away they seem'd,
      But on a near inspect their vapid Miens—
    Very alike,—at once themselves redeem'd
      From all suspicion of Romantic spleens—

XVIII.

How was it these same ledger-men could spy
   Fair Isabella in her downy nest?
How could they find out in Lorenzo's eye
   A straying from his toil? Hot Egypt's pest
Into their vision covetous and sly!
   How could these money-bags see east and west?—
Yet so they did—and every dealer fair
Must see behind, as doth the hunted hare.

XIX.

O eloquent and famed Boccaccio!
   Of thee we now should ask forgiving boon,
And of thy spicy myrtles as they blow,
   And of thy roses amorous of the moon,
And of thy lillies, that do paler grow
   Now they can no more hear thy ghittern's tune,
For venturing syllables that ill beseem
The quiet glooms of such a piteous theme.

XX.

Grant thou a pardon here, and then the tale
   Shall move on soberly, as it is meet;
There is no other crime, no mad assail
   To make old prose in modern rhyme more sweet:
But it is done—succeed the verse or fail—
   To honour thee. and thy gone spirit greet;
To stead thee as a verse in English tongue,
An echo of thee in the north-wind sung.

No fault of theirs, for their good Mother dream'd
   In the longing time of Units in their teens
Of proudly bas'd addition and of net—
   And both their backs were mark'd with tare and tret.
XIX 1 O eloquent Boccace of green Arno! *Holograph.*

   7–8 For venturing one word unseemly mean,
      In such a place, on such a daring theme. *Holograph.*
  XX. *In the holograph the closing couplet was written as published;*
but Keats substituted for the first line of it, in the Woodhouse transcript,
      Thy Muse's Vicar in the english tongue;
and afterwards rejected that for the original reading.

XXI.

These brethren having found by many signs
  What love Lorenzo for their sister had,
And how she lov'd him too, each unconfines
  His bitter thoughts to other, well nigh mad
That he, the servant of their trade designs,
  Should in their sister's love be blithe and glad,
When 'twas their plan to coax her by degrees
To some high noble and his olive-trees.

XXII.

And many a jealous conference had they,
  And many times they bit their lips alone,
Before they fix'd upon a surest way
  To make the youngster for his crime atone ;
And at the last, these men of cruel clay
  Cut Mercy with a sharp knife to the bone ;
For they resolved in some forest dim
To kill Lorenzo, and there bury him.

XXIII.

So on a pleasant morning, as he leant
  Into the sun-rise, o'er the balustrade
Of the garden-terrace, towards him they bent
  Their footing through the dews ; and to him said,
"You seem there in the quiet of content,
  "Lorenzo, and we are most loth to invade
"Calm speculation ; but if you are wise,
"Bestride your steed while cold is in the skies.

XXIV.

"To-day we purpose, aye, this hour we mount
  "To spur three leagues towards the Apennine ;
"Come down, we pray thee, ere the hot sun count
  "His dewy rosary on the eglantine."
Lorenzo, courteously as he was wont,
  Bow'd a fair greeting to these serpents' whine ;
And went in haste, to get in readiness,
With belt, and spur, and bracing huntsman's dress.

XXI 8 olive] forest *Holograph, cancelled.*
XXIV 3, 5 pry'thee *and* courteous *Holograph.*

XXV.

And as he to the court-yard pass'd along,
  Each third step did he pause, and listen'd oft
If he could hear his lady's matin-song,
  Or the light whisper of her footstep soft;
And as he thus over his passion hung,
  He heard a laugh full musical aloft;
When, looking up, he saw her features bright
Smile through an in-door lattice, all delight.

XXVI.

"Love, Isabel!" said he, "I was in pain
  "Lest I should miss to bid thee a good morrow:
"Ah! what if I should lose thee, when so fain
  "I am to stifle all the heavy sorrow
"Of a poor three hours' absence? but we'll gain
  "Out of the amorous dark what day doth borrow.
"Good bye! I'll soon be back."—"Good bye!" said she:—
And as he went she chanted merrily.

XXVII.

So the two brothers and their murder'd man
  Rode past fair Florence, to where Arno's stream
Gurgles through straiten'd banks, and still doth fan
  Itself with dancing bulrush, and the bream
Keeps head against the freshets. Sick and wan
  The brothers' faces in the ford did seem,
Lorenzo's flush with love.—They pass'd the water
Into a forest quiet for the slaughter.

XXV *A fragment of the draft (at Welbeck Abbey) has the lovely reading*—
    And looking up he saw her smiling through
    A little indoor Lattice, morning new—
The holograph leaves the same couplet unfinished, ending with Lattice. *In the transcript Woodhouse left a blank for the couplet, and Keats inserted*
    When, looking up, he saw her features fair
    Smile through an indoor lattice, debonair.
Some one, probably Taylor, took exception to this, and suggested
    When lo an indoor lattice met his view,
    And her fair features smiling playful through.
Keats altered his own couplet to that of the text. A propos of the word debonair, *he added the note*—As I have used this word before in the poem you may use your judgement between your lines and mine.—I think my last alteration will do. *This would seem to indicate that, at that stage in the proceedings, he had not thought of altering the couplet of Stanza VII and striking out the original Stanza VIII.*

XXVIII.

There was Lorenzo slain and buried in,
   There in that forest did his great love cease;
Ah! when a soul doth thus its freedom win,
   It aches in loneliness—is ill at peace
As the break-covert blood-hounds of such sin:
   They dipp'd their swords in the water, and did tease
Their horses homeward, with convulsed spur,
Each richer by his being a murderer.

XXIX.

They told their sister how, with sudden speed,
   Lorenzo had ta'en ship for foreign lands,
Because of some great urgency and need
   In their affairs, requiring trusty hands.
Poor Girl! put on thy stifling widow's weed,
   And 'scape at once from Hope's accursed bands;
To-day thou wilt not see him, nor to-morrow,
And the next day will be a day of sorrow.

XXX.

She weeps alone for pleasures not to be;
   Sorely she wept until the night came on,
And then, instead of love, O misery!
   She brooded o'er the luxury alone:
His image in the dusk she seem'd to see,
   And to the silence made a gentle moan,
Spreading her perfect arms upon the air,
And on her couch low murmuring "Where? O where?"

XXXI.

But Selfishness, Love's cousin, held not long
   Its fiery vigil in her single breast;
She fretted for the golden hour, and hung
   Upon the time with feverish unrest—
Not long—for soon into her heart a throng
   Of higher occupants, a richer zest,

XXVIII 6 water] River *Holograph.*

XXX 5 What might have been too plainly did she see...
                                   MS. Fragment.

XXXI 2–3   Its fiery vigil in her native Mind
            For joy escap'd she mourn'd—
                               MS. Fragment, cancelled.

Came tragic; passion not to be subdued,
And sorrow for her love in travels rude.

XXXII.

In the mid days of autumn, on their eves
  The breath of Winter comes from far away,
And the sick west continually bereaves
  Of some gold tinge, and plays a roundelay
Of death among the bushes and the leaves,
  To make all bare before he dares to stray
From his north cavern. So sweet Isabel
By gradual decay from beauty fell,

XXXIII.

Because Lorenzo came not. Oftentimes
  She ask'd her brothers, with an eye all pale,
Striving to be itself, what dungeon climes
  Could keep him off so long? They spake a tale
Time after time, to quiet her. Their crimes
  Came on them, like a smoke from Hinnom's vale;
And every night in dreams they groan'd aloud,
To see their sister in her snowy shroud.

XXXIV.

And she had died in drowsy ignorance,
  But for a thing more deadly dark than all;
It came like a fierce potion, drunk by chance,
  Which saves a sick man from the feather'd pall
For some few gasping moments; like a lance,
  Waking an Indian from his cloudy hall
With cruel pierce, and bringing him again
Sense of the gnawing fire at heart and brain.

XXXV.

It was a vision.—In the drowsy gloom,
  The dull of midnight, at her couch's foot

XXXI 8 Exalting her to patient Fortitude...
                        MS. Fragment, cancelled.
XXXIII 5 Time after time] Month after Month...
                    MS. Fragment and Holograph.
XXXIV 4 Which saves the sick some moments from the Pall.
                        MS. Fragment, cancelled.
  XXXV *In line 1 the manuscript fragment reads* heavy *for* drowsy;
and I cannot but think this application of the same adjective to ignorance
and to gloom *in the same page was a printer's or copyist's error. In*

Lorenzo stood, and wept : the forest tomb
　　Had marr'd his glossy hair which once could shoot
Lustre into the sun, and put cold doom
　　Upon his lips, and taken the soft lute
From his lorn voice, and past his loamed ears
Had made a miry channel for his tears.

XXXVI.

Strange sound it was, when the pale shadow spake ;
　　For there was striving, in its piteous tongue,
To speak as when on earth it was awake,
　　And Isabella on its music hung :
Languor there was in it, and tremulous shake,
　　As in a palsied Druid's harp unstrung ;
And through it moan'd a ghostly under-song,
Like hoarse night-gusts sepulchral briars among.

XXXVII.

Its eyes, though wild, were still all dewy bright
　　With love, and kept all phantom fear aloof
From the poor girl by magic of their light,
　　The while it did unthread the horrid woof
Of the late darken'd time,—the murderous spite
　　Of pride and avarice,—the dark pine roof
In the forest,—and the sodden turfed dell,
Where, without any word, from stabs he fell.

XXXVIII.

Saying moreover, " Isabel, my sweet !
　　" Red whortle-berries droop above my head,
" And a large flint-stone weighs upon my feet ;
　　" Around me beeches and high chestnuts shed
" Their leaves and prickly nuts ; a sheep-fold bleat
　　" Comes from beyond the river to my bed :

line 3, His *has been struck out in favour of* The ; *and lines* 4 *to* 7
originally read—

　　　　Had marr'd his glossy hair, that once could shoot
　　　　Bright gold into the Sun, and stamp'd his doom
　　　　Upon his soiled lips, and took the mellow Lute
　　From his deep voice, and down past his loamed ears...

But the readings put cold doom, *and* taken the soft Lute *were
afterwards substituted ; and the redundant words* soiled *and* down
were struck out.

"Go, shed one tear upon my heather-bloom,
"And it shall comfort me within the tomb.

XXXIX.

"I am a shadow now, alas! alas!
"Upon the skirts of human-nature dwelling
"Alone: I chant alone the holy mass,
"While little sounds of life are round me knelling,
"And glossy bees at noon do fieldward pass,
"And many a chapel bell the hour is telling,
"Paining me through: those sounds grow strange to me,
"And thou art distant in Humanity.

XL.

"I know what was, I feel full well what is,
"And I should rage, if spirits could go mad;
"Though I forget the taste of earthly bliss,
"That paleness warms my grave, as though I had
"A Seraph chosen from the bright abyss
"To be my spouse: thy paleness makes me glad;
"Thy beauty grows upon me, and I feel
"A greater love through all my essence steal."

XLI.

The Spirit mourn'd "Adieu!"—dissolv'd and left
The atom darkness in a slow turmoil;
As when of healthful midnight sleep bereft,
Thinking on rugged hours and fruitless toil,
We put our eyes into a pillowy cleft,
And see the spangly gloom froth up and boil:
It made sad Isabella's eyelids ache,
And in the dawn she started up awake;

XLII.

"Ha! ha!" said she, "I knew not this hard life,
"I thought the worst was simple misery;
"I thought some Fate with pleasure or with strife
"Portion'd us—happy days, or else to die;

XXXVIII 7-8 Go shed a tear upon my hether bloom
And I shall turn a diamond in my tomb.
MS. Fragment and Holograph.
XL 3 Though I forget what Pleasure was a kiss...
MS. Fragment.
Though I forget the heaven of a Kiss... *Holograph.*

"But there is crime—a brother's bloody knife!
　"Sweet Spirit, thou hast school'd my infancy:
"I'll visit thee for this, and kiss thine eyes,
"And greet thee morn and even in the skies."

XLIII.

When the full morning came, she had devised
　How she might secret to the forest hie;
How she might find the clay, so dearly prized,
　And sing to it one latest lullaby;
How her short absence might be unsurmised,
　While she the inmost of the dream would try.
Resolv'd, she took with her an aged nurse,
And went into that dismal forest-hearse.

XLIV.

See, as they creep along the river side,
　How she doth whisper to that aged Dame,
And, after looking round the champaign wide,
　Shows her a knife.—"What feverous hectic flame
"Burns in thee, child?—What good can thee betide,
　"That thou should'st smile again?"—The evening
　　came,
And they had found Lorenzo's earthy bed;
The flint was there, the berries at his head.

XLV.

Who hath not loiter'd in a green church-yard,
　And let his spirit, like a demon-mole,
Work through the clayey soil and gravel hard,
　To see scull, coffin'd bones, and funeral stole;
Pitying each form that hungry Death hath marr'd,
　And filling it once more with human soul?
Ah! this is holiday to what was felt
When Isabella by Lorenzo knelt.

XLVI.

She gaz'd into the fresh-thrown mould, as though
　One glance did fully all its secrets tell;
Clearly she saw, as other eyes would know
　Pale limbs at bottom of a crystal well;
Upon the murderous spot she seem'd to grow,
　Like to a native lilly of the dell:
Then with her knife, all sudden, she began
To dig more fervently than misers can.

XLVII.

Soon she turn'd up a soiled glove, whereon
　Her silk had play'd in purple phantasies,
She kiss'd it with a lip more chill than stone,
　And put it in her bosom, where it dries
And freezes utterly unto the bone
　Those dainties made to still an infant's cries:
Then 'gan she work again; nor stay'd her care,
But to throw back at times her veiling hair.

XLVIII.

That old nurse stood beside her wondering,
　Until her heart felt pity to the core
At sight of such a dismal labouring,
　And so she kneeled, with her locks all hoar,
And put her lean hands to the horrid thing:
　Three hours they labour'd at this travail sore;
At last they felt the kernel of the grave,
And Isabella did not stamp and rave.

XLIX.

Ah! wherefore all this wormy circumstance?
　Why linger at the yawning tomb so long?
O for the gentleness of old Romance,
　The simple plaining of a minstrel's song!
Fair reader, at the old tale take a glance,
　For here, in truth, it doth not well belong
To speak:—O turn thee to the very tale,
And taste the music of that vision pale.

L.

With duller steel than the Perséan sword
　They cut away no formless monster's head,
But one, whose gentleness did well accord
　With death, as life. The ancient harps have said,
Love never dies, but lives, immortal Lord:
　If Love impersonate was ever dead,
Pale Isabella kiss'd it, and low moan'd.
'Twas love; cold,—dead indeed, but not dethroned.

L 1-3 With duller sliver than the Persean sword
　　　They cut away—no foul Medusa's head
　　　But one's... *Holograph*.
　6 If ever any piece of Love was dead... *Holograph*.

LI.

In anxious secrecy they took it home,
　　And then the prize was all for Isabel:
She calm'd its wild hair with a golden comb,
　　And all around each eye's sepulchral cell
Pointed each fringed lash; the smeared loam
　　With tears, as chilly as a dripping well,
She drench'd away:—and still she comb'd, and kept
Sighing all day—and still she kiss'd, and wept.

LII.

Then in a silken scarf,—sweet with the dews
　　Of precious flowers pluck'd in Araby,
And divine liquids come with odorous ooze
　　Through the cold serpent-pipe refreshfully,—
She wrapp'd it up; and for its tomb did choose
　　A garden-pot, wherein she laid it by,
And cover'd it with mould, and o'er it set
Sweet Basil, which her tears kept ever wet.

LIII.

And she forgot the stars, the moon, and sun,
　　And she forgot the blue above the trees,
And she forgot the dells where waters run,
　　And she forgot the chilly autumn breeze;
She had no knowledge when the day was done,
　　And the new morn she saw not: but in peace
Hung over her sweet Basil evermore,
And moisten'd it with tears unto the core.

LIV.

And so she ever fed it with thin tears,
　　Whence thick, and green, and beautiful it grew,
So that it smelt more balmy than its peers
　　Of Basil-tufts in Florence; for it drew
Nurture besides, and life, from human fears,
　　From the fast mouldering head there shut from
　　　view:
So that the jewel, safely casketed,
Came forth, and in perfumed leafits spread.

LI 5 fringed] single *Holograph.*

LV.

O Melancholy, linger here awhile!
  O Music, Music, breathe despondingly!
O Echo, Echo, from some sombre isle,
  Unknown, Lethean, sigh to us—O sigh!
Spirits in grief, lift up your heads, and smile;
  Lift up your heads, sweet Spirits, heavily,
And make a pale light in your cypress glooms,
Tinting with silver wan your marble tombs.

LVI.

Moan hither, all ye syllables of woe,
  From the deep throat of sad Melpomene!
Through bronzed lyre in tragic order go,
  And touch the strings into a mystery;
Sound mournfully upon the winds and low;
  For simple Isabel is soon to be
Among the dead: She withers, like a palm
Cut by an Indian for its juicy balm.

LVII.

O leave the palm to wither by itself;
  Let not quick Winter chill its dying hour!—
It may not be—those Baälites of pelf,
  Her brethren, noted the continual shower
From her dead eyes; and many a curious elf,
  Among her kindred, wonder'd that such dower
Of youth and beauty should be thrown aside
By one mark'd out to be a Noble's bride.

LVIII.

And, furthermore, her brethren wonder'd much
  Why she sat drooping by the Basil green,
And why it flourish'd, as by magic touch;
  Greatly they wonder'd what the thing might mean:
They could not surely give belief, that such
  A very nothing would have power to wean
Her from her own fair youth, and pleasures gay,
And even remembrance of her love's delay.

LVII 5 From] Of *Holograph.*

LIX.

Therefore they watch'd a time when they might sift
    This hidden whim; and long they watch'd in vain;
For seldom did she go to chapel-shrift,
    And seldom felt she any hunger-pain;
And when she left, she hurried back, as swift
    As bird on wing to breast its eggs again;
And, patient as a hen-bird, sat her there
Beside her Basil, weeping through her hair.

LX.

Yet they contriv'd to steal the Basil-pot,
    And to examine it in secret place;
The thing was vile with green and livid spot,
    And yet they knew it was Lorenzo's face:
The guerdon of their murder they had got,
    And so left Florence in a moment's space,
Never to turn again.—Away they went,
With blood upon their heads, to banishment.

LXI.

O Melancholy, turn thine eyes away!
    O Music, Music, breathe despondingly!
O Echo, Echo, on some other day,
    From isles Lethean, sigh to us—O sigh!
Spirits of grief, sing not your "Well-a-way!"
    For Isabel, sweet Isabel, will die;
Will die a death too lone and incomplete,
Now they have ta'en away her Basil sweet.

LXII.

Piteous she look'd on dead and senseless things,
    Asking for her lost Basil amorously;
And with melodious chuckle in the strings
    Of her lorn voice, she oftentimes would cry
After the Pilgrim in his wanderings,
    To ask him where her Basil was; and why
'Twas hid from her: "For cruel 'tis," said she,
"To steal my Basil-pot away from me."

LX 6–7 *The punctuation of the holograph brings out a shade of difference in the sense, thus—*
> And so left Florence in a moment's space—
> Never to turn again away they went...

LXIII.

And so she pined, and so she died forlorn,
   Imploring for her Basil to the last.
No heart was there in Florence but did mourn
   In pity of her love, so overcast.
And a sad ditty of this story born
   From mouth to mouth through all the country pass'd:
Still is the burthen sung—"O cruelty,
"To steal my Basil-pot away from me!"

THE EVE OF ST. AGNES

I.

St. Agnes' Eve—Ah, bitter chill it was !
The owl, for all his feathers, was a-cold ;
The hare limp'd trembling through the frozen grass,
And silent was the flock in woolly fold :
Numb were the Beadsman's fingers, while he told
His rosary, and while his frosted breath,
Like pious incense from a censer old,
Seem'd taking flight for heaven, without a death,
Past the sweet Virgin's picture, while his prayer he
   saith.

II.

His prayer he saith, this patient, holy man ;
Then takes his lamp, and riseth from his knees,
And back returneth, meagre, barefoot, wan,
Along the chapel aisle by slow degrees :
The sculptur'd dead, on each side, seem to freeze,
Emprison'd in black, purgatorial rails :
Knights, ladies, praying in dumb orat'ries,
He passeth by ; and his weak spirit fails
To think how they may ache in icy hoods and mails.

III.

Northward he turneth through a little door,
And scarce three steps, ere Music's golden tongue
Flatter'd to tears this aged man and poor ;
But no—already had his deathbell rung :
The joys of all his life were said and sung :
His was harsh penance on St. Agnes' Eve :
Another way he went, and soon among
Rough ashes sat he for his soul's reprieve,
And all night kept awake, for sinners' sake to grieve.

III 7, 8 went ... Rough] turn'd ... Black *Woodhouse transcript.*

IV.

That ancient Beadsman heard the prelude soft;
And so it chanc'd, for many a door was wide,
From hurry to and fro. Soon, up aloft,
The silver, snarling trumpets 'gan to chide:
The level chambers, ready with their pride,
Were glowing to receive a thousand guests:
The carved angels, ever eager-eyed,
Star'd, where upon their heads the cornice rests,
With hair blown back, and wings put cross-wise on
    their breasts.

v.

At length burst in the argent revelry,
With plume, tiara, and all rich array,
Numerous as shadows haunting faerily
The brain, new stuff'd, in youth, with triumphs gay
Of old romance. These let us wish away,
And turn, sole-thoughted, to one Lady there,
Whose heart had brooded, all that wintry day,
On love, and wing'd St. Agnes' saintly care,
As she had heard old dames full many times declare.

IV *After Stanza III the Woodhouse **transcript** has the following
stanza, suppressed in the poem as printed*—

> But there are ears may hear sweet melodies,
> And there are eyes to brighten festivals,
> And there are feet for nimble minstrelsies,
> And many a lip that for the red wine calls.—
> Follow, then follow to the illumined halls,
> Follow me youth—and leave the eremite—
> Give him a tear—then trophied banneral[s]
> And many a brilliant tasseling of light
> Shall droop from arched ways this high baronial night.

In what is now Stanza IV, Woodhouse *has* and now aloft *for* Soon,
up aloft, *in line* 3, *and* Seem'd anxious *for* Were glowing *in line*
6. *G. Keats's transcript reads* High-lamped *for* The level *in line* 5.

    V 1 At length step in the urgent revelers *Woodhouse.*
      2 With tiard [*error for* tiara] and plume and rich array
        G. Keats.
  3–6   Ah what are they? the idle pulse scarce stirs,
         The muse should never make the spirit gay ;
         Away, bright dulness, laughing fools away,—
         And let me tell of one sweet lady there... *Woodhouse.*

VI.

They told her how, upon St. Agnes' Eve,
  Young virgins might have visions of delight,
And soft adorings from their loves receive
  Upon the honey'd middle of the night,
  If ceremonies due they did aright;
As, supperless to bed they must retire,
  And couch supine their beauties, lilly white;
Nor look behind, nor sideways, but require
Of Heaven with upward eyes for all that they desire.

VII.

Full of this whim was thoughtful Madeline:
  The music, yearning like a God in pain,
She scarcely heard: her maiden eyes divine,
  Fix'd on the floor, saw many a sweeping train
  Pass by—she heeded not at all: in vain
Came many a tiptoe, amorous cavalier,
  And back retir'd; not cool'd by high disdain,
But she saw not: her heart was otherwhere:
She sigh'd for Agnes' dreams, the sweetest of the
    year.

  VI *Between Stanzas VI and VII G. Keats has the following stanza,
not in the printed text—*

    'Twas said her future lord would there appear
    Offering as sacrifice—all in the dream—
    Delicious food even to her lips brought near:
    Viands and wine and fruit and sugar'd cream,
    To touch her palate with the fine extreme
    Of relish: then soft music heard; and then
    More pleasures followed in a dizzy stream
    Palpable almost: then to wake again
    Warm in the virgin morn, no weeping Magdalen.

  VII *In a letter to Taylor dated the 11th of June 1820 Keats says he
has been reading the proofs, and has found* "*what appears*" *to be an
alteration here, namely—*

                    her maiden eyes incline
    Still on the floor, while many a sweeping train
    Pass by.

"My meaning," *says the poet,* "is quite destroyed by the
alteration. I do not use ʻtrainʼ for ʻconcourse of passers by,ʼ
but for ʻskirtsʼ sweeping along the floor."

VIII.

She danc'd along with vague, regardless eyes,
Anxious her lips, her breathing quick and short :
The hallow'd hour was near at hand : she sighs
Amid the timbrels, and the throng'd resort
Of whisperers in anger, or in sport ;
'Mid looks of love, defiance, hate, and scorn,
Hoodwink'd with faery fancy ; all amort,
Save to St. Agnes and her lambs unshorn,
And all the bliss to be before to-morrow morn.

IX.

So, purposing each moment to retire,
She linger'd still. Meantime, across the moors,
Had come young Porphyro, with heart on fire
For Madeline. Beside the portal doors,
Buttress'd from moonlight, stands he, and implores
All saints to give him sight of Madeline,
But for one moment in the tedious hours,
That he might gaze and worship all unseen ;
Perchance speak, kneel, touch, kiss—in sooth such
        things have been.

X.

He ventures in : let no buzz'd whisper tell :
All eyes be muffled, or a hundred swords
Will storm his heart, Love's fev'rous citadel :
For him, those chambers held barbarian hordes,

VIII *The holograph shows the following variation—*
        She danc'd along with vague uneager eyes
            Her anxious mouth full pulp'd with rosy thought
        The hour was near at hand—and she sighs...
*but the reading of the text is substituted in the case of lines 2 and 3. In
line 7 the reading* She was hoodwink'd with fancy *is superseded by
that of the text. G. Keats's transcript has* uneager *in line* 1, *and in*
sport *in line* 5, *and* a la mort *in line* 7.

IX 3 Porphyro] Lionel *Holograph.*
        4–5   Most piteous he implores
                All saints, *Holograph, cancelled.*

X *The opening line was first written in the holograph thus—*
        He ventures in wrapped in a dark disguise...
and then we get the reading,
            He ventures in cloak'd up in dark disguise
            Let no Man see him—or a hundred swords
            Will storm his heart for all his amorous sighs.

Hyena foemen, and hot-blooded lords,
Whose very dogs would execrations howl
Against his lineage : not one breast affords
Him any mercy, in that mansion foul,
Save one old beldame, weak in body and in soul.

XI.

Ah, happy chance ! the aged creature came,
Shuffling along with ivory-headed wand,
To where he stood, hid from the torch's flame,
Behind a broad hall-pillar, far beyond
The sound of merriment and chorus bland :
He startled her ; but soon she knew his face,
And grasp'd his fingers in her palsied hand,
Saying, " Mercy, Porphyro ! hie thee from this place :
"They are all here to-night, the whole blood-thirsty race !

XII.

" Get hence ! get hence ! there 's dwarfish Hildebrand ;
" He had a fever late, and in the fit
" He cursed thee and thine, both house and land :
" Then there 's that old Lord Maurice, not a whit
" More tame for his gray hairs—Alas me ! flit !
" Flit like a ghost away."—" Ah, Gossip dear,
" We're safe enough ; here in this arm-chair sit,
" And tell me how "—" Good Saints ! not here, not
    here ;
"Follow me, child, or else these stones will be thy
    bier."

Next we have
      In ventures he—let no damn'd whisper tell...
then the reading of the text, except the word buzz'd (*for* damn'd) *which
is not in the manuscript.*
    XI 2 Tottering along with ivory headed staff.
                                                Holograph, cancelled.
      8 Mercy, Porphyro !] Mercy Jesu ! *Holograph and G. Keats.*
    XII 1 Hildebrand] Ferdinand *Holograph, cancelled.*
      4–5   There's old Francesco Mendez not a wit [sic]
            Tamer for all his palsy...
            Then there's old Lord Maurice Lacey not a wit
            More tame for his gray hairs... *Holograph, cancelled.*
            Then there is old Lord Maurice... *Woodhouse.*
      8 Good Saints !] Good God ! *Holograph, cancelled.*

XIII.

He follow'd through a lowly arched way,
Brushing the cobwebs with his lofty plume.
And as she mutter'd "Well-a—well-a-day!"
He found him in a little moonlight room,
Pale, lattic'd, chill, and silent as a tomb.
"Now tell me where is Madeline," said he,
"O tell me, Angela, by the holy loom
"Which none but secret sisterhood may see,
"When they St. Agnes' wool are weaving piously."

XIV.

"St. Agnes! Ah! it is St. Agnes' Eve—
"Yet men will murder upon holy days:
"Thou must hold water in a witch's sieve,
"And be liege-lord of all the Elves and Fays,
"To venture so: it fills me with amaze
"To see thee, Porphyro!—St. Agnes' Eve!
"God's help! my lady fair the conjuror plays
"This very night: good angels her deceive!
"But let me laugh awhile, I've mickle time to grieve"

XV.

Feebly she laugheth in the languid moon,
While Porphyro upon her face doth look,
Like puzzled urchin on an aged crone
Who keepeth clos'd a wond'rous riddle-book,
As spectacled she sits in chimney nook.
But soon his eyes grew brilliant, when she told
His lady's purpose; and he scarce could brook
Tears, at the thought of those enchantments cold,
And Madeline asleep in lap of legends old.

XIV 2 holy days] holidays, *Holograph.*
    5-6   in truth it doth amaze
        Young Signor Porphyro. *Holograph, cancelled.*
                        about these thorny Ways
            At[t]empting Be'lzebub. *G. Keats.*
        To see thee Lionel *Woodhouse.*
XV 2 Porphyro] Lionel *Woodhouse.*

XVI.

Sudden a thought came like a full-blown rose,
Flushing his brow, and in his pained heart
Made purple riot: then doth he propose
A stratagem, that makes the beldame start:
"A cruel man and impious thou art:
"Sweet lady, let her pray, and sleep, and dream
"Alone with her good angels, far apart
"From wicked men like thee. Go, go!—I deem
"Thou canst not surely be the same that thou didst
    seem."

XVII.

"I will not harm her, by all saints I swear,"
Quoth Porphyro: "O may I ne'er find grace
"When my weak voice shall whisper its last prayer,
"If one of her soft ringlets I displace,
"Or look with ruffian passion in her face: .
"Good Angela, believe me by these tears;
"Or I will, even in a moment's space,
"Awake, with horrid shout, my foemen's ears,
"And beard them, though they be more fang'd than
    wolves and bears."

XVI 1-3 Sudden a thought more rosy than the rose
            Flush'd his young Cheek, and in his painfle head
            Made riot fierce—and then doth he propose...
         Sudden a rosy thought
            Heated his Brow and in his painfle head
            Made purple riot: then doth he propose... *Holograph.*
    8-9   by Christ I deem
            Thou canst not be the youth...
                                O Christ I deem
            Thou canst not surely be the same as thou didst
                seem—*Holograph.*
         9 seem "] *turned commas wanting* 1820.
XVII 1-4 'I will not harm her, by the great St. Paul;
            Swear'th Porphyro,—O may I ne'er find grace
            When my weak voice shall unto heaven call
            If one of her soft ringlets I misplace...
                                        Holograph.
         Swears Lionel *Woodhouse.*

XVIII.

"Ah! why wilt thou affright a feeble soul?
"A poor, weak, palsy-stricken, churchyard thing,
"Whose passing-bell may ere the midnight toll;
"Whose prayers for thee, each morn and evening,
"Were never miss'd."—Thus plaining, doth she bring
A gentler speech from burning Porphyro;
So woful, and of such deep sorrowing,
That Angela gives promise she will do
Whatever he shall wish, betide her weal or woe.

XIX.

Which was, to lead him, in close secrecy,
Even to Madeline's chamber, and there hide
Him in a closet, of such privacy
That he might see her beauty unespied,
And win perhaps that night a peerless bride,
While legion'd faeries pac'd the coverlet,
And pale enchantment held her sleepy-eyed.
Never on such a night have lovers met,
Since Merlin paid his Demon all the monstrous debt.

XX.

"It shall be as thou wishest," said the Dame:
"All cates and dainties shall be stored there
"Quickly on this feast-night: by the tambour frame
"Her own lute thou wilt see: no time to spare,
"For I am slow and feeble, and scarce dare
"On such a catering trust my dizzy head.
"Wait here, my child, with patience; kneel in prayer
"The while: Ah! thou must needs the lady wed,
"Or may I never leave my grave among the dead."

XXI.

So saying, she hobbled off with busy fear.
The lover's endless minutes slowly pass'd;

XVIII 1 How canst thou terrify *G. Keats.*
       8 That the old Beldam promises to do *Holograph.*
XIX 9 his Demon] the Demons *Holograph.*
XXI 1-2 So saying she hobbled out busily
       And we will pass the Lover's endless hour;...
       The Lover's endless minutes, quickly pass'd;
                 Holograph, rejected.

The dame return'd, and whisper'd in his ear
To follow her ; with aged eyes aghast
From fright of dim espial. Safe at last,
Through many a dusky gallery, they gain
The maiden's chamber, silken, hush'd, and chaste;
Where Porphyro took covert, pleas'd amain.
His poor guide hurried back with agues in her brain.

XXII.

Her falt'ring hand upon the balustrade,
Old Angela was feeling for the stair,
When Madeline, St. Agnes' charmed maid,
Rose, like a mission'd spirit, unaware :
With silver taper's light, and pious care,
She turn'd, and down the aged gossip led
To a safe level matting. Now prepare,

XXI 6   Through loneliest passages and they gain'd,...
       Through lonely oaken Galleries they reach...
                        Holograph, rejected.

   7–9   The maiden's chamber, silken hush'd & chaste
        There he in panting covert will remain
       From Purgatory sweet to view what he may attain.
                  Keats in Woodhouse transcript.

       There in a panting covert to remain...

       Where he in panting covert must remain,

       Upon the frontier...
       Love, purgatory sweet...
       From purgatory sweet to view love's own domain.
       In purgatory sweet to what may he attain. *Holograph.*

XXII 1–6   There secreted...
       Scarce had old Angela the Staircase found
       Ere Madeline, like an affrighted Bird
       Flew past her...
       Scarcely had...

       Rose like a spirit to her unaware
       And with her taper's light and gentle care
       She turn'd and led the aged gossip down...
                  Holograph, cancelled.

       Rose, like a spirit to her, unaware :
       With silver taper light, and pious care, *G. Keats.*

Young Porphyro, for gazing on that bed ;
She comes, she comes again, like ring-dove fray'd
    and fled.

XXIII.

Out went the taper as she hurried in ;
Its little smoke, in pallid moonshine, died :
She clos'd the door, she panted, all akin
To spirits of the air, and visions wide :
No uttered syllable, or, woe betide !
But to her heart, her heart was voluble,
Paining with eloquence her balmy side ;
As though a tongueless nightingale should swell
Her throat in vain, and die, heart-stifled, in her dell.

XXIV.

A casement high and triple-arch'd there was,
All garlanded with carven imag'ries
Of fruits, and flowers, and bunches of knot-grass,
And diamonded with panes of quaint device,
Innumerable of stains and splendid dyes,
As are the tiger-moth's deep-damask'd wings ;
And in the midst, 'mong thousand heraldries,
And twilight saints, and dim emblazonings,
A shielded scutcheon blush'd with blood of queens
    and kings.

XXV.

Full on this casement shone the wintry moon,
And threw warm gules on Madeline's fair breast,
As down she knelt for heaven's grace and boon ;

XXII 8 Porphyro] Lionel *Holograph and Woodhouse.*
      Young Porphyro ; a gazing on that Bed. *G. Keats.*

XXIV 1-7 A Casement tripple arch'd and diamonded
        With many coloured glass fronted the Moon
          In midst w[h]ereof a shi[e]lded scutcheon shed
          High blushing gules ; she kneeled saintly down
          And inly prayed for grace and heavenly boon ;
        The blood red gules fell on her silver cross
        And her white hands devout.
    6-8 As is the wing of evening tiger moths
        And in the midst 'mong many heraldries
        And dim twilight... *Holograph, cancelled.*

Rose-bloom fell on her hands, together prest,
And on her silver cross soft amethyst,
And on her hair a glory, like a saint:
She seem'd a splendid angel, newly drest,
Save wings, for heaven:—Porphyro grew faint:
She knelt, so pure a thing, so free from mortal taint.

XXVI.

Anon his heart revives : her vespers done,
Of all its wreathed pearls her hair she frees ;
Unclasps her warmed jewels one by one ;
Loosens her fragrant boddice ; by degrees
Her rich attire creeps rustling to her knees :
Half-hidden, like a mermaid in sea-weed,
Pensive awhile she dreams awake, and sees,
In fancy, fair St. Agnes in her bed,
But dares not look behind, or all the charm is fled.

XXV 4 Tinging her pious hands together prest,...
       Tinging with red her hands together prest,...
       And rose bloom on her hands together prest....
                              Holograph, cancelled.
     8 Porphyro] Lionel *Holograph.*
XXVI   But soon his heart revives—her prayers said
          She lays aside her veil
          She strips her hair of all its wreathed pearl
       Unclasps her bosom jewels...
          And twists it in one knot upon her head...

       But soon his heart revives—her praying done
          Of all its wreathed pearl she strips her hair
       Unclasps her warmed jewels one by one
          Loosens the boddice from her...

          Loosens her bursting boddice...
          Loosens her Boddice lace-strings...
          Loosens her Boddice, and her bosom bare...
          Loosens her fragrant boddice and doth bare
       Her...
       But soon his heart revives—her praying done
          Of all its wreathed pearls her hair she strips
       Unclasps her warmed jewels one by one
          Loosens her fragrant boddice ; and down slips
       Her sweet attire...
                         to her knees
       Her sweet attire falls light.
       Half hidden like a Syren of the sea
       And more melodious...*Holograph, cancelled.*
     7 She stands awhile in dreamy thought and sees...
                              Holograph.

XXVII.

Soon, trembling in her soft and chilly nest,
In sort of wakeful swoon, perplex'd she lay,
Until the poppied warmth of sleep oppress'd
Her soothed limbs, and soul fatigued away ;
Flown, like a thought, until the morrow-day ;
Blissfully haven'd both from joy and pain ;
Clasp'd like a missal where swart Paynims pray ;
Blinded alike from sunshine and from rain,
As though a rose should shut, and be a bud again.

XXVIII.

Stol'n to this paradise, and so entranced,
Porphyro gazed upon her empty dress,
And listen'd to her breathing, if it chanced
To wake into a slumberous tenderness ;
Which when he heard, that minute did he bless,
And breath'd himself : then from the closet crept,
Noiseless as fear in a wide wilderness,
And over the hush'd carpet, silent, stept,
And 'tween the curtains peep'd, where, lo !—how fast
she slept.

XXIX.

Then by the bed-side, where the faded moon
Made a dim, silver twilight, soft he set
A table, and, half anguish'd, threw thereon

XXVII 1-2 Then stepping forth she slips
The charm fled not—she did not look behind...
She lay and had not seen her...
She lay and till the poppied warmth of sleep...
She lay in sort of wakeful swoon perplext...
Holograph, rejected.
  4-5 Her soothed limbs, and soul fatigued, away
Flown like a thought until the morrow's day,
Woodhouse.
XXVIII 1-5 The listening Porphyro her breathing heard...
The entranced Porphyro stol'n to Paradise...
Which when he heard he breath'd himself...
Holograph, cancelled.
  XXIX 1-3 Then by the bed side where the fading Moon
Made an illumed twilight soft he set
A Table, and with anguish spread thereon... *Holograph.*
A Table light, and stilly threw thereon...
Holograph, cancelled.
A table and with care quick spread thereon... *Woodhouse.*

A cloth of woven crimson, gold, and jet :—
O for some drowsy Morphean amulet !
The boisterous, midnight, festive clarion,
The kettle-drum, and far-heard clarinet,
    Affray his ears, though but in dying tone :—
The hall door shuts again, and all the noise is gone.

XXX.

And still she slept an azure-lidded sleep,
In blanched linen, smooth, and lavender'd,
While he from forth the closet brought a heap
Of candied apple, quince, and plum, and gourd ;
With jellies soother than the creamy curd,
And lucent syrops, tinct with cinnamon ;
Manna and dates, in argosy transferr'd
    From Fez ; and spiced dainties, every one,
From silken Samarcand to cedar'd Lebanon.

XXXI.

These delicates he heap'd with glowing hand
On golden dishes and in baskets bright
Of wreathed silver : sumptuous they stand
In the retired quiet of the night,
    Filling the chilly room with perfume light.—
" And now, my love, my seraph fair, awake !
"Thou art my heaven, and I thine eremite :
    " Open thine eyes, for meek St. Agnes' sake,
"Or I shall drowse beside thee, so my soul doth ache."

XXIX 7   clarinet *Holograph, Woodhouse, and G. Keats :* clarionet
1820.
  XXX 3 While he brought from the cabinet a heap... *G. Keats.*
     7–8   And sugar'd dates from...
               And sugar'd dates that o'er Euphrates fared
               And manna mead and...
               And sugar'd dates and manna mead transferred
               In Brigantine from Fez...
               Manna and dates in Brigantine transferred...
                                           Holograph, rejected.
  XXXI 4   Amid the quiet of St. Agnes' night *Holograph.*
              And now, saith he, my Seraph with perfume light
              Teeming... *Holograph, cancelled.*

XXXII.

Thus whispering, his warm, unnerved arm
Sank in her pillow. Shaded was her dream
By the dusk curtains:—'twas a midnight charm
Impossible to melt as iced stream :
The lustrous salvers in the moonlight gleam ;
Broad golden fringe upon the carpet lies:
It seem'd he never, never could redeem
From such a stedfast spell his lady's eyes ;
So mus'd awhile, entoil'd in woofed phantasies.

XXXIII.

Awakening up, he took her hollow lute,—
Tumultuous,—and, in chords that tenderest be,
He play'd an ancient ditty, long since mute,
In Provence call'd, " La belle dame sans mercy : "
Close to her ear touching the melody ;—
Wherewith disturb'd, she utter'd a soft moan :
He ceased—she panted quick—and suddenly
Her blue affrayed eyes wide open shone :
Upon his knees he sank, pale as smooth-sculptured
  stone.

XXXIV.

Her eyes were open, but she still beheld,
Now wide awake, the vision of her sleep :
There was a painful change, that nigh expell'd
The blisses of her dream so pure and deep
At which fair Madeline began to weep,
And moan forth witless words with many a sigh ;
While still her gaze on Porphyro would keep ;
Who knelt, with joined hands and piteous eye,
Fearing to move or speak, she look'd so dreamingly.

XXXV.

"Ah, Porphyro !" said she, " but even now
"Thy voice was at sweet tremble in mine ear,

XXXIII 7 she panted quick] her breathing ceased
                                        Holograph, rejected.
        8 affrayed] half-frayed *Holograph and Woodhouse.*
XXXIV 7 Porphyro] Lionel *Woodhouse.*
  XXXV 1 She speaks—" Ah Lionel, but even now...*Woodhouse.*

" Made tuneable with every sweetest vow;
" And those sad eyes were spiritual and clear:
" How chang'd thou art! how pallid, chill, and
    drear!
" Give me that voice again, my Porphyro,
" Those looks immortal, those complainings dear!
" Oh leave me not in this eternal woe,
"For if thou diest, my Love, I know not where to go."

XXXVI.

Beyond a mortal man impassion'd far
At these voluptuous accents, he arose,
Ethereal, flush'd, and like a throbbing star
Seen mid the sapphire heaven's deep repose;
Into her dream he melted, as the rose
Blendeth its odour with the violet,—
Solution sweet: meantime the frost-wind blows
Like Love's alarum pattering the sharp sleet
Against the window-panes; St. Agnes' moon hath set.

XXXVII.

'Tis dark: quick pattereth the flaw-blown sleet:
" This is no dream, my bride, my Madeline!"
'Tis dark: the iced gusts still rave and beat:
" No dream, alas! alas! and woe is mine!
" Porphyro will leave me here to fade and pine.—

XXXV 3 And tim'd [*error for* tun'd], devout with every softest
    vow. *G. Keats.*

    8-9 See while she speaks his arms encroaching slow
      Have zon'd her, heart to heart—loud, loud the dark
      winds blow. *G. Keats.*

XXXVI 1 Impassion'd far beyond a mortal man—
                           Holograph, rejected.

    1-7 For on the midnight came a tempest fell.
      More sooth for that his close rejoinder flows
      Into her burning ear;—and still the spell
      Unbroken guards her in serene repose.
      With her wild dream he mingled as a rose
      Marryeth its odour to a violet.
      Still, still she dreams—louder the frost wind blows...
                            G. Keats.

    9 Against the windows dark. St. Agnes moon had set.
                             Holograph.

XXXVII 5 Porphyro] Lionel *Woodhouse.*

"Cruel! what traitor could thee hither bring?
"I curse not, for my heart is lost in thine,
"Though thou forsakest a deceived thing;—
"A dove forlorn and lost with sick unpruned wing."

XXXVIII.

"My Madeline! sweet dreamer! lovely bride!
"Say, may I be for aye thy vassal blest?
"Thy beauty's shield, heart-shap'd and vermeil dyed?
"Ah, silver shrine, here will I take my rest
"After so many hours of toil and quest,
"A famish'd pilgrim,—sav'd by miracle.
"Though I have found, I will not rob thy nest
"Saving of thy sweet self; if thou think'st well
"To trust, fair Madeline, to no rude infidel.

XXXIX.

"Hark! 'tis an elfin-storm from faery land,
"Of haggard seeming, but a boon indeed:
"Arise—arise! the morning is at hand;—
"The bloated wassaillers will never heed:—
"Let us away, my love, with happy speed;
"There are no ears to hear, or eyes to see,—
"Drown'd all in Rhenish and the sleepy mead:
"Awake! arise! my love, and fearless be,
"For o'er the southern moors I have a home for thee."

XXXVIII 6 With features pale and mournful Pilgrim's weeds
              Holograph, cancelled.
           Pale featured and in weeds of Pilgrimage—
              Holograph.
       7 I have found, but will not rob thy downy nest!
              Holograph, rejected.
     7-9 Though I have found but cannot rob thy nest!
           Soft Nightingale, I'll keep thee in a cage
           To sing to me—but hark! the blinded tempest's
           rage! *Holograph.*
Inverted commas wrongly closed at end of stanza, Woodhouse and 1820.
XXXIX 7 sleepy mead *1820:* drench of mead *and* drenching
           mead *Holograph, cancelled.*
     8-9 Put on warm cloathing, sweet, and fearless be
           Over the dartmoor bl[e]ak I have a home for thee.
              Holograph.
       9 Over the bleak Dartmoor *Holograph, cancelled.*

XL.

She hurried at his words, beset with fears,
For there were sleeping dragons all around,
At glaring watch, perhaps, with ready spears—
Down the wide stairs a darkling way they found.—
In all the house was heard no human sound.
A chain-droop'd lamp was flickering by each door :
The arras, rich with horseman, hawk, and hound,
Flutter'd in the besieging wind's uproar ;
And the long carpets rose along the gusty floor.

XLI.

They glide, like phantoms, into the wide hall ;
Like phantoms, to the iron porch, they glide ;
Where lay the Porter, in uneasy sprawl,
With a huge empty flaggon by his side :
The wakeful bloodhound rose, and shook his hide,
But his sagacious eye an inmate owns :
By one, and one, the bolts full easy slide :—
The chains lie silent on the footworn stones ;—
The key turns, and the door upon its hinges groans.

XL 3 Or perhaps at glaring watch with ready spears—
Holograph, cancelled.

6–8 But noise of winds besieging the high towers...
But the besieging Storm...
The Lamps were flickering death shades on the walls
Without, the Tempest kept a hollow roar...
The Lamps were flickering...
The Lamps were dying in...
But here and there a Lamp was flickering out...
A drooping Lamp was flickering here and there.
Holograph, rejected.

XLI 1, 2 Like Spirits into the wide-paven hall
They glide,—and to the iron porch in haste ;
Holograph, rejected.

4 a large empty beaker *Woodhouse.*
6 And paced round Madeline all angerless,...
But with a calmed eye his mistress owns,
Holograph, rejected.

But quick his calmed eye its mistress owns... *Woodhouse.*
8 The chain lay silent on the footway stones *Woodhouse.*

XLII.

And they are gone: aye, ages long ago
These lovers fled away into the storm.
That night the Baron dreamt of many a woe,
And all his warrior-guests, with shade and form
Of witch, and demon, and large coffin-worm,
Were long be-nightmar'd. Angela the old
Died palsy-twitch'd, with meagre face deform ;
The Beadsman, after thousand aves told,
For aye unsought for slept among his ashes cold.

XLII 6-9   Angela went off
          Twitch'd with the Palsy ; and with face deform
          The beadsman stiffen'd, twixt a sigh and laugh
          Ta'en sudden from his beads by one weak little
          cough. *G. Keats.*

POEMS

ODE TO A NIGHTINGALE

I.

My heart aches, and a drowsy numbness pains
  My sense, as though of hemlock I had drunk,
Or emptied some dull opiate to the drains
  One minute past, and Lethe-wards had sunk:
'Tis not through envy of thy happy lot,
  But being too happy in thine happiness,—
    That thou, light-winged Dryad of the trees,
      In some melodious plot
  Of beechen green, and shadows numberless,
    Singest of summer in full-throated ease.

II.

O, for a draught of vintage! that hath been
  Cool'd a long age in the deep-delved earth,
Tasting of Flora and the country green,
  Dance, and Provençal song, and sunburnt mirth!
O for a beaker full of the warm South,
  Full of the true, the blushful Hippocrene,
    With beaded bubbles winking at the brim,
      And purple-stained mouth;
  That I might drink, and leave the world unseen,
    And with thee fade away into the forest dim:

Title] the *for* a *Draft, Transcripts, and Annals.*
I 1 Small winged Dryad *Draft, rejected opening:* painful
    numbness falls *Draft, rejected.*
  4 past] hence *Draft, cancelled.*
II 2 Cooling an age *Draft, rejected.*
  6 true, the] true and *Draft, Dilke, Museum, and Annals:*
    blissful *for* blushful *Museum.*
  7 beaded] cluster'd *Draft.*
  10 fade away *Draft and 1820;* away *omitted by Woodhouse, Dilke,*
    Museum, and Annals.

III.

Fade far away, dissolve, and quite forget
  What thou among the leaves hast never known,
The weariness, the fever, and the fret
  Here, where men sit and hear each other groan ;
Where palsy shakes a few, sad, last gray hairs,
  Where youth grows pale, and spectre-thin, and dies ;
    Where but to think is to be full of sorrow
      And leaden-eyed despairs,
  Where Beauty cannot keep her lustrous eyes,
    Or new Love pine at them beyond to-morrow.

IV.

Away ! away ! for I will fly to thee,
  Not charioted by Bacchus and his pards,
But on the viewless wings of Poesy,
  Though the dull brain perplexes and retards :
Already with thee ! tender is the night,
  And haply the Queen-Moon is on her throne,
    Cluster'd around by all her starry Fays ;
      But here there is no light,
Save what from heaven is with the breezes blown
  Through verdurous glooms and winding mossy
    ways.

V.

I cannot see what flowers are at my feet,
  Nor what soft incense hangs upon the boughs,
But, in embalmed darkness, guess each sweet
  Wherewith the seasonable month endows
The grass, the thicket, and the fruit-tree wild ;
  White hawthorn, and the pastoral eglantine ;
    Fast fading violets cover'd up in leaves ;
      And mid-May's eldest child,
The coming musk-rose, full of dewy wine,
  The murmurous haunt of flies on summer eves.

III 6 Where youth grows pale and thin and old and dies
    Draft, but the variation rejected.
  7 sorrow] grief *Draft, cancelled.*
IV 1 to] with *Draft, cancelled.*
  7 Cluster'd] Clusted *Draft, rejected, but nothing substituted.*
  10 Sidelong *stands cancelled in Draft before* Through.
V 1 See *1820 and Draft :* tell *Woodhouse.*
  2 *In the Draft* blooms *is cancelled after* what.
  9 dewy] sweetest *Draft, Dilke, Museum, and Annals.*

VI.

Darkling I listen ; and, for many a time
    I have been half in love with easeful Death,
Call'd him soft names in many a mused rhyme,
    To take into the air my quiet breath ;
Now more than ever seems it rich to die,
    To cease upon the midnight with no pain,
        While thou art pouring forth thy soul abroad
            In such an ecstasy !
    Still wouldst thou sing, and I have ears in vain—
        To thy high requiem become a sod.

VII.

Thou wast not born for death, immortal Bird !
    No hungry generations tread thee down ;
The voice I hear this passing night was heard
    In ancient days by emperor and clown :
Perhaps the self-same song that found a path
    Through the sad heart of Ruth, when, sick for home,
        She stood in tears amid the alien corn ;
            The same that oft-times hath
    Charm'd magic casements, opening on the foam
        Of perilous seas, in faery lands forlorn.

VIII.

Forlorn ! the very word is like a bell
    To toll me back from thee to my sole self!
Adieu ! the fancy cannot cheat so well
    As she is fam'd to do, deceiving elf.

VI 4 quiet] painless *Draft : there is absolutely no ground for giving
        this as a variant of* easeful *in line 2 as Mr. de Sélincourt does.*
    7 forth] thus *Draft, &c. and Annals.*
    8 ecstasy !] Extacy *Draft.*
    9 wouldst] would *Draft.*
   10 To *Draft and 1820 :* For *Draft, rejected, Transcripts, and
        Annals. The Draft has a cancelled opening,* But requiem'd.
VII 5 song] voice *Draft, cancelled.*
    9 magic] the wide *Draft, cancelled.*
   10 perilous] keelless *Draft, cancelled :* faery *1820,* fairy *Draft,
        Dilke, Museum, and Annals.*
VIII 1 Forlorn ! . . . word] Folorn ! . . . world *Draft.*
     2 me back] to me *Draft rejected :* my sole self! *1820 ;* unto
        myself *Draft and Woodhouse.*
     4 deceiving] deceitful *Draft, rejected.*

Adieu! adieu! thy plaintive anthem fades
  Past the near meadows, over the still stream,
    Up the hill-side; and now 'tis buried deep
      In the next valley-glades:
Was it a vision, or a waking dream?
Fled is that music:—Do I wake or sleep?

ODE ON A GRECIAN URN

I.

THOU still unravish'd bride of quietness,
  Thou foster-child of silence and slow time,
Sylvan historian, who canst thus express
  A flowery tale more sweetly than our rhyme:
What leaf-fring'd legend haunts about thy shape
  Of deities or mortals, or of both,
    In Tempe or the dales of Arcady?
What men or gods are these? What maidens loth?
What mad pursuit? What struggle to escape?
    What pipes and timbrels? What wild ecstasy?

II.

Heard melodies are sweet, but those unheard
  Are sweeter; therefore, ye soft pipes, play on;
Not to the sensual ear, but, more endear'd,
  Pipe to the spirit ditties of no tone:
Fair youth, beneath the trees, thou canst not leave
  Thy song, nor ever can those trees be bare;
    Bold Lover, never, never canst thou kiss,
Though winning near the goal—yet, do not grieve;

VIII 9–10 Was it a vision real or waking dream
   -       Fled is that Music—do I wake or sleep? *Draft.*
           Was it a vision? or a waking dream?
           Fled is that music? do I wake or sleep.
            Dilke, and Museum save that there is a ? at the end.
           Was it a vision? Or a waking dream?
           Fled is that music? Do I wake or sleep? *Annals.*
            The 1820 text (adopted here) is of course right.
Title]   On a Grecian Urn *Annals.*
  I   8 men or gods] Gods or Men *Annals.*
       9 What love? what dance? what struggle to escape?
            Dilke, Museum, and Annals.
II 5, 6 Fair Youth, beneath the trees thou can'st not leave
        Thy song, nor ever bid the spring adieu; *Annals.*
     8 yet,] O *Dilke, Museum, and Annals.*

* I 3

She cannot fade, though thou hast not thy bliss,
  For ever wilt thou love, and she be fair!

III.

Ah, happy, happy boughs! that cannot shed
  Your leaves, nor ever bid the Spring adieu;
And, happy melodist, unwearied,
  For ever piping songs for ever new;
More happy love! more happy, happy love!
  For ever warm and still to be enjoy'd,
    For ever panting, and for ever young;
All breathing human passion far above,
  That leaves a heart high-sorrowful and cloy'd,
    A burning forehead, and a parching tongue.

IV.

Who are these coming to the sacrifice?
  To what green altar, O mysterious priest,
Lead'st thou that heifer lowing at the skies,
  And all her silken flanks with garlands drest?
What little town by river or sea shore,
  Or mountain-built with peaceful citadel,
    Is emptied of this folk, this pious morn?
And, little town, thy streets for evermore
  Will silent be; and not a soul to tell
    Why thou art desolate, can e'er return.

V.

O Attic shape! Fair attitude! with brede
  Of marble men and maidens overwrought,
With forest branches and the trodden weed;
  Thou, silent form, dost tease us out of thought
As doth eternity: Cold Pastoral!
  When old age shall this generation waste,
    Thou shalt remain, in midst of other woe
Than ours, a friend to man, to whom thou say'st,
  "Beauty is truth, truth beauty,"—that is all
    Ye know on earth, and all ye need to know.

III 2 ever] never *Annals.*
IV 4 flanks] sides *Dilke and Museum.*
  7 this] *Dilke, Museum, Annals, and 1820;* its *Smith 1840 and 1841 and Houghton.*
  10 e'er] ne'er *Dilke.*
V 7 shalt] wilt *Dilke, Museum, and Annals.*
  8 a] as *Museum.*

ODE TO PSYCHE

O GODDESS! hear these tuneless numbers, wrung
  By sweet enforcement and remembrance dear,
And pardon that thy secrets should be sung
  Even into thine own soft-conched ear:
Surely I dreamt to-day, or did I see
  The wingèd Psyche with awaken'd eyes?
I wander'd in a forest thoughtlessly,
  And, on the sudden, fainting with surprise,
Saw two fair creatures, couched side by side
  In deepest grass, beneath the whisp'ring roof   10
  Of leaves and trembled blossoms, where there ran
    A brooklet, scarce espied:

'Mid hush'd, cool-rooted flowers, fragrant-eyed,
  Blue, silver-white, and budded Tyrian,
They lay calm-breathing on the bedded grass;
  Their arms embraced, and their pinions too;
  Their lips touch'd not, but had not bade adieu,
As if disjoined by soft-handed slumber,
And ready still past kisses to outnumber
  At tender eye-dawn of aurorean love: 20
      The wingèd boy I knew;
  But who wast thou, O happy, happy dove?
    His Psyche true!

O latest born and loveliest vision far
  Of all Olympus' faded hierarchy!
Fairer than Phœbe's sapphire-region'd star,
  Or Vesper, amorous glow-worm of the sky;

The textual variations in the Ode to Psyche are from two holographs,
one on a separate quarto sheet, the other embodied in a letter.
  6 awaken'd] awaked *Letter.*
  10 roof] fan *Letter.*
  13 'Mid] In *Quarto, rejected.*
  14 Blue, freckle-pink, and budded Syrian, *Letter.*
  20 eye-dawn] dawning *Quarto, rejected.*
  23 true!] true? *Letter.*
  26 Phœbe's] Night's nude, Night's full, *and* Night's orb'd
Quarto, rejected.

Fairer than these, though temple thou hast none,
    Nor altar heap'd with flowers ;
Nor virgin-choir to make delicious moan   30
    Upon the midnight hours ;
No voice, no lute, no pipe, no incense sweet
  From chain-swung censer teeming ;
No shrine, no grove, no oracle, no heat
  Of pale-mouth'd prophet dreaming.

O brightest ! though too late for antique vows,
    Too, too late for the fond believing lyre,
When holy were the haunted forest boughs,
    Holy the air, the water, and the fire ;
Yet even in these days so far retir'd   40
  From happy pieties, thy lucent fans,
    Fluttering among the faint Olympians,
I see, and sing, by my own eyes inspir'd.
So let me be thy choir, and make a moan
    Upon the midnight hours ;
Thy voice, thy lute, thy pipe, thy incense sweet
  From swinged censer teeming ;
Thy shrine, thy grove, thy oracle, thy heat
  Of pale-mouth'd prophet dreaming.

Yes, I will be thy priest, and build a fane   50
    In some untrodden region of my mind,
Where branched thoughts, new grown with pleasant
    pain,
    Instead of pines shall murmur in the wind :
Far, far around shall those dark-cluster'd trees
    Fledge the wild-ridged mountains steep by steep ;
And there by zephyrs, streams, and birds, and bees,
  The moss-lain Dryads shall be lull'd to sleep ;
And in the midst of this wide quietness
A rosy sanctuary will I dress

28 hast] hadst *Letter.*
32 *and* 34 No (8 times)] Nor (8 times) *Quarto, rejected.*
36 brightest !] Bloomiest ! *Letter.*
42 among] above *Quarto, rejected.*
43 own] clear *Quarto, rejected.*
44 So] O *Letter.*
47 From] Thy *Quarto, rejected.*
      Thy altar heap'd with flowers *Margin of Quarto.*
57 lull'd] charm'd *Letter, cancelled.*

With the wreath'd trellis of a working brain,   60
  With buds, and bells, and stars without a name,
With all the gardener Fancy e'er could feign,
  Who breeding flowers, will never breed the same:
And there shall be for thee all soft delight
  That shadowy thought can win,
A bright torch, and a casement ope at night,
  To let the warm Love in!

FANCY

Ever let the fancy roam,
Pleasure never is at home:
At a touch sweet Pleasure melteth,
Like to bubbles when rain pelteth;
Then let winged Fancy wander
Through the thought still spread beyond her:
Open wide the mind's cage-door,
She'll dart forth, and cloudward soar.
O sweet Fancy! let her loose;
Summer's joys are spoilt by use,   10
And the enjoying of the Spring
Fades as does its blossoming;
Autumn's red-lipp'd fruitage too,
Blushing through the mist and dew,
Cloys with tasting: What do then?
Sit thee by the ingle, when
The sear faggot blazes bright,
Spirit of a winter's night;
When the soundless earth is muffled,
And the caked snow is shuffled   20

62 feign] frame *Letter.*
64 So bower'd goddess will I worship thee *Quarto, rejected.*
67 To let warm Love glide in *Quarto, rejected.*
After the closing line Keats wrote playfully in the letter—Here
endethe ye Ode to Psyche.

*The variations noted below are from two manuscripts, the holograph in
a journal-letter sent to George Keats and his wife* (*winter of 1818–19*),
and that in Sir Charles Dilke's " *Endymion.*"
  6 Towards heaven still spread beyond her. *MSS.*
  15 tasting] kissing *MSS.*
  16 by the ingle] in an ingle *MSS.*

From the ploughboy's heavy shoon ;
When the Night doth meet the Noon
In a dark conspiracy
To banish Even from her sky.
Sit thee there, and send abroad,
With a mind self-overaw'd,
Fancy, high-commission'd :—send her !
She has vassals to attend her :
She will bring, in spite of frost,
Beauties that the earth hath lost ;   30
She will bring thee, all together,
All delights of summer weather ;
All the buds and bells of May,
From dewy sward or thorny spray ;
All the heaped Autumn's wealth,
With a still, mysterious stealth :
She will mix these pleasures up
Like three fit wines in a cup,
And thou shalt quaff it :—thou shalt hear
Distant harvest-carols clear ;   40
Rustle of the reaped corn ;
Sweet birds antheming the morn :
And, in the same moment—hark !
'Tis the early April lark,
Or the rooks, with busy caw,
Foraging for sticks and straw.
Thou shalt, at one glance, behold
The daisy and the marigold ;
White-plum'd lillies, and the first
Hedge-grown primrose that hath burst ;   50
Shaded hyacinth, alway
Sapphire queen of the mid-May ;
And every leaf, and every flower
Pearled with the self-same shower.

24 Even] vesper *Holograph.*   28 She has] She'll have *MSS.*
29   She will bring thee spite of frost... *MSS.*
33-4   All the faery buds of May
            On spring turf or scented spray ; *Holograph.*
43-5   And in the same moment hark
            To the early April lark
            And the rooks with busy caw... *MSS.*
50 Hedge-row primrose *MSS.*   54 same soft shower *MSS.*

Thou shalt see the field-mouse peep
Meagre from its celled sleep;
And the snake all winter-thin
Cast on sunny bank its skin;
Freckled nest-eggs thou shalt see
Hatching in the hawthorn-tree,   60
When the hen-bird's wing doth rest
Quiet on her mossy nest;
Then the hurry and alarm
When the bee-hive casts its swarm;
Acorns ripe down-pattering,
While the autumn breezes sing.

    Oh, sweet Fancy! let her loose;
Every thing is spoilt by use:
Where's the cheek that doth not fade,
Too much gaz'd at? Where's the maid   70
Whose lip mature is ever new?
Where's the eye, however blue,
Doth not weary? Where's the face
One would meet in every place?
Where's the voice, however soft,
One would hear so very oft?
At a touch sweet Pleasure melteth
Like to bubbles when rain pelteth.
Let, then, winged Fancy find
·Thee a mistress to thy mind: 80
Dulcet-eyed as Ceres' daughter,
Ere the God of Torment taught her
How to frown and how to chide;
With a waist and with a side

55 peep] creep *Holograph.*
57–8   And the snake all winter-shrank
        Cast its skin on sunny bank... *MSS.*
66 *Additional couplet after this line :*
        For the same sleek-throated mouse
        To store up in its winter house. *MSS.*
67–8 *Instead of this couplet the manuscripts have four lines :*
        O sweet fancy let her loose !
        Every sweet is spoilt by use
        Every pleasure every joy
        Not a mistress but doth cloy...
76 too oft and oft *MSS.*

White as Hebe's, when her zone
Slipt its golden clasp, and down
Fell her kirtle to her feet,
While she held the goblet sweet,
And Jove grew languid.—Break the mesh
Of the Fancy's silken leash;   90
Quickly break her prison-string
And such joys as these she'll bring.—
Let the winged Fancy roam,
Pleasure never is at home.

ODE

[*Written on the blank page before Beaumont and Fletcher's*
Tragi-Comedy " The Fair Maid of the Inn."]

BARDS of Passion and of Mirth,
Ye have left your souls on earth!
Have ye souls in heaven too,
Double lived in regions new?
Yes, and those of heaven commune
With the spheres of sun and moon;
With the noise of fountains wond'rous,
And the parle of voices thund'rous;
With the whisper of heaven's trees
And one another, in soft ease   10

89–91 *Instead of these three lines the manuscripts have the following
seventeen :*

> And Jove grew languid. Mistress fair !
> Thou shalt have that tressed hair
> Adonis tangled all for spite
> And the mouth he would not kiss
> And the treasure he would miss :
> And the hand he would not press
> And the warmth he would distress
> O the ravishment—the bliss—
> Fancy has her—there she is !
> Never fulsome—ever new
> There she steps ! and tell me who
> Has a mistress so divine ?
> Be the palate ne'er so fine
> She cannot sicken. Break the mesh
> Of the Fancy's silken leash
> Where she's tether'd to the heart—
> Quick break her prison string...

4 *Cancelled line in the Beaumont and Fletcher manuscript after line 4—*

> With the earth ones I am talking.

Seated on Elysian lawns
Brows'd by none but Dian's fawns;
Underneath large blue-bells tented,
Where the daisies are rose-scented,
And the rose herself has got
Perfume which on earth is not;
Where the nightingale doth sing
Not a senseless, tranced thing,
But divine melodious truth;
Philosophic numbers smooth;   20
Tales and golden histories
Of heaven and its mysteries.

Thus ye live on high, and then
On the earth ye live again;
And the souls ye left behind you
Teach us, here, the way to find you,
Where your other souls are joying,
Never slumber'd, never cloying.
Here, your earth-born souls still speak
To mortals, of their little week;   30
Of their sorrows and delights;
Of their passions and their spites;
Of their glory and their shame;
What doth strengthen and what maim.
Thus ye teach us, every day,
Wisdom, though fled far away.

Bards of Passion and of Mirth,
Ye have left your souls on earth!
Ye have souls in heaven too,
Double-lived in regions new!   40

19–20   But melodious truth divine
          Philosophic numbers fine,... *Holographs.*
21 Tales] Stories *Holographs, rejected.*
29 souls] loves *Holographs, rejected.*
30–1   To mortals of the little Week
          They must sojourn...
                    Beaumont and Fletcher and Woodhouse.
31 and delights] with their cares *Holograph and Woodhouse.*

LINES ON THE MERMAID TAVERN

SOULS of Poets dead and gone,
What Elysium have ye known,
Happy field or mossy cavern,
Choicer than the Mermaid Tavern?
Have ye tippled drink more fine
Than mine host's Canary wine?
Or are fruits of Paradise
Sweeter than those dainty pies
Of venison? O generous food!
Drest as though bold Robin Hood   10
Would, with his maid Marian,
Sup and bowse from horn and can.

I have heard that on a day
Mine host's sign-board flew away,
Nobody knew whither, till
An astrologer's old quill
To a sheepskin gave the story,
Said he saw you in your glory,
Underneath a new old sign
Sipping beverage divine,   20
And pledging with contented smack
The Mermaid in the Zodiac.

Souls of Poets dead and gone,
What Elysium have ye known,
Happy field or mossy cavern,
Choicer than the Mermaid Tavern?

Title] Ode, 1818 *Museum*
4 Choicer] Fairer *Dilke and Woodhouse.*
8 Sweeter] Richer *Museum.*
9 O generous] delicious *Museum.*
15 *The Museum holograph shows a slip here*—know wither *for*
knew whither.
19 *Instead of* new old-sign, *the reading of the first edition, the
Museum holograph and Woodhouse read* new old sign, *and the Dilke
copy* new-old sign.
23-6 Souls of Poets dead and gone,
        Are the winds a sweeter home,
        Richer is uncellar'd cavern
        Than the Merry Mermaid Tavern? *Dilke and Woodhouse.*

ROBIN HOOD

TO A FRIEND

No! those days are gone away,
And their hours are old and gray,
And their minutes buried all
Under the down-trodden pall
Of the leaves of many years:
Many times have winter's shears,
Frozen North, and chilling East,
Sounded tempests to the feast
Of the forest's whispering fleeces,
Since men knew nor rent nor leases.   10

No, the bugle sounds no more,
And the twanging bow no more;
Silent is the ivory shrill
Past the heath and up the hill;
There is no mid-forest laugh,
Where lone Echo gives the half
To some wight, amaz'd to hear
Jesting, deep in forest drear.

On the fairest time of June
You may go, with sun or moon,   20
Or the seven stars to light you,
Or the polar ray to right you;

Title]   To John Reynolds,
        In answer to his Robin Hood Sonnets—
                        Dilke and Woodhouse.
            To John Reynolds
        In answer to his Sonnets on Robin Hood. *Museum.*
6–7   Many times old Winter's shears
        Frozen North and chilly east,... *Draft, cancelled.*
10 Since Men paid no Rent and Leases. *Draft.*
13 And the whistle shrill is... *Draft, cancelled.*
16 *Cancelled* **reading**, No old hermit with his... *Probably it was
meant to finish the line with* staff.
18   Jests { deep in / within } a forest drear. *Draft.*
        No more barbed arrows fly
        Through one's own roof to the sky... *Draft, cancelled.*
19   { In / On } the fairest { time / day } of June... *Draft.*
21–2 Planets seven *and* polar beam *Draft, rejected.*

But you never may behold
Little John, or Robin bold ;
Never one, of all the clan,
Thrumming on an empty can
Some old hunting ditty, while
He doth his green way beguile
To fair hostess Merriment,
Down beside the pasture Trent ;   30
For he left the merry tale
Messenger for spicy ale.

    Gone, the merry morris din ;
Gone, the song of Gamelyn ;
Gone, the tough-belted outlaw
Idling in the "grenè shawe" ;
All are gone away and past !
And if Robin should be cast
Sudden from his turfed grave,
And if Marian should have   40
Once again her forest days,
She would weep, and he would craze :
He would swear, for all his oaks,
Fall'n beneath the dockyard strokes,
Have rotted on the briny seas ;
She would weep that her wild bees
Sang not to her—strange ! that honey
Can't be got without hard money !

25-7   Never meet one of all the clan
        Rattling on an empty can
        An old hunting ditty... *Draft, rejected.*
        Never any of the clan. *Woodhouse.*
29 hostess] Mistress *Draft.*
33-42 No those times are flown and past.
        What if Robin should be cast
        Sudden from his turfed grave ?
        How would Marian behave
        In the forest now a days ?
        She would weep and he would craze. *Draft, rejected.*
37   All are gone and all is past ! *Draft.*
39 turfed] tufted *Draft.*
44   Fallen beneath the Woodma[n]'s strokes... *Draft.*
46 her] his *Museum.*

So it is : yet let us sing,
Honour to the old bow-string !   50
Honour to the bugle-horn !
Honour to the woods unshorn !
Honour to the Lincoln green !
Honour to the archer keen !
Honour to tight little John,
And the horse he rode upon !
Honour to bold Robin Hood,
Sleeping in the underwood !
Honour to maid Marian,
And to all the Sherwood-clan !   60
Though their days have hurried by
Let us two a burden try.

TO AUTUMN

I.

Season of mists and mellow fruitfulness,
  Close bosom-friend of the maturing sun ;
Conspiring with him how to load and bless
  With fruit the vines that round the thatch-eves run ;
To bend with apples the moss'd cottage-trees,
  And fill all fruit with ripeness to the core ;
    To swell the gourd, and plump the hazel shells
With a sweet kernel ; to set budding more,
And still more, later flowers for the bees,
Until they think warm days will never cease,
    For Summer has o'er-brimm'd their clammy cells.

II.

Who hath not seen thee oft amid thy store ?
  Sometimes whoever seeks abroad may find

49 yet] then *Draft, cancelled.*
61 Though their Pleasures *Draft, rejected.*
62   You and I a stave will try. *Draft.*

I 4 The vines with fruit that round the thatch-eves run ;
               Holograph and Museum.
  6 ripeness] sweetness *Holograph and Museum.*
  fruit] fruits *Museum.*
  8 sweet] white *Holograph.*
II 1 Who hath not seen thee, for thy haunts are many
               Holograph.
  2 abroad] for thee *Holograph.*

Thee sitting careless on a granary floor,
  Thy hair soft-lifted by the winnowing wind;
Or on a half-reap'd furrow sound asleep,
    Drows'd with the fume of poppies, while thy hook
      Spares the next swath and all its twined flowers:
And sometimes like a gleaner thou dost keep
    Steady thy laden head across a brook;
  Or by a cyder-press, with patient look,
      Thou watchest the last oozings hours by hours.

III.

Where are the songs of Spring? Ay, where are they?
  Think not of them, thou hast thy music too,—
While barred clouds bloom the soft-dying day,
  And touch the stubble-plains with rosy hue;
Then in a wailful choir the small gnats mourn
    Among the river sallows, borne aloft
      Or sinking as the light wind lives or dies;
And full-grown lambs loud bleat from hilly bourn;
    Hedge-crickets sing; and now with treble soft
    The red-breast whistles from a garden-croft;
      And gathering swallows twitter in the skies.

II 5-8 While bright the sun slants through the husky barn
      Or sound asleep in a half reaped field
      Dozed with red poppies while thy reaping hook
        Spares from some slumbrous minutes while warm
        slumbers creep... *Holograph.*
  6, 7 Dozéd with a fume of poppies, while thy hook
        Spares the next sheath and all its honied flowers;
                                        Museum.
  7 Spares for some slumbrous minutes the next swath;
                                        Holograph.
  9 laden] leaden *Museum.*
  11 oozings] oozing *Holograph and Museum.*

III 3 While a gold cloud gilds the soft dying day *Holograph.*
  4 And touch] Touching *Holograph.*
  6 borne aloft] on thee borne aloft *Holograph.*
  7 or dies] and dies *Holograph.*
  9 with treble] again full *Holograph and Museum.*
  11 And new flock still *Holograph, rejected.*

ODE ON MELANCHOLY

I.

No. no, go not to Lethe, neither twist
  Wolf's-bane, tight-rooted, for its poisonous wine;
Nor suffer thy pale forehead to be kiss'd
  By nightshade, ruby grape of Proserpine;
Make not your rosary of yew-berries,
    Nor let the beetle, nor the death-moth be
      Your mournful Psyche, nor the downy owl
A partner in your sorrow's mysteries;
    For shade to shade will come too drowsily,
      And drown the wakeful anguish of the soul.

II.

But when the melancholy fit shall fall
  Sudden from heaven like a weeping cloud,
That fosters the droop-headed flowers all,
  And hides the green hill in an April shroud;
Then glut thy sorrow on a morning rose,
    Or on the rainbow of the salt sand-wave,
      Or on the wealth of globed peonies;
Or if thy mistress some rich anger shows,
    Emprison her soft hand, and let her rave,
      And feed deep, deep upon her peerless eyes.

Of the Ode on Melancholy Lord Houghton gives the following stanza as a rejected opening from the original manuscript:

    Though you should build a bark of dead men's bones,
      And rear a phantom gibbet for a mast,
    Stitch shrouds together for a sail, with groans
      To fill it out, blood-stained and aghast;
    Although your rudder be a dragon's tail
      Long sever'd, yet still hard with agony,
        Your cordage large uprootings from the skull
    Of bald Medusa, certes you would fail
      To find the Melancholy—whether she
        Dreameth in any isle of Lethe dull...

II 4 hill] hills *Museum.*

III.

She dwells with Beauty—Beauty that must die;
  And Joy, whose hand is ever at his lips
Bidding adieu; and aching Pleasure nigh,
  Turning to Poison while the bee-mouth sips:
Ay, in the very temple of delight
  Veil'd Melancholy has her sovran shrine,
    Though seen of none save him whose strenuous
      tongue
Can burst Joy's grape against his palate fine;
His soul shall taste the sadness of her might,
    And be among her cloudy trophies hung.

III 1 dwells with] lives in *Museum.*

HYPERION

BOOK I

DEEP in the shady sadness of a vale
Far sunken from the healthy breath of morn,
Far from the fiery noon, and eve's one star,
Sat gray-hair'd Saturn, quiet as a stone,
Still as the silence round about his lair ;
Forest on forest hung about his head
Like cloud on cloud.   No stir of air was there,
Not so much life as on a summer's day
Robs not one light seed from the feather'd grass,
But where the dead leaf fell, there did it rest.   10
A stream went voiceless by, still deadened more
By reason of his fallen divinity
Spreading a shade : the Naiad 'mid her reeds
Press'd her cold finger closer to her lips.

Along the margin-sand large foot-marks went,
No further than to where his feet had stray'd,
And slept there since.   Upon the sodden ground
His old right hand lay nerveless, listless, dead,
Unsceptred ; and his realmless eyes were closed ;

Heading] Hyperion—Book I^{st} *MS : compare II and III.*
3 eve's one] evening *MS., cancelled.*
6 about *1820 :* above *MS.*
7 Like clouds that whose bosoms thunderous bosoms *MS.,*
cancelled.
8-9 Not so much Life as { a young vulture's wing / what an eagles wing
    Would spread upon a field of green-ear'd corn :
                                    MS., cancelled.
9 Robs not at all the dandelion's fleece ; *MS. and Woodhouse.*
13 Spreading a shade] Spreading across it *MS., cancelled.*
16 stray'd] stay'd *MS. and Woodhouse.*
17 And slept without a motion : since that time *MS., cancelled.*
18 nerveless, listless, dead,] { nerveless, dead, supine, / nerveless on the ground.
                                    MS., cancelled.
19 realmless] { ancient / white-brow'd } *MS., cancelled.*

While his bow'd head seem'd list'ning to the Earth,
His ancient mother, for some comfort yet.   21

It seem'd no force could wake him from his place ;
But there came one, who with a kindred hand
Touch'd his wide shoulders, after bending low
With reverence, though to one who knew it not.
She was a Goddess of the infant world ;
By her in stature the tall Amazon
Had stood a pigmy's height : she would have ta'en
Achilles by the hair and bent his neck ;
Or with a finger stay'd Ixion's wheel.   30
Her face was large as that of Memphian sphinx,
Pedestal'd haply in a palace court,
When sages look'd to Egypt for their lore.
But oh ! how unlike marble was that face :
How beautiful, if sorrow had not made
Sorrow more beautiful than Beauty's self.
There was a listening fear in her regard,
As if calamity had but begun ;
As if the vanward clouds of evil days
Had spent their malice, and the sullen rear   40
Was with its stored thunder labouring up.
One hand she press'd upon that aching spot
Where beats the human heart, as if just there,
Though an immortal, she felt cruel pain :
The other upon Saturn's bended neck
She laid, and to the level of his ear
Leaning with parted lips, some words she spake
In solemn tenour and deep organ tone :
Some mourning words, which in our feeble tongue
Would come in these like accents ; O how frail   50
To that large utterance of the early Gods !

21 *After line 21 the following four stand in the holograph, but are
cancelled in the Woodhouse transcript :*
   Thus the old Eagle drowsy with great grief,
   Sat moulting his weak Plumage never more
   To be restored or soar against the Sun,
   While his three Sons upon Olympus stood—
27-8 Placed by her side the tallest Amazon
   Had stood a little child : *MS., cancelled.*
30 stay'd Ixion's wheel] eased Ixion's toil *MS. and Woodhouse.*
48 tone] tune *MS. and Woodhouse.*

"Saturn, look up!—though wherefore, poor old King?
" I have no comfort for thee, no not one :
" I cannot say, 'O wherefore sleepest thou?'
" For heaven is parted from thee, and the earth
" Knows thee not, thus afflicted, for a God ;
" And ocean too, with all its solemn noise,
" Has from thy sceptre pass'd ; and all the air
" Is emptied of thine hoary majesty.
" Thy thunder, conscious of the new command,   60
" Rumbles reluctant o'er our fallen house ;
" And thy sharp lightning in unpractis'd hands
" Scorches and burns our once serene domain.
" O aching time ! O moments big as years !
" All as ye pass swell out the monstrous truth,
" And press it so upon our weary griefs
" That unbelief has not a space to breathe.
" Saturn, sleep on :—O thoughtless, why did I
" Thus violate thy slumbrous solitude ?
" Why should I ope thy melancholy eyes ?   70
" Saturn, sleep on ! while at thy feet I weep."

    As when, upon a tranced summer-night,
Those green-rob'd senators of mighty woods,
Tall oaks, branch-charmed by the earnest stars,
Dream, and so dream all night without a stir,
Save from one gradual solitary gust
Which comes upon the silence, and dies off,
As if the ebbing air had but one wave ;
So came these words and went ; the while in tears
She touch'd her fair large forehead to the ground,

62 unpractis'd] impetuous *MS., cancelled.*

65 All . . . monstrous] Each . . . rebel *MS., but* rebel *cancelled.*

67 *Followed by* Or a brief dream to find its way to heaven. *MS., rejected.*

74-8 *Originally written in the holograph manuscript thus :*
    The Oaks stand charmed by the earnest Stars :
    And thus all night without a stir they rest
    Save from one sudden momentary gust
    Which comes upon the silence and dies off
    As if the Sea of Air had but one wave :
in line 75 Keats first substituted remain *for* they rest, *and finally got the splendid reading of the text, substituting* solitary *for* momentary *in line 76 and* ebbing *for* Sea of *in line 78.*

Just where her falling hair might be outspread   81
A soft and silken mat for Saturn's feet.
One moon, with alteration slow, had shed
Her silver seasons four upon the night,
And still these two were postured motionless,
Like natural sculpture in cathedral cavern ;
The frozen God still couchant on the earth,
And the sad Goddess weeping at his feet :
Until at length old Saturn lifted up
His faded eyes, and saw his kingdom gone,   90
And all the gloom and sorrow of the place,
And that fair kneeling Goddess ; and then spake,
As with a palsied tongue, and while his beard
Shook horrid with such aspen-malady :
" O tender spouse of gold Hyperion,
" Thea, I feel thee ere I see thy face ;
" Look up, and let me see our doom in it ;
" Look up, and tell me if this feeble shape
" Is Saturn's ; tell me, if thou hear'st the voice
" Of Saturn ; tell me, if this wrinkling brow,   100
" Naked and bare of its great diadem,
" Peers like the front of Saturn. Who had power
" To make me desolate ? whence came the strength ?
" How was it nurtur'd to such bursting forth,
" While Fate seem'd strangled in my nervous grasp ?
" But it is so ; and I am smother'd up,
" And buried from all godlike exercise
" Of influence benign on planets pale,
" Of admonitions to the winds and seas,
" Of peaceful sway above man's harvesting,   110

81 falling] fallen MS.   be outspread] make (remains of
a rejected thought, make a mat) MS.
87 earth] sand MS., cancelled.
90 His eyes and saw his royal kingdom gone
        His faint blue eyes and saw his kingdom gone
                                            MS., rejected.
92 then spake] he said MS., cancelled.
96 Thea] Thiia MS.   98 Look up see if thou... MS., rejected.
102 Two lines in the holograph :
        Peers like the front of Saturn ! What dost think ?
        Am I that same—O Chaos who had power...
106 But it is so] And yet and But so it is MS., rejected.
108 on planets] on Sun MS., cancelled.

"And all those acts which Deity supreme
"Doth ease its heart of love in.—I am gone
"Away from my own bosom: I have left
"My strong identity, my real self,
"Somewhere between the throne, and where I sit
"Here on this spot of earth. Search, Thea, search!
"Open thine eyes eterne, and sphere them round
"Upon all space: space starr'd, and lorn of light;
"Space region'd with life-air; and barren void;
"Spaces of fire, and all the yawn of hell.—   120
"Search, Thea, search! and tell me, if thou seest
"A certain shape or shadow, making way
"With wings or chariot fierce to repossess
"A heaven he lost erewhile: it must—it must
"Be of ripe progress—Saturn must be King.
"Yes, there must be a golden victory;
"There must be Gods thrown down, and trumpets
            blown
"Of triumph calm, and hymns of festival
"Upon the gold clouds metropolitan,
"Voices of soft proclaim, and silver stir   130
"Of strings in hollow shells; and there shall be
"Beautiful things made new, for the surprise
"Of the sky-children; I will give command:
"Thea! Thea! Thea! where is Saturn?"

    This passion lifted him upon his feet,
And made his hands to struggle in the air,
His Druid locks to shake and ooze with sweat,
His eyes to fever out, his voice to cease.
He stood, and heard not Thea's sobbing deep;
A little time, and then again he snatch'd   140
Utterance thus.—"But cannot I create?

    112   Must do to ease itself, lest two [sic] hot grown
            Doth ease its heart of Love in just as tears
            Leave a calm pleasure in the human breast.—
            O Thea I must burn—my Spirit gasps
        Written in the MS., but all struck out, save the words of the text.
    115 the] my *MS., cancelled.*   116 spot] bit *MS. and Woodhouse.*
    118 lorn] lone *MS., rejected.*
    125 Be going on—Saturn must still be king— *MS., rejected.*
    134 where is] am I *MS., cancelled.*
    139 and heard not] not hearing *MS., cancelled.*

"Cannot I form? Cannot I fashion forth
"Another world, another universe,
"To overbear and crumble this to naught?
"Where is another chaos? Where?"—That word
Found way unto Olympus, and made quake
The rebel three.—Thea was startled up,
And in her bearing was a sort of hope,
As thus she quick-voic'd spake, yet full of awe.
"This cheers our fallen house: come to our friends, 150
"O Saturn! come away, and give them heart;
"I know the covert, for thence came I hither."
Thus brief; then with beseeching eyes she went
With backward footing through the shade a space:
He follow'd, and she turn'd to lead the way
Through aged boughs, that yielded like the mist
Which eagles cleave upmounting from their nest.

Meanwhile in other realms big tears were shed,
More sorrow like to this, and such like woe,
Too huge for mortal tongue or pen of scribe: 160
The Titans fierce, self-hid, or prison-bound,
Groan'd for the old allegiance once more,
And listen'd in sharp pain for Saturn's voice.
But one of the whole mammoth-brood still kept
His sov'reignty, and rule, and majesty;—
Blazing Hyperion on his orbed fire
Still sat, still snuff'd the incense, teeming up
From man to the sun's God; yet unsecure:
For as among us mortals omens drear
Fright and perplex, so also shuddered he—   170
Not at dog's howl, or gloom-bird's hated screech,
Or the familiar visiting of one
Upon the first toll of his passing-bell,
Or prophesyings of the midnight lamp;

145 That word] that word—that sound *MS., rejected.*
147 startled] started *MS.*
154 backward] backford *MS. ; and* gloom *rejected for* shade.
156 Through aged boughs which to them gave like Air
                                        MS., cancelled.
     Through aged boughs that gave to them like Mist
                                        MS. and Woodhouse.
173 Just at the tolling *MS., cancelled.*

But horrors, portion'd to a giant nerve,
Oft made Hyperion ache.   His palace bright
Bastion'd with pyramids of glowing gold,
And touch'd with shade of bronzed obelisks,
Glar'd a blood-red through all its thousand courts,
Arches, and domes, and fiery galleries ;   180
And all its curtains of Aurorian clouds
Flush'd angerly : while sometimes eagle's wings,
Unseen before by Gods or wondering men,
Darken'd the place ; and neighing steeds were heard,
Not heard before by Gods or wondering men.
Also, when he would taste the spicy wreaths
Of incense, breath'd aloft from sacred hills,
Instead of sweets, his ample palate took
Savour of poisonous brass and metal sick :
And so, when harbour'd in the sleepy west,   190
After the full completion of fair day,—
For rest divine upon exalted couch
And slumber in the arms of melody,
He pac'd away the pleasant hours of ease
With stride colossal, on from hall to hall ;
While far within each aisle and deep recess,
His winged minions in close clusters stood,
Amaz'd and full of fear ; like anxious men

175–6 But warnings portioned to his giant sense—
   Oft $\left\{\begin{array}{l}\text{pressed his curly chin upon his Breast}\\ \text{made his Chin}\end{array}\right.$ *MS., rejected.*

178 With $\left\{\begin{array}{l}\text{shading}\\ \text{chequers}\end{array}\right\}$ black of bronsed Obelisks
   Touched with the shade of bronsed Obelisks
                       MS., rejected for reading of text.

181 all its] through *MS., cancelled.*

185 by either Gods or Men *MS., rejected.*

186 Sometimes when he would $\left\{\begin{array}{l}\text{take}\\ \text{taste}\end{array}\right\}$ *MS., rejected.*

189 A $\left\{\begin{array}{l}\text{nauseous}\\ \text{nausea}\end{array}\right\}$ feel of brass *MS., rejected.*
   A poison feel of brass and metal sick *MS. and Woodhouse.*

190 So that, when he had harbour'd in the West *MS., rejected.*

192 Instead of rest upon exalted Couch *MS., rejected.*

196 deep aisle and wide recess *MS., rejected.*

198 For fear and sad $\left\{\begin{array}{l}\text{surprise}\\ \text{amaze}\end{array}\right\}$ like $\left\{\begin{array}{l}\text{trooped men}\\ \text{men at gaze}\end{array}\right\}$
                       MS., rejected.

Who on wide plains gather in panting troops,
When earthquakes jar their battlements and towers. 200
Even now, while Saturn, rous'd from icy trance,
Went step for step with Thea through the woods,
Hyperion, leaving twilight in the rear,
Came slope upon the threshold of the west ;
Then, as was wont, his palace-door flew ope
In smoothest silence, save what solemn tubes,
Blown by the serious Zephyrs, gave of sweet
And wandering sounds, slow-breathed melodies ;
And like a rose in vermeil tint and shape,
In fragrance soft, and coolness to the eye,   210
That inlet to severe magnificence
Stood full blown, for the God to enter in.

He enter'd, but he enter'd full of wrath ;
His flaming robes stream'd out beyond his heels,
And gave a roar, as if of earthly fire,
That scar'd away the meek ethereal Hours
And made their dove-wings tremble. On he flared,
From stately nave to nave, from vault to vault,

   199 Who on a wide plain gather in sad troops *MS., rejected.*
        plains] plain *MS.*
   200 When an Earthquake hath shook their city towers.   *MS.
   and Woodhouse ; but the revision of the text stands substituted in the
   Common-place book.*
   202 Thea] Thiea *MS.*
   203 He of the Sun just lighted from the Air *MS., cancelled.*
   205 Then, as] As it *MS., cancelled.*
        A curious simile is rejected here : the next line written was
            As opes a Rose bud to a farae's [*sic*] Lute
   which Keats changed by substituting successively (1) As open Rose
   buds, (2) As doth a Rose bud, *and* (3) Most like a Rose bud.
   Woodhouse reads
            Most like a rose bud to a faery's lute.
   209 Yes, like a Rose { in teint and in vermeil *MS., cancelled.*
                         { in vermeil tint and shape *MS.*
   211 That inlet] The Sun's inlet *MS., rejected.*
   214 flaming] fiery *MS., cancelled.*
   217 dove-wings] dove-wing *MS.*   flared] went *MS., cancelled.*
   218-22 From gorgeous vault to vault, from space to space
            Untill he reached the great main Copula:
            There standing fierce }
            And there he stood   } beneath, he stampt his foot
                                             MS., cancelled.

Through bowers of fragrant and enwreathed light,
And diamond-paved lustrous long arcades,   220
Until he reach'd the great main cupola;
There standing fierce beneath, he stamped his foot,
And from the basements deep to the high towers
Jarr'd his own golden region ; and before
The quavering thunder thereupon had ceas'd,
His voice leapt out, despite of godlike curb,
To this result : " O dreams of day and night !
" O monstrous forms ! O effigies of pain !
" O spectres busy in a cold, cold gloom !
" O lank-ear'd Phantoms of black-weeded pools !   230
" Why do I know ye? why have I seen ye? why
" Is my eternal essence thus distraught
" To see and to behold these horrors new ?
" Saturn is fallen, am I too to fall?
" Am I to leave this haven of my rest,
" This cradle of my glory, this soft clime,
" This calm luxuriance of blissful light,
" These crystalline pavilions, and pure fanes,
" Of all my lucent empire? It is left
" Deserted, void, nor any haunt of mine.   240
" The blaze, the splendor, and the symmetry,
" I cannot see—but darkness, death and darkness.
" Even here, into my centre of repose,
" The shady visions come to domineer,
" Insult, and blind, and stifle up my pomp.—
" Fall !—No, by Tellus and her briny robes !
" Over the fiery frontier of my realms
" I will advance a terrible right arm
" Shall scare that infant thunderer, rebel Jove,
" And bid old Saturn take his throne again."—   250
He spake, and ceas'd, the while a heavier threat
Held struggle with his throat but came not forth ;
For as in theatres of crowded men

219 wreathed fragrant light *MS.*, *cancelled.*
220 paved *1820 :* paned *MS.*
223 basements deep] deep foundations *MS.*, *rejected.*
233 see] mark *MS.*, *cancelled.*
243 into my centre] in my sanctuary *MS.*, *rejected.*
247 Over] Upon *MS.*, *cancelled.*
250 take] seize *MS.*, *cancelled.*

Hubbub increases more they call out "Hush!"
So at Hyperion's words the Phantoms pale
Bestirr'd themselves, thrice horrible and cold;
And from the mirror'd level where he stood
A mist arose, as from a scummy marsh.
At this, through all his bulk an agony
Crept gradual, from the feet unto the crown,   260
Like a lithe serpent vast and muscular
Making slow way, with head and neck convuls'd
From over-strained might. Releas'd, he fled
To the eastern gates, and full six dewy hours
Before the dawn in season due should blush,
He breath'd fierce breath against the sleepy portals,
Clear'd them of heavy vapours, burst them wide
Suddenly on the ocean's chilly streams.
The planet orb of fire, whereon he rode
Each day from east to west the heavens through, 270
Spun round in sable curtaining of clouds;
Not therefore veiled quite, blindfold, and hid,

255 So] So as wind *MS., cancelled.*
256 horrible] horribly *MS., rejected.*
257 mirror'd *1820 :* mirrour'd *MS. :* glossy *MS., cancelled.*
258 scummy] stagnant *MS., cancelled.*
260 gradual] slowly *MS., cancelled.*
261 lithe] vast *MS., cancelled.*
263 With spite *MS. opening, cancelled :* From over strained gripe *rejected.*
264 six] three *MS., cancelled.*
267 vapours] clouds, and *MS., cancelled.*
267–8 *Woodhouse has a colon after* wide, *and reads* And, sudden on the Ocean's chilly streams, The planet orb, *&c. But the holograph reads clearly*

burst them wide
And sudden on the Ocean's chilly streams.

271 Spun round in { duskest / blackest } curtaining of clouds
MS., cancelled.

272–84 Not therefore hidden up and muffled quite
{ But / For } ever and anon the glancing spheres

{ Shot / Glow'd } { through and still } { about / within / upon } { the / this } sable shroud

Made sweet shap'd lightning: wings this splendent orb
Possess for glory, *MS., cancelled save* wings this orb
Possess for glory. *In a second attempt, written opposite, the word* hid
(272) *was only reached after* dun, dim, *and* veil'd *had been rejected.*

But ever and anon the glancing spheres,
Circles, and arcs, and broad-belting colure,
Glow'd through, and wrought upon the muffling dark
Sweet-shaped lightnings from the nadir deep
Up to the zenith,—hieroglyphics old
Which sages and keen-eyed astrologers
Then living on the earth, with labouring thought
Won from the gaze of many centuries :   280
Now lost, save what we find on remnants huge
Of stone, or marble swart ; their import gone,
Their wisdom long since fled.—Two wings this orb
Possess'd for glory, two fair argent wings,
Ever exalted at the God's approach :
And now, from forth the gloom their plumes immense
Rose, one by one, till all outspreaded were ;
While still the dazzling globe maintain'd eclipse,
Awaiting for Hyperion's command.
Fain would he have commanded, fain took throne 290
And bid the day begin, if but for change.
He might not:—No, though a primeval God :
The sacred seasons might not be disturb'd.
Therefore the operations of the dawn
Stay'd in their birth, even as here 'tis told.
Those silver wings expanded sisterly,
Eager to sail their orb ; the porches wide
Open'd upon the dusk demesnes of night ;

275 Glow'd through and $\left\{ \begin{array}{l} \text{shot} \\ \text{struck} \end{array} \right\}$ throughout the muffling blind MS., *rejected*.
281 Now lost with all their Wisdom and import MS., *cancelled*.
283 $\left\{ \begin{array}{l} \text{Their} \\ \text{And all their} \end{array} \right\}$ wisdom long since fled. Wings this Orb MS.
284 Possess'd] Possess MS.   285 Ever] Always MS., *cancelled*.
287 Rose] Came MS., *cancelled*.
292 No, though] no, not even though MS., *rejected*.
293 $\left\{ \begin{array}{l} \text{Disturb} \\ \text{Break through} \end{array} \right\}$ the sacred Seasons MS., *rejected*.
might] could MS., *cancelled*.
295 here 'tis told] it is writ MS., *cancelled*.
296 Those Silver wings of the Sun were full outspread MS., *rejected*
297 Eager] Ready MS., *cancelled*.
298 Were opened on the dusk domain of night, MS., *rejected for text*.

And the bright Titan, phrenzied with new woes,
Unus'd to bend, by hard compulsion bent   300
His spirit to the sorrow of the time;
And all along a dismal rack of clouds,
Upon the boundaries of day and night,
He stretch'd himself in grief and radiance faint.
There as he lay, the Heaven with its stars
Look'd down on him with pity, and the voice
Of Cœlus, from the universal space,
Thus whisper'd low and solemn in his ear.
"O brightest of my children dear, earth-born
"And sky-engendered, Son of Mysteries   310
"All unrevealed even to the powers
"Which met at thy creating; at whose joys
"And palpitations sweet, and pleasures soft,
"I, Cœlus, wonder, how they came and whence;
"And at the fruits thereof what shapes they be,
"Distinct, and visible; symbols divine,
"Manifestations of that beauteous life
"Diffus'd unseen throughout eternal space:
"Of these new-form'd art thou, oh brightest child!
"Of these, thy brethren and the Goddesses!   320
"There is sad feud among ye, and rebellion
"Of son against his sire. I saw him fall,
"I saw my first-born tumbled from his throne!
"To me his arms were spread, to me his voice
"Found way from forth the thunders round his head!
"Pale wox I, and in vapours hid my face.

299 bright] enraged MS., cancelled.
300 hard] stern MS., cancelled.
304 He laid himself supine, and in radiance faint—MS., rejected.
306 Look'd] Look MS.
314 came] could come MS., rejected.
316 and visible] in form MS., cancelled.
317 beauteous life] Life and Beauty MS., cancelled.
319 art] at MS.
319–20 Against these lines in the Woodhouse transcript is a pencilled
"Qy." On the blank page opposite are written the following words:
    Of these new formd thou art one
    Of these also are thy brethren and the goddesses.
The writing seems to be Keats's in its loose pencilled form; and his
intent was, of course, not thus to revise the lines of the text, but to answer
the question put to him as to the meaning, by Woodhouse, or perhaps Taylor.
323 tumbled] hurtled MS., cancelled.

" Art thou, too, near such doom ? vague fear there is :
" For I have seen my sons most unlike Gods.
" Divine ye were created, and divine
" In sad demeanour, solemn, undisturb'd,   330
" Unruffled, like high Gods, ye liv'd and ruled :
" Now I behold in you fear, hope, and wrath ;
" Actions of rage and passion ; even as
" I see them, on the mortal world beneath,
" In men who die.—This is the grief, O Son !
" Sad sign of ruin, sudden dismay, and fall !
" Yet do thou strive ; as thou art capable,
" As thou canst move about, an evident God ;
" And canst oppose to each malignant hour
" Ethereal presence :—I am but a voice ;   340
" My life is but the life of winds and tides,
" No more than winds and tides can I avail :—
" But thou canst.—Be thou therefore in the van
" Of circumstance ; yea, seize the arrow's barb
" Before the tense string murmur.—To the earth !
" For there thou wilt find Saturn, and his woes.
" Meantime I will keep watch on thy bright sun,
" And of thy seasons be a careful nurse."—
Ere half this region-whisper had come down,
Hyperion arose, and on the stars   350
Lifted his curved lids, and kept them wide
Until it ceas'd ; and still he kept them wide :
And still they were the same bright, patient stars.
Then with a slow incline of his broad breast,
Like to a diver in the pearly seas,
Forward he stoop'd over the airy shore,
And plung'd all noiseless into the deep night.

331 Unruffled] Passionless MS., cancelled.

332 Woodhouse reads ye for you ; but in the holograph Keats has actually altered ye into you.

334 In widest speculation I do see MS., cancelled.

337 art] wert MS., cancelled.   343 But] Yet MS., cancelled.

345 murmur] murmurs MS. and Woodhouse.

349 come down] gone by MS., cancelled.

351 Lifted] Opened MS., cancelled.

353 And still they all were the same patient stars
    And still he saw the same bright patient stars
                    MS., rejected for text.

HYPERION. BOOK II

Just at the self-same beat of Time's wide wings
Hyperion slid into the rustled air,
And Saturn gain'd with Thea that sad place
Where Cybele and the bruised Titans mourn'd.
It was a den where no insulting light
Could glimmer on their tears ; where their own groans
They felt, but heard not, for the solid roar
Of thunderous waterfalls and torrents hoarse,
Pouring a constant bulk, uncertain where.
Crag jutting forth to crag, and rocks that seem'd 10
Ever as if just rising from a sleep,
Forehead to forehead held their monstrous horns ;
And thus in thousand hugest phantasies
Made a fit roofing to this nest of woe.
Instead of thrones, hard flint they sat upon,
Couches of rugged stone, and slaty ridge
Stubborn'd with iron. All were not assembled :
Some chain'd in torture, and some wandering.
Cœus, and Gyges, and Briareüs,
Typhon, and Dolor, and Porphyrion,   20
With many more, the brawniest in assault,
Were pent in regions of laborious breath ;
Dungeon'd in opaque element, to keep
Their clenched teeth still clench'd, and all their limbs
Lock'd up like veins of metal, crampt and screw'd ;

Book II] Canto 2nd MS.

1 Upon $\left\{ \begin{array}{l} \text{the} \\ \text{that} \end{array} \right\}$ very point of winged time

  That saw Hyperion...
  Hyperion slid...   MS., two cancelled openings.
1 beat] struck out in MS. and move substituted.
4 Cybele and her bruised children MS., rejected.
5 It was a den] It was a place was first written, and was left
standing in the holograph, but with Den written above the line.
  16 Rough stones...cancelled opening.
    slaty ridge] edge of slate and shoulder (?) of slate MS.,
rejected.
  17 assembled] here and hidden here MS., cancelled.
  21 brawniest in] brawniest of MS. : hugest of rejected.
  23 to keep] that keep MS., cancelled.
  25 Metal veins with cramp and screw MS., rejected.

Without a motion, save of their big hearts
Heaving in pain, and horribly convuls'd
With sanguine feverous boiling gurge of pulse.
Mnemosyne was straying in the world ;
Far from her moon had Phœbe wandered ;   30
And many else were free to roam abroad,
But for the main, here found they covert drear.
Scarce images of life, one here, one there,
Lay vast and edgeways ; like a dismal cirque
Of Druid stones, upon a forlorn moor,
When the chill rain begins at shut of eve,
In dull November, and their chancel vault,
The Heaven itself, is blinded throughout night.
Each one kept shroud, nor to his neighbour gave
Or word, or look, or action of despair.   40
Creüs was one ; his ponderous iron mace
Lay by him, and a shatter'd rib of rock
Told of his rage, ere he thus sank and pined.
Iäpetus another ; in his grasp,
A serpent's plashy neck ; its barbed tongue
Squeez'd from the gorge, and all its uncurl'd length
Dead ; and because the creature could not spit
Its poison in the eyes of conquering Jove.
Next Cottus : prone he lay, chin uppermost,
As though in pain ; for still upon the flint   50
He ground severe his skull, with open mouth
And eyes at horrid working. Nearest him
Asia, born of most enormous Caf,
Who cost her mother Tellus keener pangs,
Though feminine, than any of her sons :

27 Heaving] Labouring *MS.*, *cancelled.*
28 boiling] whelming *MS.*, *cancelled.*
30 Far] And *MS.*, *cancelled.*
32 The others here found grief and respite sad *MS.*, *rejected.*
    main] rest *MS.*, *cancelled.*
35 stones] temple *MS.*, *cancelled.*
38 throughout] through $\begin{Bmatrix} \text{the} \\ \text{long} \end{Bmatrix}$ *MS.*, *cancelled.*
43 sank] sunk *MS. and Woodhouse.*
46 the gorge] its gorge *MS.*, *rejected.*
48 poison] venom *Woodhouse, Extract.*
50 As though in pain] Pained he seem'd *MS.*, *cancelled.*
    flint] floor *Woodhouse, Extract.*

More thought than woe was in her dusky face,
For she was prophesying of her glory ;
And in her wide imagination stood
Palm-shaded temples, and high rival fanes,
By Oxus or in Ganges' sacred isles.   60
Even as Hope upon her anchor leans,
So leant she, not so fair, upon a tusk
Shed from the broadest of her elephants.
Above her, on a crag's uneasy shelve,
Upon his elbow rais'd, all prostrate else,
Shadow'd Enceladus ; once tame and mild
As grazing ox unworried in the meads ;
Now tiger-passion'd, lion-thoughted, wroth,
He meditated, plotted, and even now
Was hurling mountains in that second war,   70
Not long delay'd, that scar'd the younger Gods
To hide themselves in forms of beast and bird.
Not far hence Atlas ; and beside him prone
Phorcus, the sire of Gorgons. Neighbour'd close
Oceanus, and Tethys, in whose lap
Sobb'd Clymene among her tangled hair.
In midst of all lay Themis, at the feet
Of Ops the queen all clouded round from sight ;
No shape distinguishable, more than when
Thick night confounds the pine-tops with the clouds :
And many else whose names may not be told.   81
For when the Muse's wings are air-ward spread,
Who shall delay her flight? And she must chaunt
Of Saturn, and his guide, who now had climb'd
With damp and slippery footing from a depth
More horrid still. Above a sombre cliff
Their heads appear'd, and up their stature grew

60 From Tigris unto Ganges and far north *MS., cancelled.*
    Oxus]Tigris *MS., cancelled :* sacred] shaded *MS. and Woodhouse.*
62 a] the *MS., cancelled.*
68 wroth] wrath *MS. and* sour'd *cancelled.*
72 themselves] themself *MS., altered.*
74 Neighbour'd] Next *MS., cancelled.*
81 else] more *MS., cancelled.*   83 chaunt] tell *MS., cancelled.*
86 More horrid still and now was slowly come *MS., rejected
for text.*
        sombre] gnarled *MS., cancelled.*

Till on the level height their steps found ease:
Then Thea spread abroad her trembling arms
Upon the precincts of this nest of pain,   90
And sidelong fix'd her eye on Saturn's face :
There saw she direst strife ; the supreme God
At war with all the frailty of grief,
Of rage, of fear, anxiety, revenge,
Remorse, spleen, hope, but most of all despair.
Against these plagues he strove in vain ; for Fate
Had pour'd a mortal oil upon his head,
A disanointing poison : so that Thea,
Affrighted, kept her still, and let him pass
First onwards in, among the fallen tribe.   100

    As with us mortal men, the laden heart
Is persecuted more, and fever'd more,
When it is nighing to the mournful house
Where other hearts are sick of the same bruise ;
So Saturn, as he walk'd into the midst,
Felt faint, and would have sunk among the rest,
But that he met Enceladus's eye,
Whose mightiness, and awe of him, at once
Came like an inspiration ; and he shouted,
"Titans, behold your God !" at which some groan'd :
Some started on their feet ; some also shouted ;   111
Some wept, some wail'd, all bow'd with reverence ;
And Ops, uplifting her black folded veil,
Show'd her pale cheeks, and all her forehead wan,
Her eye-brows thin and jet, and hollow eyes.
There is a roaring in the bleak-grown pines
When Winter lifts his voice ; there is a noise
Among immortals when a God gives sign,
With hushing finger, how he means to load
His tongue with the full weight of utterless thought,
With thunder, and with music, and with pomp : 121

88 Till their feet *MS., cancelled.*
89 *A pencilled note in the Woodhouse book, apparently Keats's,
explains thus*—motioning to him to go in first.
  101 with us] among *MS., cancelled.*
  103 house] spot *MS., cancelled.*
  108 mightiness] mightliness *MS.*
  112 Some wept, some sat up, *MS., rejected for text.*
  115 Her hollow eyes and eyebrows thin and jet— *MS., rejected.*

Such noise is like the roar of bleak-grown pines:
Which, when it ceases in this mountain'd world,
No other sound succeeds; but ceasing here,
Among these fallen, Saturn's voice therefrom
Grew up like organ, that begins anew
Its strain, when other harmonies, stopt short,
Leave the dinn'd air vibrating silverly.
Thus grew it up—"Not in my own sad breast,
"Which is its own great judge and searcher out,
"Can I find reason why ye should be thus: 131
"Not in the legends of the first of days,
"Studied from that old spirit-leaved book
"Which starry Uranus with finger bright
"Sav'd from the shores of darkness, when the waves
"Low-ebb'd still hid it up in shallow gloom;—
"And the which book ye know I ever kept
"For my firm-based footstool:—Ah, infirm!
"Not there, nor in sign, symbol, or portent
"Of element, earth, water, air, and fire,—   140
"At war, at peace, or inter-quarreling
"One against one, or two, or three, or all
"Each several one against the other three,
"As fire with air loud warring when rain-floods
"Drown both, and press them both against earth's face,
"Where, finding sulphur, a quadruple wrath
"Unhinges the poor world;—not in that strife,
"Wherefrom I take strange lore, and read it deep,
"Can I find reason why ye should be thus:
"No, no-where can unriddle, though I search,   150

128 And leave the Air vibrated silverly— *altered to* leave the
din'd Air vibrated [*not* vibrating] silverly— *MS. The word* vibrated
appears in the Woodhouse book; but it is altered in pencil to vibrating,
seemingly by Keats.

134 Which starr'd Uranus with his finger bright *MS. and*
Woodhouse. A reading which involves the misplacement of the accent on
the second syllable of Uranus. *No doubt the error was pointed out to*
Keats in discussion; for the reading of the text is supplied in pencil.
Thus we owe, it seems, to a mere chance one of the most beautiful single
lines in the whole poem.

136 hid it up] secretly touch'd *MS., cancelled.*
137 Nor in that book nor in the *MS., rejected opening.*
144 loud warring] engaging *MS., cancelled.*
150 unriddle] { discover / I find it } *MS., cancelled.*

"And pore on Nature's universal scroll
"Even to swooning, why ye, Divinities,
"The first-born of all shap'd and palpable Gods.
"Should cower beneath what, in comparison,
"Is untremendous might. Yet ye are here,
"O'erwhelm'd, and spurn'd, and batter'd, ye are here !
"O Titans, shall I say, 'Arise !'—Ye groan :
"Shall I say 'Crouch !'—Ye groan. What can I then ?
"O Heaven wide ! O unseen parent dear !
"What can I ? Tell me, all ye brethren Gods,   160
"How we can war, how engine our great wrath !
"O speak your counsel now, for Saturn's ear
"Is all a-hunger'd. Thou, Oceanus,
"Ponderest high and deep ; and in thy face
"I see, astonied, that severe content
"Which comes of thought and musing : give us help ! "

  So ended Saturn ; and the God of the Sea,
Sophist and sage, from no Athenian grove,
But cogitation in his watery shades,
Arose, with locks not oozy, and began,   170
In murmurs, which his first-endeavouring tongue
Caught infant-like from the far-foamed sands.
"O ye, whom wrath consumes ! who, passion-stung,
"Writhe at defeat, and nurse your agonies !
"Shut up your senses, stifle up your ears,
"My voice is not a bellows unto ire.
"Yet listen, ye who will, whilst I bring proof
"How ye, perforce, must be content to stoop :
"And in the proof much comfort will I give,
"If ye will take that comfort in its truth.   180

151 wide *cancelled in MS. before* universal.
156 spurn'd] spur'd *MS.*
157 groan] groan—thus ! *MS., rejected.*
161 we can] can we *MS., rejected.*
165 astonied] astonish'd *MS., rejected.*
167 God o' the Sea *MS. and Woodhouse.*

169 in his watery shades] beneath $\left\{ \begin{array}{c} \text{wat'ry} \\ \text{watery} \end{array} \right\}$ gloom
                                        MS., rejected.
173-4   whom passion stings
        Shut up your senses *MS., rejected.*
179 Healthy content *MS., cancelled opening.*
    will I give] may be felt *MS., cancelled.*

"We fall by course of Nature's law, not force
"Of thunder, or of Jove. Great Saturn, thou
"Hast sifted well the atom-universe ;
"But for this reason, that thou art the King,
"And only blind from sheer supremacy,
"One avenue was shaded from thine eyes,
"Through which I wandered to eternal truth.
"And first, as thou wast not the first of powers,
"So art thou not the last ; it cannot be :
"Thou art not the beginning nor the end.   190
"From chaos and parental darkness came
"Light, the first fruits of that intestine broil,
"That sullen ferment, which for wondrous ends
"Was ripening in itself. The ripe hour came,
"And with it light, and light, engendering
"Upon its own producer, forthwith touch'd
"The whole enormous matter into life.
"Upon that very hour, our parentage,
"The Heavens and the Earth, were manifest :
"Then thou first born, and we the giant race,   200
"Found ourselves ruling new and beauteous realms.
"Now comes the pain of truth, to whom 'tis pain ;
"O folly ! for to bear all naked truths,
"And to envisage circumstance, all calm,
"That is the top of sovereignty. Mark well !
"As Heaven and Earth are fairer, fairer far
"Than Chaos and blank Darkness, though once chiefs ;
"And as we show beyond that Heaven and Earth
"In form and shape compact and beautiful,
"In will, in action free, companionship,   210

185 only] being MS., cancelled.   188 wast] was MS.
191-3 Darkness was first and then a light there was ;
        From Chaos came the Heavens and the Earth
        The first grand Parent MS., cancelled.
192 Light, 'twas the first of all MS., rejected.
193 which for wondrous ends] grown unto its height MS., cancelled.
194 Was at strange boil MS., rejected.
200 In the 1820 volume first-born and giant-race were hyphenated, probably by the printer. Neither the holograph nor Woodhouse gives the hyphens ; and sense and movement alike are better without them.
207 chiefs] Kings MS., cancelled.
210 action free] action, voice, MS., rejected.

"And thousand other signs of purer life ;
"So on our heels a fresh perfection treads,
"A power more strong in beauty, born of us
"And fated to excel us, as we pass
"In glory that old Darkness: nor are we
"Thereby more conquer'd, than by us the rule
"Of shapeless Chaos. Say, doth the dull soil
"Quarrel with the proud forests it hath fed,
"And feedeth still, more comely than itself?
"Can it deny the chiefdom of green groves?   220
"Or shall the tree be envious of the dove
"Because it cooeth, and hath snowy wings
"To wander wherewithal and find its joys?
"We are such forest-trees, and our fair boughs
"Have bred forth, not pale solitary doves,
"But eagles golden-feather'd, who do tower
"Above us in their beauty, and must reign
"In right thereof; for 'tis the eternal law
"That first in beauty should be first in might :
"Yea, by that law, another race may drive   230
"Our conquerors to mourn as we do now.
"Have ye beheld the young God of the Seas,
"My dispossessor? Have ye seen his face?
"Have ye beheld his chariot, foam'd along
"By noble winged creatures he hath made?
"I saw him on the calmed waters scud,
"With such a glow of beauty in his eyes,
"That it enforc'd me to bid sad farewell
"To all my empire: farewell sad I took,
"And hither came, to see how dolorous fate   240
"Had wrought upon ye ; and how I might best
"Give consolation in this woe extreme.
"Receive the truth, and let it be your balm."

   Whether through poz'd conviction, or disdain,
They guarded silence, when Oceanus

   214 we pass] do *is cancelled between these words in the MS.*
   217 Say, &c.] Strife indeed there was *and* Say, shall $\left\{ \begin{array}{l} \text{the} \\ \text{life's} \end{array} \right\}$
senseless soil *MS., rejected for text.*
   231 we] ye *MS.*   232 God o' the Seas *MS.*
   237 of beauty] bleauty (*no of*) *MS.*
   239 took] gave *MS., cancelled.*

Left murmuring, what deepest thought can tell?
But so it was, none answer'd for a space,
Save one whom none regarded, Clymene;
And yet she answer'd not, only complain'd,
With hectic lips, and eyes up-looking mild,   250
Thus wording timidly among the fierce:
"O Father, I am here the simplest voice,
"And all my knowledge is that joy is gone,
"And this thing woe crept in among our hearts,
"There to remain for ever, as I fear:
"I would not bode of evil, if I thought
"So weak a creature could turn off the help
"Which by just right should come of mighty Gods;
"Yet let me tell my sorrow, let me tell
"Of what I heard, and how it made me weep,   260
"And know that we had parted from all hope.
"I stood upon a shore, a pleasant shore,
"Where a sweet clime was breathed from a land
"Of fragrance, quietness, and trees, and flowers.
"Full of calm joy it was, as I of grief;
"Too full of joy and soft delicious warmth;
"So that I felt a movement in my heart
"To chide, and to reproach that solitude
"With songs of misery, music of our woes;
"And sat me down, and took a mouthed shell   270
"And murmur'd into it, and made melody—
"O melody no more! for while I sang,
"And with poor skill let pass into the breeze
"The dull shell's echo, from a bowery strand
"Just opposite, an island of the sea,
"There came enchantment with the shifting wind,
"That did both drown and keep alive my ears.
"I threw my shell away upon the sand,
"And a wave fill'd it, as my sense was fill'd
"With that new blissful golden melody.   280
"A living death was in each gush of sounds,
"Each family of rapturous hurried notes,

263 Where a sweet clime came breathing from inland *MS.,*
rejected.
271 melody] what till then *MS., cancelled.*
273 into] unto *MS., cancelled.*
281 gush] pour *MS., cancelled.*

"That fell, one after one, yet all at once,
"Like pearl beads dropping sudden from their string:
"And then another, then another strain,
"Each like a dove leaving its olive perch,
"With music wing'd instead of silent plumes,
"To hover round my head, and make me sick
"Of joy and grief at once.   Grief overcame,
"And I was stopping up my frantic ears,   290
"When, past all hindrance of my trembling hands,
"A voice came sweeter, sweeter than all tune,
"And still it cried, 'Apollo! young Apollo!
"'The morning-bright Apollo! young Apollo!'
"I fled, it follow'd me, and cried 'Apollo!'
"O Father, and O Brethren, had ye felt
"Those pains of mine; O Saturn, hadst thou felt,
"Ye would not call this too indulged tongue
"Presumptuous, in thus venturing to be heard."

So far her voice flow'd on, like timorous brook 300
That, lingering along a pebbled coast,
Doth fear to meet the sea: but sea it met,
And shudder'd; for the overwhelming voice
Of huge Enceladus swallow'd it in wrath:
The ponderous syllables, like sullen waves
In the half-glutted hollows of reef-rocks,
Came booming thus, while still upon his arm
He lean'd; not rising, from supreme contempt.
"Or shall we listen to the over-wise,
"Or to the over-foolish, Giant-Gods?   310
"Not thunderbolt on thunderbolt, till all
"That rebel Jove's whole armoury were spent,
"Not world on world upon these shoulders piled,
"Could agonize me more than baby-words
"In midst of this dethronement horrible.
"Speak! roar! shout! yell! ye sleepy Titans all.
"Do ye forget the blows, the buffets vile?

294 The bright Apollo *MS.*, *rejected opening.*
308 from supreme contempt] from contempt of that mild
speech *MS.*, *rejected.*
310 Giant-Gods? *MS.* : giant, Gods? *1820.*
312 were] was *MS. and Woodhouse.*
313 piled] poure'd *MS.* : lain *cancelled* : pour'd *Woodhouse.*
316 Speak! Roar! Shout ye Titans all, *MS., rejected.*

" Are ye not smitten by a youngling arm ?
" Dost thou forget, sham Monarch of the Waves,
" Thy scalding in the seas ? What, have I rous'd 320
" Your spleens with so few simple words as these ?
" O joy ! for now I see ye are not lost :
" O joy ! for now I see a thousand eyes
" Wide-glaring for revenge ! "—As this he said,
He lifted up his stature vast, and stood,
Still without intermission speaking thus :
" Now ye are flames, I'll tell you how to burn,
" And purge the ether of our enemies ;
" How to feed fierce the crooked stings of fire,
" And singe away the swollen clouds of Jove,   330
" Stifling that puny essence in its tent.
" O let him feel the evil he hath done ;
" For though I scorn Oceanus's lore,
" Much pain have I for more than loss of realms :
" The days of peace and slumberous calm are fled ;
" Those days, all innocent of scathing war,
" When all the fair Existences of heaven
" Came open-eyed to guess what we would speak :—
" That was before our brows were taught to frown,
" Before our lips knew else but solemn sounds ; 340
" That was before we knew the winged thing,
" Victory, might be lost, or might be won.
" And be ye mindful that Hyperion,
" Our brightest brother, still is undisgraced—
" Hyperion, lo ! his radiance is here ! "

    All eyes were on Enceladus's face,
And they beheld, while still Hyperion's name
Flew from his lips up to the vaulted rocks,
A pallid gleam across his features stern :

323 thousand] hundred *MS.*, *cancelled.*
324 Wide-glaring *MS.* : *no hyphen 1820.*
325 He arose *MS.*, *rejected opening.*
326 $\begin{Bmatrix} \text{And standing} \\ \text{And stood,} \end{Bmatrix}$ continuing thus : *MS.*, *cancelled.*
327 you how] ye how *Woodhouse.*
330 And $\begin{Bmatrix} \text{lick} \\ \text{singe} \end{Bmatrix}$ away the cloudy tent of Jove, *MS.*, *rejected.*
333 Oceanus's *1820 :* Oceanus' *MS.*
335 slumberous *1820 :* slumbrous *MS.*
348 from] through *MS.*, *cancelled.*

Not savage, for he saw full many a God   350
Wroth as himself. He look'd upon them all,
And in each face he saw a gleam of light,
But splendider in Saturn's, whose hoar locks
Shone like the bubbling foam about a keel
When the prow sweeps into a midnight cove.
In pale and silver silence they remain'd,
Till suddenly a splendour, like the morn,
Pervaded all the beetling gloomy steeps,
All the sad spaces of oblivion,
And every gulf, and every chasm old,   360
And every height, and every sullen depth,
Voiceless, or hoarse with loud tormented streams:
And all the everlasting cataracts,
And all the headlong torrents far and near,
Mantled before in darkness and huge shade,
Now saw the light and made it terrible.
It was Hyperion:—a granite peak
His bright feet touch'd, and there he stay'd to view
The misery his brilliance had betray'd
To the most hateful seeing of itself.   370
Golden his hair of short Numidian curl,
Regal his shape majestic, a vast shade
In midst of his own brightness, like the bulk

351 Wroth] Wrath *MS.*
355 sweeps] turns *MS., cancelled.*
357 *et seq.* Till suddenly a full-blown Splendour fill'd
    Those native spaces of oblivion
    And every glulph [*sic*] $\left\{ \begin{matrix} \text{and every} \\ \text{was seen and} \end{matrix} \right\}$ chasm old
    And every height and every sullen depth
    Voiceless or filled with hoarse tormented Streams ;
    And all the everlasting Cataracts
    And all the headlong torrents far and near,
    And all the Caverns soft with moss and weed
    Or $\left\{ \begin{matrix} \text{blazon'd} \\ \text{dazzling} \end{matrix} \right\}$ with $\left\{ \begin{matrix} \text{clear spar} \\ \text{bright} \end{matrix} \right\}$ and barren gems;
    And all the giant-Gods. It was Hyperion :
    He stood upon a granite peak aloof
    With golden hair of short numidian curl,
    Rich as the colchian fleece,   *MS., cancelled.*
366 saw] shamed *MS., cancelled.*   368 view] see *MS., cancelled.*
369 brilliance] Brilliant *MS.*
373 bulk] shade *MS., cancelled.*

Of Memnon's image at the set of sun
To one who travels from the dusking East :
Sighs, too, as mournful as that Memnon's harp
He utter'd, while his hands contemplative
He press'd together, and in silence stood.
Despondence seiz'd again the fallen Gods
At sight of the dejected King of Day,   380
And many hid their faces from the light :
But fierce Enceladus sent forth his eyes
Among the brotherhood; and, at their glare,
Uprose Iäpetus, and Creüs too,
And Phorcus, sea-born, and together strode
To where he towered on his eminence.
There those four shouted forth old Saturn's name ;
Hyperion from the peak loud answered, "Saturn!"
Saturn sat near the Mother of the Gods,
In whose face was no joy, though all the Gods 390
Gave from their hollow throats the name of "Saturn!"

HYPERION. BOOK III

THUS in alternate uproar and sad peace,
Amazed were those Titans utterly.
O leave them, Muse ! O leave them to their woes ;
For thou art weak to sing such tumults dire :
A solitary sorrow best befits
Thy lips, and antheming a lonely grief.
Leave them, O Muse ! for thou anon wilt find
Many a fallen old Divinity
Wandering in vain about bewildered shores.
Meantime touch piously the Delphic harp,   10
And not a wind of heaven but will breathe

376 Sighs too melodious as Memnon's harp *MS., rejected.*
387 Their [*sic*] whispered they bewildered, while despair
MS., cancelled.
389 sat] stood *and* put for... *MS., cancelled.*
Heading] Canto 3 *MS.*
2 Amazed] Perplexed *MS., cancelled.*
3 O leave them Muse ! for they have succour none *MS., rejected.*
6 { Thy / Thine } anthem'd lips *MS., cancelled opening.*
8 fallen] lonely *and* mateless *MS., cancelled.*
10 touch deftly *MS., rejected.*

In aid soft warble from the Dorian flute ;
For lo! 'tis for the Father of all verse.
Flush every thing that hath a vermeil hue,
Let the rose glow intense and warm the air,
And let the clouds of even and of morn
Float in voluptuous fleeces o'er the hills ;
Let the red wine within the goblet boil,
Cold as a bubbling well ; let faint-lipp'd shells,
On sands, or in great deeps, vermilion turn   20
Through all their labyrinths ; and let the maid
Blush keenly, as with some warm kiss surpris'd.
Chief isle of the embowered Cyclades,
Rejoice, O Delos, with thine olives green,
And poplars, and lawn-shading palms, and beech,
In which the Zephyr breathes the loudest song,
And hazels thick, dark-stemm'd beneath the shade :
Apollo is once more the golden theme !
Where was he, when the Giant of the Sun
Stood bright, amid the sorrow of his peers?   30
Together had he left his mother fair
And his twin-sister sleeping in their bower,
And in the morning twilight wandered forth
Beside the osiers of a rivulet,
Full ankle-deep in lillies of the vale.
The nightingale had ceas'd, and a few stars
Were lingering in the heavens, while the thrush
Began calm-throated. Throughout all the isle
There was no covert, no retired cave
Unhaunted by the murmurous noise of waves,   40
Though scarcely heard in many a green recess.
He listen'd, and he wept, and his bright tears
Went trickling down the golden bow he held.
Thus with half-shut suffused eyes he stood,

13 'tis for] thou sing'st *MS.*, *cancelled.*
14 Let a warm rosy hue distain *MS.*, *rejected opening.*
    vermeil *1820 :* vermil *MS. :* rosy *cancelled.*
16 And the corn haunting poppy *MS.*, *cancelled.*
19 faint lipp'd] red lip'd *MS.*, *rejected.*
22 Blush keenly, as] Blush as she did *MS.*, *rejected.*
27 hazels] Hzle's [*for* Hazles] *MS. :* Hyle's *Woodhouse.*
33 wandered] roamed *MS.*, *cancelled.*
44-5 So kept his [*sic for* he] with his eyes suffus'd halfshut
    While from *MS.*, *cancelled.*

While from beneath some cumbrous boughs hard by
With solemn step an awful Goddess came,
And there was purport in her looks for him,
Which he with eager guess began to read
Perplex'd, the while melodiously he said:
"How cam'st thou over the unfooted sea? 　　　　50
"Or hath that antique mien and robed form
"Mov'd in these vales invisible till now?
"Sure I have heard those vestments sweeping o'er
" The fallen leaves, when I have sat alone
"In cool mid-forest. Surely I have traced
"The rustle of those ample skirts about
"These grassy solitudes, and seen the flowers
"Lift up their heads, as still the whisper pass'd.
"Goddess! I have beheld those eyes before,
"And their eternal calm, and all that face, 　　　　60
"Or I have dream'd."—"Yes," said the supreme shape,
"Thou hast dream'd of me; and awaking up
"Didst find a lyre all golden by thy side,
" Whose strings touch'd by thy fingers, all the vast
" Unwearied ear of the whole universe
"Listen'd in pain and pleasure at the birth
"Of such new tuneful wonder. Is't not strange
"That thou shouldst weep, so gifted? Tell me, youth,
"What sorrow thou canst feel; for I am sad
"When thou dost shed a tear: explain thy griefs
"To one who in this lonely isle hath been 　　　　71
"The watcher of thy sleep and hours of life,
"From the young day when first thy infant hand

45 boughs] shade *and* oaks *MS.*, *cancelled.*
49 the while] and while *MS. and Woodhouse.*
50 cam'st . . . unfooted] camest . . . pathless *MS.*, *rejected.*
52 Mov'd] Walked *MS.*, *cancelled.*
53 o'er] by *MS.*, *cancelled.*　　　　55 cool] the *MS.*, *cancelled.*
56–7　　　　　　　　　　　　　　　　　　along
　　　　These solitudes seeing the grass and flowers *MS.*, *rejected.*
58 pass'd] went *MS.*, *cancelled.*
61 dream'd] dreampt *MS.*, *rejected.*
62 hast dream'd] dreamedst *MS.*, *cancelled.*
63 lyre all golden] golden Lyre *MS.*, *rejected.*
64 The whi[ch] *MS.*, *cancelled opening :* touch'd] swept *MS.*,
cancelled.
69 thou canst] canst thou *MS.*, *rejected.*

"Pluck'd witless the weak flowers, till thine arm
"Could bend that bow heroic to all times.
"Show thy heart's secret to an ancient Power
"Who hath forsaken old and sacred thrones
"For prophecies of thee, and for the sake
"Of loveliness new born."—Apollo then,
With sudden scrutiny and gloomless eyes,   80
Thus answer'd, while his white melodious throat
Throbb'd with the syllables.—"Mnemosyne!
"Thy name is on my tongue, I know not how;
"Why should I tell thee what thou so well seest?
"Why should I strive to show what from thy lips
"Would come no mystery? For me, dark, dark,
"And painful vile oblivion seals my eyes:
"I strive to search wherefore I am so sad,
"Until a melancholy numbs my limbs;
"And then upon the grass I sit, and moan,   90
"Like one who once had wings.—O why should I
"Feel curs'd and thwarted, when the liegeless air
"Yields to my step aspirant? why should I
"Spurn the green turf as hateful to my feet?
"Goddess benign, point forth some unknown thing:
"Are there not other regions than this isle?
"What are the stars? There is the sun, the sun!
"And the most patient brilliance of the moon!
"And stars by thousands! Point me out the way
"To any one particular beauteous star,   100
"And I will flit into it with my lyre,
"And make its silvery splendour pant with bliss.

74 weak] mead *MS., cancelled.*
76 Show *1820:* Shew *MS.:* Develop *cancelled.*
79 Apollo then] To whom the God *MS., cancelled.*
81 Thus *1820:* This *MS., where the line originally stood thus:*
       Answer'd, ~~while~~ while his white melodious throat,
the first while *having no doubt been written prematurely and struck out
with the intention of substituting the.*
83 Thy name] That sound *MS., cancelled.*
84 Thou knowest knowest better *MS., cancelled.*
    seest?] knowest *MS., cancelled.*
92 liegeless] leigeless *MS.*
100 any one] *MS.* any any one—*as if Keats meant to write the line*
       To any—any one particular star
and forgot to cancel one any *as the line of the text bloomed in his mind.*
102 And make it pant *MS., rejected.*

"I have heard the cloudy thunder : Where is power ?
"Whose hand, whose essence, what divinity
"Makes this alarum in the elements,
"While I here idle listen on the shores
"In fearless yet in aching ignorance ?
"O tell me, lonely Goddess, by thy harp,
"That waileth every morn and eventide,
"Tell me why thus I rave, about these groves !   110
"Mute thou remainest—mute ! yet I can read
"A wondrous lesson in thy silent face :
"Knowledge enormous makes a God of me.
"Names, deeds, grey legends, dire events, rebellions,
"Majesties, sovran voices, agonies,
"Creations and destroyings, all at once
"Pour into the wide hollows of my brain,
"And deify me, as if some blithe wine
"Or bright elixir peerless I had drunk,
"And so become immortal."—Thus the God,   120
While his enkindled eyes, with level glance
Beneath his white soft temples, stedfast kept
Trembling with light upon Mnemosyne.
Soon wild commotions shook him, and made flush
All the immortal fairness of his limbs ;

106 here] am *MS., cancelled.*   107 yet] but *MS., cancelled.*
111 mute ! *MS. :* Mute ! *1820.*
112 Matte[r] *MS., cancelled opening.*
114 dire events, rebellions] fier[ce] events, loud voices *MS., rejected.*
116 Creations, visages of...
    Creations, and destroyings, and calm peace *MS., rejected.*
118 And like some *MS., rejected.*
    deify] deifies *MS., cancelled.*   119 drunk] drank *MS.*
121-2 While his...
    While level-glanced beneath his temples soft
    His eyes were stedfast on Mnemosyne,
                                      MS., cancelled.
123 Upon Mnemosyne and *MS., rejected opening.*
124 And while throughout his $\begin{Bmatrix} \text{frame} \\ \text{limbs} \end{Bmatrix}$ *MS., cancelled.*
    And wild commotion throughout...
    And his white... *MS., cancelled.*
125 All his white *MS., rejected. After this line is one, cancelled,*
    Roseate and pained as $\begin{Bmatrix} \text{a} \\ \text{any} \end{Bmatrix}$ ravish'd nymph—

Most like the struggle at the gate of death;
Or liker still to one who should take leave
Of pale immortal death, and with a pang
As hot as death's is chill, with fierce convulse
Die into life: so young Apollo anguish'd :   130
His very hair, his golden tresses famed
Kept undulation round his eager neck.
During the pain Mnemosyne upheld
Her arms as one who prophesied.—At length
Apollo shriek'd ;—and lo! from all his limbs
Celestial   *   *   *   *   *   *   *
*   *   *   *   *   *   *   *   *

THE END.

and then the following four uncancelled, also given in Woodhouse's book :
    Into a hue more roseate than sweet pain
    Gives to a ravish'd nymph when her warm tears
    Gush luscious with no sob. Or more severe ;—
    More like the struggle at the gate of death,
but in Woodhouse the first three lines are marked through with a pencil ;
and And is substituted for More in the fourth.   Most is what Keats
printed.

    131 His very] Even his MS., rejected.

    132 Kept undulation] Keep graceful undulation MS., rejected.

    135 There are several trials for this truncated conclusion : first Keats
wrote and cancelled the one word Phœbus : then—
    Apollo shreikd—and lo he was the God !
    And god like
which he altered into the reading of the 1820 text (above), save for the
spelling and punctuation.   The unfinished line and sentence is filled up
in pencil in the Woodhouse transcript, wherein we read :
                             At length
    Apollo shriek'd—and lo from all his limbs
    Celestial Glory dawn'd : he was a god !
The words may be confidently attributed to Keats ; and it must be
assumed that he deliberately preferred to let the fragment given to the
public end abruptly, as it does with the word Celestial.

POSTHUMOUS

AND

FUGITIVE POEMS

POSTHUMOUS AND FUGITIVE POEMS

ON DEATH

I.

Can death be sleep, when life is but a dream,
And scenes of bliss pass as a phantom by?
The transient pleasures as a vision seem,
And yet we think the greatest pain's to die.

II.

How strange it is that man on earth should roam,
And lead a life of woe, but not forsake
His rugged path; nor dare he view alone
His future doom which is but to awake.

WOMEN, WINE, AND SNUFF

Give me women, wine and snuff
Until I cry out "hold, enough!"
You may do so sans objection
Till the day of resurrection;
For bless my beard they aye shall be
My beloved Trinity.

FILL FOR ME A BRIMMING BOWL

Fill for me a brimming bowl
And let me in it drown my soul:
But put therein some drug, designed
To Banish Women from my mind:
For I want not the stream inspiring
That fills the mind with—fond desiring,
But I want as deep a draught
As e'er from Lethe's wave was quaff'd;
From my despairing heart to charm

The Image of the fairest form   10
That e'er my reveling eyes beheld,
That e'er my wandering fancy spell'd.
In vain! away I cannot chace
The melting softness of that face,
The beaminess of those bright eyes,
That breast—earth's only Paradise.
My sight will never more be blest;
For all I see has lost its zest:
Nor with delight can I explore
The Classic page, or Muse's lore.   20
Had she but known how beat my heart,
And with one smile reliev'd its smart
I should have felt a sweet relief,
I should have felt "the joy of grief."
Yet as the Tuscan mid the snow
Of Lapland thinks on sweet Arno,
Even so for ever shall she be
The Halo of my Memory.

Aug. 1814.

SONNET

ON PEACE

O PEACE! and dost thou with thy presence bless
    The dwellings of this war-surrounded Isle;
Soothing with placid brow our late distress,
    Making the triple kingdom brightly smile?
Joyful I hail thy presence; and I hail
    The sweet companions that await on thee;
Complete my joy—let not my first wish fail,
    Let the sweet mountain nymph thy favourite be,
With England's happiness proclaim Europa's Liberty.
O Europe! let not sceptred tyrants see   10
    That thou must shelter in thy former state;
Keep thy chains burst, and boldly say thou art free;
    Give thy kings law—leave not uncurbed the great;
    So with the horrors past thou'lt win thy happier fate!

14 horrors] honors *Notes and Queries:* honours *Poems de Sélincourt.*
No doubt horrors *is right.*

SONNET TO BYRON

Byron! how sweetly sad thy melody!
  Attuning still the soul to tenderness,
  As if soft Pity, with unusual stress,
Had touch'd her plaintive lute, and thou, being by,
Hadst caught the tones, nor suffer'd them to die.
  O'ershadowing sorrow doth not make thee less
  Delightful : thou thy griefs dost dress
With a bright halo, shining beamily,
As when a cloud the golden moon doth veil,
  Its sides are ting'd with a resplendent glow,   10
Through the dark robe oft amber rays prevail,
  And like fair veins in sable marble flow ;
Still warble, dying swan! still tell the tale,
  The enchanting tale, the tale of pleasing woe.

SONNET TO CHATTERTON

O Chatterton! how very sad thy fate!
  Dear child of sorrow—son of misery!
  How soon the film of death obscur'd that eye,
Whence Genius mildly flash'd, and high debate.
How soon that voice, majestic and elate,
  Melted in dying numbers! Oh! how nigh
  Was night to thy fair morning. Thou didst die
A half-blown flow'ret which cold blasts amate.
But this is past : thou art among the stars
  Of highest Heaven : to the rolling spheres   10
Thou sweetly singest : naught thy hymning mars,
  Above the ingrate world and human fears.
On earth the good man base detraction bars
  From thy fair name, and waters it with tears.

SONNET TO SPENSER

Spenser! a jealous honourer of thine,
  A forester deep in thy midmost trees,
Did last eve ask my promise to refine
  Some English that might strive thine ear to please.
But Elfin Poet 'tis impossible
  For an inhabitant of wintry earth
To rise like Phœbus with a golden quell
  Fire-wing'd and make a morning in his mirth.

It is impossible to escape from toil
  O' the sudden and receive thy spiriting:
The flower must drink the nature of the soil
  Before it can put forth its blossoming:
Be with me in the summer days and I
Will for thine honour and his pleasure try.

ODE TO APOLLO

In thy western halls of gold
    When thou sittest in thy state,
Bards, that erst sublimely told
    Heroic deeds, and sang of fate,
With fervour seize their adamantine lyres,
Whose chords are solid rays, and twinkle radiant fires.

Here Homer with his nervous arms
    Strikes the twanging harp of war,
And even the western splendour warms,
    While the trumpets sound afar :   10
But, what creates the most intense surprise,
His soul looks out through renovated eyes.

Then, through thy Temple wide, melodious swells
    The sweet majestic tone of Maro's lyre :
The soul delighted on each accent dwells,—
    Enraptur'd dwells,—not daring to respire,
The while he tells of grief around a funeral pyre.

'Tis awful silence then again ;
    Expectant stand the spheres ;
    Breathless the laurell'd peers,   20
Nor move, till ends the lofty strain,
Nor move till Milton's tuneful thunders cease,
And leave once more the ravish'd heavens in peace.

Thou biddest Shakspeare wave his hand,
    And quickly forward spring
The Passions—a terrific band—
    And each vibrates the string
That with its tyrant temper best accords,
While from their Master's lips pour forth the inspiring
    words.

A silver trumpet Spenser blows,   30
   And, as its martial notes to silence flee,
From a virgin chorus flows
   A hymn in praise of spotless Chastity.
'Tis still! Wild warblings from the Æolian lyre
Enchantment softly breathe, and tremblingly expire.

Next thy Tasso's ardent numbers
   Float along the pleased air,
Calling youth from idle slumbers,
   Rousing them from Pleasure's lair :—
Then o'er the strings his fingers gently move,
And melt the soul to pity and to love.   41

But when *Thou* joinest with the Nine,
And all the powers of song combine,
   We listen here on earth:
The dying tones that fill the air,
And charm the ear of evening fair,
From thee, great God of Bards, receive their heavenly
   birth.

SONNET

TO A YOUNG LADY WHO SENT ME A LAUREL CROWN

FRESH morning gusts have blown away all fear
   From my glad bosom,—now from gloominess
   I mount for ever—not an atom less
Than the proud laurel shall content my bier.
No! by the eternal stars! or why sit here
   In the Sun's eye, and 'gainst my temples press
   Apollo's very leaves, woven to bless
By thy white fingers and thy spirit clear.   8
Lo! who dares say, "Do this"? Who dares call down
   My will from its high purpose? Who say, "Stand,"
Or "Go"? This mighty moment I would frown
   On abject Cæsars—not the stoutest band
Of mailed heroes should tear off my crown:
   Yet would I kneel and kiss thy gentle hand.

Sonnet 11 mighty] very *Woodhouse.*

SONNET

ON RECEIVING A LAUREL CROWN FROM LEIGH HUNT

MINUTES are flying swiftly, and as yet
  Nothing unearthly has enticed my brain
  Into a delphic Labyrinth—I would fain
Catch an unmortal thought to pay the debt
I owe to the kind Poet who has set
  Upon my ambitious head a glorious gain.
  Two bending laurel Sprigs—'tis nearly pain
To be conscious of such a Coronet.
Still time is fleeting, and no dream arises
  Gorgeous as I would have it—only I see   10
A Trampling down of what the world most prizes
  Turbans and Crowns, and blank regality ;
And then I run into most wild surmises
  Of all the many glories that may be.

SONNET

TO THE LADIES WHO SAW ME CROWN'D

WHAT is there in the universal Earth
  More lovely than a Wreath from the bay tree ?
  Haply a Halo round the Moon—a glee
Circling from three sweet pair of Lips in Mirth ;
And haply you will say the dewy birth
  Of morning Roses—riplings tenderly
  Spread by the Halcyon's breast upon the Sea—
But these Comparisons are nothing worth—
Then is there nothing in the world so fair ?
  The silvery tears of April ?—Youth of May ?   10
Or June that breaths out life for butterflies ?
  No—none of these can from my favourite bear
Away the Palm—yet shall it ever pay
  Due Reverence to your most sovereign eyes.

HYMN TO APOLLO

God of the golden bow,
  And of the golden lyre,
And of the golden hair,
  And of the golden fire,
     Charioteer
     Of the patient year,
  Where—where slept thine ire,
When like a blank idiot I put on thy wreath,
  Thy laurel, thy glory,
  The light of thy story,   10
Or was I a worm—too low crawling, for death?
  O Delphic Apollo!

The Thunderer grasp'd and grasp'd,
  The Thunderer frown'd and frown'd;
The eagle's feathery mane
  For wrath became stiffen'd—the sound
     Of breeding thunder
     Went drowsily under,
  Muttering to be unbound.
O why didst thou pity, and for a worm   20
  Why touch thy soft lute
  Till the thunder was mute,
Why was not I crush'd—such a pitiful germ?
  O Delphic Apollo!

The Pleiades were up,
  Watching the silent air;
The seeds and roots in the Earth
  Were swelling for summer fare;
     The Ocean, its neighbour,
     Was at its old labour,   30
  When, who—who did dare
To tie, like a madman, thy plant round his brow,
  And grin and look proudly,
  And blaspheme so loudly,
And live for that honour, to stoop to thee now?
  O Delphic Apollo!

SONNET

As from the darkening gloom a silver dove
　Upsoars, and darts into the Eastern light,
　On pinions that naught moves but pure delight,
So fled thy soul into the realms above,
Regions of peace and everlasting love ;
　Where happy spirits, crown'd with circlets bright
　Of starry beam, and gloriously bedight,
Taste the high joy none but the blest cǎn prove.
There thou or joinest the immortal quire
　In melodies that even Heaven fair
Fill with superior bliss, or, at desire
　Of the omnipotent Father, cleavest the air
On holy message sent—What pleasures higher ?
　Wherefore does any grief our joy impair ?

STANZAS TO MISS WYLIE

O come Georgiana ! the rose is full blown,
The riches of Flora are lavishly strown,
The air is all softness, and crystal the streams,
The West is resplendently clothed in beams.

O come ! let us haste to the freshening shades,
The quaintly carv'd seats, and the opening glades ;
Where the faeries are chanting their evening hymns,
And in the last sun-beam the sylph lightly swims.

And when thou art weary I'll find thee a bed,
Of mosses and flowers to pillow thy head :　　　　10
And there Georgiana I'll sit at thy feet,
While my story of love I enraptur'd repeat.

So fondly I'll breathe, and so softly I'll sigh,
Thou wilt think that some amorous Zephyr is nigh :
Yet no—as I breathe I will press thy fair knee,
And then thou wilt know that the sigh comes from me.

Ah ! why dearest girl should we lose all these blisses?
That mortal 's a fool who such happiness misses :
So smile acquiescence, and give me thy hand,
With love-looking eyes, and with voice sweetly bland.　20

Title] Stanzas to Miss Wylie *G. Keats's transcript* : To Emma,
Woodhouse's.
　I 1 Georgiana !] my dear Emma ! *Woodhouse.*
　III 3 There, beauteous Emma, *Woodhouse.*

SONNET

OH! how I love, on a fair summer's eve,
  When streams of light pour down the golden west,
  And on the balmy zephyrs tranquil rest
The silver clouds, far—far away to leave
All meaner thoughts, and take a sweet reprieve
  From little cares ; to find, with easy quest,
  A fragrant wild, with Nature's beauty drest,
And there into delight my soul deceive.
There warm my breast with patriotic lore,
  Musing on Milton's fate—on Sydney's bier—   10
    Till their stern forms before my mind arise :
Perhaps on wing of Poesy upsoar,
  Full often dropping a delicious tear,
    When some melodious sorrow spells mine eyes.

SONNET

BEFORE he went to feed with owls and bats
  Nebuchadnezzar had an ugly dream,
  Worse than an Hus'if's when she thinks her cream
Made a Naumachia for mice and rats.
So scared, he sent for that "Good King of Cats"
  Young Daniel, who soon did pluck away the beam
  From out his eye, and said he did not deem
The sceptre worth a straw—his Cushions old door-mats.
A horrid nightmare similar somewhat
  Of late has haunted a most motley crew,   10
    Most loggerheads and Chapmen—we are told
That any Daniel tho' he be a sot
  Can make the lying lips turn pale of hue
    By belching out "ye are that head of Gold."

SONNET

WRITTEN IN DISGUST OF VULGAR SUPERSTITION

THE church bells toll a melancholy round,
  Calling the people to some other prayers,
  Some other gloominess, more dreadful cares,
More hearkening to the sermon's horrid sound.
Surely the mind of man is closely bound
  In some black spell ; seeing that each one tears
  Himself from fireside joys, and Lydian airs,
And converse high of those with glory crown'd.

Still, still they toll, and I should feel a damp,—
  A chill as from a tomb, did I not know   10
That they are dying like an outburnt lamp;
    That 'tis their sighing, wailing ere they go
    Into oblivion;—that fresh flowers will grow,
And many glories of immortal stamp.

SONNET

AFTER dark vapors have oppress'd our plains
  For a long dreary season, comes a day
  Born of the gentle South, and clears away
From the sick heavens all unseemly stains.
The anxious month, relieved of its pains,
    Takes as a long-lost right the feel of May;
    The eyelids with the passing coolness play
Like rose leaves with the drip of Summer rains.
The calmest thoughts come round us; as of leaves
  Budding—fruit ripening in stillness—Autumn suns
Smiling at eve upon the quiet sheaves—   11
Sweet Sappho's cheek—a smiling infant's breath—
  The gradual sand that through an hour-glass runs—
A woodland rivulet—a Poet's death.

SONNET

[*Written at the end of " The Floure and the Lefe"*]

THIS pleasant tale is like a little copse:
  The honied lines do freshly interlace
  To keep the reader in so sweet a place,
So that he here and there full-hearted stops;
And oftentimes he feels the dewy drops
  Come cool and suddenly against his face,
  And by the wandering melody may trace
Which way the tender-legged linnet hops.
Oh! what a power hath white Simplicity!
  What mighty power has this gentle story!   10
  I that for ever feel athirst for glory
Could at this moment be content to lie
  Meekly upon the grass, as those whose sobbings
  Were heard of none beside the mournful robins.

TWO SONNETS

I

TO HAYDON, WITH A SONNET WRITTEN ON SEEING THE ELGIN MARBLES

HAYDON! forgive me that I cannot speak
  Definitively on these mighty things;
  Forgive me that I have not Eagle's wings—
That what I want I know not where to seek:
And think that I would not be over meek
  In rolling out upfollow'd thunderings,
  Even to the steep of Heliconian springs,
Were I of ample strength for such a freak—
Think too, that all those numbers should be thine;
  Whose else? In this who touch thy vesture's hem?
For when men star'd at what was most divine   11
  With browless idiotism—o'erwise phlegm—
Thou hadst beheld the Hesperean shine
  Of their star in the East, and gone to worship them.

II

ON SEEING THE ELGIN MARBLES

MY spirit is too weak—mortality
  Weighs heavily on me like unwilling sleep,
  And each imagin'd pinnacle and steep
Of godlike hardship, tells me I must die
Like a sick Eagle looking at the sky.
  Yet 'tis a gentle luxury to weep
  That I have not the cloudy winds to keep,
Fresh for the opening of the morning's eye.
Such dim-conceived glories of the brain
  Bring round the heart an undescribable feud;
So do these wonders a most dizzy pain,   11
  That mingles Grecian grandeur with the rude
Wasting of old Time—with a billowy main—
  A sun—a shadow of a magnitude.

SONNET

ON A PICTURE OF LEANDER

Come hither all sweet maidens soberly,
   Down-looking aye, and with a chasten'd light,
   Hid in the fringes of your eyelids white,
And meekly let your fair hands joined be,
As if so gentle that ye could not see,
   Untouch'd, a victim of your beauty bright,
   Sinking away to his young spirit's night,—
Sinking bewilder'd 'mid the dreary sea:
'Tis young Leander toiling to his death;
   Nigh swooning, he doth purse his weary lips   10
     For Hero's cheek, and smiles against her smile.
O horrid dream! see how his body dips
     Dead-heavy; arms and shoulders gleam awhile:
He's gone: up bubbles all his amorous breath!

TO ———

Think not of it, sweet one, so;—
   Give it not a tear;
Sigh thou mayst, and bid it go
   Any, any where.

Do not look so sad, sweet one,—
   Sad and fadingly;
Shed one drop, then it is gone,
   O 'twas born to die.

Still so pale? then dearest weep;
   Weep, I'll count the tears,   10
And each one shall be a bliss
   For thee in after years.

Brighter has it left thine eyes
   Than a sunny rill;
And thy whispering melodies
   Are tenderer still.

Yet—as all things mourn awhile
   At fleeting blisses,
Let us too! but be our dirge
   A dirge of kisses.   20

LINES

I.

UNFELT, unheard, unseen,
　　I've left my little queen,
Her languid arms in silver slumber lying:
　　Ah! through their nestling touch,
　　Who—who could tell how much
There is for madness—cruel, or complying?

II.

　　Those faery lids how sleek!
　　Those lips how moist!—they speak,
In ripest quiet, shadows of sweet sounds:
　　Into my fancy's ear
　　Melting a burden dear,
How "Love doth know no fullness nor no bounds."

III.

　　True!—tender monitors!
　　I bend unto your laws:
This sweetest day for dalliance was born!
　　So, without more ado,
　　I'll feel my heaven anew,
For all the blushing of the hasty morn.

SONNET

ON THE SEA

It keeps eternal whisperings around
　　Desolate shores, and with its mighty swell
　　Gluts twice ten thousand Caverns, till the spell
Of Hecate leaves them their old shadowy sound.
Often 'tis in such gentle temper found,
　　That scarcely will the very smallest shell
　　Be mov'd for days from where it sometime fell,
When last the winds of Heaven were unbound.
Oh ye! who have your eye-balls vex'd and tir'd,
　　Feast them upon the wideness of the Sea;　　10
　　Oh ye! whose ears are dinn'd with uproar rude,
Or fed too much with cloying melody—
　　Sit ye near some old Cavern's Mouth, and brood
Until ye start, as if the sea-nymphs quir'd!

SONNET

ON LEIGH HUNT'S POEM "THE STORY OF RIMINI"

WHO loves to peer up at the morning sun,
   With half-shut eyes and comfortable cheek,
   Let him, with this sweet tale, full often seek
For meadows where the little rivers run;
Who loves to linger with that brightest one
   Of Heaven—Hesperus—let him lowly speak
   These numbers to the night, and starlight meek,
Or moon, if that her hunting be begun.
He who knows these delights, and too is prone
   To moralize upon a smile or tear,   10
Will find at once a region of his own,
   A bower for his spirit, and will steer
To alleys where the fir-tree drops its cone,
   Where robins hop, and fallen leaves are sear.

ON OXFORD

A PARODY

I.

THE Gothic looks solemn,
   The plain Doric column
Supports an old Bishop and Crosier;
   The mouldering arch,
   Shaded o'er by a larch
Stands next door to Wilson the Hosier.

II.

Vicè—that is, by turns,—
   O'er pale faces mourns
The black tassell'd trencher and common hat;
   The Chantry boy sings,
   The Steeple-bell rings,
And as for the Chancellor—*dominat*.

III.

There are plenty of trees,
   And plenty of ease,
And plenty of fat deer for Parsons;
   And when it is venison,
   Short is the benison,—
Then each on a leg or thigh fastens.

THE POET

A FRAGMENT

WHERE's the Poet? show him! show him,
Muses nine! that I may know him!
'Tis the man who with a man
  Is an equal, be he King,
Or poorest of the beggar-clan,
  Or any other wondrous thing
A man may be 'twixt ape and Plato;
  'Tis the man who with a bird,
Wren or Eagle, finds his way to
  All its instincts; he hath heard   10
The Lion's roaring, and can tell
  What his horny throat expresseth,
And to him the Tiger's yell
  Comes articulate and presseth
On his ear like mother-tongue.

MODERN LOVE

AND what is love? It is a doll dress'd up
For idleness to cosset, nurse, and dandle;
A thing of soft misnomers, so divine
That silly youth doth think to make itself
Divine by loving, and so goes on
Yawning and doting a whole summer long,
Till Miss's comb is made a pearl tiara,
And common Wellingtons turn Romeo boots;
Then Cleopatra lives at number seven,
And Antony resides in Brunswick Square.   10
Fools! if some passions high have warm'd the world,
If Queens and Soldiers have play'd deep for hearts,
It is no reason why such agonies
Should be more common than the growth of weeds.
Fools! make me whole again that weighty pearl
The Queen of Egypt melted, and I'll say
That ye may love in spite of beaver hats.

THE CASTLE BUILDER

FRAGMENTS OF A DIALOGUE

CASTLE BUILDER.

*   *   *   *   *   *   *

In short, convince you that however wise
You may have grown from Convent libraries,
I have, by many yards at least, been carding
A longer skein of wit in Convent garden.

BERNARDINE.

A very Eden that same place must be!
Pray what demesne? Whose Lordship's legacy?
What, have you convents in that Gothic Isle?
Pray pardon me, I cannot help but smile.

*   *   *   *   *   *   *

CASTLE BUILDER.

Sir, Convent Garden is a monstrous beast
From morning, four o'clock, to twelve at noon,   10
It swallows cabbages without a spoon,
And then, from twelve till two, this Eden made is
A promenade for cooks and ancient ladies;
And then for supper, 'stead of soup and poaches,
It swallows chairmen, damns, and Hackney coaches.
In short, Sir, 'tis a very place for monks,
For it containeth twenty thousand punks,
Which any man may number for his sport,
By following fat elbows up a court.

*   *   *   *   *   *   *

In such like nonsense would I pass an hour   20
With random Friar, or Rake upon his tour,
Or one of few of that imperial host
Who came unmaimed from the Russian frost

*   *   *   *   *   *   *

To-night I'll have my friar—let me think
About my room,—I'll have it in the pink;
It should be rich and sombre, and the moon,
Just in its mid-life in the midst of June,
Should look thro' four large windows and display
Clear, but for gold-fish vases in the way,
Their glassy diamonding on Turkish floor;   30
The tapers keep aside, an hour and more,

To see what else the moon alone can show;
While the night-breeze doth softly let us know
My terrace is well bower'd with oranges.
Upon the floor the dullest spirit sees
A guitar-ribband and a lady's glove
Beside a crumple-leaved tale of love;
A tambour-frame, with Venus sleeping there,
All finish'd but some ringlets of her hair;
A viol-bow, strings torn, cross-wise upon   40
A glorious folio of Anacreon;
A skull upon a mat of roses lying,
Ink'd purple with a song concerning dying;
An hour-glass on the turn, amid the trails
Of passion-flower;—just in time there sails
A cloud across the moon,—the lights bring in!
And see what more my phantasy can win.
It is a gorgeous room, but somewhat sad;
The draperies are so, as tho' they had
Been made for Cleopatra's winding-sheet;   50
And opposite the stedfast eye doth meet
A spacious looking-glass, upon whose face,
In letters raven-sombre, you may trace
Old "Mene, Mene, Tekel, Upharsin."
Greek busts and statuary have ever been
Held, by the finest spirits, fitter far
Than vase grotesque and Siamesian jar;
Therefore 'tis sure a want of Attic taste
That I should rather love a Gothic waste
Of eyesight on cinque-coloured potter's clay,   6C
Than on the marble fairness of old Greece.
My table-coverlits of Jason's fleece
And black Numidian sheep-wool should be wrought,
Gold, black, and heavy, from the Lama brought.
My ebon sofas should delicious be
With down from Leda's cygnet progeny.
My pictures all Salvator's, save a few
Of Titian's portraiture, and one, though new,
Of Haydon's in its fresh magnificence.
My wine—O good! 'tis here at my desire,   70
And I must sit to supper with my friar.

    *   *   *   *   *   *   *

40 A viol, bow-strings torn, *Houghton*.

A SONG OF OPPOSITES

"Under the flag
Of each his faction, they to battle bring
Their embryon atoms."—MILTON.

WELCOME joy, and welcome sorrow,
　Lethe's weed and Hermes' feather;
Come to-day, and come to-morrow,
　I do love you both together!
I love to mark sad faces in fair weather;
And hear a merry laugh amid the thunder;
　Fair and foul I love together.
Meadows sweet where flames are under,
And a giggle at a wonder;
Visage sage at pantomime;　　　　　　　10
Funeral, and steeple-chime;
Infant playing with a skull;
Morning fair, and shipwreck'd hull;
Nightshade with the woodbine kissing;
Serpents in red roses hissing;
Cleopatra regal-dress'd
With the aspic at her breast;
Dancing music, music sad,
Both together, sane and mad;
Muses bright and muses pale;　　　　　　20
Sombre Saturn, Momus hale;—
Laugh and sigh, and laugh again;
Oh the sweetness of the pain!
Muses bright, and muses pale,
Bare your faces of the veil;
Let me see; and let me write
Of the day, and of the night—
Both together:—let me slake
All my thirst for sweet heart-ache!
Let my bower be of yew,　　　　　　　30
Interwreath'd with myrtles new;
Pines and lime-trees full in bloom,
And my couch a low grass-tomb.

SONNET

TO A CAT

CAT! who hast pass'd thy grand climacteric,
  How many mice and rats hast in thy days
  Destroy'd?—How many tit bits stolen? Gaze
With those bright languid segments green, and prick
Those velvet ears—but pr'ythee do not stick
  Thy latent talons in me—and upraise
  Thy gentle mew—and tell me all thy frays
Of fish and mice, and rats and tender chick.
Nay, look not down, nor lick thy dainty wrists—
  For all the wheezy asthma,—and for all   10
Thy tail's tip is nick'd off—and though the fists
  Of many a maid have given thee many a maul,
Still is that fur as soft as when the lists
  In youth thou enter'dst on glass bottled wall.

LINES ON SEEING A LOCK OF MILTON'S HAIR

CHIEF of organic numbers!
  Old Scholar of the Spheres!
Thy spirit never slumbers,
  But rolls about our ears,
For ever, and for ever!
O what a mad endeavour
      Worketh he,
Who to thy sacred and ennobled hearse
Would offer a burnt sacrifice of verse
      And melody.   10

How heavenward thou soundest,
  Live Temple of sweet noise,
And Discord unconfoundest,
  Giving Delight new joys,
And Pleasure nobler pinions!
O, where are thy dominions?
      Lend thine ear

Sonnet to a Cat] Sonnet on Mrs. Reynolds's Cat. *Woodhouse.*
Milton's Hair] 12 O living fane of Sounds— *Draft, cancelled.*

To a young Delian oath,—aye, by thy soul,
By all that from thy mortal lips did roll,
And by the kernel of thine earthly love,   20
Beauty, in things on earth, and things above
     I swear!

   When every childish fashion
     Has vanish'd from my rhyme,
   Will I, grey-gone in passion,
     Leave to an after-time,
       Hymning and harmony
Of thee, and of thy works, and of thy life;
But vain is now the burning and the strife,
Pangs are in vain, until I grow high-rife   30
     With old Philosophy,
And mad with glimpses of futurity!

For many years my offering must be hush'd;
  When I do speak, I'll think upon this hour,
Because I feel my forehead hot and flush'd,
   Even at the simplest vassal of thy power,—
     A lock of thy bright hair,—
     Sudden it came,
And I was startled, when I caught thy name
     Coupled so unaware;   40
Yet, at the moment, temperate was my blood.
I thought I had beheld it from the flood.

SONNET

ON SITTING DOWN TO READ KING LEAR ONCE AGAIN

O golden tongued Romance, with serene lute!
  Fair plumed Syren, Queen of far-away!
  Leave melodizing on this wintry day,
Shut up thine olden pages, and be mute:
Adieu! for, once again, the fierce dispute
  Betwixt damnation and impassion'd clay
  Must I burn through; once more humbly assay
The bitter-sweet of this Shakespearian fruit:

Chief Poet! and ye clouds of Albion,
  Begetters of our deep eternal theme!   10
When through the old oak Forest I am gone,
  Let me not wander in a barren dream,
But, when I am consumed in the fire,
Give me new Phœnix wings to fly at my desire.

SONNET

WHEN I have fears that I may cease to be
  Before my pen has glean'd my teeming brain,
Before high-piled books, in charactery,
  Hold like rich garners the full ripen'd grain ;
When I behold, upon the night's starr'd face,
  Huge cloudy symbols of a high romance,
And think that I may never live to trace
  Their shadows, with the magic hand of chance ;
And when I feel, fair creature of an hour,
  That I shall never look upon thee more,   10
Never have relish in the faery power
  Of unreflecting love ;—then on the shore
Of the wide world I stand alone, and think
Till love and fame to nothingness do sink.

SHARING EVE'S APPLE

I.

O BLUSH not so! O blush not so!
  Or I shall think you knowing ;
And if you smile the blushing while,
  Then maidenheads are going.

II.

There 's a blush for won't, and a blush for shan't,
  And a blush for having done it:
There 's a blush for thought and a blush for naught,
  And a blush for just begun it.

King Lear] 11 When I am through the old oak forest gone—
Letter to G. and T. Keats.

III.

O sigh not so! O sigh not so!
  For it sounds of Eve's sweet pippin;
By these loosen'd lips you have tasted the pips
  And fought in an amorous nipping.

IV.

Will you play once more at nice-cut-core,
  For it only will last our youth out,
And we have the prime of the kissing time,
  We have not one sweet tooth out.

V.

There's a sigh for yes, and a sigh for no,
  And a sigh for I can't bear it!
O what can be done, shall we stay or run?
  O cut the sweet apple and share it!

A DRAUGHT OF SUNSHINE

HENCE Burgundy, Claret, and Port,
  Away with old Hock and Madeira,
Too earthly ye are for my sport;
  There's a beverage brighter and clearer.
Instead of a pitiful rummer,
My wine overbrims a whole summer;
  My bowl is the sky,
  And I drink at my eye,
  Till I feel in the brain
  A Delphian pain—   10
Then follow, my Caius! then follow:
  On the green of the hill
  We will drink our fill
  Of golden sunshine,
  Till our brains intertwine
With the glory and grace of Apollo!
  God of the Meridian,
    And of the East and West,
  To thee my soul is flown,
    And my body is earthward press'd.—   20
It is an awful mission,
  A terrible division;

And leaves a gulph austere
To be fill'd with worldly fear.
Aye, when the soul is fled
To high above our head,
Affrighted do we gaze
After its airy maze,
As doth a mother wild,
When her young infant child   30
Is in an eagle's claws—
And is not this the cause
Of madness?—God of Song,
Thou bearest me along
Through sights I scarce can bear:
O let me, let me share
With the hot lyre and thee,
The staid Philosophy.
Temper my lonely hours,
And let me see thy bowers   40
More unalarm'd!

SONNET

TO THE NILE

Son of the old moon-mountains African!
  Chief of the Pyramid and Crocodile!
  We call thee fruitful, and, that very while,
A desert fills our seeing's inward span;
Nurse of swart nations since the world began,
  Art thou so fruitful? or dost thou beguile
  Such men to honour thee, who, worn with toil,
Rest for a space 'twixt Cairo and Decan?
O may dark fancies err! they surely do;
  'Tis ignorance that makes a barren waste   10
Of all beyond itself, thou dost bedew
  Green rushes like our rivers, and dost taste
The pleasant sun-rise, green isles hast thou too,
  And to the sea as happily dost haste.

6-8   Art thou so beautiful, or a wan smile
       Pleasant but to those men who, sick with toil,
    Rest them a space 'twixt Cairo and Dekan? *Woodhouse.*
10 And ignorance doth make a barren waste... *Woodhouse.*

SONNET

TO A LADY SEEN FOR A FEW MOMENTS AT VAUXHALL

TIME'S sea hath been five years at its slow ebb,
　　Long hours have to and fro let creep the sand,
Since I was tangled in thy beauty's web,
　　And snared by the ungloving of thine hand.
And yet I never look on midnight sky,
　　But I behold thine eyes' well memory'd light;
I cannot look upon the rose's dye,
　　But to thy cheek my soul doth take its flight.
I cannot look on any budding flower,
　　But my fond ear, in fancy at thy lips　　10
And hearkening for a love-sound, doth devour
　　Its sweets in the wrong sense:—Thou dost eclipse
Every delight with sweet remembering,
And grief unto my darling joys dost bring.

SONNET

WRITTEN IN ANSWER TO A SONNET ENDING THUS:—

> Dark eyes are dearer far
> Than those that mock the hyacinthine bell—
> > By J. H. REYNOLDS.

BLUE! 'Tis the life of heaven,—the domain
　　Of Cynthia,—the wide palace of the sun,—
The tent of Hesperus, and all his train,—
　　The bosomer of clouds, gold, grey and dun.
Blue! 'Tis the life of waters:—Ocean
　　And all its vassal streams, pools numberless,
May rage, and foam, and fret, but never can
　　Subside, if not to dark blue nativeness.

1 Life's sea hath been five times at its slow ebb,
　　　　　　　Hood's Magazine.
13–14 Other delights with thy remembering
　　And sorrow to my darling joys doth bring.
　　　　　　　Hood's Magazine.
6 With all its tributary streams, pools numberless,
　　　　　　　Athenæum.
8 Subside but to a dark blue Nativeness. *Draft.*

Blue! Gentle cousin of the forest-green,
　Married to green in all the sweetest flowers,— 10
Forget-me-not,—the Blue bell,—and, that Queen
　Of secrecy, the Violet: what strange powers
Hast thou, as a mere shadow! But how great,
When in an Eye thou art, alive with fate!

SONNET

TO JOHN HAMILTON REYNOLDS

O THAT a week could be an age, and we
　Felt parting and warm meeting every week,
Then one poor year a thousand years would be,
　The flush of welcome ever on the cheek:
So could we live long life in little space,
　So time itself would be annihilate,
So a day's journey in oblivious haze
　To serve our joys would lengthen and dilate.
O to arrive each Monday morn from Ind!
　To land each Tuesday from the rich Levant!　10
In little time a host of joys to bind,
　And keep our souls in one eternal pant!
This morn, my friend, and yester-evening taught
Me how to harbour such a happy thought.

WHAT THE THRUSH SAID

LINES FROM A LETTER TO JOHN HAMILTON REYNOLDS

O THOU whose face hath felt the Winter's wind,
　Whose eye has seen the snow-clouds hung in mist,
　And the black elm tops 'mong the freezing stars,
To thee the spring will be a harvest-time.
O thou, whose only book has been the light
　Of supreme darkness which thou feddest on
Night after night when Phœbus was away,
　To thee the Spring shall be a triple morn.
O fret not after knowledge—I have none,
　And yet my song comes native with the warmth.
O fret not after knowledge—I have none,　11
　And yet the Evening listens. He who saddens
At thought of idleness cannot be idle,
And he's awake who thinks himself asleep.

SONNET

THE HUMAN SEASONS

FOUR seasons fill the measure of the year;
   There are four seasons in the mind of man:
He has his lusty Spring, when fancy clear
   Takes in all beauty with an easy span:
He has his Summer, when luxuriously
   Spring's honied cud of youthful thought he loves
To ruminate, and by such dreaming nigh
   His nearest unto heaven: quiet coves
His soul has in its Autumn, when his wings
   He furleth close; contented so to look   10
On mists in idleness—to let fair things
   Pass by unheeded as a threshold brook.
He has his Winter too of pale misfeature,
Or else he would forego his mortal nature.

EXTRACTS FROM AN OPERA

O! WERE I one of the Olympian twelve,
Their godships should pass this into a law,—
That when a man doth set himself in toil
After some beauty veiled far away,
Each step he took should make his lady's hand
More soft, more white, and her fair cheek more fair;
And for each briar-berry he might eat,
A kiss should bud upon the tree of love,
And pulp and ripen richer every hour,
To melt away upon the traveller's lips.   10

*   *   *   *   *   *

The text of the Sonnet is that contributed by Keats to Hunt's "Literary Pocket-Book." An earlier version is preserved by Woodhouse.
  2 Four seasons are there. *Woodhouse.*
  6–10 He chews the honied cud of fair spring thoughts,
     Till in his soul, dissolv'd, they come to be
       Part of himself: He hath his Autumn Ports
    And havens of repose, when his tired wings
       Are folded up, and he content to look *Woodhouse.*

DAISY'S SONG

I.

The sun, with his great eye,
Sees not so much as I;
And the moon, all silver-proud,
Might as well be in a cloud.

II.

And O the spring—the spring!
I lead the life of a king!
Couch'd in the teeming grass,
I spy each pretty lass.

III.

I look where no one dares,
And I stare where no one stares,
And when the night is nigh,
Lambs bleat my lullaby.

*   *   *   *   *   *

FOLLY'S SONG

When wedding fiddles are a-playing,
   Huzza for folly O!
And when. maidens go a-maying,
   Huzza, &c.
When a milk-pail is upset,
   Huzza, &c.
And the clothes left in the wet,
   Huzza, &c.
When the barrel's set abroach,
   Huzza, &c.
When Kate Eyebrow keeps a coach,
   Huzza, &c.
When the pig is over-roasted,
   Huzza, &c.
And the cheese is over-toasted,
   Huzza, &c.
When Sir Snap is with his lawyer,
   Huzza, &c.
And Miss Chip has kiss'd the sawyer,
   Huzza, &c.

10

20

*   *   *   *   *   *

Oh, I am frighten'd with most hateful thoughts!
Perhaps her voice is not a nightingale's,
Perhaps her teeth are not the fairest pearl;
Her eye-lashes may be, for aught I know,
Not longer than the May-fly's small fan-horns;
There may not be one dimple on her hand;
And freckles many; ah! a careless nurse,
In haste to teach the little thing to walk,
May have crumpt up a pair of Dian's legs,
And warpt the ivory of a Juno's neck.

*   *   *   *   *   *   *

SONG

I.

The stranger lighted from his steed,
    And ere he spake a word,
He seiz'd my lady's lilly hand,
    And kiss'd it all unheard.

II.

The stranger walk'd into the hall,
    And ere he spake a word,
He kiss'd my lady's cherry lips,
    And kiss'd 'em all unheard.

III.

The stranger walk'd into the bower,—
    But my lady first did go,—
Aye hand in hand into the bower,
    Where my lord's roses blow.

IV.

My lady's maid had a silken scarf,
    And a golden ring had she,
And a kiss from the stranger, as off he went
    Again on his fair palfrey.

*   *   *   *   *

Asleep! O sleep a little while, white pearl!
And let me kneel, and let me pray to thee,
And let me call Heaven's blessing on thine eyes,
And let me breathe into the happy air,
That doth enfold and touch thee all about,
Vows of my slavery, my giving up,
My sudden adoration, my great love!

FAERY SONGS

I.

SHED no tear—O shed no tear!
The flower will bloom another year.
Weep no more—O weep no more!
Young buds sleep in the root's white core.
Dry your eyes—O dry your eyes,
For I was taught in Paradise
To ease my breast of melodies—
     Shed no tear.

Overhead—look overhead
'Mong the blossoms white and red—   10
Look up, look up—I flutter now
On this flush pomegranate bough—
See me—'tis this silvery bill
Ever cures the good man's ill—
Shed no tear—O shed no tear!
The flower will bloom another year.
Adieu—Adieu—I fly, adieu,
I vanish in the heaven's blue—
     Adieu, Adieu!

II.

Ah! woe is me! poor silver-wing!
  That I must chant thy lady's dirge,
And death to this fair haunt of spring,
  Of melody, and streams of flowery verge,—
Poor silver-wing! ah! woe is me!
     That I must see
These blossoms snow upon thy lady's pall!
  Go, pretty page! and in her ear
  Whisper that the hour is near!
  Softly tell her not to fear   10
Such calm favonian burial!
  Go, pretty page! and soothly tell,—
  The blossoms hang by a melting spell,
And fall they must, ere a star wink thrice
     Upon her closed eyes,
That now in vain are weeping their last tears,
  At sweet life leaving, and these arbours green,—
Rich dowry from the Spirit of the Spheres,—
     Alas! poor Queen!

SONNET

TO HOMER

STANDING aloof in giant ignorance,
  Of thee I hear and of the Cyclades,
As one who sits ashore and longs perchance
  To visit dolphin-coral in deep seas.
So thou wast blind;—but then the veil was rent,
  For Jove uncurtain'd Heaven to let thee live,
And Neptune made for thee a spumy tent,
  And Pan made sing for thee his forest-hive;
Aye on the shores of darkness there is light,
  And precipices show untrodden green,   10
There is a budding morrow in midnight,
  There is a triple sight in blindness keen;
Such seeing hadst thou, as it once befel
To Dian, Queen of Earth, and Heaven, and Hell.

SONG

[*Written on a blank page in Beaumont and Fletcher's
    Works, between "Cupid's Revenge" and "The Two
    Noble Kinsmen."*]

I.

SPIRIT here that reignest!
Spirit here that painest!
Spirit here that burnest!
Spirit here that mournest!
    Spirit, I bow
    My forehead low,
  Enshaded with thy pinions.
    Spirit, I look
    All passion-struck
  Into thy pale dominions.

II.

Spirit here that laughest!
Spirit here that quaffest!
Spirit here that dancest!
Noble soul that prancest!
    Spirit, with thee
    I join in the glee

A-nudging the elbow of Momus.
  Spirit, I flush
  With a Bacchanal blush
Just fresh from the Banquet of Comus.

TEIGNMOUTH

"SOME DOGGEREL" SENT IN A LETTER TO B. R. HAYDON

I.

HERE all the summer could I stay,
  For there's Bishop's teign
  And King's teign
And Coomb at the clear teign head—
  Where close by the stream
  You may have your cream
All spread upon barley bread.

II.

  There's arch Brook
  And there's larch Brook
Both turning many a mill;
  And cooling the drouth
  Of the salmon's mouth,
And fattening his silver gill.

III.

  There is Wild wood,
  A Mild hood
To the sheep on the lea o' the down,
  Where the golden furze,
  With its green, thin spurs,
Doth catch at the maiden's gown.

IV.

  There is Newton marsh
  With its spear grass harsh—
A pleasant summer level
  Where the maidens sweet
  Of the Market Street,
Do meet in the dusk to revel.

v.

There 's the Barton rich
With dyke and ditch
And hedge for the thrush to live in
And the hollow tree
For the buzzing bee
And a bank for the wasp to hive in.

vi.

And O, and O
The daisies blow
And the primroses are waken'd,
And violets white
Sit in silver plight,
And the green bud's as long as the spike end.

vii.

Then who would go
Into dark Soho,
And chatter with dack'd hair'd critics,
When he can stay
For the new-mown hay,
And startle the dappled Prickets?

THE DEVON MAID

STANZAS SENT IN A LETTER TO B. R. HAYDON

i.

Where be ye going, you Devon Maid?
And what have ye there in the Basket?
Ye tight little fairy just fresh from the dairy,
Will ye give me some cream if I ask it?

ii.

I love your Meads, and I love your flowers,
And I love your junkets mainly,
But 'hind the door I love kissing more,
O look not so disdainly.

III.

I love your hills, and I love your dales,
　And I love your flocks a-bleating—
But O, on the heather to lie together,
　With both our hearts a-beating!

IV.

I'll put your Basket all safe in a nook,
　Your shawl I hang up on the willow,
And we will sigh in the daisy's eye
　And kiss on a grass green pillow.

EPISTLE TO JOHN HAMILTON REYNOLDS

Dear Reynolds! as last night I lay in bed,
There came before my eyes that wonted thread
Of shapes, and shadows, and remembrances,
That every other minute vex and please:
Things all disjointed come from north and south,—
Two Witch's eyes above a Cherub's mouth,
Voltaire with casque and shield and habergeon,
And Alexander with his nightcap on;
Old Socrates a-tying his cravat,
And Hazlitt playing with Miss Edgeworth's cat;　10
And Junius Brutus, pretty well so so,
Making the best of 's way towards Soho.

　Few are there who escape these visitings,—
Perhaps one or two whose lives have patent wings,
And thro' whose curtains peeps no hellish nose,
No wild-boar tushes, and no Mermaid's toes;
But flowers bursting out with lusty pride,
And young Æolian harps personified;
Some Titian colours touch'd into real life,—
The sacrifice goes on; the pontiff knife　　　　20
Gleams in the Sun, the milk-white heifer lows,
The pipes go shrilly, the libation flows:
A white sail shows above the green-head cliff,
Moves round the point, and throws her anchor stiff;
The mariners join hymn with those on land.

You know the Enchanted Castle,—it doth stand
Upon a rock, on the border of a Lake,
Nested in trees, which all do seem to shake
From some old magic-like Urganda's Sword.
O Phœbus! that I had thy sacred word   30
To show this Castle, in fair dreaming wise,
Unto my friend, while sick and ill he lies!

You know it well enough, where it doth seem
A mossy place, a Merlin's Hall, a dream;
You know the clear Lake, and the little Isles,
The mountains blue, and cold near neighbour rills,
All which elsewhere are but half animate;
There do they look alive to love and hate,
To smiles and frowns; they seem a lifted mound
Above some giant, pulsing underground.   40

Part of the Building was a chosen See,
Built by a banish'd Santon of Chaldee;
The other part, two thousand years from him,
Was built by Cuthbert de Saint Aldebrim;
Then there's a little wing, far from the Sun,
Built by a Lapland Witch turn'd maudlin Nun;
And many other juts of aged stone
Founded with many a mason-devil's groan.

The doors all look as if they op'd themselves,
The windows as if latch'd by Fays and Elves,   50
And from them comes a silver flash of light,
As from the westward of a Summer's night;
Or like a beauteous woman's large blue eyes
Gone mad thro' olden songs and poesies.

See! what is coming from the distance dim!
A golden Galley all in silken trim!
Three rows of oars are lightening, moment whiles,
Into the verd'rous bosoms of those isles;
Towards the shade, under the Castle wall,
It comes in silence,—now 'tis hidden all.   60
The Clarion sounds, and from a Postern-gate
An echo of sweet music doth create
A fear in the poor Herdsman, who doth bring
His beasts to trouble the enchanted spring,—

He tells of the sweet music, and the spot,
To all his friends, and they believe him not.

O that our dreamings all, of sleep or wake,
Would all their colours from the sunset take:
From something of material sublime,
Rather than shadow our own soul's day-time   70
In the dark void of night. For in the world
We jostle,—but my flag is not unfurl'd
On the Admiral-staff,—and so philosophize
I dare not yet! Oh, never will the prize,
High reason, and the love of good and ill,
Be my award! Things cannot to the will
Be settled, but they tease us out of thought;
Or is it that imagination brought
Beyond its proper bound, yet still confin'd,
Lost in a sort of Purgatory blind,   80
Cannot refer to any standard law
Of either earth or heaven? It is a flaw
In happiness, to see beyond our bourn,—
It forces us in summer skies to mourn,
It spoils the singing of the Nightingale.

Dear Reynolds! I have a mysterious tale,
And cannot speak it: the first page I read
Upon a Lampit rock of green sea-weed
Among the breakers; 'twas a quiet eve,
The rocks were silent, the wide sea did weave   90
An untumultuous fringe of silver foam
Along the flat brown sand; I was at home
And should have been most happy,—but I saw
Too far into the sea, where every maw
The greater on the less feeds evermore.—
But I saw too distinct into the core
Of an eternal fierce destruction,
And so from happiness I far was gone.
Still am I sick of it, and tho', to-day,
I've gather'd young spring-leaves, and flowers gay
Of periwinkle and wild strawberry,   101
Still do I that most fierce destruction see,—
The Shark at savage prey,—the Hawk at pounce,—
The gentle Robin, like a Pard or Ounce,

Ravening a worm,—Away, ye horrid moods!
Moods of one's mind! You know I hate them well.
You know I'd sooner be a clapping Bell
To some Kamtschatcan Missionary Church,
Than with these horrid moods be left i' the lurch.

DAWLISH FAIR

Over the Hill and over the Dale,
    And over the Bourne to Dawlish,
Where ginger-bread wives have a scanty sale,
    And ginger-bread nuts are smallish.

FRAGMENT OF AN ODE TO MAIA, WRITTEN ON MAY DAY, 1818

Mother of Hermes! and still youthful Maia!
        May I sing to thee
As thou wast hymned on the shores of Baiæ?
        Or may I woo thee
In earlier Sicilian? or thy smiles
Seek as they once were sought, in Grecian isles,
By bards who died content on pleasant sward,
    Leaving great verse unto a little clan?
O, give me their old vigour, and unheard
    Save of the quiet Primrose, and the span   10
        Of heaven and few ears,
Rounded by thee, my song should die away
        Content as theirs,
Rich in the simple worship of a day.

ACROSTIC

GEORGIANA AUGUSTA KEATS

Give me your patience Sister while I frame
Exact in Capitals your golden name
Or sue the fair Apollo and he will
Rouse from his heavy slumber and instil
Great love in me for thee and Poesy.
Imagine not that greatest mastery
And kingdom over all the Realms of verse
Nears more to Heaven in aught than when we nurse
And surety give to love and Brotherhood.

Anthropophagi in Othello's mood ;   10
Ulysses stormed, and his enchanted belt
Glow with the Muse, but they are never felt
Unbosom'd so and so eternal made,
Such tender incense in their Laurel shade,
To all the regent sisters of the Nine
As this poor offering to you, sister mine.

Kind sister ! aye, this third name says you are ;
Enchanted has it been the Lord knows where.
And may it taste to you like good old wine,
Take you to real happiness and give   20
Sons, daughters and a home like honied hive.

SONNET

ON VISITING THE TOMB OF BURNS

THE town, the churchyard, and the setting sun,
   The clouds, the trees, the rounded hills all seem,
   Though beautiful, cold—strange—as in a dream,
I dreamed long ago, now new begun.
The short-liv'd, paly Summer is but won
   From Winter's ague, for one hour's gleam ;
   Though sapphire-warm, their stars do never beam:
All is cold Beauty ; pain is never done :
For who has mind to relish, Minos-wise,
   The Real of Beauty, free from that dead hue   10
     Sickly imagination and sick pride
   Cast wan upon it ! Burns ! with honour due
     I oft have honour'd thee. Great shadow, hide
Thy face ; I sin against thy native skies.

MEG MERRILIES

I.

OLD MEG she was a Gipsy,
   And liv'd upon the Moors :
Her bed it was the brown heath turf,
   And her house was out of doors.

II.

Her apples were swart blackberries,
    Her currants pods o' broom;
Her wine was dew of the wild white rose,
    Her book a churchyard tomb.

III.

Her Brothers were the craggy hills,
    Her Sisters larchen trees—
Alone with her great family
    She liv'd as she did please.

IV.

No breakfast had she many a morn,
    No dinner many a noon,
And 'stead of supper she would stare
    Full hard against the Moon.

V.

But every morn of woodbine fresh
    She made her garlanding,
And every night the dark glen Yew
    She wove, and she would sing.

VI.

And with her fingers old and brown
    She plaited Mats o' Rushes,
And gave them to the Cottagers
    She met among the Bushes.

VII.

Old Meg was brave as Margaret Queen
    And tall as Amazon:
An old red blanket cloak she wore;
    A chip hat had she on.
God rest her aged bones somewhere—
    She died full long agone!

A SONG ABOUT MYSELF

FROM A LETTER TO FANNY KEATS

I.

THERE was a naughty Boy,
A naughty boy was he,
He would not stop at home,
He could not quiet be—
He took
In his Knapsack
A Book
Full of vowels
And a shirt
With some towels—
A slight cap
For night cap—
A hair brush,
Comb ditto,
New Stockings
For old ones
Would split O !
This Knapsack
Tight at 's back
He rivetted close
And followéd his Nose
To the North,
To the North,
And follow'd his nose
To the North.

II.

There was a naughty boy
And a naughty boy was he,
For nothing would he do
But scribble poetry—
He took
An ink stand
In his hand
And a pen
Big as ten

KEATS   * M

In the other.
And away
In a Pother
He ran
To the mountains
And fountains
And ghostes
And Postes
And witches
And ditches
And wrote
In his coat
When the weather
Was cool,
Fear of gout,
And without
When the weather
Was warm—
Och the charm
When we choose
To follow one's nose
To the north,
To the north,
To follow one's nose
To the north!

III.

There was a naughty boy
And a naughty boy was he,
He kept little fishes
In washing tubs three
In spite
Of the might
Of the Maid
Nor afraid
Of his Granny-good—
He often would
Hurly burly
Get up early
And go
By hook or crook
To the brook

And bring home
Miller's thumb,
Tittlebat
Not over fat,
Minnows small
As the stall
Of a glove,
Not above
The size
Of a nice
Little Baby's
Little fingers—
O he made
'Twas his trade
Of Fish a pretty Kettle
A Kettle—
A Kettle
Of Fish a pretty Kettle
A Kettle!

IV.

There was a naughty Boy,
 And a naughty Boy was he,
He ran away to Scotland
 The people for to see—
 Then he found
 That the ground
 Was as hard,
 That a yard
 Was as long,
 That a song
 Was as merry,
 That a cherry
 Was as red—
 That lead
 Was as weighty,
 That fourscore
 Was as eighty,
 That a door
 Was as wooden
 As in England--

So he stood in his shoes
And he wonder'd,
He wonder'd,
He stood in his shoes
And he wonder'd.

A GALLOWAY SONG

FROM A LETTER TO TOM KEATS

Ah! ken ye what I met the day
  Out oure the Mountains
A coming down by craggi[e]s grey
  An mossie fountains—
A[h] goud hair'd Marie yeve I pray
  Ane minute's guessing—
For that I met upon the way
  Is past expressing.
As I stood where a rocky brig
  A torrent crosses   10
I spied upon a misty rig
  A troup o' Horses—
And as they trotted down the glen
  I sped to meet them
To see if I might know the Men
  To stop and greet them.
First Willie on his sleek mare came
  At canting gallop
His long hair rustled like a flame
  On board a shallop.   20
Then came his brother Rab and then
  Young Peggy's Mither
And Peggy too—adown the glen
  They went togither—
I saw her wrappit in her hood
  Fra wind and raining—
Her cheek was flush wi' timid blood
  Twixt growth and waning—
She turn'd her dazed head full oft
  For there her Brithers   30
Came riding with her Bridegroom soft
  And mony ithers.

Young Tam came up an' eyed me quick
  With reddened cheek—
Braw Tam was daffed like a chick—
  He coud na speak—
Ah Marie they are all gane hame
  Through blustering weather
An' every heart is full on flame
  An' light as feather.   40
Ah! Marie they are all gone hame
  Fra happy wedding,
Whilst I—Ah is it not a shame?
  Sad tears am shedding.

SONNET

TO AILSA ROCK

HEARKEN, thou craggy ocean pyramid!
  Give answer from thy voice, the sea-fowls' screams!
  When were thy shoulders mantled in huge streams?
When, from the sun, was thy broad forehead hid?
How long is 't since the mighty power bid
  Thee heave to airy sleep from fathom dreams?
  Sleep in the lap of thunder or sunbeams,
Or when grey clouds are thy cold coverlid.
Thou answer'st not; for thou art dead asleep;
  Thy life is but two dead eternities—   10
The last in air, the former in the deep;
  First with the whales, last with the eagle-skies—
Drown'd wast thou till an earthquake made thee steep,
  Another cannot wake thy giant size.

SONNET

WRITTEN IN THE COTTAGE WHERE BURNS WAS BORN

THIS mortal body of a thousand days
  Now fills, O Burns, a space in thine own room,
Where thou didst dream alone on budded bays,
  Happy and thoughtless of thy day of doom!
My pulse is warm with thine own Barley-bree,
  My head is light with pledging a great soul,
My eyes are wandering, and I cannot see,
  Fancy is dead and drunken at its goal;

Yet can I stamp my foot upon thy floor,
  Yet can I ope thy window-sash to find   10
The meadow thou hast tramped o'er and o'er,—
  Yet can I think of thee till thought is blind,—
Yet can I gulp a bumper to thy name,—
O smile among the shades, for this is fame!

LINES WRITTEN IN THE HIGHLANDS AFTER A VISIT TO BURNS'S COUNTRY

THERE is a charm in footing slow across a silent plain,
Where patriot battle has been fought, where glory had
    the gain ;
There is a pleasure on the heath where Druids old have
    been,
Where mantles grey have rustled by and swept the
    nettles green ;
There is a joy in every spot made known by times
    of old,
New to the feet, although each tale a hundred times
    be told ;
There is a deeper joy than all, more solemn in the
    heart,
More parching to the tongue than all, of more divine
    a smart,
When weary steps forget themselves upon a pleasant
    turf,
Upon hot sand, or flinty road, or sea-shore iron scurf, 10
Toward the castle or the cot, where long ago was born
One who was great through mortal days, and died of
    fame unshorn,
Light heather-bells may tremble then, but they are far
    away ;
Wood-lark may sing from sandy fern,—the Sun may
    hear his lay ;
Runnels may kiss the grass on shelves and shallows
    clear,
But their low voices are not heard, though come on
    travels drear ;

Blood-red the Sun may set behind black mountain
    peaks ;
Blue tides may sluice and drench their time in caves
    and weedy creeks ;
Eagles may seem to sleep wing-wide upon the air ;
Ring-doves may fly convuls'd across to some high-cedar'd
    lair ;   20
But the forgotten eye is still fast lidded to the ground,
As Palmer's, that with weariness, mid-desert shrine
    hath found.
At such a time the soul 's a child, in childhood is the
    brain ;
Forgotten is the worldly heart—alone, it beats in vain.—
Aye, if a madman could have leave to pass a healthful
    day
To tell his forehead's swoon and faint when first began
    decay,
He might make tremble many a one whose spirit had
    gone forth
To find a Bard's low cradle-place about the silent North !
Scanty the hour and few the steps beyond the bourn
    of care,
Beyond the sweet and bitter world,—beyond it un-
    aware !   30
Scanty the hour and few the steps, because a longer
    stay
Would bar return, and make a man forget his mortal
    way :
O horrible ! to lose the sight of well remember'd face,
Of Brother's eyes, of Sister's brow—constant to every
    place ;
Filling the air, as on we move, with portraiture intense ;
More warm than those heroic tints that pain a painter's
    sense,
When shapes of old come striding by, and visages of old,
Locks shining black, hair scanty grey, and passions
    manifold.
No, no, that horror cannot be, for at the cable's length
Man feels the gentle anchor pull and gladdens in its
    strength :—   40
One hour, half-idiot, he stands by mossy waterfall,
But in the very next he reads his soul's memorial :—

He reads it on the mountain's height, where chance he
    may sit down
Upon rough marble diadem—that hill's eternal crown.
Yet be his anchor e'er so fast, room is there for a prayer
That man may never lose his mind on mountains black
    and bare ;
That he may stray league after league some great birth-
    place to find
And keep his vision clear from speck, his inward sight
    unblind.

THE GADFLY

FROM A LETTER TO TOM KEATS

I.

ALL gentle folks who owe a grudge
    To any living thing
Open your ears and stay your t[r]udge
    Whilst I in dudgeon sing.

II.

The Gadfly he hath stung me sore—
    O may he ne'er sting you !
But we have many a horrid bore
    He may sting black and blue.

III.

Has any here an old grey Mare
    With three legs all her store,
O put it to her Buttocks bare
    And straight she'll run on four.

IV.

Has any here a Lawyer suit
    Of Seventeen-Forty-Three,
Take Lawyer's nose and put it to 't
    And you the end will see.

v.

Is there a Man in Parliament
  Dum[b-]founder'd in his speech,
O let his neighbour make a rent
  And put one in his breech.

vi.

O Lowther how much better thou
  Hadst figur'd t' other day
When to the folks thou mad'st a bow
  And hadst no more to say

vii.

If lucky Gadfly had but ta'en
  His seat *   *   *
And put thee to a little pain
  To save thee from a worse.

viii.

Better than Southey it had been,
  Better than Mr. D——,
Better than Wordsworth too, I ween,
  Better than Mr. V——.

ix.

Forgive me pray good people all
  For deviating so—
In spirit sure I had a call—
  And now I on will go.

x.

Has any here a daughter fair
  Too fond of reading novels,
Too apt to fall in love with care
  And charming Mister Lovels,

xi.

O put a Gadfly to that thing
  She keeps so white and pert—
I mean the finger for the ring,
  And it will breed a wort.

* M 3

XII.

Has any here a pious spouse
　Who seven times a day
Scolds as King David pray'd, to chouse
　And have her holy way—

XIII.

O let a Gadfly's little sting
　Persuade her sacred tongue
That noises are a common thing,
　But that her bell has rung.

XIV.

And as this is the summum bo-
　num of all conquering,
I leave "withouten wordes mo"
　The Gadfly's little sting.

SONNET

ON HEARING THE BAG-PIPE AND SEEING "THE
STRANGER" PLAYED AT INVERARY

Of late two dainties were before me plac'd
　Sweet, holy, pure, sacred and innocent,
　From the ninth sphere to me benignly sent
That Gods might know my own particular taste :
First the soft Bag-pipe mourn'd with zealous haste,
　The Stranger next with head on bosom bent
　Sigh'd ; rueful again the piteous Bag-pipe went,
Again the Stranger sighings fresh did waste.
O Bag-pipe thou didst steal my heart away—
　O Stranger thou my nerves from Pipe didst charm—
O Bag-pipe thou didst re-assert thy sway—　　　11
　Again thou Stranger gav'st me fresh alarm—
Alas ! I could not choose. Ah ! my poor heart,
Mum chance art thou with both oblig'd to part.

STAFFA

Not Aladdin magian
Ever such a work began ;
Not the wizard of the Dee
Ever such a dream could see ;
Not St. John, in Patmos' Isle,
In the passion of his toil,
When he saw the churches seven,
Golden aisl'd, built up in heaven,
Gaz'd at such a rugged wonder.
As I stood its roofing under,   10
Lo ! I saw one sleeping there,
On the marble cold and bare.
While the surges wash'd his feet,
And his garments white did beat

What appears to have been the first draft of the Staffa poem was written in the fresh enthusiasm inspired by the spectacle. A copy of the draft was made by Brown and sent to Severn : it ended with line 49 of the text,—lines 50 and 51 being added in pencil. In writing to his brother Tom, Keats vividly described Staffa, including Fingal's Cave, and, after saying "But it is impossible to describe it," *inserted a matured version of the poem, with the following lines added to what Brown had copied for Severn :*

> 'Tis now free to stupid face,
> To cutters, and to Fashion boats,
> To cravats and to petticoats :—
> The great sea shall war it down,
> For its fame shall not be blown
> At each farthing Quadrille dance.
> So saying with a spirit's glance
> He dived.

He resumed prose with "I am sorry I am so indolent as to write such stuff as this," *meaning, probably, the six lines of doggerel added there and then in a wholly different mood from that of the poem. Woodhouse transcribed* "Staffa" *in his Common-place book to line 49, adding the rest in pencil. The holograph letter to Tom reads (by a slip) in line 45* stupid *for* dulled, *and by another in line 27* architected. *The circumstances do not warrant the restoration of the doggerel lines to the text. The Brown transcript has some trifling textual variations. In line 9 it reads* on *for* at,—*for line 31*

> Here his dolphins, one and all,

in line 41 Here *for* Where (*lines 39 and 40 not being there*), *and for line 46*

> Has dar'd to pass the rocky portal.

Drench'd about the sombre rocks,
On his neck his well-grown locks,
Lifted dry above the main,
Were upon the curl again.
"What is this? and what art thou?"
Whisper'd I, and touch'd his brow;   20
"What art thou? and what is this?"
Whisper'd I, and strove to kiss
The spirit's hand, to wake his eyes;
Up he started in a trice:
"I am Lycidas," said he,
"Fam'd in funeral minstrelsy!
This was architectur'd thus
By the great Oceanus!—
Here his mighty waters play
Hollow organs all the day;   30
Here by turns his dolphins all,
Finny palmers great and small,
Come to pay devotion due—
Each a mouth of pearls must strew.
Many a mortal of these days,
Dares to pass our sacred ways,
Dares to touch audaciously
This Cathedral of the Sea!
I have been the pontiff-priest
Where the waters never rest,   40
Where a fledgy sea-bird choir
Soars for ever; holy fire
I have hid from mortal man;
Proteus is my Sacristan.
But the dulled eye of mortal
Hath pass'd beyond the rocky portal;
So for ever will I leave
Such a taint, and soon unweave
All the magic of the place."

  *   *   *   *   *   *

So saying, with a Spirit's glance   50
He dived!

SONNET

WRITTEN UPON THE TOP OF BEN NEVIS

READ me a lesson, Muse, and speak it loud
  Upon the top of Nevis, blind in mist!
I look into the chasms, and a shroud
  Vapourous doth hide them,—just so much I wist
Mankind do know of hell; I look o'erhead,
  And there is sullen mist,—even so much
Mankind can tell of heaven; mist is spread
  Before the earth, beneath me,—even such,
Even so vague is man's sight of himself!
  Here are the craggy stones beneath my feet,—   10
Thus much I know that, a poor witless elf,
  I tread on them,—that all my eye doth meet
Is mist and crag, not only on this height,
But in the world of thought and mental might!

BEN NEVIS

A DIALOGUE

[PERSONS: MRS. CAMERON AND BEN NEVIS]

MRS. C.

UPON my life Sir Nevis I am pique'd
That I have so far panted tugg'd and reek'd
To do an hono[u]r to your old bald pate
And now am sitting on you just to bate,
Without your paying me one compliment.
Alas 'tis so with all, when our intent
Is plain, and in the eye of all Mankind
We fair ones show a preference, too blind!
You Gentle man immediately turn tail—
O let me then my hapless fate bewail!   10

The Ben Nevis dialogue is from a letter to Tom. Keats describes the
ascent, and adds—After all there was one Mrs. Cameron of 50
years of age and the fattest woman in all Invernessshire who
got up this Mountain some few years ago—true she had her
servants—but then she had herself . . . 'Tis said a little conversation took place between the mountain and the Lady.
After taking a glass of W[h]iskey as she was tolerably seated
at ease she thus began.

Ungrateful Baldpate, have I not disdain'd
The pleasant Valleys—have I not, madbrain'd,
Deserted all my Pickles and preserves,
My China closet too—with wretched Nerves
To boot—say, wretched ingrate, have I not
Le[f]t my soft cushion chair and caudle pot?
'Tis true I had no corns—no! thank the fates,
My Shoemaker was always Mr. Bates.
And if not Mr. Bates why I'm not old!
Still dumb, ungrateful Nevis—still so cold!   20

Here the Lady took some more w[h]iskey and was
putting even more to her lips when she dashed [it] to
the Ground for the Mountain began to grumble—
which continued for a few minutes before he thus began,

BEN NEVIS.

What whining bit of tongue and Mouth thus dares
Disturb my slumber of a thousand years?
Even so long my sleep has been secure—
And to be so awaked I'll not endure.
Oh pain—for since the Eagle's earliest scream
I've had a dam[n]'d confounded ugly dream,
A Nightmare sure.   What, Madam, was it you?
It cannot be!   My old eyes are not true!
Red-Crag, my Spectacles!   Now let me see!
Good Heavens, Lady, how the gemini   30
Did you get here?   O I shall split my sides!
I shall earthquake——

MRS. C.

Sweet Nevis, do not quake, for though I love
You[r] honest Countenance all things above,
Truly I should not like to be convey'd
So far into your Bosom—gentle Maid
Loves not too rough a treatment, gentle Sir—
Pray thee be calm and do not quake nor stir,
No not a Stone, or I shall go in fits—

22 Disturb] distur'd *Letter.*

26 *It is not quite clear whether the word in the letter is* dam'd *or* darn'd.

29 *As regards* Red-Crag, *Keats explains* A domestic of Ben's.

BEN NEVIS.

I must—I shall—I meet not such tit bits—   40
I meet not such sweet creatures every day—
By my old night-cap, night-cap night and day,
I must have one sweet Buss—I must and shall !
Red-Crag !—What, Madam, can you then repent
Of all the toil and vigour you have spent
To see Ben Nevis and to touch his nose ?
Red-Crag, I say ! O I must have them close !
Red-Crag, there lies beneath my farthest toe
A vein of Sulphur—go dear Red-Crag, go—
And rub your flinty back against it—budge !   50
Dear Madam, I must kiss you, faith I must !
I must Embrace you with my dearest gust !
Block-head, d'ye hear—Block-head, I'll make her feel—
There lies beneath my east leg's northern heel
A cave of young earth dragons—well, my boy,
Go thither quick and so complete my joy ;
Take you a bundle of the largest pines
And when the sun on fiercest Phosphor shines
Fire them and ram them in the Dragon's nest,
Then will the dragons fry and fizz their best   60
Until ten thousand now no bigger than
Poor Al[l]igators—poor things of one span—
Will each one swell to twice ten times the size
Of northern whale—then for the tender prize—
The moment then—for then will Red-Crag rub
His flinty back—and I shall kiss and snub
And press my dainty morsel to my breast.
Block-head, make haste !

                O Muses weep the rest—
The Lady fainted and he thought her dead
So pulled the clouds again about his head   70
And went to sleep again—soon she was rous'd
By her affrighted servants—next day hous'd
Safe on the lowly ground she bless'd her fate
That fainting fit was not delayed too late.

53 *Keats explains that* Block-head *is* Another domestic of Ben's.
74 *He adds here in plain prose :* But what surprises me above
all is how this Lady got down again.   I felt it horribly.   'Twas
the most vile descent—shook me all to pieces.

TRANSLATION FROM A SONNET OF RONSARD

NATURE withheld Cassandra in the skies,
  For more adornment, a full thousand years ;
She took their cream of Beauty's fairest dyes,
  And shap'd and tinted her above all Peers :
Meanwhile Love kept her dearly with his wings,
  And underneath their shadow fill'd her eyes
With such a richness that the cloudy Kings
  Of high Olympus utter'd slavish sighs.
When from the Heavens I saw her first descend,
  My heart took fire, and only burning pains, 10
They were my pleasures—they my Life's sad end ;
  Love pour'd her beauty into my warm veins...

   *   *   *   *   *   *   *   *
   *   *   *   *   *   *   *   *

A PROPHECY: TO GEORGE KEATS IN AMERICA

'TIS the witching hour of night,
  Orbed is the moon and bright,
  And the stars they glisten, glisten,
  Seeming with bright eyes to listen—
    For what listen they ?
For a song and for a charm,
  See they glisten in alarm,
  And the moon is waxing warm
    To hear what I shall say.
Moon ! keep wide thy golden ears—   10
Hearken, stars ! and hearken, spheres !—
Hearken, thou eternal sky !
I sing an infant's lullaby,
    A pretty lullaby.
Listen, listen, listen, listen,
Glisten, glisten, glisten, glisten,
    And hear my lullaby !
Though the rushes that will make
Its cradle still are in the lake—

Sonnet 3 dyes] dies *MS*.

Though the linen that will be   20
Its swathe, is on the cotton tree—
Though the woollen that will keep
It warm, is on the silly sheep—
Listen, starlight, listen, listen,
Glisten, glisten, glisten, glisten,
     And hear my lullaby!
Child, I see thee! Child, I've found thee
Midst of the quiet all around thee!
Child, I see thee! Child, I spy thee!
And thy mother sweet is nigh thee!   30
Child, I know thee! Child no more,
But a Poet evermore!
See, see, the lyre, the lyre,
In a flame of fire,
Upon the little cradle's top
Flaring, flaring, flaring,
Past the eyesight's bearing.
Awake it from its sleep,
And see if it can keep
Its eyes upon the blaze—   40
     Amaze, amaze!
It stares, it stares, it stares,
It dares what no one dares!
It lifts its little hand into the flame
Unharm'd, and on the strings
Paddles a little tune, and sings,
With dumb endeavour sweetly—
Bard art thou completely!
     Little child
     O' th' western wild,   50
Bard art thou completely!
Sweetly with dumb endeavour,
A Poet now or never,
     Little child
     O' th' western wild,
A Poet now or never!

STANZAS

I.

In a drear-nighted December,
　　Too happy, happy tree,
Thy branches ne'er remember
　　Their green felicity:
　　The north cannot undo them,
　　With a sleety whistle through them;
　　Nor frozen thawings glue them
　　　　From budding at the prime.

II.

In a drear-nighted December,
　　Too happy, happy brook,
Thy bubblings ne'er remember
　　Apollo's summer look;
　　But with a sweet forgetting,
　　They stay their crystal fretting,
　　Never, never petting
　　　　About the frozen time.

III.

Ah! would 'twere so with many
　　A gentle girl and boy!
But were there ever any
　　Writh'd not at passed joy?
　　To know the change and feel it,
　　When there is none to heal it,
　　Nor numbed sense to steel it,
　　　　Was never said in rhyme.

SPENSERIAN STANZA

[*Written at the close of Canto II, Book V, of
"The Faerie Queene."*]

In after-time, a sage of mickle lore
Yclep'd Typographus, the Giant took,
And did refit his limbs as heretofore,
And made him read in many a learned book,

I 1 and II 1 In a drear-nighted] In drear-nighted *Holograph.*
III 5 The feel of not to feel it, *Holograph.*
　　7 steel *Woodhouse*: steal "*The Gem*," &c.

And into many a lively legend look;
Thereby in goodly themes so training him,
That all his brutishness he quite forsook,
When, meeting Artegall and Talus grim,
The one he struck stone-blind, the other's eyes wox
    dim.

THE EVE OF SAINT MARK

Upon a Sabbath-day it fell;
Twice holy was the Sabbath-bell,
That call'd the folk to evening prayer;
The city streets were clean and fair
From wholesome drench of April rains;
And, on the western window panes,
The chilly sunset faintly told
Of unmatur'd green vallies cold,
Of the green thorny bloomless hedge,
Of rivers new with spring-tide sedge,   10
Of primroses by shelter'd rills,
And daisies on the aguish hills.
Twice holy was the Sabbath-bell:
The silent streets were crowded well
With staid and pious companies,
Warm from their fire-side orat'ries;
And moving, with demurest air,
To even-song, and vesper prayer.
Each arched porch, and entry low,
Was fill'd with patient folk and slow,   20
With whispers hush, and shuffling feet,
While play'd the organ loud and sweet.

The bells had ceas'd, the prayers begun,
And Bertha had not yet half done

*There are two extant holographs of "The Eve of St. Mark," one embodied
in a letter to George Keats which I have not had an opportunity of
collating with the text, and the other in the Keats Manuscript Book at
the British Museum. The variations noted are from the Museum MS.*
  1 It was on a twice holiday *MS., cancelled*
  7 *The word* blaz'd *stands cancelled after* sunset.
  22 organ] organs *MS.*

A curious volume, patch'd and torn,
That all day long, from earliest morn,
Had taken captive her two eyes,
Among its golden broideries;
Perplex'd her with a thousand things,—
The stars of Heaven, and angels' wings,   30
Martyrs in a fiery blaze,
Azure saints in silver rays,
Moses' breastplate, and the seven
Candlesticks John saw in Heaven,
The winged Lion of Saint Mark,
And the Covenantal Ark,
With its many mysteries,
Cherubim and golden mice.

Bertha was a maiden fair,
Dwelling in the old Minster-square;   40
From her fire-side she could see,
Sidelong, its rich antiquity,
Far as the Bishop's garden-wall;
Where sycamores and elm-trees tall,
Full-leav'd, the forest had outstript,
By no sharp north-wind ever nipt,
So shelter'd by the mighty pile.
Bertha arose, and read awhile,
With forehead 'gainst the window-pane.
Again she try'd, and then again,   50
Until the dusk eve left her dark
Upon the legend of St. Mark.
From plaited lawn-frill, fine and thin,
She lifted up her soft warm chin,
With aching neck and swimming eyes,
And daz'd with saintly imageries.

All was gloom, and silent all,
Save now and then the still foot-fall

40 the old *MS.* : th' old *Houghton.*
52 Upon] Amid *MS., cancelled.*
53–4 She look abroa . . .
        She rais'd her head and all was gloom
        S[h]e rais'd he[r] swimming eyes and all
        Was hidden in a cloudy pall *MS., cancelled.*

Of one returning homewards late,
Past the echoing minster-gate. 60

The clamorous daws, that all the day
Above tree-tops and towers play,
Pair by pair had gone to rest,
Each in its ancient belfry-nest,
Where asleep they fall betimes,
To music of the drowsy chimes.

All was silent, all was gloom,
Abroad and in the homely room:
Down she sat, poor cheated soul!
And struck a lamp from the dismal coal; 70
Lean'd forward, with bright drooping hair
And slant book, full against the glare.
Her shadow, in uneasy guise,
Hover'd about, a giant size,
On ceiling-beam and old oak chair,
The parrot's cage, and panel square;
And the warm angled winter screen,
On which were many monsters seen,
Call'd doves of Siam, Lima mice,
And legless birds of Paradise, 80
Macaw, and tender Avadavat,
And silken-furr'd Angora cat.
Untir'd she read, her shadow still
Glower'd about, as it would fill
The room with wildest forms and shades,
As though some ghostly queen of spades
Had come to mock behind her back,
And dance, and ruffle her garments black.

60   By   } the [now?] echoing Minster gate *MS., rejected.*
      Through }
63 Were gone long ago, *MS., cancelled.*
66 *The reading* of the *for* and the *is from the manuscript.*
68 Both abroad and in the room : *MS., rejected.*
69-70 The Maiden lost in dizzy maze
        Tu[r]n'd to the fire and made a blaze *MS., cancelled.*
77 And angled screen *MS., cancelled.*
79 Java Pheasants, Doves of Siam *cancelled for* Doves of Siam,
Lima Mice *MS.*
83 She read untird *MS., cancelled.*
86 some] three *MS., cancelled :* Queens *MS.*
88 her] their *MS., cancelled.*

Untir'd she read the legend page,
Of holy Mark, from youth to age,   90
On land, on sea, in pagan chains,
Rejoicing for his many pains.
Sometimes the learned eremite,
With golden star, or dagger bright,
Referr'd to pious poesies
Written in smallest crow-quill size
Beneath the text; and thus the rhyme
Was parcell'd out from time to time:
——"Als writith he of swevenis,
Men han beforne they wake in bliss,   100
Whanne that hir friendes thinke hem bound
In crimped shroude farre under grounde;
And how a litling child mote be
A saint er its nativitie,
Gif that the modre (God her blesse!)
Kepen in solitarinesse,
And kissen devoute the holy croce.
Of Goddes love, and Sathan's force,—
He writith; and thinges many mo:
Of swiche thinges I may not show.   110
Bot I must tellen verilie
Somdel of Saintè Cicilie,
And chieflie what he auctorethe
Of Saintè Markis life and dethe:"

At length her constant eyelids come
Upon the fervent martyrdom;
Then lastly to his holy shrine,
Exalt amid the tapers' shine
At Venice,—

89 page] tales MS., cancelled.
93 eremite] Monk referr'd MS., cancelled.
95 poesies] Madrigal MS., cancelled.
101 hem MS.: him Houghton.   102 crimped] crimpid MS.
104 nativitie] nativity MS., rejected.
105 If altered to Gif MS.   108 Goddis MS.

ODE TO FANNY

I.

PHYSICIAN Nature! let my spirit blood!
  O ease my heart of verse and let me rest;
Throw me upon thy Tripod, till the flood
  Of stifling numbers ebbs from my full breast.
A theme! a theme! great nature! give a theme;
    Let me begin my dream.
I come—I see thee, as thou standest there,
Beckon me not into the wintry air.

II.

Ah! dearest love, sweet home of all my fears,
  And hopes, and joys, and panting miseries,—
To-night, if I may guess, thy beauty wears
    A smile of such delight,
    As brilliant and as bright,
  As when with ravished, aching, vassal eyes,
    Lost in soft amaze,
    I gaze, I gaze!

III.

Who now, with greedy looks, eats up my feast?
What stare outfaces now my silver moon!
Ah! keep that hand unravished at the least;
    Let, let, the amorous burn—
    But, pr'ythee, do not turn
  The current of your heart from me so soon.
    O! save, in charity,
    The quickest pulse for me.

IV.

Save it for me, sweet love! though music breathe
  Voluptuous visions into the warm air;
Though swimming through the dance's dangerous
      wreath,
    Be like an April day,
    Smiling and cold and gay,
  A temperate lilly, temperate as fair;
    Then, Heaven! there will be
    A warmer June for me.

I 8 not] *probably a mistake for* out.
II 7 Lost in a soft amaze *would be more Keats like.*

V.

Why, this—you'll say, my Fanny! is not true :
  Put your soft hand upon your snowy side,
Where the heart beats : confess—'tis nothing new—
      Must not a woman be
      A feather on the sea,
  Sway'd to and fro by every wind and tide ?
      Of as uncertain speed
      As blow-ball from the mead ?

VI.

I know it—and to know it is despair
  To one who loves you as I love, sweet Fanny !
Whose heart goes fluttering for you every where,
      Nor, when away you roam,
      Dare keep its wretched home,
  Love, love alone, his pains severe and many :
      Then, loveliest ! keep me free,
      From torturing jealousy.

VII.

Ah ! if you prize my subdued soul above
  The poor, the fading, brief, pride of an hour ;
Let none profane my Holy See of love,
      Or with a rude hand break
      The sacramental cake :
  Let none else touch the just new-budded flower ;
      If not—may my eyes close,
      Love ! on their lost repose.

SONNET

TO SLEEP

O soft embalmer of the still midnight,
  Shutting, with careful fingers and benign,
Our gloom-pleas'd eyes, embower'd from the light,
  Enshaded in forgetfulness divine :
O soothest Sleep ! if so it please thee, close
  In midst of this thine hymn my willing eyes,

Sonnet 4 As wearisome as darkness is divine *Dilke, draft.*
     6 My willing eyes in midst of this thine hymn *Draft.*

Or wait the "Amen," ere thy poppy throws
   Around my bed its lulling charities.
Then save me, or the passed day will shine
Upon my pillow, breeding many woes,—   10
   Save me from curious Conscience, that still lords
Its strength for darkness, burrowing like a mole ;
   Turn the key deftly in the oiled wards,
And seal the hushed Casket of my Soul.

SONG

I.

Hush, hush ! tread softly ! hush, hush my dear !
   All the house is asleep, but we know very well
That the jealous, the jealous old bald-pate may hear,
   Tho' you've padded his night-cap—O sweet Isabel !
      Tho' your feet are more light than a Fairy's feet,
      Who dances on bubbles where brooklets meet,—
Hush, hush ! soft tiptoe ! hush, hush my dear !
For less than a nothing the jealous can hear.

II.

No leaf doth tremble, no ripple is there
   On the river,—all 's still, and the night's sleepy eye
Closes up, and forgets all its Lethean care,
   Charm'd to death by the drone of the humming
      Mayfly ;
      And the Moon, whether prudish or complaisant,
      Has fled to her bower, well knowing I want
No light in the dusk, no torch in the gloom,
But my Isabel's eyes, and her lips pulp'd with bloom.

Sonnet 8 lulling *Houghton :* dewy *G. Keats and Dilke, fair copy.*
    8–12 Its sweet-death dews o'er every pulse and limb—
       Then shut the hushed Casket of my soul
         And turn the key round in the oiled wards
         And let it rest until the morn has stole,
           Bright tressed From the grey east's shuddering
           bourn... *Draft.*
    12 From the west's shuddering bourn . . . *Draft, rejected.*

III.

Lift the latch! ah gently! ah tenderly—sweet!
  We are dead if that latchet gives one little clink!
Well done—now those lips, and a flowery seat—
    The old man may sleep, and the planets may wink;
      The shut rose shall dream of our loves, and awake
      Full blown, and such warmth for the morning's take,
The stock-dove shall hatch her soft brace and shall coo,
While I kiss to the melody, aching all through!

SONG

I HAD a dove and the sweet dove died;
  And I have thought it died of grieving:
O, what could it grieve for? Its feet were tied,
  With a silken thread of my own hand's weaving;
Sweet little red feet! why should you die—
Why should you leave me, sweet bird! why?
You liv'd alone in the forest-tree,
Why, pretty thing! would you not live with me?
I kiss'd you oft and gave you white peas;
Why not live sweetly, as in the green trees?   10

ODE ON INDOLENCE

"They toil not, neither do they spin."

I.

ONE morn before me were three figures seen,
  With bowed necks, and joined hands, side-faced;
And one behind the other stepp'd serene,
  In placid sandals, and in white robes graced;
They pass'd, like figures on a marble urn,
    When shifted round to see the other side;
      They came again; as when the urn once more
Is shifted round, the first seen shades return;
    And they were strange to me, as may betide
      With vases, to one deep in Phidian lore.

Song 3 O what could it mourn for? it was tied ... MS.

II.

How is it, Shadows! that I knew ye not?
  How came ye muffled in so hush a mask?
Was it a silent deep-disguised plot
  To steal away, and leave without a task
My idle days? Ripe was the drowsy hour;
  The blissful cloud of summer-indolence
    Benumb'd my eyes; my pulse grew less and less;
Pain had no sting, and pleasure's wreath no flower:
  O, why did ye not melt, and leave my sense
    Unhaunted quite of all but—nothingness?

III.

A third time pass'd they by, and, passing, turn'd
  Each one the face a moment whiles to me;
Then faded, and to follow them I burn'd
  And ach'd for wings because I knew the three;
The first was a fair Maid, and Love her name;
  The second was Ambition, pale of cheek,
    And ever watchful with fatigued eye;
The last, whom I love more, the more of blame
  Is heap'd upon her, maiden most unmeek,—
    I knew to be my demon Poesy.

IV.

They faded, and, forsooth! I wanted wings:
  O folly! What is love! and where is it?
And for that poor Ambition! it springs
  From a man's little heart's short fever-fit;
For Poesy!—no,—she has not a joy,—
  At least for me,—so sweet as drowsy noons,
    And evenings steep'd in honied indolence;
O, for an age so shelter'd from annoy,
  That I may never know how change the moons,
    Or hear the voice of busy common-sense!

V.

And once more came they by;—alas! wherefore?
  My sleep had been embroider'd with dim dreams;
My soul had been a lawn besprinkled o'er
  With flowers, and stirring shades, and baffled beams:

The morn was clouded, but no shower fell,
  Tho' in her lids hung the sweet tears of May;
    The open casement press'd a new-leav'd vine,
  Let in the budding warmth and throstle's lay;
O Shadows! 'twas a time to bid farewell!
    Upon your skirts had fallen no tears of mine.

VI.

So, ye three Ghosts, adieu! Ye cannot raise
  My head cool-bedded in the flowery grass;
For I would not be dieted with praise,
  A pet-lamb in a sentimental farce!
Fade softly from my eyes, and be once more
  In masque-like figures on the dreamy urn;
    Farewell! I yet have visions for the night,
And for the day faint visions there is store;
    Vanish, ye Phantoms! from my idle spright,
  Into the clouds, and never more return!

SONNET

WHY did I laugh to-night? No voice will tell:
  No God, no Demon of severe response,
Deigns to reply from heaven or from Hell.
  Then to my human heart I turn at once.
Heart! Thou and I are here sad and alone;
  I say, why did I laugh! O mortal pain!
O Darkness! Darkness! ever must I moan,
  To question Heaven and Hell and Heart in vain.
Why did I laugh? I know this Being's lease,
  My fancy to its utmost blisses spreads;   10
Yet would I on this very midnight cease,
  And the world's gaudy ensigns see in shreds;
Verse, Fame, and Beauty are intense indeed,
But Death intenser—Death is Life's high meed.

Sonnet 6 Say, wherefore did I laugh? *MS.*   11 would] could *MS.*

SONNET

A DREAM, AFTER READING DANTE'S EPISODE OF
PAULO AND FRANCESCA

As Hermes once took to his feathers light,
  When lulled Argus, baffled, swoon'd and slept,
So on a Delphic reed, my idle spright
  So play'd, so charm'd, so conquer'd, so bereft
The dragon-world of all its hundred eyes ;
  And, seeing it asleep, so fled away—
Not to pure Ida with its snow-cold skies,
  Nor unto Tempe where Jove griev'd a day ;
But to that second circle of sad hell,
  Where 'mid the gust, the whirlwind, and the flaw
Of rain and hail-stones, lovers need not tell   11
  Their sorrows.   Pale were the sweet lips I saw,
Pale were the lips I kiss'd, and fair the form
I floated with, about that melancholy storm.

AN EXTEMPORE

FROM A LETTER TO GEORGE KEATS AND HIS WIFE

When they were come into the Faery's Court
They rang—no one at home—all gone to sport
And dance and kiss and love as faeries do
For Fa[e]ries be as humans, lovers true—
Amid the woods they were, so lone and wild,
Where even the Robin feels himself exil'd
And where the very brooks as if afraid
Hurry along to some less magic shade.
"No one at home ! " the fretful princess cried
"And all for nothing such a dre[a]ry ride,   10
And all for nothing my new diamond cross,
No one to see my Persian feathers toss,

Sonnet 1–3 Full in the midst of bloomless hours my { spright
                                                 { soul
                Seeing one night the dragon world asleep
                Arose like Hermes . . . *Pocket Dante, rejected opening.*
    3   But not olympus-ward to serene skies . . .
                                  Pocket Dante, cancelled.

No one to see my Ape, my Dwarf, my Fool,
Or how I pace my Otaheitan mule.
Ape, Dwarf and Fool, why stand you gaping there?
Burst the door open, quick—or I declare
I'll switch you soundly and in pieces tear."
The Dwarf began to tremble and the Ape
Star'd at the Fool, the Fool was all agape,
The Princess grasp'd her switch, but just in time 20
The dwarf with piteous face began to rhyme.
"O mighty Princess did you ne'er hear tell
What your poor servants know but too too well?
Know you the three great crimes in faery land?
The first, alas! poor Dwarf, I understand—
I made a whipstock of a faery's wand—
The next is snoring in their company—
The next, the last, the direst of the three
Is making free when they are not at home.
I was a Prince—a baby prince—my doom 30
You see, I made a whipstock of a wand—
My top has henceforth slept in faery land.
He was a Prince, the Fool, a grown up Prince,
But he has never been a King's son since
He fell a-snoring at a faery Ball—
Your poor Ape was a prince and he, poor thing,
Picklock'd a faery's boudour—now no king,
But ape—so pray your highness stay awhile;
'Tis sooth indeed, we know it to our sorrow—
Persist and *you* may be an ape tomorrow— 40
While the Dwarf spake the Princess all for spite
Peal'd [sic] the brown hazel twig to lilly white,
Clench'd her small teeth, and held her lips apart,
Try'd to look unconcern'd with beating heart.
They saw her highness had made up her mind
And quaver'd like the reeds before the wind,
And they had had it, but, O happy chance!
The Ape for very fear began to dance
And grin'd as all his ugliness did ache—
She staid her vixen fingers for his sake, 50
He was so very ugly: then she took
Her pocket glass mirror and began to look
First at herself and [then] at him and then
She smil'd at her own beauteous face again.

Yet for all this—for all her pretty face
She took it in her head to see the place.
Women gain little from experience
Either in Lovers, husbands or expense.
The more the beauty, the more fortune too,
Beauty before the wide world never knew.   60
So each fair reasons—tho' it oft miscarries.
She thought *her* pretty face would please the fa[e]ries.
"My darling Ape I won't whip you today—
Give me the Picklock, sirrah, and go play."
They all three wept—but counsel was as vain
As crying cup biddy to drops of rain.
Yet lingeringly did the sad Ape forth draw
The Picklock from the Pocket in his Jaw.
The Princess took it and dismounting straight
Trip'd in blue silver'd slippers to the gate   70
And touch'd the wards, the Door opes full cou[r]teou[s]ly
Opened—she enter'd with her servants three.
Again it clos'd and there was nothing seen
But the Mule grazing on the herbage green.

End of Canto xii

Canto the xiii

The Mule no sooner saw himself alone
Than he prick'd up his Ears—and said "well done!
At least, unhappy Prince, I may be free—
No more a Princess shall side-saddle me.
O King of Othaietè—tho' a Mule
'Aye every inch a King'—tho' 'Fortune's fool'— 80
Well done—for by what Mr. Dwarfy said
I would not give a sixpence for her head."
Even as he spake he trotted in high glee
To the knotty side of an old Pollard tree
And rub['d] his sides against the mossed bark
Till his Girths burst and left him naked stark
Except his Bridle—how get rid of that,
Buckled and tied with many a twist and plait?
At last it struck him to pretend to sleep
And then the thievish Monkeys down would creep 90
And filch the unpleasant trammels quite away.
No sooner thought of than adown he lay,

Sham'd a good snore—the Monkey-men descended
And whom they thought to injure they befriended.
They hung his Bridle on a topmost bough
And of[f] he went, run, trot, or anyhow—
    Brown is gone to bed—and I am tired of rhyming...

SPENSERIAN STANZAS
ON CHARLES ARMITAGE BROWN

I.

HE is to weet a melancholy carle:
Thin in the waist, with bushy head of hair,
As hath the seeded thistle when in parle
It holds the Zephyr, ere it sendeth fair
Its light balloons into the summer air;
Therto his beard had not begun to bloom,
No brush had touch'd his chin or razor sheer;
No care had touch'd his cheek with mortal doom,
But new he was and bright as scarf from Persian loom.

II.

Ne cared he for wine, or half-and-half
Ne cared he for fish or flesh or fowl,
And sauces held he worthless as the chaff;
He 'sdeigned the swine-head at the wassail-bowl;
Ne with lewd ribbalds sat he cheek by jowl;
Ne with sly Lemans in the scorner's chair;
But after water-brooks this Pilgrim's soul
Panted, and all his food was woodland air
Though he would oft-times feast on gilliflowers rare.

III.

The slang of cities in no wise he knew,
Tipping the wink to him was heathen Greek;
He sipp'd no olden Tom or ruin blue,
Or nantz or cherry-brandy drank full meek
By many a damsel hoarse and rouge of cheek;
Nor did he know each aged watchman's beat,
Nor in obscured purlieus would he seek
For curled Jewesses, with ankles neat,
Who as they walk abroad make tinkling with their feet.

TWO OR THREE

FROM A LETTER TO HIS SISTER

Two or three Posies
With two or three simples—
Two or three Noses
With two or three pimples—
Two or three wise men
And two or three ninny's—
Two or three purses
And two or three guineas—
Two or three raps
At two or three doors—   10
Two or three naps
Of two or three hours—
Two or three Cats
And two or three mice—
Two or three sprats
At a very great price—
Two or three sandies
And two or three tabbies—
Two or three dandies
And two Mrs ————   mum!   20
Two or three Smiles
And two or three frowns—
Two or three Miles
To two or three towns—
Two or three pegs
For two or three bonnets—
Two or three dove eggs
To hatch into sonnets.

20 *The omission of Mrs. Abbey's name was probably a part of the joke.*

LA BELLE DAME SANS MERCI

I.

AH, what can ail thee, wretched wight,
    Alone and palely loitering;
The sedge is wither'd from the lake,
    And no birds sing.

II.

Ah, what can ail thee, wretched wight,
    So haggard and so woe-begone?
The squirrel's granary is full,
    And the harvest 's done.

III.

I see a lilly on thy brow,
    With anguish moist and fever dew;
And on thy cheek a fading rose
    Fast withereth too.

IV.

I met a lady in the meads
    Full beautiful, a faery's child;
Her hair was long, her foot was light,
    And her eyes were wild.

" La Belle Dame sans Merci " in its earliest known form was written into a journal-letter to George Keats and his wife in the latter half of April 1819, without any prelude, but with the heading—

Wednesday Evening—
La belle dame sans merci—

and written in a way that indicates fresh composition; for there are many corrections. This version was first published by Mr. Colvin in "Macmillan's Magazine" for August 1888. A revised version was published by Hunt in "The Indicator" on the 10th of May 1820. In Woodhouse's Common-place book is a transcript of the poem, which is probably the source of the version printed by Lord Houghton among the Literary Remains in 1848. The " Indicator " version is here adopted in the text, variations of more than ordinary interest being noted.

I and II 1 O what can ail thee, Knight at arms *Draft.*
    III I see death's lilly on thy brow
          With anguish moist and fever dew
          And on thy cheeks death's fading rose
          Withereth too. *Draft.*

The word **death's,** *however, is struck out in favour of a both in line 1 and in line 3 ; and* **Fast** *is put in before* withereth *in line 4.*

IV *In this stanza line 1 originally ended with* Wilds (*not* Wolds *as in " Macmillan's Magazine "*) *instead of* Meads.

V.

I set her on my pacing steed,
  And nothing else saw all day long;
For sideways would she lean, and sing
  A faery's song.

VI.

I made a garland for her head,
  And bracelets too, and fragrant zone ;
She look'd at me as she did love,
  And made sweet moan.

VII.

She found me roots of relish sweet,
  And honey wild, and manna dew ;
And sure in language strange she said,
  I love thee true.

VIII.

She took me to her elfin grot,
  And there she gaz'd and sighed deep,
And there I shut her wild sad eyes—
  So kiss'd to sleep.

IX.

And there we slumber'd on the moss,
  And there I dream'd, ah woe betide,
The latest dream I ever dream'd
  On the cold hill side.

V *This and the next stanza are transposed in the Draft and the
Woodhouse version ; and in the third line we read* sidelong would she
bend.

VII *Line 2 originally stood thus—*
    And honey wild and honey dew.
The only change made in the Draft in this stanza is the substitution of
manna dew *for* honey dew. *There is no trace of the word* once
given in "Macmillan's Magazine" in line 3.

VIII–IX *In Lord Houghton's version (following that of the journal-
letter and Woodhouse)—*
    She took me to her elfin grot,
      And there she wept, and sigh'd full sore,
    And there I shut her wild wild eyes
      With kisses four.
    And there she lulled me asleep, . . .
In the second line of stanza VIII is the cancelled reading
    And there she wept and there she sigh'd . . .
And in line 4 of stanzas IX and XI, we have hill's side *for* hill side.
The kisses four *perhaps struck Keats, upon review, as a little quaint ; and
the other changes are an organic consequence of that made here. Indeed,*

X.

I saw pale kings, and princes too,
　　Pale warriors, death-pale were they all;
Who cry'd—"La belle Dame sans merci
　　Hath thee in thrall!"

XI.

I saw their starv'd lips in the gloam
　　With horrid warning gaped wide,
And I awoke, and found me here
　　On the cold hill side.

XII.

And this is why I sojourn here
　　Alone and palely loitering,
Though the sedge is wither'd from the lake,
　　And no birds sing.

SONG OF FOUR FAERIES,

FIRE, AIR, EARTH, AND WATER,

SALAMANDER, ZEPHYR, DUSKETHA, AND BREAMA.

SALAMANDER.

HAPPY, happy glowing fire!

ZEPHYR.

Fragrant air! delicious light!

DUSKETHA.

Let me to my glooms retire!

in the journal-letter Keats says—"Why four kisses—you will say
—why four because I wish to restrain the headlong impetu-
osity of my Muse—she would have fain said 'score' without
hurting the rhyme—but we must temper the Imagination as
the Critics say with Judgment."

　　X *The Draft reads* They *for* Who *in line 3, and*
　　　　　Thee hath in thrall.
　　XI 1 gloam *Draft, Woodhouse, and Houghton :* gloom " *Indicator.*"
*Hunt probably made that small change.　Line 2 of the stanza had been
begun with* All tremble *and had then been written*
　　　　　With horrid warning wide agape
before the reading of the text was adopted.
　　XII 1　　And this is why I wither.— *Draft, rejected.*
　　*The " Song of Four Faeries " also occurs in the journal-letter con-
taining " La Belle Dame."*

BREAMA.

I to green-weed rivers bright!

SALAMANDER.

Happy, happy glowing fire!
Dazzling bowers of soft retire,
Ever let my nourish'd wing,
Like a bat's, still wandering,
Faintless fan your fiery spaces,
Spirit sole in deadly places.   10
In unhaunted roar and blaze,
Open eyes that never daze,
Let me see the myriad shapes
Of men, and beasts, and fish, and apes,
Portray'd in many a fiery den,
And wrought by spumy bitumen.
On the deep intenser roof,
Arched every way aloof,
Let me breathe upon their skies,
And anger their live tapestries;   20
Free from cold, and every care,
Of chilly rain, and shivering air.

ZEPHYR.

Spirit of Fire! away! away!
Or your very roundelay
Will sear my plumage newly budded
From its quilled sheath, all studded
With the self-same dews that fell
On the May-grown Asphodel.
Spirit of Fire—away! away!

BREAMA.

Spirit of Fire—away! away!   30
Zephyr, blue-eyed Faery, turn,
And see my cool sedge-bury'd urn,
Where it rests its mossy brim
'Mid water-mint and cresses dim;
And the flowers, in sweet troubles,
Lift their eyes above the bubbles,
Like our Queen, when she would please
To sleep, and Oberon *will* teaze.

Love me, blue-eyed Faery, true!
Soothly I am sick for you.   40

ZEPHYR.

Gentle Breama! by the first
Violet young nature nurst,
I will bathe myself with thee,
So you sometimes follow me
To my home, far, far, in west,
Beyond the nimble-wheeled quest
Of the golden-browed sun:
Come with me, o'er tops of trees,
To my fragrant palaces,
Where they ever floating are   50
Beneath the cherish of a star
Call'd Vesper, who with silver veil
Ever hides his brilliance pale,
Ever gently-drows'd doth keep
Twilight for the Fayes to sleep.
Fear not that your watery hair
Will thirst in drouthy ringlets there;
Clouds of stored summer rains
Thou shalt taste, before the stains
Of the mountain soil they take,   60
And too unlucent for thee make.
I love thee, crystal Faery, true!
Sooth I am as sick for you!

SALAMANDER.

Out, ye aguish Faeries, out!
Chilly lovers, what a rout
Keep ye with your frozen breath,
Colder than the mortal death.
Adder-eyed Dusketha, speak,
Shall we leave these, and go seek
In the earth's wide entrails old   70
Couches warm as their's are cold?
O for a fiery gloom and thee,
Dusketha, so enchantingly
Freckle-wing'd and lizard-sided!

46 Far beyond the search and quest *Journal-letter.*
65 Chillier than the water *Journal-letter, cancelled.*

DUSKETHA.

By thee, Sprite, will I be guided!
I care not for cold or heat;
Frost and flame, or sparks, or sleet,
To my essence are the same;—
But I honour more the flame.
Sprite of Fire, I follow thee   80
Wheresoever it may be,
To the torrid spouts and fountains,
Underneath earth-quaked mountains;
Or, at thy supreme desire,
Touch the very pulse of fire
With my bare unlidded eyes.

SALAMANDER.

Sweet Dusketha! paradise!
Off, ye icy Spirits, fly!
Frosty creatures of the sky!

DUSKETHA.

Breathe upon them, fiery sprite!   90

ZEPHYR AND BREAMA.

Away! away to our delight!

SALAMANDER.

Go, feed on icicles, while we
Bedded in tongue-flames will be.

DUSKETHA.

Lead me to those feverous glooms,
Sprite of Fire!

BREAMA.

       Me to the blooms,
Blue-eyed Zephyr, of those flowers
Far in the west where the May-cloud lowers;
And the beams of still Vesper, when winds
    are all wist,
Are shed thro' the rain and the milder mist,
And twilight your floating bowers.   100

82 To the very torrid fountains— *Journal-letter, rejected.*
98 when] where *Journal-letter.*

TWO SONNETS ON FAME

I

FAME, like a wayward Girl, will still be coy
  To those who woo her with too slavish knees,
But makes surrender to some thoughtless Boy,
  And dotes the more upon a heart at ease ;
She is a Gipsey, will not speak to those
  Who have not learnt to be content without her ;
A Jilt, whose ear was never whisper'd close,
  Who thinks they scandal her who talk about her;
A very Gipsey is she, Nilus-born,
  Sister-in-law to jealous Potiphar ;   10
Ye love-sick Bards, repay her scorn for scorn,
  Ye Artists lovelorn, madmen that ye are !
Make your best bow to her and bid adieu,
Then, if she likes it, she will follow you.

II

"You cannot eat your cake and have it too."—*Proverb.*

How fever'd is the man, who cannot look
  Upon his mortal days with temperate blood,
Who vexes all the leaves of his life's book,
  And robs his fair name of its maidenhood;
It is as if the rose should pluck herself,
  Or the ripe plum finger its misty bloom,
As if a Naiad, like a meddling elf,
  Should darken her pure grot with muddy gloom,
But the rose leaves herself upon the briar,
  For winds to kiss and grateful bees to feed,   10
And the ripe plum still wears its dim attire,
    The undisturbed lake has crystal space,
    Why then should man, teasing the world for grace,
Spoil his salvation for a fierce miscreed ?

These two sonnets also occur in the Journal-letter.

II 7-8 As if a clear Lake meddling with itself
        Should cloud its pureness with a muddy gloom
                              Journal-letter.

13-14 Why then should man his own bright name deface
      And burn our pleasures in his selfish fire
                          Journal-letter, rejected.

SONNET

ON THE SONNET

If by dull rhymes our English must be chain'd,
And, like Andromeda, the Sonnet sweet
Fetter'd, in spite of pained loveliness,
Let us find out, if we must be constrain'd,
Sandals more interwoven and complete
To fit the naked foot of Poesy:
Let us inspect the Lyre, and weigh the stress
Of every chord, and see what may be gain'd
By ear industrious, and attention meet;
Misers of sound and syllable, no less   10
Than Midas of his coinage, let us be
Jealous of dead leaves in the bay wreath crown;
So, if we may not let the Muse be free,
She will be bound with garlands of her own.

APOLLO AND THE GRACES

WRITTEN TO THE TUNE OF THE AIR IN "DON GIOVANNI"

APOLLO.

Which of the fairest three
To-day will ride with me?
My steeds are all pawing at the threshold of the morn:
Which of the fairest three
To-day will ride with me
Across the gold Autumn's whole Kingdom of corn?

THE GRACES *all answer.*

I will, I— I— I—
O young Apollo let me fly
Along with thee,
I will—I, I, I,   10
The many wonders see
I— I— I— I—
And thy lyre shall never have a slackened string:
I, I, I, I,
Thro' the golden day will sing.

* N 3

YOU SAY YOU LOVE

I.

You say you love ; but with a voice
   Chaster than a nun's, who singeth
The soft Vespers to herself
   While the chime-bell ringeth—
     O love me truly !

II.

You say you love ; but with a smile
   Cold as sunrise in September,
As you were Saint Cupid's nun,
   And kept his weeks of Ember.
     O love me truly !

III.

You say you love—but then your lips
   Coral tinted teach no blisses.
More than coral in the sea—
   They never pout for kisses—
     O love me truly !

IV.

You say you love ; but then your hand
   No soft squeeze for squeeze returneth,
It is like a statue's dead—
   While mine to passion burneth—
     O love me truly !

V.

O breathe a word or two of fire !
   Smile, as if those words should burn me,
Squeeze as lovers should—O kiss
   And in thy heart inurn me !
     O love me truly !

OTHO THE GREAT

A TRAGEDY

IN FIVE ACTS

DRAMATIS PERSONÆ

OTHO THE GREAT, *Emperor of Germany.*
LUDOLPH, *his Son.*
CONRAD, *Duke of Franconia.*
ALBERT, *a Knight, favoured by Otho.*
SIGIFRED, *an Officer, friend of Ludolph.*
THEODORE, } *Officers.*
GONFRED, }
ETHELBERT, *an Abbot.*
GERSA, *Prince of Hungary.*
An Hungarian Captain.
Physician.
Page.
Nobles, Knights, Attendants, and Soldiers.
ERMINIA, *Niece of Otho.*
AURANTHE, *Conrad's Sister.*
Ladies and Attendants.

SCENE. *The Castle of Friedburg, its vicinity, and the Hungarian Camp.*

TIME. *One Day.*

OTHO THE GREAT

ACT I.

SCENE I.—*An Apartment in the Castle.* *Enter* CONRAD.

Conrad. So, I am safe emerged from these broils!
Amid the wreck of thousands I am whole ;
For every crime I have a laurel-wreath,
For every lie a lordship. Nor yet has
My ship of fortune furl'd her silken sails,—
Let her glide on ! This danger'd neck is saved,
By dexterous policy, from the rebel's axe ;
And of my ducal palace not one stone
Is bruised by the Hungarian petards.
Toil hard, ye slaves, and from the miser-earth   10
Bring forth once more my bullion, treasured deep,
With all my jewell'd salvers, silver and gold,
And precious goblets that make rich the wine.
But why do I stand babbling to myself?
Where is Auranthe ? I have news for her
Shall—

Enter AURANTHE.

Auranthe. Conrad ! what tidings ? Good, if I may
   guess
From your alert eyes and high-lifted brows.
What tidings of the battle? Albert? Ludolph? Otho ?
   Conrad. You guess aright. And, sister, slurring o'er
Our by-gone quarrels, I confess my heart   20
Is beating with a child's anxiety,
To make our golden fortune known to you.
   Auranthe. So serious ?
   Conrad.   Yes, so serious, that before
I utter even the shadow of a hint
Concerning what will make that sin-worn cheek
Blush joyous blood through every lineament,
You must make here a solemn vow to me.
   Auranthe. I prythee, Conrad, do not overact

The hypocrite—what vow would you impose?

Conrad. Trust me for once,—that you may be assur'd
'Tis not confiding to a broken reed,   31
A poor Court-bankrupt, outwitted and lost,
Revolve these facts in your acutest mood,
In such a mood as now you listen to me :—
A few days since, I was an open rebel
Against the Emperor, had suborn'd his son,
Drawn off his nobles to revolt, and shown
Contented fools causes for discontent
Fresh hatch'd in my ambition's eagle nest—
So thriv'd I as a rebel, and behold   40
Now I am Otho's favourite, his dear friend,
His right hand, his brave Conrad.

   Auranthe.   I confess
You have intrigued with these unsteady times
To admiration ; but to be a favourite——

   Conrad. I saw my moment. The Hungarians,
Collected silently in holes and corners,
Appear'd, a sudden host, in the open day.
I should have perish'd in our empire's wreck,
But, calling interest loyalty, swore faith
To most believing Otho ; and so help'd   50
His blood-stain'd ensigns to the victory
In yesterday's hard fight, that it has turn'd
The edge of his sharp wrath to eager kindness.

   Auranthe. So far yourself. But what is this to me
More than that I am glad ? I gratulate you.

   Conrad. Yes, sister, but it does regard you greatly,
Nearly, momentously,—aye, painfully !
Make me this vow—

   Auranthe.   Concerning whom or what ?

   Conrad. Albert !

   Auranthe.   I would inquire somewhat of him :
You had a letter from me touching him ?   60
No treason 'gainst his head in deed or word !
Surely you spar'd him at my earnest prayer ?
Give me the letter—it should not exist !

   Conrad. At one pernicious charge of the enemy,
I, for a moment-whiles, was prisoner ta'en
And rifled,—stuff ! the horses' hoofs have minc'd it !

   Auranthe. He is alive ?

Conrad.   He is! but here make oath
To alienate him from your scheming brain,
Divorce him from your solitary thoughts,
And cloud him in such utter banishment,   70
That when his person meets again your eye,
Your vision shall quite lose its memory,
And wander past him as through vacancy.
    Auranthe. I'll not be perjured.
    Conrad.   No, nor great, nor mighty;
You would not wear a crown, or rule a kingdom.
To you it is indifferent.
    Auranthe.   What means this?
    Conrad. You'll not be perjured! Go to Albert then,
That camp-mushroom—dishonour of our house.
Go, page his dusty heels upon a march,
Furbish his jingling baldric while he sleeps,   80
And share his mouldy ration in a siege.
Yet stay,—perhaps a charm may call you back,
And make the widening circlets of your eyes
Sparkle with healthy fevers.—The Emperor
Hath given consent that you should marry Ludolph!
    Auranthe. Can it be, brother? For a golden crown
With a queen's awful lips I doubly thank you!
This is to wake in Paradise! Farewell
Thou clod of yesterday—'twas not myself!
Not till this moment did I ever feel   90
My spirit's faculties! I'll flatter you
For this, and be you ever proud of it;
Thou, Jove-like, struck'dst thy forehead,
And from the teeming marrow of thy brain
I spring complete Minerva! But the prince—
His highness Ludolph—where is he?
    Conrad.   I know not:
When, lackeying my counsel at a beck,
The rebel lords, on bended knees, received
The Emperor's pardon, Ludolph kept aloof,
Sole, in a stiff, fool-hardy, sulky pride;   100
Yet, for all this, I never saw a father
In such a sickly longing for his son.
We shall soon see him, for the Emperor
He will be here this morning.
    Auranthe.   That I heard

Among the midnight rumours from the camp.
    Conrad. You give up Albert to me?
    Auranthe.   Harm him not!
E'en for his highness Ludolph's sceptry hand,
I would not Albert suffer any wrong.
    Conrad. Have I not laboured, plotted—?
    Auranthe.   See you spare him:
Nor be pathetic, my kind benefactor,   110
On all the many bounties of your hand,—
'Twas for yourself you laboured—not for me!
Do you not count, when I am queen, to take
Advantage of your chance discoveries
Of my poor secrets, and so hold a rod
Over my life?
    Conrad.   Let not this slave—this villain—
Be cause of feud between us. See! he comes!
Look, woman, look, your Albert is quite safe!
In haste it seems. Now shall I be in the way,
And wish'd with silent curses in my grave,   120
Or side by side with 'whelmed mariners.

Enter ALBERT.

    Albert. Fair on your graces fall this early morrow!
So it is like to do, without my prayers,
For your right noble names, like favourite tunes,
Have fall'n full frequent from our Emperor's lips,
High commented with smiles.
    Auranthe.   Noble Albert!
    Conrad (aside).   Noble!
    Auranthe. Such salutation argues a glad heart
In our prosperity. We thank you, sir.
    Albert. Lady! O, would to Heaven your poor servant
Could do you better service than mere words!   130
But I have other greeting than mine own,
From no less man than Otho, who has sent
This ring as pledge of dearest amity;
'Tis chosen I hear from Hymen's jewel'ry,
And you will prize it, lady, I doubt not,
Beyond all pleasures past, and all to come.
To you great duke—
    Conrad.   To me! What of me, ha?
    Albert. What pleas'd your grace to say?

Conrad.   Your message, sir !
Albert. You mean not this to me ?
Conrad.   Sister, this way ;
For there shall be no "gentle Alberts" now,   [*Aside.*
No "sweet Auranthes !"   141

                    [*Exeunt* CONRAD *and* AURANTHE.

Albert (*solus*). The duke is out of temper ; if he knows
More than a brother of a sister ought,
I should not quarrel with his peevishness.
Auranthe—Heaven preserve her always fair !—
Is in the heady, proud, ambitious vein ;
I bicker not with her,—bid her farewell !
She has taken flight from me, then let her soar,—
He is a fool who stands at pining gaze !
But for poor Ludolph, he is food for sorrow: 150
No levelling bluster of my licens'd thoughts,
No military swagger of my mind,
Can smother from myself the wrong I've done him,—
Without design, indeed,—yet it is so,—
And opiate for the conscience have I none !   [*Exit.*

          SCENE II.—*The Court-yard of the Castle.*

Martial Music.   Enter, from the outer gate, OTHO, *Nobles,
     Knights, and Attendants.   The Soldiers halt at the
     gate, with Banners in sight.*

     Otho. Where is my noble herald ?

Enter CONRAD, *from the Castle, attended by two Knights
          and Servants.* ALBERT *following.*

                              Well, hast told
Auranthe our intent imperial ?
Lest our rent banners, too o' the sudden shown,
Should fright her silken casements, and dismay
Her household to our lack of entertainment.
A victory !
     Conrad. God save illustrious Otho !
     Otho. Aye, Conrad, it will pluck out all grey hairs ;
It is the best physician for the spleen ;
The courtliest inviter to a feast ;

The subtlest excuser of small faults;   10
And a nice judge in the age and smack of wine.

Enter, from the Castle, AURANTHE, *followed by Pages
     holding up her robes, and a train of Women. She
     kneels.*

Hail my sweet hostess! I do thank the stars,
Or my good soldiers, or their ladies' eyes,
That, after such a merry battle fought,
I can, all safe in body and in soul,
Kiss your fair hand and lady fortune's too.
My ring! now, on my life, it doth rejoice
These lips to feel 't on this soft ivory!
Keep it, my brightest daughter; it may prove
The little prologue to a line of kings.   20
I strove against thee and my hot-blood son,
Dull blockhead that I was to be so blind,
But now my sight is clear; forgive me, lady.
     Auranthe. My lord, I was a vassal to your frown,
And now your favour makes me but more humble;
In wintry winds the simple snow is safe,
But fadeth at the greeting of the sun:
Unto thine anger I might well have spoken,
Taking on me a woman's privilege,
But this so sudden kindness makes me dumb.   30
     Otho. What need of this? Enough, if you will be
A potent tutoress to my wayward boy,
And teach him, what it seems his nurse could not,
To say, for once, I thank you. Sigifred!
     Albert. He has not yet return'd, my gracious liege.
     Otho. What then! No tidings of my friendly Arab?
     Conrad. None, mighty Otho.
                          [*To one of his Knights, who goes out.*
                              Send forth instantly
An hundred horsemen from my honoured gates,
To scour the plains and search the cottages.
Cry a reward, to him who shall first bring   40
News of that vanished Arabian,
A full-heap'd helmet of the purest gold.
     Otho. More thanks, good Conrad; for, except my son's,

10 subtlest] subtelest *MS.*

There is no face I rather would behold
Than that same quick-eyed pagan's. By the saints,
This coming night of banquets must not light
Her dazzling torches; nor the music breathe
Smooth, without clashing cymbal, tones of peace
And in-door melodies; nor the ruddy wine
Ebb spouting to the lees; if I pledge not,   50
In my first cup, that Arab!
   Albert.   Mighty Monarch,
I wonder not this stranger's victor-deeds
So hang upon your spirit. Twice in the fight
It was my chance to meet his olive brow,
Triumphant in the enemy's shatter'd rhomb;
And, to say truth, in any Christian arm
I never saw such prowess.
   Otho.   Did you ever?
O, 'tis a noble boy!—tut!—what do I say?
I mean a triple Saladin, whose eyes,
When in the glorious scuffle they met mine,   60
Seem'd to say—"Sleep, old man, in safety sleep;
I am the victory!"
   Conrad.   Pity he's not here.
   Otho. And my son too, pity he is not here.
Lady Auranthe, I would not make you blush,
But can you give a guess where Ludolph is?
Know you not of him?
   Auranthe.   Indeed, my liege, no secret—
   Otho. Nay, nay, without more words, dost know
     of him?
   Auranthe. I would I were so over-fortunate,
Both for his sake and mine, and to make glad
A father's ears with tidings of his son.   70
   Otho. I see 'tis like to be a tedious day.
Were Theodore and Gonfred and the rest
Sent forth with my commands?
   Albert.   Aye, my lord.
   Otho. And no news! No news! 'Faith! 'tis very
     strange
He thus avoids us. Lady, is't not strange?
Will he be truant to you too? It is a shame.
   Conrad. Will't please your highness enter, and accept
The unworthy welcome of your servant's house?

Leaving your cares to one whose diligence
May in few hours make pleasures of them all.   80
  Otho. Not so tedious, Conrad. No, no, no,—
I must see Ludolph or the—What's that shout!
  Voices without. Huzza! huzza! Long live the Emperor!
  Other Voices. Fall back! Away there!
  Otho.   Say, what noise is that?

> [ALBERT *advancing from the back of the Stage,
> whither he had hastened on hearing the
> cheers of the soldiery.*

  Albert. It is young Gersa, the Hungarian prince,
Pick'd like a red stag from the fallow herd
Of prisoners. Poor prince, forlorn he steps,
Slow, and demure, and proud in his despair.
If I may judge by his so tragic bearing,
His eye not downcast, and his folded arm,   90
He doth this moment wish himself asleep
Among his fallen captains on yon plains.

> *Enter* GERSA, *in chains, and guarded.*

  Otho. Well said, Sir Albert.
  Gersa.   Not a word of greeting,
No welcome to a princely visitor,
Most mighty Otho? Will not my great host
Vouchsafe a syllable, before he bids
His gentlemen conduct me with all care
To some securest lodging?—cold perhaps!
  Otho. What mood is this? Hath fortune touch'd
      thy brain?
  Gersa. O kings and princes of this fev'rous world,
What abject things, what mockeries must ye be, 101
What nerveless minions of safe palaces!
When here, a monarch, whose proud foot is used
To fallen princes' necks, as to his stirrup,
Must needs exclaim that I am mad forsooth,
Because I cannot flatter with bent knees
My conqueror!
  Otho.   Gersa, I think you wrong me:
I think I have a better fame abroad.
  Gersa. I prythee mock me not with gentle speech,
But, as a favour, bid me from thy presence;   110

Let me no longer be the wondering food
Of all these eyes ; prythee command me hence !
   Otho. Do not mistake me, Gersa. That you may not,
Come, fair Auranthe, try if your soft hands
Can manage those hard rivets to set free
So brave a prince and soldier.
   Auranthe (*sets him free*).   Welcome task !
   Gersa. I am wound up in deep astonishment !
Thank you, fair lady. Otho ! emperor !
You rob me of myself ; my dignity
Is now your infant ; I am a weak child.   120
   Otho. Give me your hand, and let this kindly grasp
Live in our memories.   In mine it will.
   Gersa.
I blush to think of my unchasten'd tongue ;
But I was haunted by the monstrous ghost
Of all our slain battalions. Sire, reflect,
And pardon you will grant, that, at this hour,
The bruised remnants of our stricken camp
Are huddling undistinguish'd my dear friends,
With common thousands, into shallow graves.
   Otho. Enough, most noble Gersa. You are free
To cheer the brave remainder of your host   131
By your own healing presence, and that too,
Not as their leader merely, but their king ;
For, as I hear, the wily enemy,
Who eas'd the crownet from your infant brows,
Bloody Taraxa, is among the dead.
   Gersa. Then I retire, so generous Otho please,
Bearing with me a weight of benefits
Too heavy to be borne.
   Otho.   It is not so ;
Still understand me, King of Hungary,   140
Nor judge my open purposes awry.
Though I did hold you high in my esteem
For your self's sake, I do not personate
The stage-play emperor to entrap applause,
To set the silly sort o' the world agape,
And make the politic smile ; no, I have heard
How in the Council you condemn'd this war,
Urging the perfidy of broken faith,—
For that I am your friend.

Gersa. If ever, sire,
You are mine enemy, I dare here swear 150
'Twill not be Gersa's fault. Otho, farewell!
   Otho. Will you return, Prince, to our banqueting?
   Gersa. As to my father's board I will return.
   Otho. Conrad, with all due ceremony, give
The prince a regal escort to his camp;
Albert, go thou and bear him company.
Gersa, farewell!
   Gersa. All happiness attend you!
   Otho. Return with what good speed you may; for soon
We must consult upon our terms of peace.

     [*Exeunt* GERSA *and* ALBERT *with others.*

And thus a marble column do I build 160
To prop my empire's dome. Conrad, in thee
I have another stedfast one, to uphold
The portals of my state; and, for my own
Pre-eminence and safety, I will strive
To keep thy strength upon its pedestal.
For, without thee, this day I might have been
A show-monster about the streets of Prague,
In chains, as just now stood that noble prince:
And then to me no mercy had been shown,
For when the conquer'd lion is once dungeon'd, 170
Who lets him forth again? or dares to give
An old lion sugar-cates of mild reprieve?
Not to thine ear alone I make confession,
But to all here, as, by experience,
I know how the great basement of all power
Is frankness, and a true tongue to the world;
And how intriguing secrecy is proof
Of fear and weakness, and a hollow state.
Conrad, I owe thee much.
   Conrad. To kiss that hand,
My emperor, is ample recompense, 180
For a mere act of duty.
   Otho. Thou art wrong;
For what can any man on earth do more?
We will make trial of your house's welcome,
My bright Auranthe!
   Conrad. How is Friedburg honoured!

Enter ETHELBERT *and six Monks.*

Ethelbert. The benison of heaven on your head,
Imperial Otho !

Otho.   Who stays me ? Speak ! Quick !

Ethelbert. Pause but one moment, mighty conqueror
Upon the threshold of this house of joy.

Otho. Pray, do not prose, good Ethelbert, but speak
What is your purpose.   190

Ethelbert. The restoration of some captive maids,
Devoted to Heaven's pious ministries,
Who, being driven from their religious cells,
And kept in thraldom by our enemy,
When late this province was a lawless spoil,
Still weep amid the wild Hungarian camp,
Though hemm'd around by thy victorious arms.

Otho. Demand the holy sisterhood in our name
From Gersa's tents. Farewell, old Ethelbert.   199

Ethelbert. The saints will bless you for this pious care.

Otho. Daughter, your hand ; Ludolph's would fit it
best.

Conrad. Ho ! let the music sound !

> [*Music.* ETHELBERT *raises his hands, as in
> benediction of* OTHO. *Exeunt severally.
> The scene closes on them.*

SCENE III.—*The Country, with the Castle in the distance.*

Enter LUDOLPH *and* SIGIFRED.

Ludolph. You have my secret ; let it not be breath'd.

Sigifred. Still give me leave to wonder that the Prince
Ludolph and the swift Arab are the same ;
Still to rejoice that 'twas a German arm
Death doing in a turban'd masquerade.

Ludolph. The Emperor must not know it, Sigifred.

Sigifred. I prythee, why ? What happier hour of time
Could thy pleas'd star point down upon from heaven
With silver index, bidding thee make peace ?

Ludolph. Still it must not be known, good Sigifred ;

193 Who, driven forth from their religious cells, *Houghton.*

The star may point oblique.   11
    Sigifred.   If Otho knew
His son to be that unknown Mussulman
After whose spurring heels he sent me forth,
With one of his well-pleas'd Olympian oaths,
The charters of man's greatness, at this hour
He would be watching round the castle walls,
And, like an anxious warder, strain his sight
For the first glimpse of such a son return'd—
Ludolph, that blast of the Hungarians,
That Saracenic meteor of the fight,   20
That silent fury, whose fell scymitar
Kept danger all aloof from Otho's head,
And left him space for wonder.
    Ludolph.   Say no more.
Not as a swordsman would I pardon claim,
But as a son. The bronz'd centurion,
Long toil'd in foreign wars, and whose high deeds
Are shaded in a forest of tall spears,
Known only to his troop, hath greater plea
Of favour with my sire than I can have.   29
    Sigifred. My lord, forgive me that I cannot see
How this proud temper with clear reason squares.
What made you then, with such an anxious love,
Hover around that life, whose bitter days
You vext with bad revolt? Was 't opium,
Or the mad-fumed wine? Nay, do not frown,
I rather would grieve with you than upbraid.
    Ludolph. I do believe you. No, 'twas not to make
A father his son's debtor, or to heal
His deep heart-sickness for a rebel child.
'Twas done in memory of my boyish days,   40
Poor cancel for his kindness to my youth,
For all his calming of my childish griefs,
And all his smiles upon my merriment.
No, not a thousand foughten fields could sponge
Those days paternal from my memory,
Though now upon my head he heaps disgrace.
    Sigifred. My Prince, you think too harshly—
    Ludolph.   Can I so?

44-5 Ever will those bright days live in my heart
    Though he still *MS.*, *cancelled.*

Hath he not gall'd my spirit to the quick?
And with a sullen rigour obstinate
Pour'd out a phial of wrath upon my faults?   50
Hunted me as the Tartar does the boar,
Driven me to the very edge o' the world,
And almost put a price upon my head?

    Sigifred. Remember how he spar'd the rebel lords.

    Ludolph. Yes, yes, I know he hath a noble nature
That cannot trample on the fallen. But his
Is not the only proud heart in his realm.
He hath wrong'd me, and I have done him wrong;
He hath lov'd me, and I have shown him kindness;
We should be almost equal.

    Sigifred.   Yet, for all this,   60
I would you had appear'd among those lords,
And ta'en his favour.

    Ludolph.   Ha! till now I thought
My friend had held poor Ludolph's honour dear.
What! would you have me sue before his throne
And kiss the courtier's missal, its silk steps?
Or hug the golden housings of his steed,
Amid a camp, whose steeled swarms I dar'd
But yesterday? And, at the trumpet sound,
Bow like some unknown mercenary's flag,
And lick the soiled grass? No, no, my friend,   70
I would not, I, be pardon'd in the heap,
And bless indemnity with all that scum,—
Those men I mean, who on my shoulders propp'd
Their weak rebellion, winning me with lies,
And pitying forsooth my many wrongs;
Poor self-deceived wretches, who must think
Each one himself a king in embryo,
Because some dozen vassals cry'd—my lord!
Cowards, who never knew their little hearts,
Till flurried danger held the mirror up,   80
And then they own'd themselves without a blush,
Curling, like spaniels, round my father's feet.
Such things deserted me and are forgiven,
While I, least guilty, am an outcast still,

55 He hath a noble nature, well I know. *MS., rejected.*
65 missal] Bible *MS., cancelled.*
66 steed] horse *MS., cancelled.*

And will be, for I love such fair disgrace.

Sigifred. I know the clear truth ; so would Otho see,
For he is just and noble. Fain would I
Be pleader for you—

    Ludolph.   He'll hear none of it ;
You know his temper, hot, proud, obstinate ;
Endanger not yourself so uselessly.   90
I will encounter his thwart spleen myself,
To-day, at the Duke Conrad's, where he keeps
His crowded state after the victory.
There will I be, a most unwelcome guest,
And parley with him, as a son should do,
Who doubly loathes a father's tyranny ;
Tell him how feeble is that tyranny ;
How the relationship of father and son
Is no more valid than a silken leash
Where lions tug adverse, if love grow not   100
From interchanged love through many years.
Aye, and those turreted Franconian walls,
Like to a jealous casket, hold my pearl—
My fair Auranthe ! Yes, I will be there.

    Sigifred. Be not so rash ; wait till his wrath shall pass,
Until his royal spirit softly ebbs
Self-influenced ; then, in his morning dreams
He will forgive thee, and awake in grief
To have not thy good morrow.

    Ludolph.   Yes, to-day
I must be there, while her young pulses beat   110
Among the new-plum'd minions of the war.
Have you seen her of late ? No ? Auranthe,
Franconia's fair sister, 'tis I mean.
She should be paler for my troublous days—
And there it is—my father's iron lips
Have sworn divorcement 'twixt me and my right.

    Sigifred (*aside*). Auranthe ! I had hop'd this whim
      had pass'd.

    Ludolph. And, Sigifred, with all his love of justice,
When will he take that grandchild in his arms,
That, by my love I swear, shall soon be his ?   120

101 From mutual benefits *MS.*, *rejected.*
112–13 Auranthe 'tis I mean, the Duke's fair sister
                                   MS., *cancelled.*

This reconcilement is impossible,
For see—but who are these?

 Sigifred.   They are messengers
From our great emperor; to you, I doubt not,
For couriers are abroad to seek you out.

    Enter THEODORE *and* GONFRED.

 Theodore. Seeing so many vigilant eyes explore
The province to invite your highness back
To your high dignities, we are too happy.

 Gonfred. We have no eloquence to colour justly
The emperor's anxious wishes.

 Ludolph.   Go. I follow you.

    [*Exeunt* THEODORE *and* GONFRED.

I play the prude: it is but venturing—   130
Why should he be so earnest? Come, my friend,
Let us to Friedburg castle.

ACT II.

SCENE I.—*An Ante-chamber in the Castle.*

Enter LUDOLPH *and* SIGIFRED.

 Ludolph. No more advices, no more cautioning:
I leave it all to fate—to any thing!
I cannot square my conduct to time, place,
Or circumstance; to me 'tis all a mist!

 Sigifred. I say no more.

 Ludolph.   It seems I am to wait
Here in the ante-room;—that may be a trifle.
You see now how I dance attendance here,
Without that tyrant temper, you so blame,
Snapping the rein. You have medicin'd me
With good advices; and I here remain,   10
In this most honourable ante-room,
Your patient scholar.

 Sigifred.   Do not wrong me, Prince.
By Heavens, I'd rather kiss Duke Conrad's slipper,
When in the morning he doth yawn with pride,
Than see you humbled but a half-degree!

Truth is, the Emperor would fain dismiss
The nobles ere he sees you.

Enter GONFRED *from the Council-room.*

    Ludolph.   Well, sir! what?
    Gonfred. Great honour to the Prince! The Emperor,
Hearing that his brave son had re-appeared,
Instant dismiss'd the Council from his sight,   20
As Jove fans off the clouds.   Even now they pass.
                                         [*Exit.*

Enter the Nobles from the Council-room.   They cross the
    stage, bowing with respect to LUDOLPH, *he frowning on*
    them. CONRAD *follows.   Exeunt Nobles.*

    Ludolph. Not the discoloured poisons of a fen,
Which he who breathes feels warning of his death,
Could taste so nauseous to the bodily sense,
As these prodigious sycophants disgust
The soul's fine palate.
    Conrad.   Princely Ludolph, hail!
Welcome, thou younger sceptre to the realm!
Strength to thy virgin crownet's golden buds,
That they, against the winter of thy sire,
May burst, and swell, and flourish round thy brows,   30
Maturing to a weighty diadem!
Yet be that hour far off; and may he live,
Who waits for thee, as the chapp'd earth for rain.
Set my life's star! I have lived long enough,
Since under my glad roof, propitiously,
Father and son each other re-possess.
    Ludolph. Fine wording, Duke! but words could
        never yet
Forestall the fates; have you not learnt that yet?
Let me look well: your features are the same;
Your gait the same; your hair of the same shade;   40
As one I knew some passed weeks ago,
Who sung far different notes into mine ears.
I have mine own particular comments on 't;

---

24 Not the death watch tickling a Beldam's ear
                                  MS., cancelled.
26 The relish of my soul's invisible tongue *MS., rejected.*

You have your own, perhaps.

Conrad.   My gracious Prince,
All men may err. In truth I was deceived
In your great father's nature, as you were.
Had I known that of him I have since known,
And what you soon will learn, I would have turn'd
My sword to my own throat, rather than held
Its threatening edge against a good King's quiet :   50
Or with one word fever'd you, gentle Prince,
Who seem'd to me, as rugged times then went,
Indeed too much oppress'd. May I be bold
To tell the Emperor you will haste to him?

   Ludolph. Your Dukedom's privilege will grant so
     much.   [*Exit* CONRAD.
He's very close to Otho, a tight leech!
Your hand—I go. Ha! here the thunder comes
Sullen against the wind! If in two angry brows
My safety lies, then Sigifred, I'm safe.

       Enter OTHO *and* CONRAD.

   Otho. Will you make Titan play the lackey-page   60
To chattering pigmies? I would have you know
That such neglect of our high Majesty
Annuls all feel of kindred. What is son,—
Or friend,—or brother,—or all ties of blood,—
When the whole kingdom, centred in ourself,
Is rudely slighted? Who am I to wait?
By Peter's chair! I have upon my tongue
A word to fright the proudest spirit here!—
Death!—and slow tortures to the hardy fool,
Who dares take such large charter from our smiles! 70
Conrad, we would be private. Sigifred!
Off! And none pass this way on pain of death!
           [*Exeunt* CONRAD *and* SIGIFRED.

   Ludolph. This was but half expected, my good sire,
Yet I am griev'd at it, to the full height,
As though my hopes of favour had been whole.

   Otho. How you indulge yourself! What can you
     hope for?

---

51 And with one word put fever in your heart *MS., cancelled.*

Ludolph. Nothing, my liege; I have to hope for
   nothing.
I come to greet you as a loving son,
And then depart, if I may be so free,
Seeing that blood of yours in my warm veins   80
Has not yet mitigated into milk.
   Otho. What would you, sir?
   Ludolph.   A lenient banishment;
So please you let me unmolested pass
This Conrad's gates, to the wide air again.
I want no more. A rebel wants no more.
   Otho. And shall I let a rebel loose again
To muster kites and eagles 'gainst my head?
No, obstinate boy, you shall be kept cag'd up,
Serv'd with harsh food, with scum for Sunday-drink.
   Ludolph. Indeed!
   Otho.   And chains too heavy for your life:
I'll choose a gaoler, whose swart monstrous face 91
Shall be a hell to look upon, and she—
   Ludolph.   Ha!
   Otho. Shall be your fair Auranthe.
   Ludolph.   Amaze! Amaze!
   Otho. To-day you marry her.
   Ludolph.   This is a sharp jest!
   Otho. No. None at all. When have I said a lie?
   Ludolph. If I sleep not, I am a waking wretch.
   Otho. Not a word more. Let me embrace my child.
   Ludolph. I dare not. 'Twould pollute so good a
   father!
O heavy crime! that your son's blinded eyes
Could not see all his parent's love aright,   100
As now I see it. Be not kind to me—
Punish me not with favour.
   Otho.   Are you sure,
Ludolph, you have no saving plea in store?
   Ludolph. My father, none!
   Otho.   Then you astonish me.
   Ludolph. No, I have no plea. Disobedience,
Rebellion, obstinacy, blasphemy,

89 Serv'd with harsh food, with puddle for your drink
                         MS., rejected.

Are all my counsellors. If they can make
My crooked deeds show good and plausible,
Then grant me loving pardon, but not else,
Good Gods! not else, in any way, my liege!   110
    Otho. You are a most perplexing, noble boy.
    Ludolph. You not less a perplexing noble father.
    Otho. Well, you shall have free passport through
      the gates.
Farewell!
    Ludolph. Farewell! and by these tears believe,
And still remember, I repent in pain
All my misdeeds!
    Otho.   Ludolph, I will! I will!
But, Ludolph, ere you go, I would enquire
If you, in all your wandering, ever met
A certain Arab haunting in these parts.
    Ludolph. No, my good lord, I cannot say I did.   120
    Otho. Make not your father blind before his time;
Nor let these arms paternal hunger more
For an embrace, to dull the appetite
Of my great love for thee, my supreme child!
Come close, and let me breathe into thine ear.
I knew you through disguise. You are the Arab!
You can't deny it.   [*Embracing him.*
    Ludolph.   Happiest of days!
    Otho. We'll make it so.
    Ludolph.   'Stead of one fatted calf
Ten hecatombs shall bellow out their last,
Smote 'twixt the horns by the death-stunning mace   130
Of Mars, and all the soldiery shall feast
Nobly as Nimrod's masons, when the towers
Of Nineveh new kiss'd the parted clouds!
    Otho. Large as a God speak out, where all is thine.
    Ludolph. Aye, father, but the fire in my sad breast
Is quench'd with inward tears! I must rejoice
For you, whose wings so shadow over me
In tender victory, but for myself
I still must mourn. The fair Auranthe mine!
Too great a boon! I prythee let me ask   140
What more than I know of could so have changed
Your purpose touching her?
    Otho.   At a word, this:

In no deed did you give me more offence
Than your rejection of Erminia.
To my appalling, I saw too good proof
Of your keen-eyed suspicion,—she is naught!
    Ludolph. You are convinc'd?
    Otho.   Aye, spite of her sweet looks.
O, that my brother's daughter should so fall!
Her fame has pass'd into the grosser lips
Of soldiers in their cups.
    Ludolph.   'Tis very sad.   150
    Otho. No more of her.   Auranthe—Ludolph, come!
This marriage be the bond of endless peace! [*Exeunt.*

SCENE II.—*The Entrance of* GERSA'S *Tent in the*
Hungarian Camp.

Enter ERMINIA.

Erminia. Where! where! where shall I find a
    messenger?
A trusty soul? A good man in the camp?
Shall I go myself? Monstrous wickedness!
O cursed Conrad! devilish Auranthe!
Here is proof palpable as the bright sun!
O for a voice to reach the Emperor's ears!
                       [*Shouts in the Camp.*

Enter an HUNGARIAN CAPTAIN.

Captain. Fair prisoner, hear you those joyous shouts?
The king—aye, now our king,—but still your slave,
Young Gersa, from a short captivity
Has just return'd. He bids me say, bright Dame, 10
That even the homage of his ranged chiefs
Cures not his keen impatience to behold
Such beauty once again. What ails you, lady?
    Erminia. Say, is not that a German, yonder? There!
    Captain. Methinks by his stout bearing he should be—
Yes—'tis one Albert; a brave German knight,
And much in the emperor's favour.
    Erminia.   I would fain
Enquire of friends and kinsfolk; how they fared
In these rough times. Brave soldier, as you pass

To royal Gersa with my humble thanks,   20
Will you send yonder knight to me?
    Captain.   I will. [*Exit.*
    Erminia. Yes, he was ever known to be a man
Frank, open, generous; Albert I may trust.
O proof! proof! proof! Albert's an honest man;
Not Ethelbert the monk, if he were here,
Would I hold more trustworthy. Now!

Enter ALBERT.

    Albert.   Good Gods!
Lady Erminia! are you prisoner
In this beleaguer'd camp? Or are you here
Of your own will? You pleas'd to send for me.
By Venus, 'tis a pity I knew not   30
Your plight before, and, by her Son, I swear
To do you every service you can ask.
What would the fairest—?
    Erminia.   Albert, will you swear?
    Albert. I have. Well?
    Erminia.   Albert, you have fame to lose.
If men, in court and camp, lie not outright,
You should be, from a thousand, chosen forth
To do an honest deed. Shall I confide—?
    Albert. Aye, anything to me, fair creature. Do;
Dictate my task. Sweet woman,—
    Erminia.   Truce with that.
You understand me not; and, in your speech, 40
I see how far the slander is abroad.
Without proof could you think me innocent?
    Albert. Lady, I should rejoice to know you so.
    Erminia. If you have any pity for a maid,
Suffering a daily death from evil tongues;
Any compassion for that Emperor's niece,
Who, for your bright sword and clear honesty,
Lifted you from the crowd of common men
Into the lap of honour;—save me, knight!
    Albert. How? Make it clear; if it be possible, 50
I, by the banner of Saint Maurice, swear
To right you.
    Erminia. Possible!—Easy. O my heart!
This letter's not so soil'd but you may read it:—

Possible! There—that letter! Read—read it.
                              [*Gives him a letter.*

    Albert (reading). "To the Duke Conrad.—Forget the
threat you made at parting, and I will forget to send
the Emperor letters and papers of your's I have become
possessed of. His life is no trifle to me ; his death you
shall find none to yourself." (*Speaks to himself:*) 'Tis
me—my life that's pleaded for! (*Reads.*) "He, for
his own sake, will be dumb as the grave. Erminia has
my shame fix'd upon her, sure as a wen. We are safe.
                        AURANTHE."
A she-devil! A dragon! I her imp!
Fire of Hell! Auranthe—lewd demon!
Where got you this? Where? When?
    Erminia. I found it in the tent, among some spoils
Which, being noble, fell to Gersa's lot.
Come in, and see.   [*They go in and return.*
    Albert.   Villainy! Villainy!
Conrad's sword, his corslet, and his helm,   70
And his letter. Caitiff, he shall feel—
    Erminia. I see you are thunderstruck. Haste, haste
      away!
    Albert. O I am tortured by this villainy.
    Erminia. You needs must be. Carry it swift to Otho;
Tell him, moreover, I am prisoner
Here in this camp, where all the sisterhood,
Forc'd from their quiet cells, are parcell'd out
For slaves among these Huns. Away! Away!
    Albert. I am gone.
    Erminia.   Swift be your steed! Within this hour
The Emperor will see it.
    Albert.   Ere I sleep :   80
That I can swear.   [*Hurries out.*
    Gersa (without). Brave captains! thanks. Enough
Of loyal homage now!

             Enter GERSA.

    Erminia.   Hail, royal Hun!
    Gersa. What means this, fair one? Why in such
      alarm?
Who was it hurried by me so distract?
It seem'd you were in deep discourse together;

Your doctrine has not been so harsh to him
As to my poor deserts. Come, come, be plain.
I am no jealous fool to kill you both,
Or, for such trifles, rob the adorned world
Of such a beauteous vestal.
    Erminia.   I grieve, my Lord,   90
To hear you condescend to ribald phrase.
    Gersa. This is too much ! Hearken, my lady pure !
    Erminia. Silence ! and hear the magic of a name—
Erminia ! I am she,—the Emperor's niece !
Prais'd be the Heavens, I now dare own myself !
    Gersa. Erminia ! Indeed ! I've heard of her.
Prythee, fair lady, what chance brought you here ?
    Erminia. Ask your own soldiers.
    Gersa.   And you dare own your name.
For loveliness you may—and for the rest
My vein is not censorious.
    Erminia.   Alas ! poor me !   100
'Tis false indeed.
    Gersa.   Indeed you are too fair :
The swan, soft leaning on her fledgy breast,
When to the stream she launches, looks not back
With such a tender grace ; nor are her wings
So white as your soul is, if that but be
Twin-picture to your face. Erminia !
To-day, for the first day, I am a king,
Yet would I give my unworn crown away
To know you spotless.
    Erminia.   Trust me one day more,
Generously, without more certain guarantee,   110
Than this poor face you deign to praise so much ;
After that, say and do whate'er you please.
If I have any knowledge of you, sir,
I think, nay I am sure, you will grieve much
To hear my story. O be gentle to me,
For I am sick and faint with many wrongs,

96-100 Then you dare do no more than women dare
         Who dare the devil on his 'vantage ground
         Yet if some strange report I heard hold good
         You are in truth no coward. Ha ! Erminia !
                  MS., last two words cancelled.

Tir'd out, and weary-worn with contumelies.

   Gersa. Poor lady!

Enter ETHELBERT.

   Erminia.   Gentle Prince, 'tis false indeed.
Good morrow, holy father! I have had
Your prayers, though I look'd for you in vain.   120
   Ethelbert. Blessings upon you, daughter! Sure you look
Too cheerful for these foul pernicious days.
Young man, you heard this virgin say 'twas false, –
'Tis false, I say. What! can you not employ
Your temper elsewhere, 'mong these burly tents,
But you must taunt this dove, for she hath lost
The Eagle Otho to beat off assault?
Fie! fie! But I will be her guard myself;
In the Emperor's name. I here demand of you
Herself, and all her sisterhood. She false!   130
   Gersa. Peace! peace, old man! I cannot think she is.
   Ethelbert. Whom I have known from her first infancy,
Baptiz'd her in the bosom of the Church,
Watch'd her, as anxious husbandmen the grain,
From the first shoot till the unripe mid-May,
Then to the tender ear of her June days,
Which, lifting sweet abroad its timid green,
Is blighted by the touch of calumny;
You cannot credit such a monstrous tale.
   Gersa. I cannot. Take her. Fair Erminia,   140
I follow you to Friedburg,—is't not so?
   Erminia. Aye, so we purpose.
   Ethelbert.   Daughter, do you so?
How's this? I marvel! Yet you look not mad.
   Erminia. I have good news to tell you, Ethelbert.
   Gersa. Ho! ho, there! Guards!
Your blessing, father! Sweet Erminia,
Believe me, I am well nigh sure—
   Erminia.   Farewell!
Short time will show.   [*Enter Chiefs.*
        Yes, father Ethelbert,
I have news precious as we pass along.
   Ethelbert. Dear daughter, you shall guide me.   149
   Erminia.   To no ill.

Gersa. Command an escort to the Friedburg lines.
  [*Exeunt Chiefs.*
Pray let me lead.   Fair lady, forget not
Gersa, how he believ'd you innocent.
I follow you to Friedburg with all speed.   [*Exeunt.*

ACT III.

Scene I.—*The Country.*

Enter ALBERT.

Albert. O that the earth were empty, as when Cain
Had no perplexity to hide his head !
Or that the sword of some brave enemy
Had put a sudden stop to my hot breath,
And hurl'd me down the illimitable gulph
Of times past, unremember'd !   Better so
Than thus fast-limed in a cursed snare,
The white limbs of a wanton.   This the end
Of an aspiring life !   My boyhood past
In feud with wolves and bears, when no eye saw
The solitary warfare, fought for love   11
Of honour 'mid the growling wilderness.
My sturdier youth, maturing to the sword,
Won by the syren-trumpets, and the ring
Of shields upon the pavement, when bright-mail'd
Henry the Fowler pass'd the streets of Prague.
Was 't to this end I louted and became.
The menial of Mars, and held a spear
Sway'd by command, as corn is by the wind ?
Is it for this, I now am lifted up   20
By Europe's throned Emperor, to see
My honour be my executioner,—
My love of fame, my prided honesty
Put to the torture for confessional ?
Then the damn'd crime of blurting to the world
A woman's secret !—Though a fiend she be,
Too tender of my ignominious life ;
But then to wrong the generous Emperor
In such a searching point, were to give up
My soul for foot-ball at Hell's holiday !   30

I must confess,—and cut my throat,—to-day?
To-morrow?   Ho! some wine!

Enter SIGIFRED.

Sigifred.   A fine humour—
  Albert. Who goes there? Count Sigifred? Ha! Ha!
  Sigifred. What, man, do you mistake the hollow sky
For a throng'd tavern,—and these stubbed trees
For old serge hangings,—me, your humble friend,
For a poor waiter?   Why, man, how you stare!
What gipsies have you been carousing with?
No, no more wine; methinks you've had enough.
  Albert. You well may laugh and banter. What a fool
An injury may make of a staid man!   41
You shall know all anon.
  Sigifred.   Some tavern brawl?
  Albert. 'Twas with some people out of common reach;
Revenge is difficult.
  Sigifred.   I am your friend;
We meet again to-day, and can confer
Upon it. For the present I'm in haste.
  Albert. Whither?
  Sigifred.   To fetch King Gersa to the feast.
The Emperor on this marriage is so hot,
Pray Heaven it end not in apoplexy!
The very porters, as I pass'd the doors,   50
Heard his loud laugh, and answer'd in full choir.
I marvel, Albert, you delay so long
From those bright revelries; go, show yourself.
You may be made a duke.
  Albert.   Aye, very like:
Pray, what day has his Highness fix'd upon?
  Sigifred. For what?
  Albert.   The marriage. What else can I mean?
  Sigifred. To-day! O, I forgot, you could not know;
The news is scarce a minute old with me.
  Albert. Married to-day! To-day! You did not say so?
  Sigifred. Now, while I speak to you, their comely
    heads   60
Are bow'd before the mitre.
  Albert.   O! monstrous!
  Sigifred. What is this?

Albert.   Nothing, Sigifred.   Farewell!
We'll meet upon our subject.   Farewell, count!
[*Exit.*

Sigifred. Is this clear-headed Albert ? He brain-turn'd!
'Tis as portentous as a meteor.   [*Exit.*

SCENE II.—*An Apartment in the Castle.*

Enter, as from the Marriage, OTHO, LUDOLPH, AURANTHE,
CONRAD, *Nobles, Knights, Ladies, &c.   Music.*

Otho. Now, Ludolph! Now, Auranthe! Daughter fair!
What can I find to grace your nuptial day
More than my love, and these wide realms in fee ?
    Ludolph. I have too much.
    Auranthe.   And I, my liege, by far.
    Ludolph. Auranthe! I have! O, my bride, my love!
Not all the gaze upon us can restrain
My eyes, too long poor exiles from thy face,
From adoration, and my foolish tongue
From uttering soft responses to the love
I see in thy mute beauty beaming forth !   10
Fair creature, bless me with a single word !
All mine !
    Auranthe. Spare, spare me, my Lord ; I swoon else.
    Ludolph. Soft beauty ! by to-morrow I should die,
Wert thou not mine.   [*They talk apart.*
    First Lady.   How deep she has bewitch'd him !
    First Knight. Ask you for her recipe for love philtres.
    Second Lady. They hold the Emperor in admiration.
    Otho. If ever king was happy, that am I !
What are the cities 'yond the Alps to me,
The provinces about the Danube's mouth,
The promise of fair soil beyond the Rhone ;   20
Or routing out of Hyperborean hordes,
To these fair children, stars of a new age ?
Unless perchance I might rejoice to win

64 Is] To *Houghton :* Is *is conjectural.*
64-5 Farewell and nothing—but this nothing is
    Something I'll take my oath on—He is mad.
Exit Sigifred. *MS.*
9-10 From uttering soft responses to thy mute
    But eloquent Beauty. *MS., rejected.*

This little ball of earth, and chuck it them
To play with!

    Auranthe.   Nay, my Lord, I do not know.

    Ludolph. Let me not famish.

    Otho (to Conrad).   Good Franconia,
You heard what oath I sware, as the sun rose,
That unless Heaven would send me back my son,
My Arab,—no soft music should enrich
The cool wine, kiss'd off with a soldier's smack; 30
Now all my empire, barter'd for one feast,
Seems poverty.

    Conrad.   Upon the neighbour-plain
The heralds have prepar'd a royal lists;
Your knights, found war-proof in the bloody field,
Speed to the game.

    Otho.   Well, Ludolph, what say you?

    Ludolph. My lord!

    Otho.   A tourney?

    Conrad.   Or, if 't please you best—

    Ludolph. I want no more!

    First Lady.   He soars!

    Second Lady.   Past all reason.

    Ludolph. Though heaven's choir
Should in a vast circumference descend
And sing for my delight, I'd stop my ears! 40
Though bright Apollo's car stood burning here,
And he put out an arm to bid me mount,
His touch an immortality, not I!
This earth, this palace, this room, Auranthe!

    Otho. This is a little painful; just too much.
Conrad, if he flames longer in this wise,
I shall believe in wizard-woven loves
And old romances; but I'll break the spell.
Ludolph!

    Conrad. He will be calm, anon.

    Ludolph.   You call'd?
Yes, yes, yes, I offend. You must forgive me; 50
Not being quite recover'd from the stun
Of your large bounties. A tourney, is it not?

                       [*A senet heard faintly.*

    Conrad. The trumpets reach us.

Ethelbert (without).   On your peril, sirs,
Detain us !
    First Voice (without). Let not the abbot pass.
    Second Voice (without).   No,
On your lives !
    First Voice (without). Holy father, you must not.
    Ethelbert (without). Otho !
    Otho.   Who calls on Otho ?
    Ethelbert (without).   Ethelbert !
    Otho. Let him come in.

          [*Enter* ETHELBERT *leading in* ERMINIA.
          Thou cursed abbot, why
Hast brought pollution to our holy rites ?
Hast thou no fear of hangman, or the faggot ?   59
    Ludolph. What portent—what strange prodigy is this?
    Conrad. Away !
    Ethelbert.   You, Duke ?
    Erminia.   Albert has surely fail'd me !
Look at the Emperor's brow upon me bent !
    Ethelbert. A sad delay !
    Conrad.   Away, thou guilty thing !
    Ethelbert. You again, Duke ? Justice, most mighty
    Otho !
You—go to your sister there and plot again,
A quick plot, swift as thought to save your heads ;
For lo ! the toils are spread around your den,
The world is all agape to see dragg'd forth
Two ugly monsters.
    Ludolph.   What means he, my lord ?
    Conrad. I cannot guess.
    Ethelbert.   Best ask your lady sister, 70
Whether the riddle puzzles her beyond
The power of utterance.
    Conrad.   Foul barbarian, cease ;
The Princess faints !
    Ludolph.   Stab him ! O, sweetest wife !
          [*Attendants bear off* AURANTHE.
    Erminia. Alas !
    Ethelbert. Your wife ?
    Ludolph.   Aye, Satan ! does that yerk ye ?

59 Mad Churchman wouldst thou be impal'd alive ? *MS.*

Ethelbert. Wife! so soon!

Ludolph.   Aye, wife! Oh, impudence!
Thou bitter mischief! Venomous mad priest!
How dar'st thou lift those beetle brows at me?
Me—the prince Ludolph, in this presence here,
Upon my marriage-day, and scandalize
My joys with such opprobrious surprise?   80
Wife! Why dost linger on that syllable,
As if it were some demon's name pronounc'd
To summon harmful lightning, and make roar
The sleepy thunder? Hast no sense of fear?
No ounce of man in thy mortality?
Tremble! for, at my nod, the sharpen'd axe
Will make thy bold tongue quiver to the roots,
Those grey lids wink, and thou not know it more!

    Ethelbert. O, poor deceived Prince! I pity thee!
Great Otho! I claim justice—

    Ludolph.   Thou shalt have 't!
Thine arms from forth a pulpit of hot fire   91
Shall sprawl distracted! O that that dull cowl
Were some most sensitive portion of thy life,
That I might give it to my hounds to tear!
Thy girdle some fine zealous-pained nerve
To girth my saddle! And those devil's beads
Each one a life, that I might, every day,
Crush one with Vulcan's hammer!

    Otho.   Peace, my son;
You far outstrip my spleen in this affair.
Let us be calm, and hear the abbot's plea   100
For this intrusion.

    Ludolph.   I am silent, sire.

    Otho. Conrad, see all depart not wanted here.

                        [*Exeunt Knights, Ladies, &c.*

Ludolph, be calm. Ethelbert, peace awhile.
This mystery demands an audience
Of a just judge, and that will Otho be.

    Ludolph. Why has he time to breathe another word?

    Otho. Ludolph, old Ethelbert, be sure, comes not
To beard us for no cause; he's not the man

                    92 sprawl] spawl *MS.*

To cry himself up an ambassador
Without credentials.

  Ludolph.   I'll chain up myself. 110

  Otho. Old Abbot, stand here forth. Lady Erminia,
Sit. And now, Abbot! what have you to say?
Our ear is open. First we here denounce
Hard penalties against thee, if't be found
The cause for which you have disturb'd us here,
Making our bright hours muddy, be a thing
Of little moment.

  Ethelbert. See this innocent!
Otho! thou father of the people call'd,
Is her life nothing? Her fair honour nothing?
Her tears from matins until even-song 120
Nothing? Her burst heart nothing? Emperor!
Is this your gentle niece—the simplest flower
Of the world's herbal—this fair lilly blanch'd
Still with the dews of piety, this meek lady
Here sitting like an angel newly-shent,
Who veils its snowy wings and grows all pale,—
Is she nothing?

  Otho.   What more to the purpose, abbot?

  Ludolph. Whither is he winding?

  Conrad.   No clue yet!

  Ethelbert. You have heard, my Liege, and so, no
    doubt, all here,
Foul, poisonous, malignant whisperings; 130
Nay open speech, rude mockery grown common,
Against the spotless nature and clear fame
Of the princess Erminia, your niece.
I have intruded here thus suddenly,
Because I hold those base weeds, with tight hand,
Which now disfigure her fair growing stem,
Waiting but for your sign to pull them up
By the dark roots, and leave her palpable,
To all men's sight, a Lady, innocent.
The ignominy of that whisper'd tale 140
About a midnight gallant, seen to climb
A window to her chamber neighbour'd near,
I will from her turn off, and put the load

 120 Her tears at matin and at even-song *MS., rejected.*

On the right shoulders; on that wretch's head,
Who, by close stratagems, did save herself,
Chiefly by shifting to this lady's room
A rope-ladder for false witness.

    Ludolph.   Most atrocious!

    Otho. Ethelbert, proceed.

    Ethelbert.   With sad lips I shall:
For, in the healing of one wound, I fear
To make a greater. His young highness here   150
To-day was married.

    Ludolph.   Good.

    Ethelbert.   Would it were good!
Yet why do I delay to spread abroad
The names of those two vipers, from whose jaws
A deadly breath went forth to taint and blast
This guileless lady?

    Otho.   Abbot, speak their names.

    Ethelbert. A minute first. It cannot be—but may
I ask, great judge, if you to-day have put
A letter by unread?

    Otho.   Does 't end in this?

    Conrad. Out with their names!

    Ethelbert.   Bold sinner, say you so?

    Ludolph. Out, tedious monk!

    Otho.   Confess, or by the wheel—

    Ethelbert. My evidence cannot be far away;   161
And, though it never come, be on my head
The crime of passing an attaint upon
The slanderers of this virgin.

    Ludolph.   Speak aloud!

    Ethelbert. Auranthe, and her brother there.

    Conrad.   Amaze!

    Ludolph. Throw them from the windows!

    Otho. Do what you will!

    Ludolph.   What shall I do with them?
Something of quick dispatch, for should she hear,
My soft Auranthe, her sweet mercy would
Prevail against my fury. Damned priest!   170
What swift death wilt thou die? As to the lady
I touch her not.

    154 A poisonous breath went forth to blast and taint
                                MS., rejected.

Ethelbert.   Illustrious Otho, stay!
An ample store of misery thou hast,
Choak not the granary of thy noble mind
With more bad bitter grain, too difficult
A cud for the repentance of a man
Grey-growing. To thee only I appeal,
Not to thy noble son, whose yeasting youth
Will clear itself, and crystal turn again.
A young man's heart, by Heaven's blessing, is   180
A wide world, where a thousand new-born hopes
Empurple fresh the melancholy blood:
But an old man's is narrow, tenantless
Of hopes, and stuff'd with many memories,
Which, being pleasant, ease the heavy pulse—
Painful, clog up and stagnate. Weigh this matter
Even as a miser balances his coin;
And, in the name of mercy, give command
That your knight Albert be brought here before you.
He will expound this riddle; he will show   190
A noon-day proof of bad Auranthe's guilt.
    Otho. Let Albert straight be summon'd.

                    [*Exit one of the Nobles.*
    Ludolph.   Impossible!
I cannot doubt—I will not—no—to doubt
Is to be ashes!—wither'd up to death!
    Otho. My gentle Ludolph, harbour not a fear;
You do yourself much wrong.
    Ludolph.   O, wretched dolt!
Now, when my foot is almost on thy neck,
Wilt thou infuriate me? Proof! Thou fool!
Why wilt thou teaze impossibility
With such a thick-skull'd persevering suit?   200
Fanatic obstinacy! Prodigy!
Monster of folly! Ghost of a turn'd brain!
You puzzle me,—you haunt me,—when I dream
Of you my brain will split! Bald sorcerer!
Juggler! May I come near you? On my soul
I know not whether to pity, curse, or laugh.

        Enter ALBERT, *and the Nobleman.*

Here, Albert, this old phantom wants a proof!
Give him his proof! A camel's load of proofs!

Otho. Albert, I speak to you as to a man
Whose words once utter'd pass like current gold ; 210
And therefore fit to calmly put a close
To this brief tempest. Do you stand possess'd
Of any proof against the honourableness
Of Lady Auranthe, our new-spoused daughter ?
    Albert. You chill me with astonishment. How 's
      this ?
My Liege, what proof should I have 'gainst a fame
Impossible of slur ?   [OTHO *rises.*
    Erminia.   O wickedness !
    Ethelbert. Deluded monarch, 'tis a cruel lie.
    Otho. Peace, rebel-priest !
    Conrad.   Insult beyond credence !
    Erminia. Almost a dream !
    Ludolph.   We have awaken'd from 220
A foolish dream that from my brow hath wrung
A wrathful dew. O folly ! why did I
So act the lion with this silly gnat ?
Let them depart. Lady Erminia !
I ever griev'd for you, as who did not ?
But now you have, with such a brazen front,
So most maliciously, so madly striven
To dazzle the soft moon, when tenderest clouds
Should be unloop'd around to curtain her ;
I leave you to the desert of the world   230
Almost with pleasure. Let them be set free
For me ! I take no personal revenge
More than against a nightmare, which a man
Forgets in the new dawn.   [*Exit* LUDOLPH.
    Otho. Still in extremes ! No, they must not be loose.
    Ethelbert. Albert, I must suspect thee of a crime
So fiendish—
    Otho.   Fear'st thou not my fury, monk ?
Conrad, be they in your sure custody
Till we determine some fit punishment.
It is so mad a deed, I must reflect   240
And question them in private ; for perhaps,
By patient scrutiny, we may discover

220 Then we are quite awakend from this dream
                         MS., cancelled.

Whether they merit death, or should be placed
In care of the physicians.

        [Exeunt OTHO *and Nobles,* ALBERT *following.*
Conrad. My guards, ho !
    Erminia.   Albert, wilt thou follow there ?
Wilt thou creep dastardly behind his back,
And slink away from a weak woman's eye ?
Turn, thou court-Janus ! thou forget'st thyself ;
Here is the Duke, waiting with open arms,

                  [Enter Guards.
To thank thee ; here congratulate each other ;   250
Wring hands ; embrace ; and swear how lucky 'twas
That I, by happy chance, hit the right man
Of all the world to trust in.
    Albert.   Trust ! to me !
    Conrad (*aside*). He is the sole one in this mystery.
    Erminia. Well, I give up, and save my prayers for
      Heaven !
You, who could do this deed, would ne'er relent,
Though, at my words, the hollow prison-vaults
Would groan for pity.
    Conrad.   Manacle them both !
    Ethelbert. I know it—it must be—I see it all !
Albert, thou art the minion !
    Erminia.   Ah ! too plain—   260
    Conrad. Silence ! Gag up their mouths ! I cannot bear
More of this brawling. That the Emperor
Had plac'd you in some other custody !
Bring them away.   *[Exeunt all but* ALBERT.
    Albert. Though my name perish from the book of
      honour,
Almost before the recent ink is dry,
And be no more remember'd after death,
Than any drummer's in the muster-roll ;
Yet shall I season high my sudden fall
With triumph o'er that evil-witted duke !   270
He shall feel what it is to have the hand
Of a man drowning, on his hateful throat.

  272 *Here the manuscript has the two following lines :*
    Erminia ! dream tonight of better days
    Tomorrow makes them real—Once more good morrow.

Enter GERSA *and* SIGIFRED.

Gersa. What discord is at ferment in this house?

Sigifred. We are without conjecture; not a soul
We met could answer any certainty.

Gersa. Young Ludolph, like a fiery arrow, shot
By us.

Sigifred. The Emperor, with cross'd arms, in thought.

Gersa. In one room music, in another sadness,
Perplexity every where!

Albert.   A trifle more!
Follow; your presences will much avail   280
To tune our jarred spirits. I'll explain.   [*Exeunt.*

ACT IV.

SCENE I.—AURANTHE's *Apartment.*

AURANTHE *and* CONRAD *discovered.*

Conrad. Well, well, I know what ugly jeopardy
We are cag'd in; you need not pester that
Into my ears. Prythee, let me be spared
A foolish tongue, that I may bethink me
Of remedies with some deliberation.
You cannot doubt but 'tis in Albert's power
To crush or save us?

Auranthe.   No, I cannot doubt.
He has, assure yourself, by some strange means,
My secret; which I ever hid from him,
Knowing his mawkish honesty.

Conrad.   Curs'd slave!   10

Auranthe. Ay, I could almost curse him now myself.
Wretched impediment! Evil genius!
A glue upon my wings, that cannot spread,
When they should span the provinces! A snake,
A scorpion, sprawling on the first gold step,
Conducting to the throne, high canopied.

Conrad. You would not hear my council, when his life
Might have been trodden out, all sure and hush'd;
Now the dull animal forsooth must be
Intreated, managed! When can you contrive   20
The interview he demands?

 Auranthe.   As speedily
It must be done as my brib'd woman can
Unseen conduct him to me ; but I fear
'Twill be impossible, while the broad day
Comes through the panes with persecuting glare.
Methinks, if 't now were night I could intrigue
With darkness, bring the stars to second me,
And settle all this trouble.
 Conrad.   Nonsense ! Child !
See him immediately ; why not now ?
 Auranthe. Do you forget that even the senseless
   door-posts   30
Are on the watch and gape through all the house ?
How many whisperers there are about,
Hungry for evidence to ruin me ;
Men I have spurn'd, and women I have taunted ?
Besides, the foolish prince sends, minute whiles,
His pages—so they tell me—to enquire
After my health, entreating, if I please,
To see me.
 Conrad. Well, suppose this Albert here ;
What is your power with him ?
 Auranthe.   He should be
My echo, my taught parrot ! but I fear   40
He will be cur enough to bark at me ;
Have his own say ; read me some silly creed
'Bout shame and pity.
 Conrad.   What will you do then ?
 Auranthe. What I shall do, I know not : what I
   would
Cannot be done ; for see, this chamber-floor
Will not yield to the pick-axe and the spade,—
Here is no quiet depth of hollow ground.
 Conrad. Sister, you have grown sensible and wise,
Seconding, ere I speak it, what is now,
I hope, resolv'd between us.
 Auranthe.   Say, what is 't ? 50
 Conrad. You need not be his sexton too : a man
May carry that with him shall make him die
Elsewhere,—give that to him ; pretend the while
You will to-morrow succumb to his wishes,
Be what they may, and send him from the Castle

On some fool's errand ; let his latest groan
Frighten the wolves!

    Auranthe.   Alas! he must not die!

    Conrad. Would you were both hears'd up in stifling
      lead!
Detested—

    Auranthe. Conrad, hold! I would not bear
The little thunder of your fretful tongue,   60
Tho' I alone were taken in these toils,
And you could free me ; but remember, sir,
You live alone in my security :
So keep your wits at work, for your own sake,
Not mine, and be more mannerly.

    Conrad.   Thou wasp!
If my domains were emptied of these folk,
And I had thee to starve—

    Auranthe.   O, marvellous!
But Conrad, now be gone; the Host is look'd for ;
Cringe to the Emperor, entertain the Lords,
And, do ye mind, above all things, proclaim   70
My sickness, with a brother's sadden'd eye,
Condoling with Prince Ludolph. In fit time
Return to me.

    Conrad.   I leave you to your thoughts. [*Exit.*

    Auranthe (sola). Down, down, proud temper! down,
      Auranthe's pride!
Why do I anger him when I should kneel?
Conrad! Albert! help! help! What can I do?
O wretched woman! lost, wreck'd, swallow'd up,
Accursed, blasted! O, thou golden Crown,
Orbing along the serene firmament
Of a wide empire, like a glowing moon ;   80
And thou, bright sceptre! lustrous in my eyes,—
There—as the fabled fair Hesperian tree,
Bearing a fruit more precious! graceful thing,
Delicate, godlike, magic! must I leave
Thee to melt in the visionary air,
Ere, by one grasp, this common hand is made
Imperial? I do not know the time
When I have wept for sorrow ; but methinks
I could now sit upon the ground, and shed
Tears, tears of misery. O, the heavy day!   90

How shall I bear my life till Albert comes?
Ludolph! Erminia! Proofs! O heavy day!
Bring me some mourning weeds, that I may 'tire
Myself, as fits one wailing her own death:
Cut off these curls, and brand this lilly hand,
And throw these jewels from my loathing sight,—
Fetch me a missal, and a string of beads,—
A cup of bitter'd water, and a crust,—
I will confess, O holy Abbot!—How!
What is this? Auranthe! thou fool, dolt,   100
Whimpering idiot! up! up! act and quell!
I am safe! Coward! why am I in fear?
Albert! he cannot stickle, chew the cud
In such a fine extreme,—impossible!
Who knocks? [*Goes to the Door, listens, and opens it.*

Enter ALBERT.

Albert, I have been waiting for you here
With such an aching heart, such swooning throbs
On my poor brain, such cruel—cruel sorrow,
That I should claim your pity! Art not well?
    Albert. Yes, lady, well.
    Auranthe.   You look not so, alas! 110
But pale, as if you brought some heavy news.
    Albert. You know full well what makes me look so pale.
    Auranthe. No! Do I? Surely I am still to learn
Some horror; all I know, this present, is
I am near hustled to a dangerous gulph,
Which you can save me from,—and therefore safe,
So trusting in thy love; that should not make
Thee pale, my Albert.
    Albert.   It doth make me freeze.
    Auranthe. Why should it, love?
    Albert.   You should not ask me that,
But make your own heart monitor, and save   120
Me the great pain of telling. You must know.
    Auranthe. Something has vext you, Albert. There
        are times
When simplest things put on a sombre cast:
A melancholy mood will haunt a man,
Until most easy matters take the shape
Of unachievable tasks; small rivulets

Then seem impassable.

Albert.   Do not cheat yourself
With hope that gloss of words, or suppliant action,
Or tears, or ravings, or self-threaten'd death,
Can alter my resolve.

Auranthe.   You make me tremble ;   120
Not so much at your threats, as at your voice,
Untun'd, and harsh, and barren of all love.

Albert. You suffocate me ! Stop this devil's parley,
And listen to me ; know me once for all.

Auranthe. I thought I did. Alas ! I am deceiv'd.

Albert. No, you are not deceiv'd. You took me for
A man detesting all inhuman crime ;
And therefore kept from me your demon's plot
Against Erminia. Silent ? Be so still ;
For ever ! Speak no more ; but hear my words,
Thy fate. Your safety I have bought to-day   141
By blazoning a lie, which in the dawn
I'll expiate with truth.

Auranthe.   O cruel traitor !

Albert. For I would not set eyes upon thy shame ;
I would not see thee dragg'd to death by the hair,
Penanc'd, and taunted on a scaffolding !
To-night, upon the skirts of the blind wood
That blackens northward of these horrid towers,
I wait for you with horses. Choose your fate.
Farewell.

Auranthe. Albert, you jest ; I'm sure you must.
You, an ambitious Soldier ! I, a Queen,   151
One who could say,—Here, rule these Provinces !
Take tribute from those cities for thyself !
Empty these armouries, these treasuries,
Muster thy warlike thousands at a nod !
Go ! conquer Italy !

Albert.   Auranthe, you have made
The whole world chaff to me. Your doom is fix'd.

Auranthe. Out, villain ! dastard !

133-4 Can Ludolph's wife hold such a devil's parley !
        Auranthe, listen ! Know me once for all ;
        Sooner would I have... *MS., rejected.*
141-3 Thy fate. Tomorrow to the public ear
        I blazon out the truth. *MS.*

Albert.　　　　　　　　　　Look there to the door!
Who is it?
　Auranthe. Conrad, traitor!
　Albert.　　　　　　　　Let him in.

　　　　　　　　　　　　　　[*Enter* CONRAD.

Do not affect amazement, hypocrite,　　　　160
At seeing me in this chamber.
　Conrad.　　　　　　　　Auranthe?
　Albert. Talk not with eyes, but speak your curses out
Against me, who would sooner crush and grind
A brace of toads, than league with them to oppress
An innocent lady, gull an Emperor,
More generous to me than autumn's sun
To ripening harvests.
　Auranthe.　　　　　No more insult, sir!
　Albert. Aye, clutch your scabbard; but, for prudence
　　sake,
Draw not the sword; 'twould make an uproar, Duke,
You would not hear the end of.　At nightfall　170
Your lady sister, if I guess aright,
Will leave this busy castle.　You had best
Take farewell too of worldly vanities.
　Conrad. Vassal!
　Albert.　　　　To-morrow, when the Emperor sends
For loving Conrad, see you fawn on him.
Good even!
　Auranthe. You'll be seen!
　Albert.　　　　　　　See the coast clear then.
　Auranthe (*as he goes*). Remorseless Albert!　Cruel,
　　cruel wretch!　　　　　　　　　　[*She lets him out.*
　Conrad. So, we must lick the dust?
　Auranthe.　　　　　　　　I follow him.
　Conrad. How? Where? The plan of your escape?
　Auranthe.　　　　　　　　　　He waits
For me with horses by the forest-side,　　　180
Northward.
　Conrad. Good, good! he dies.　You go, say you?
　Auranthe. Perforce.
　Conrad.　　　　Be speedy, darkness!　Till that comes,
Fiends keep you company!　　　　　　　[*Exit.*

　　　　170–1 The shut | Of eve *MS.*, *cancelled.*

Auranthe.   And you !   And you !
And all men !   Vanish !

          [*Retires to an inner Apartment.*

SCENE II.—*An Apartment in the Castle.*

Enter LUDOLPH *and Page.*

 Page. Still very sick, my Lord ; but now I went
Knowing my duty to so good a Prince ;
And there her women in a mournful throng
Stood in the passage whispering : if any
Mov'd 'twas with careful steps and hush'd as death ;
They bid me stop.
 Ludolph.   Good fellow, once again
Make soft enquiry ; prythee be not stay'd
By any hindrance, but with gentlest force
Break through her weeping servants, till thou com'st
E'en to her chamber door, and there, fair boy, 10
If with thy mother's milk thou hast suck'd in
Any diviner eloquence ; woo her ears
With plaints for me more tender than the voice
Of dying Echo, echoed.
 Page.   Kindest master !
To know thee sad thus, will unloose my tongue
In mournful syllables.   Let but my words reach
Her ears and she shall take them coupled with
Moans from my heart and sighs not counterfeit.
May I speed better !   [*Exit Page.*
 Ludolph.   Auranthe ! My Life !
Long have I lov'd thee, yet till now not lov'd : 20
Remembering, as I do, hard-hearted times
When I had heard even of thy death perhaps,
And thoughtless, suffered to pass alone
Into Elysium ! now I follow thee
A substance or a shadow, wheresoe'er
Thou leadest me,—whether thy white feet press,
With pleasant weight, the amorous-aching earth,
Or thro' the air thou pioneerest me,
A shade !   Yet sadly I predestinate !

---

14 Of dying echo, echoed at her death... MS., *cancelled.*

O unbenignest Love, why wilt thou let   30
Darkness steal out upon the sleepy world
So wearily ; as if night's chariot wheels
Were clog'd in some thick cloud. O, changeful Love,
Let not her steeds with drowsy-footed pace
Pass the high stars, before sweet embassage
Comes from the pillow'd beauty of that fair
Completion of all delicate nature's wit.
Pout her faint lips anew with rubious health
And with thine infant fingers lift the fringe
Of her sick eyelids ; that those eyes may glow   40
With wooing light upon me, ere the Morn
Peers with disrelish, grey, barren, and cold.

Enter GERSA *and Courtiers.*

Otho calls me his Lion—should I blush
To be so tam'd, so———
    Gersa.   Do me the courtesy
Gentlemen to pass on.
    Courtier.   We are your servants.
                           [*Exeunt Courtiers.*
    Ludolph. It seems then, Sir, you have found out the man
You would confer with ; me ?
    Gersa.   If I break not
Too much upon your thoughtful mood, I will
Claim a brief while your patience.
    Ludolph.   For what cause
Soe'er I shall be honour'd.
    Gersa.   I not less.   50
    Ludolph. What may it be ? No trifle can take place
Of such deliberate prologue, serious 'haviour.
But be it what it may I cannot fail
To listen with no common interest—
For though so new your presence is to me,
I have a soldier's friendship for your fame—
Please you explain.

  30 unbenignest] unpropitious *MS.*, *rejected.*
  34-7 Let her not take her drowsy-eyed watch
      Among the stars, before sweet embassage
      Comes from the pillow'd beauty of that fair
      Completion of all fairness and all form.
                              MS., *rejected.*

    Gersa.   As thus—for, pardon me,
I cannot in plain terms grossly assault
A noble nature; and would faintly sketch
What your quick apprehension will fill up   60
So finely I esteem you.
    Ludolph.   I attend—
    Gersa. Your generous Father, most illustrious Otho,
Sits in the Banquet room among his chiefs—
His wine is bitter, for you are not there—
His eyes are fix'd still on the open doors,
And every passer in he frowns upon
Seeing no Ludolph comes.
    Ludolph.   I do neglect—
    Gersa. And for your absence, may I guess the
    cause?
    Ludolph. Stay there! no—guess? more princely you
    must be—
Than to make guesses at me. 'Tis enough,   70
I'm sorry I can hear no more.
    Gersa.   And I
As griev'd to force it on you so abrupt;
Yet one day you must know a grief whose sting
Will sharpen more the longer 'tis conceal'd.
    Ludolph. Say it at once, sir, dead, dead, is she dead?
    Gersa. Mine is a cruel task: she is not dead—
And would for your sake she were innocent—
    Ludolph. Thou liest! thou amazest me beyond
All scope of thought; convulsest my heart's blood
To deadly churning—Gersa you are young   80
As I am; let me observe you face to face;
Not grey-brow'd like the poisonous Ethelbert,
No rheumed eyes, no furrowing of age,
No wrinkles where all vices nestle in
Like crannied vermin—no, but fresh and young
And hopeful featur'd. Ha! by heaven you weep
Tears, human tears—Do you repent you then
Of a curs'd torturer's office! Why shouldst join—
Tell me, the league of Devils? Confess—confess
The Lie.—
    Gersa. Lie!—but begone all ceremonious points   90
Of honour battailous. I could not turn
My wrath against thee for the orbed world.

Ludolph. Your wrath, weak boy ?   Tremble at mine
  unless
Retraction follow close upon the heels
Of that late stounding insult: why has my sword
Not done already a sheer judgment on thee ?
Despair, or eat thy words.   Why, thou wast nigh
Whimpering away my reason : hark ye, Sir,
It is no secret ;—that Erminia,
Erminia, Sir, was hidden in your tent ;   100
O bless'd asylum ! comfortable home !
Begone, I pity thee, thou art a Gull—
Erminia's last new puppet—
    Gersa.   Furious fire !
Thou mak'st me boil as hot as thou canst flame !
And in thy teeth I give thee back the lie !
Thou liest !   Thou, Auranthe's fool, a wittol——
    Ludolph. Look ! look at this bright sword ;
There is no part of it to the very hilt
But shall indulge itself about thine heart—
Draw—but remember thou must cower thy plumes, 110
As yesterday the Arab made thee stoop—
    Gersa. Patience ! not here, I would not spill thy blood
Here underneath this roof where Otho breathes,
Thy father—almost mine—
    Ludolph.   O faltering coward—

Re-enter PAGE.

Stay, stay, here is one I have half a word with—
Well—What ails thee child ?
    Page.   My lord,
    Ludolph.   Good fellow !
    Page. They are fled !
    Ludolph.   They—who ?
    Page.   When anxiously
I hasten'd back, your grieving messenger,
I found the stairs all dark, the lamps extinct,
And not a foot or whisper to be heard.   120
I thought her dead, and on the lowest step
Sat listening ; when presently came by
Two muffled up,—one sighing heavily,

       103 Erminia's fresh puppet *MS.*

The other cursing low, whose voice I knew
For the Duke Conrad's. Close I follow'd them
Thro' the dark ways they chose to the open air ;
And, as I follow'd, heard my lady speak.
   Ludolph. Thy life answers the truth !
   Page.   The chamber 's empty !
   Ludolph. As I will be of mercy ! So, at last,
This nail is in my temples !
   Gersa.   Be calm in this.   130
   Ludolph. I am.
   Gersa.   And Albert too has disappear'd ;
Ere I met you, I sought him everywhere ;
You would not hearken.
   Ludolph.   Which way went they, boy ?
   Gersa. I'll hunt with you.
   Ludolph.   No, no, no. My senses are
Still whole. I have surviv'd. My arm is strong—
My appetite sharp—for revenge ! I'll no sharer
In my feast ; my injury is all my own,
And so is my revenge, my lawful chattels !
Terrier, ferret them out ! Burn—burn the witch !
Trace me their footsteps ! Away !   140
                        [*Exeunt.*

ACT V.

Scene I.—*A part of the Forest.*

Enter Conrad *and* Auranthe.

   Auranthe. Go no further ; not a step more ; thou art
A master-plague in the midst of miseries.
Go—I fear thee. I tremble every limb,
Who never shook before. There 's moody death
In thy resolved looks—Yes, I could kneel
To pray thee far away. Conrad, go, go—
There ! yonder underneath the boughs I see
Our horses !
   Conrad.   Aye, and the man.
   Auranthe.   Yes, he is there.
Go, go,—no blood, no blood ; go, gentle Conrad !

   2 A plague-spot in the midst of miseries. *MS., cancelled.*

Conrad. Farewell!
Auranthe.   Farewell, for this Heaven pardon you. 10

[*Exit* AURANTHE.

Conrad. If he survive one hour, then may I die
In unimagined tortures—or breathe through
A long life in the foulest sink of the world!
He dies—'tis well she do not advertise
The caitiff of the cold steel at his back.

[*Exit* CONRAD.

Enter LUDOLPH *and* PAGE.

Ludolph. Miss'd the way, boy, say not that on your
peril!
Page. Indeed, indeed I cannot trace them further.
Ludolph. Must I stop here? Here solitary die?
Stifled beneath the thick oppressive shade
Of these dull boughs,—this oven of dark thickets,— 20

18-32   *Ludolph.* What here! here solitary must I die
Without revenge, here stifled in the shade
Of these dull Boughs? Pshaw bitter bitter end—
A bitter death! a suffocating death!
A gnawing, silent deadly, quiet death!
Must she escape me? Can I not clutch her fast?
She's gone, away, away, away—and now
Each moment brings its poison—I must die
As near a Hermit's death as patience—Oh!
War! War! War! where is that illustrious noise
To gasp away my life ⎱ of labouring breath
~~To smother up this sound~~ ⎰
This death song of the trees. Blow Trumpeters!
   sinks] O curs'd Auranthe! [*Enter* ALBERT *Wounded.*
         Albert! here is hope!
   starts up] Glorious illuminate clamour yet; Thrice
                                villainous
Tell me where that detested woman is
Or this is through ⎰ thee—
               ⎱ ~~you~~
   Albert.   My good Prince with me
The sword has done its worst—   [AURANTHE *shrieks.*
   Page.   My Lord—a noise
This way—Hark!
   Ludolph.   Yes a glorious ⎰ clamour ⎰ yet—
                              ⎱ ~~skuffle~~ ⎰
                                        exeunt.

   Scene changes to another part of the wood.
   Enter ALBERT *wounded and* LUDOLPH.

                              MS., *cancelled.*

Silent,—without revenge ?—pshaw !—bitter end,—
A bitter death,—a suffocating death,—
A gnawing—silent—deadly, quiet death !
Escap'd ?—fled ?—vanish'd ? melted into air ?
She's gone ! I cannot clutch her ! no revenge !
A muffled death, ensnar'd in horrid silence !
Suck'd to my grave amid a dreamy calm !
O, where is that illustrious noise of war,
To smother up this sound of labouring breath,
This rustle of the trees !

> [AURANTHE *shrieks at a distance.*

Page.   My Lord, a noise !
This way—hark !
     Ludolph.   Yes, yes ! A hope ! A music !
A glorious clamour ! How I live again !   [*Exeunt.*

SCENE II.—*Another part of the Forest.*

Enter ALBERT (*wounded*).

Albert. O for enough life to support me on
To Otho's feet—

Enter LUDOLPH.

Ludolph.   Thrice villainous, stay there !
Tell me where that detested woman is
Or this is through thee !
     Albert.   My good Prince, with me
The sword has done its worst ; not without worst
Done to another—Conrad has it home—
I see you know it all—
     Ludolph.   Where is his sister ?

AURANTHE *rushes in.*

Auranthe. Albert !
     Ludolph. Ha ! There ! there !—He is the paramour !—
There—hug him—dying ! O, thou innocence,
Shrine him and comfort him at his last gasp,   10
Kiss down his eyelids ! Was he not thy love ?
Wilt thou forsake him at his latest hour ?
Keep fearful and aloof from his last gaze,

His most uneasy moments, when cold death
Stands with the door ajar to let him in?
　　Albert. O that that door with hollow slam would close
Upon me sudden, for I cannot meet,
In all the unknown chambers of the dead,
Such horrors ――――
　　Ludolph.　　　　Auranthe! what can he mean?
What horrors? Is it not a joyous time?　　　　20
Am I not married to a paragon
"Of personal beauty and untainted soul?"
A blushing fair-eyed Purity! A Sylph,
Whose snowy timid hand has never sin'd
Beyond a flower pluck'd, white as itself?
Albert, you do insult my Bride—your Mistress—
To talk of horrors on our wedding night.
　　Albert. Alas! poor Prince, I would you knew my heart.
'Tis not so guilty—
　　Ludolph.　　　　Hear you he pleads not guilty—
You are not? or if so what matters it?　　　　30
You have escap'd me,—free as the dusk air—
Hid in the forest—safe from my revenge;
I cannot catch you—You should laugh at me,
Poor cheated Ludolph,—make the forest hiss
With jeers at me—You tremble; faint at once,
You will come to again. O Cockatrice,
I have you. Whither wander those fair eyes
To entice the Devil to your help, that he
May change you to a Spider, so to crawl
Into some cranny to escape my wrath?　　　　40
　　Albert. Sometimes the counsel of a dying man
Doth operate quietly when his breath is gone—
Disjoin those hands—part—part, do not destroy
Each other—forget her—our miseries
Are equal shar'd, and mercy is—
　　Ludolph.　　　　　　A boon
When one can compass it. Auranthe, try
Your oratory—your breath is not so hitch'd—
Aye, stare for help—　　　　[ALBERT *groans and dies.*
　　　　　　　　There goes a spotted soul
Howling in vain along the hollow night—

24-5 Whose snowy timid hand has never grasp'd
　　　Beyond a flower, dainty as itself, *MS., rejected.*

Hear him—he calls you—Sweet Auranthe, come ! 50
    Auranthe. Kill me.
    Ludolph.   No ! What ? upon our Marriage-night !
The earth would shudder at so foul a deed—
A fair Bride, a sweet Bride, an innocent Bride !
No, we must revel it, as 'tis in use
In times of delicate brilliant ceremony :
Come, let me lead you to our halls again—
Nay, linger not—make no resistance sweet—
Will you—Ah wretch, thou canst not, for I have
The strength of twenty lions 'gainst a lamb—
Now one adieu for Albert—come away.—   60
                           [*Exeunt.*

SCENE III.—*An inner Court of the Castle.*

Enter SIGIFRED, GONFRED, *and* THEODORE *meeting.*

    Theodore. Was ever such a night ?
    Sigifred.   What horrors more ?
Things unbeliev'd one hour, so strange they are,
The next hour stamps with credit.
    Theodore.   Your last news ?
    Gonfred. After the Page's story of the death
Of Albert and Duke Conrad ?
    Sigifred.   And the return
Of Ludolph with the Princess.
    Gonfred.   No more save
Prince Gersa's freeing Abbot Ethelbert,
And the sweet lady, fair Erminia,
From prison.
    Theodore. Where are they now ? hast yet heard ?
    Gonfred. With the sad Emperor they are closeted;
I saw the three pass slowly up the stairs,   11
The lady weeping, the old Abbot cowl'd.
    Sigifred. What next ?
    Theodore.   I ache to think on 't.
    Gonfred.   'Tis with fate.
    Theodore. One while these proud towers are hush'd
    as death.

    2 Things unbelieved for strangeness *MS., cancelled.*

Gonfred. The next our poor Prince fills the arched
    rooms
With ghastly ravings.
    Sigifred.   I do fear his brain.
    Gonfred. I will see more.   Bear you so stout a heart ?
                                [*Exeunt into the Castle.*

    SCENE IV.—*A Cabinet, opening towards a Terrace.*

OTHO, ERMINIA, ETHELBERT, *and a Physician, discovered.*

    Otho. O, my poor Boy! my Son! my Son! my
    Ludolph!
Have ye no comfort for me, ye Physicians
Of the weak Body and Soul?
    Ethelbert.   'Tis not the Medicine
Either of heaven or earth can cure unless
Fit time be chosen to administer—
    Otho. A kind forbearance, holy Abbot—come
Erminia, here sit by me, gentle Girl ;
Give me thy hand—hast thou forgiven me ?
    Erminia. Would I were with the saints to pray for
you !   9
    Otho. Why will ye keep me from my darling child ?
    Physician. Forgive me, but he must not see thy face—
    Otho. Is then a father's countenance a Gorgon ?
Hath it not comfort in it ?   Would it not
Console my poor Boy, cheer him, heal his spirits ?
Let me embrace him, let me speak to him—
I will—who hinders me ?   Who's Emperor ?
    Physician. You may not, Sire—'twould overwhelm
    him quite,
He is so full of grief and passionate wrath,
Too heavy a sigh would kill him—or do worse.
He must be sav'd by fine contrivances—   20
And most especially we must keep clear
Out of his sight a Father whom he loves—
His heart is full, it can contain no more,
And do its ruddy office.
    Ethelbert.   Sage advice ;
We must endeavour how to ease and slacken
The tight-wound energies of his despair,
Not make them tenser—

Otho.   Enough! I hear, I hear.
Yet you were about to advise more—I listen.
    Ethelbert. This learned doctor will agree with me,
That not in the smallest point should he be thwarted
Or gainsaid by one word—his very motions,   31
Nods, becks and hints, should be obey'd with care,
Even on the moment: so his troubled mind
May cure itself—
    Physician.   There is no other means.
    Otho. Open the door: let's hear if all is quiet—
    Physician. Beseech you, Sire, forbear.
    Erminia.   Do, do.
    Otho.   I command!
Open it straight—hush!—quiet—my lost Boy!
My miserable Child!
    Ludolph (*indistinctly without*). Fill, fill my goblet,—
Here's a health!
    Erminia.   O, close the door!
    Otho. Let, let me hear his voice; this cannot last—
And fain would I catch up his dying words   41
Though my own knell they be—this cannot last—
O let me catch his voice—for lo! I hear
This silence whisper me that he is dead!
It is so. Gersa?

                    Enter GERSA.

    Physician.   Say, how fares the prince?
    Gersa. More calm—his features are less wild and
        flush'd—
Once he complain'd of weariness—
    Physician.   Indeed!
'Tis good—'tis good—let him but fall asleep,
That saves him.
    Otho.   Gersa, watch him like a child—   49
Ward him from harm—and bring me better news—
    Physician. Humour him to the height. I fear
        to go;
For should he catch a glimpse of my dull garb,
It might affright him—fill him with suspicion

43 catch] hear *MS., cancelled.*
44 A whisper in this silence that he's dead! *Houghton, but
struck out in MS. for text.*

That we believe him sick, which must not be—
   Gersa. I will invent what soothing means I can.

                         [*Exit* GERSA.
   Physician. This should cheer up your Highness—
    weariness
Is a good symptom, and most favourable—
It gives me pleasant hopes. Please you walk forth
Onto the Terrace; the refreshing air
Will blow one half of your sad doubts away.   60
                            [*Exeunt.*

SCENE V.—*A Banqueting Hall, brilliantly illuminated,
and set forth with all costly magnificence, with Supper-
tables, laden with services of Gold and Silver. A door
in the back scene, guarded by two Soldiers. Lords,
Ladies, Knights, Gentlemen, &c., whispering sadly,
and ranging themselves; part entering and part discovered.*

   First Knight. Grievously are we tantaliz'd, one and
    all—
Sway'd here and there, commanded to and fro
As though we were the shadows of a dream
And link'd to a sleeping fancy. What do we here?
   Gonfred. I am no Seer—you know we must obey
The prince from A to Z—though it should be
To set the place in flames. I pray hast heard
Where the most wicked Princess is?
   First Knight.   There, Sir,
In the next room—have you remark'd those two
Stout soldiers posted at the door?
   Gonfred.   For what?   10
                          [*They whisper.*
   First Lady. How ghast a train!
   Second Lady. Sure this should be some splendid
    burial.
   First Lady. What fearful whispering! See, see,—
    Gersa there!

3-4   the shadows of a sleep,
   And link'd to a dreaming fancy. *Houghton.*

Enter GERSA.

  Gersa. Put on your brightest looks; smile if you
    can;
Behave as all were happy; keep your eyes
From the least watch upon him; if he speaks
To any one, answer collectedly,
Without surprise, his questions, howe'er strange.
Do this to the utmost,—though, alas! with me
The remedy grows hopeless! Here he comes,—   20
Observe what I have said,—show no surprise.

    Enter LUDOLPH, *followed by* SIGIFRED *and Page.*

  Ludolph. A splendid company! rare beauties here!
I should have Orphean lips, and Plato's fancy,
Amphion's utterance, toned with his lyre,
Or the deep key of Jove's sonorous mouth,
To give fit salutation. Methought I heard,
As I came in, some whispers,—what of that?
'Tis natural men should whisper; at the kiss
Of Psyche given by Love, there was a buzz
Among the gods!—and silence is as natural.   30
These draperies are fine, and, being a mortal,
I should desire no better; yet, in truth,
There must be some superior costliness,
Some wider-domed high magnificence!
I would have, as a mortal I may not,
Hanging of heaven's clouds, purple and gold,
Slung from the spheres; gauzes of silver mist,
Loop'd up with cords of twisted wreathed light,
And tassell'd round with weeping meteors!
These pendent lamps and chandeliers are bright   40
As earthly fires from dull dross can be cleansed;
Yet could my eyes drink up intenser beams
Undazzled,—this is darkness,—when I close
These lids, I see far fiercer brilliances,—
Skies full of splendid moons, and shooting stars,
And spouting exhalations, diamond fires,
And panting fountains quivering with deep glows!
Yes—this is dark—is it not dark?
  Sigifred.   My Lord,
'Tis late; the lights of festival are ever

Quench'd in the morn.

    Ludolph.   'Tis not to-morrow then?   50

    Sigifred. 'Tis early dawn.

    Gersa.   Indeed full time we slept;

Say you so, Prince?

    Ludolph.   I say I quarrell'd with you;

We did not tilt each other,—that's a blessing,—

Good gods! no innocent blood upon my head!

    Sigifred. Retire, Gersa!

    Ludolph.   There should be three more here:

For two of them, they stay away perhaps,

Being gloomy-minded, haters of fair revels,—

They know their own thoughts best.

                    As for the third,

Deep blue eyes—semi-shaded in white lids,

Finish'd with lashes fine for more soft shade,   60

Completed by her twin-arch'd ebon brows—

White temples of exactest elegance,

Of even mould felicitous and smooth—

Cheeks fashion'd tenderly on either side,

So perfect, so divine that our poor eyes

Are dazzled with the sweet proportioning,

And wonder that 'tis so,—the magic chance!

Her nostrils, small, fragrant, faery-delicate;

Her lips—I swear no human bones e'er wore

So taking a disguise—you shall behold her!   70

We'll have her presently; aye, you shall see her,

And wonder at her, friends, she is so fair—

She is the world's chief Jewel, and by heaven

She's mine by right of marriage—she is mine!

Patience, good people, in fit time I send

A Summoner—she will obey my call,

Being a wife most mild and dutiful.

First I would hear what music is prepared

To herald and receive her—let me hear!

    Sigifred. Bid the musicians soothe him tenderly.   80

                    [*A soft strain of Music*

    Ludolph. Ye have none better—no—I am content;

'Tis a rich sobbing melody, with reliefs

Full and majestic; it is well enough,

And will be sweeter, when ye see her pace

Sweeping into this presence, glisten'd o'er
With emptied caskets, and her train upheld
By ladies, habited in robes of lawn,
Sprinkled with golden crescents; (others bright
In silks, with spangles shower'd,) and bow'd to
By Duchesses and pearled Margravines—   90
Sad, that the fairest creature of the earth—
I pray you mind me not—'tis sad, I say,
That the extremest beauty of the world
Should so entrench herself away from me,
Behind a barrier of engender'd guilt!

    Second Lady. Ah! what a moan!
    First Knight.   Most piteous indeed!
    Ludolph. She shall be brought before this company,
And then—then—
    First Lady.   He muses.
    Gersa.   O, Fortune, where will this end?
    Sigifred. I guess his purpose! Indeed he must
    not have
That pestilence brought in,—that cannot be,   100
There we must stop him.
    Gersa.   I am lost! Hush, hush!
He is about to rave again.
    Ludolph. A barrier of guilt! I was the fool.
She was the cheater! Who's the cheater now,
And who the fool? The entrapp'd, the caged fool,
The bird-lim'd raven? She shall croak to death
Secure! Methinks I have her in my fist,
To crush her with my heel! Wait, wait! I marvel
My father keeps away: good friend, ah! Sigifred!
Do bring him to me—and Erminia   110
I fain would see before I sleep—and Ethelbert,
That he may bless me, as I know he will
Though I have curs'd him.
    Sigifred.   Rather suffer me
To lead you to them—
    Ludolph.   No, excuse me, no—
The day is not quite done—go bring them hither.

                         [*Exit* SIGIFRED.

Certes, a father's smile should, like sun light,
Slant on my sheafed harvest of ripe bliss—

Besides, I thirst to pledge my lovely Bride
In a deep goblet: let me see—what wine?
The strong Iberian juice, or mellow Greek?   120
Or pale Calabrian? Or the Tuscan grape?
Or of old Ætna's pulpy wine presses,
Black stain'd with the fat vintage, as it were
The purple slaughter-house, where Bacchus' self
Prick'd his own swollen veins? Where is my Page?
    Page.   Here, here!
    Ludolph. Be ready to obey me; anon thou shalt
Bear a soft message for me—for the hour
Draws near when I must make a winding up
Of bridal Mysteries—a fine-spun vengeance!
Carve it on my Tomb, that when I rest beneath   130
Men shall confess—This Prince was gull'd and cheated,
But from the ashes of disgrace he rose
More than a fiery Phœnix—and did burn
His ignominy up in purging fires—
Did I not send, Sir, but a moment past,
For my Father?
    Gersa.   You did.
    Ludolph.   Perhaps 'twould be
Much better he came not.
    Gersa.   He enters now!

    Enter OTHO, ERMINIA, ETHELBERT, SIGIFRED, *and*
                  Physician.

    Ludolph. O thou good Man, against whose sacred
    head
I was a mad conspirator, chiefly too
For the sake of my fair newly wedded wife,   140
Now to be punish'd, do not look so sad!
Those charitable eyes will thaw my heart,
Those tears will wash away a just resolve,
A verdict ten times sworn! Awake—awake—
Put on a judge's brow, and use a tongue
Made iron-stern by habit! Thou shalt see
A deed to be applauded, 'scribed in gold!
Join a loud voice to mine, and so denounce

---

128 *The word* righteous *is cancelled before* winding up *in the MS.*
133 Phœnix] dragon *Houghton.*

What I alone will execute!

Otho.   Dear son,
What is it? By your father's love, I sue   150
That it be nothing merciless!

   Ludolph.   To that demon?
Not so! No! She is in temple-stall
Being garnish'd for the sacrifice, and I,
The Priest of Justice, will immolate her
Upon the altar of wrath! She stings me through!—
Even as the worm doth feed upon the nut,
So she, a scorpion, preys upon my brain!
I feel her gnawing here! Let her but vanish,
Then, father, I will lead your legions forth,
Compact in steeled squares, and speared files,   160
And bid our trumpets speak a fell rebuke
To nations drows'd in peace!

   Otho.   To-morrow, Son,
Be your word law—forget to-day—

   Ludolph.   I will
When I have finish'd it—now! now! I'm pight,
Tight-footed for the deed!

   Erminia.   Alas! Alas!

   Ludolph. What Angel's voice is that? Erminia!
Ah! gentlest creature, whose sweet innocence
Was almost murder'd; I am penitent,
Wilt thou forgive me? And thou, holy Man,
Good Ethelbert, shall I die in peace with you?   170

   Erminia. Die, my lord!

   Ludolph.   I feel it possible.

   Otho.   Physician?

   Physician. I fear me he is past my skill.

   Otho.   Not so!

   Ludolph. I see it, I see it—I have been wandering—
Half-mad—not right here—I forget my purpose.
Bestir, bestir, Auranthe! ha! ha! ha!
Youngster! Page! go bid them drag her to me!
Obey! This shall finish it!   [*Draws a dagger.*

   Otho.   O my Son! my Son!

   Sigifred. This must not be—stop there!

   Ludolph.   Am I obey'd?
A little talk with her—no harm—haste! haste!
                    [*Exit Page.*

Set her before me—never fear I can strike. 180
   Several Voices. My Lord! My Lord!
   Gersa.   Good Prince!
   Ludolph. Why do ye trouble me? out—out—out
     away!
There she is! take that! and that! no, no—
That's not well done—Where is she?
      [*The doors open. Enter Page. Several women are
        seen grouped about Auranthe in the inner room.*
   Page. Alas! My Lord, my Lord! they cannot move
     her!
Her arms are stiff,—her fingers clench'd and cold—
   Ludolph. She's dead!
              [*Staggers and falls into their arms.*

   Ethelbert.   Take away the dagger.
   Gersa.   Softly; so!
   Otho. Thank God for that!
   Sigifred.   I fear it could not harm him.
   Gersa. No!—brief be his anguish!
   Ludolph. She's gone—I am content—Nobles, good
     night! 190
We are all weary—faint—set ope the doors—
I will to bed!—To-morrow—   [*Dies.*

        THE CURTAIN FALLS.

KING STEPHEN

A FRAGMENT OF A TRAGEDY

WRITTEN IN NOVEMBER 1819

KING STEPHEN

A FRAGMENT OF A TRAGEDY

ACT I.

Scene I.—*Field of Battle.*

Alarum. Enter King Stephen, *Knights, and Soldiers.*

Stephen. If shame can on a soldier's vein-swoll'n front
Spread deeper crimson than the battle's toil,
Blush in your casing helmets ! for see, see !
Yonder my chivalry, my pride of war,
Wrench'd with an iron hand from firm array,
Are routed loose about the plashy meads,
Of honour forfeit. O that my known voice
Could reach your dastard ears, and fright you more !
Fly, cowards, fly ! Glocester is at your backs !
Throw your slack bridles o'er the flurried manes, 10
Ply well the rowel with faint trembling heels,
Scampering to death at last !
    First Knight.   The enemy
Bears his flaunt standard close upon their rear.
    Second Knight. Sure of a bloody prey, seeing the fens
Will swamp them girth-deep.
    Stephen.   Over head and ears,
No matter ! 'Tis a gallant enemy ;
How like a comet he goes streaming on.
But we must plague him in the flank,—hey, friends ?
We are well breathed,—follow !

    Enter Earl Baldwin *and Soldiers, as defeated.*

    Stephen.   De Redvers !
What is the monstrous bugbear that can fright   20
Baldwin ?
    Baldwin. No scare-crow, but the fortunate star
Of boisterous Chester, whose fell truncheon now
Points level to the goal of victory.

This way he comes, and if you would maintain
Your person unaffronted by vile odds,
Take horse, my Lord.
    Stephen.   And which way spur for life?
Now I thank Heaven I am in the toils,
That soldiers may bear witness how my arm
Can burst the meshes.   Not the eagle more
Loves to beat up against a tyrannous blast,   30
Than I to meet the torrent of my foes.
This is a brag,—be 't so,—but if I fall,
Carve it upon my 'scutcheon'd sepulchre.
On, fellow soldiers !   Earl of Redvers, back !
Not twenty Earls of Chester shall brow-beat
The diadem.   [*Exeunt.   Alarum.*

SCENE II.—*Another part of the Field.*

Trumpets sounding a Victory.   Enter GLOCESTER,
Knights, and Forces.

    Glocester. Now may we lift our bruised vizors up,
And take the flattering freshness of the air,
While the wide din of battle dies away
Into times past, yet to be echoed sure
In the silent pages of our chroniclers.
    First Knight. Will Stephen's death be mark'd there,
      my good Lord,
Or that we gave him lodging in yon towers?
    Glocester. Fain would I know the great usurper's fate.

Enter two Captains severally.

    First Captain. My Lord !
    Second Captain.   Most noble Earl !
    First Captain.   The King—
    Second Captain. The Empress greets—
    Glocester. What of the King?
    First Captain.   He sole and lone maintains 10
A hopeless bustle mid our swarming arms,
And with a nimble savageness attacks,
Escapes, makes fiercer onset, then anew
Eludes death, giving death to most that dare
Trespass within the circuit of his sword !

He must by this have fallen. Baldwin is taken :
And for the Duke of Bretagne, like a stag
He flies, for the Welsh beagles to hunt down.
God save the Empress !
    Glocester.   Now our dreaded Queen :
What message from her Highness ?
    Second Captain.   Royal Maud 20
From the throng'd towers of Lincoln hath look'd down,
Like Pallas from the walls of Ilion,
And seen her enemies havock'd at her feet.
She greets most noble Glocester from her heart,
Intreating him, his captains, and brave knights,
To grace a banquet. The high city gates
Are envious which shall see your triumph pass ;
The streets are full of music.

Enter Second Knight.

    Glocester.   Whence come you ?
    Second Knight. From Stephen, my good Prince,—
    Stephen ! Stephen !   29
    Glocester. Why do you make such echoing of his name?
    Second Knight. Because I think, my lord, he is no
    man,
But a fierce demon, 'nointed safe from wounds,
And misbaptized with a Christian name.
    Glocester. A mighty soldier !—Does he still hold out?
    Second Knight. He shames our victory. His valour
    still
Keeps elbow-room amid our eager swords,
And holds our bladed falchions all aloof—
His gleaming battle-axe being slaughter-sick,
Smote on the morion of a Flemish knight,
Broke short in his hand ; upon the which he flung
The heft away with such a vengeful force, 41
It paunch'd the Earl of Chester's horse, who then
Spleen-hearted came in full career at him.
    Glocester. Did no one take him at a vantage then ?
    Second Knight. Three then with tiger leap upon him
    flew,
Whom, with his sword swift-drawn and nimbly held,
He stung away again, and stood to breathe.
Smiling. Anon upon him rush'd once more

A throng of foes, and in this renew'd strife,
My sword met his and snapp'd off at the hilts.   50
   Glocester. Come, lead me to this Mars—and let us
      move
In silence, not insulting his sad doom
With clamorous trumpets. To the Empress bear
My salutation as befits the time.

                [*Exeunt* GLOCESTER *and Forces.*

SCENE III.—*The Field of Battle. Enter* STEPHEN *unarmed.*

   Stephen. Another sword ! And what if I could seize
One from Bellona's gleaming armoury,
Or choose the fairest of her sheaved spears !

50 hilts *MS. :* hilt *Houghton.*
51 Mars] mars *MS. :* man *Houghton.*
*Scene II is followed in Keats's manuscript by a cancelled opening of
Scene III, thus*—

                Scene 3rd

      The field of Battle—Enter Stephen unarm'd
   Stephen. Another Sword ! for one short minute longer
That I may pepper that De Kaims and then
Yield to { ~~valliant~~   } some twenty squadrons— { Stephen say
      { ~~this army~~ }   { ~~This is gory !~~
Wouldst thou exchange this helmeted renown
To rule in qu[i]et Pylos Nestor-like ?
No !—

    Enter De Kaims Knights and Soldiers dropping in
De Kaims...

In rewriting the opening of the Scene, Keats at first put

      Another Sword ! and what if I took one
      From forth Bellona's gleaming armoury

*which stands altered to the far better reading of the text.   After line 3
the rewritten opening originally stood thus*—

      Where is my Enemy ? Aye, close at hand
      Here comes the testy Brood

but this stands changed to the reading of the text, save that comes *is not
altered to* come.   *Line 15 stands thus*—

      Yield Stephen, or my Sword's point ~~explore~~ dip in...

I scarcely think Keats meant this as an alternative present-future,

      or my sword's point dips in
    The gloomy current of a traitor's heart,

as Lord Houghton gave it : more probably he used or *for* ere *or* before.
There is certainly no s *either in* explore *or in* dip.

Where are my enemies? Here, close at hand,
Here come the testy brood. O for a sword!
I'm faint—a biting sword! A noble sword!
A hedge-stake—or a ponderous stone to hurl
With brawny vengeance, like the labourer Cain.
Come on! Farewell my kingdom, and all hail
Thou superb, plum'd, and helmeted renown,   10
All hail—I would not truck this brilliant day
To rule in Pylos with a Nestor's beard—
Come on!

Enter DE KAIMS *and Knights, &c.*

   De Kaims. Is't madness, or a hunger after death,
That makes thee thus unarm'd throw taunts at us?
Yield, Stephen, or my sword's point dip in
The gloomy current of a traitor's heart.
   Stephen. Do it, De Kaims, I will not budge an inch.
   De Kaims. Yes, of thy madness thou shalt take the
    meed.
   Stephen. Darest thou?
   De Kaims.   How dare, against a man disarm'd?
   Stephen. What weapons has the lion but himself?
Come not near me, De Kaims, for by the price   21
Of all the glory I have won this day,
Being a king, I will not yield alive
To any but the second man of the realm,
Robert of Glocester.
   De Kaims.   Thou shalt vail to me.
   Stephen. Shall I, when I have sworn against it, sir?
Thou think'st it brave to take a breathing king,
That, on a court-day bow'd to haughty Maud,
The awed presence-chamber may be bold
To whisper, there's the man who took alive   30
Stephen—me—prisoner. Certes, De Kaims,
The ambition is a noble one.
   De Kaims.   'Tis true,
And, Stephen, I must compass it.

27 a breathing king] a king alive *MS., rejected.*
30-31 To whi[s]per { there's the man who } took alive
               { there is he who }
    King...
    The stubborn Reb[el]... *MS., rejected.*

    Stephen.   No, no,
Do not tempt me to throttle you on the gorge,
Or with my gauntlet crush your hollow breast,
Just when your knighthood is grown ripe and full
For lordship.
    A Soldier. Is an honest yeoman's spear
Of no use at a need ? Take that.
    Stephen.   Ah, dastard !
    De Kaims. What, you are vulnerable ! my prisoner !
    Stephen. No, not yet. I disclaim it, and demand
Death as a sovereign right unto a king   41
Who 'sdains to yield to any but his peer,
If not in title, yet in noble deeds,
The Earl of Glocester. Stab to the hilts, De Kaims,
For I will never by mean hands be led
From this so famous field. Do ye hear ! Be quick !

    [*Trumpets. Enter the Earl of* CHESTER *and Knights.*

SCENE IV.—*A Presence Chamber. Queen* MAUD *in a
    Chair of State, the Earls of* GLOCESTER *and* CHESTER,
    Lords, Attendants.*

    Maud. Glocester, no more : I will behold that
    Boulogne :
Set him before me. Not for the poor sake
Of regal pomp and a vain-glorious hour,
As thou with wary speech, yet near enough,
Hast hinted.
    Glocester.   Faithful counsel have I given ;
If wary, for your Highness' benefit.
    Maud. The Heavens forbid that I should not think so,
For by thy valour have I won this realm,
Which by thy wisdom I will ever keep.
To sage advisers let me ever bend   10
A meek attentive ear, so that they treat
Of the wide kingdom's rule and government,
Not trenching on our actions personal.
Advis'd, not school'd, I would be ; and henceforth
Spoken to in clear, plain, and open terms,
Not side-ways sermon'd at.

                44 hilts *MS. :* hilt *Houghton.*

Glocester.   Then, in plain terms,
Once more for the fallen king—
    Maud.   Your pardon, Brother,
I would no more of that ; for, as I said,
'Tis not for worldly pomp I wish to see
The rebel, but as dooming judge to give   20
A sentence something worthy of his guilt.
    Glocester. If 't must be so, I'll bring him to your
       presence.   [*Exit* GLOCESTER.
    Maud. A meaner summoner might do as well—
My Lord of Chester, is 't true what I hear
Of Stephen of Boulogne, our prisoner,
That he, as a fit penance for his crimes,
Eats wholesome, sweet, and palatable food
Off Glocester's golden dishes—drinks pure wine,
Lodges soft ?
    Chester.   More than that, my gracious Queen,
Has anger'd me. The noble Earl, methinks,   30
Full soldier as he is, and without peer
In counsel, dreams too much among his books.
It may read well, but sure 'tis out of date
To play the Alexander with Darius.
    Maud. Truth ! I think so. By Heavens it shall not
       last !
    Chester. It would amaze your Highness now to mark
How Glocester overstrains his courtesy
To that crime-loving rebel, that Boulogne—
    Maud. That ingrate !
    Chester.   For whose vast ingratitude
To our late sovereign lord, your noble sire,   40
The generous Earl condoles in his mishaps,
And with a sort of lackeying friendliness,
Talks off the mighty frowning from his brow,
Woos him to hold a duet in a smile,
Or, if it please him, play an hour at chess—
    Maud. A perjured slave !
    Chester.   And for his perjury,
Glocester has fit rewards—nay, I believe,
He sets his bustling household's wits at work
For flatteries to ease this Stephen's hours,
And make a heaven of his purgatory ;   50
Adorning bondage with the pleasant gloss

Of feasts and music, and all idle shows
Of indoor pageantry ; while syren whispers,
Predestin'd for his ear, 'scape as half-check'd
From lips the courtliest and the rubiest
Of all the realm, admiring of his deeds.

    Maud. A frost upon his summer !

    Chester.   A queen's nod
Can make his June December.   Here he comes.

POEMS

WRITTEN LATE IN 1819

POEMS WRITTEN LATE IN 1819

A PARTY OF LOVERS:

"A few Nonsense Verses" sent in a Letter to
George Keats.

PENSIVE they sit, and roll their languid eyes,
Nibble their toast and cool their tea with sighs;
Or else forget the purpose of the night,
Forget their tea, forget their appetite.
See, with cross'd arms they sit—Ah! happy crew,
The fire is going out and no one rings
For coals, and therefore no coals Betty brings.
A fly is in the milk-pot. Must he die
Circled by a humane society?
No, no; there, Mr. Werter takes his spoon,   10
Inserts it, dips the handle, and lo! soon
The little straggler, sav'd from perils dark,
Across the teaboard draws a long wet mark.

Romeo! Arise, take snuffers by the handle,
There's a large cauliflower in each candle.
A winding sheet—ah, me! I must away
To No. 7, just beyond the circus gay.
Alas, my friend, your coat sits very well;
Where may your Tailor live? I may not tell.
O pardon me. I'm absent now and then.   20
Where *might* my Tailor live? I say again
I cannot tell, let me no more be teazed;
He lives in Wapping, might live where he pleased.

SONNET.

THE day is gone, and all its sweets are gone!
  Sweet voice, sweet lips, soft hand, and softer breast,
Warm breath, light whisper, tender semi-tone,
  Bright eyes, accomplish'd shape, and lang'rous waist!

Faded the flower and all its budded charms,
  Faded the sight of beauty from my eyes,
Faded the shape of beauty from my arms,
  Faded the voice, warmth, whiteness, paradise—
Vanish'd unseasonably at shut of eve,
  When the dusk holiday—or holinight   10
Of fragrant-curtain'd love begins to weave
  The woof of darkness thick, for hid delight ;
But, as I've read love's missal through to-day,
He'll let me sleep, seeing I fast and pray.

LINES TO FANNY.

What can I do to drive away
Remembrance from my eyes? for they have seen,
Aye, an hour ago, my brilliant Queen !
Touch has a memory. O say, love, say,
What can I do to kill it and be free
In my old liberty ?
When every fair one that I saw was fair,
Enough to catch me in but half a snare,
Not keep me there :
When, howe'er poor or particolour'd things,   10
My muse had wings,
And ever ready was to take her course
Whither I bent her force,
Unintellectual, yet divine to me ;—
Divine, I say !—What sea-bird o'er the sea
Is a philosopher the while he goes
Winging along where the great water throes ?

  How shall I do
  To get anew
Those moulted feathers, and so mount once more 20
  Above, above
  The reach of fluttering Love,
And make him cower lowly while I soar ?
Shall I gulp wine ? No, that is vulgarism,
A heresy and schism,
  Foisted into the canon law of love ;—

3 *The word* and *or but* has probably dropped out after Aye.

No,—wine is only sweet to happy men;
  More dismal cares
  Seize on me unawares,—
Where shall I learn to get my peace again? 30
To banish thoughts of that most hateful land,
Dungeoner of my friends, that wicked strand
Where they were wreck'd and live a wrecked life;
That monstrous region, whose dull rivers pour,
Ever from their sordid urns unto the shore,
Unown'd of any weedy-haired gods;
Whose winds, all zephyrless, hold scourging rods,
Iced in the great lakes, to afflict mankind;
Whose rank-grown forests, frosted, black, and blind,
Would fright a Dryad; whose harsh herbag'd meads
Make lean and lank the starv'd ox while he feeds;
There bad flowers have no scent, birds no sweet song,
And great unerring Nature once seems wrong. 43

O, for some sunny spell
To dissipate the shadows of this hell!
Say they are gone,— with the new dawning light
Steps forth my lady bright!
O, let me once more rest
My soul upon that dazzling breast!
Let once again these aching arms be plac'd, 50
The tender gaolers of thy waist!
And let me feel that warm breath here and there
To spread a rapture in my very hair,—
O, the sweetness of the pain!
Give me those lips again!
Enough! Enough! it is enough for me
To dream of thee!

33 *Probably* wrecked *should be* wretched.
35 Even *seems a likelier initial word here than* Ever.
42 *The word* bad *before* flowers *is questionable. Keats may have got as far as* bud *with the word* buds, *and then decided for* flowers (*disyllable*) *and forgotten to strike out* bud.

SONNET.

TO FANNY.

I CRY your mercy—pity—love!—aye, love!
  Merciful love that tantalizes not,
One-thoughted, never-wandering, guileless love,
  Unmask'd, and being seen—without a blot!
O! let me have thee whole,—all—all—be mine!
  That shape, that fairness, that sweet minor zest
Of love, your kiss,—those hands, those eyes divine,
  That warm, white, lucent, million-pleasured breast,—
Yourself—your soul—in pity give me all,
  Withhold no atom's atom or I die,   10
Or living on perhaps, your wretched thrall,
  Forget, in the mist of idle misery,
Life's purposes,—the palate of my mind
Losing its gust, and my ambition blind!

THE FALL OF HYPERION

A DREAM

AN ATTEMPT MADE AT THE END OF 1819 TO
RECONSTRUCT THE POEM

THE FALL OF HYPERION

A DREAM

[CANTO I.]

FANATICS have their dreams, wherewith they weave
A paradise for a sect ; the savage too
From forth the loftiest fashion of his sleep
Guesses at Heaven ; pity these have not
Trac'd upon vellum or wild Indian leaf
The shadows of melodious utterance.
But bare of laurel they live, dream, and die ;
For Poesy alone can tell her dreams,
With the fine spell of words alone can save
Imagination from the sable chain   10
And dumb enchantment. Who alive can say,
"Thou art no Poet—may'st not tell thy dreams ?"
Since every man whose soul is not a clod
Hath visions, and would speak, if he had loved,
And been well nurtured in his mother tongue.
Whether the dream now purpos'd to rehearse
Be poet's or fanatic's will be known
When this warm scribe my hand is in the grave.

Methought I stood where trees of every clime,
Palm, myrtle, oak, and sycamore, and beech,   20
With plantain, and spice-blossoms, made a screen ;
In neighbourhood of fountains (by the noise
Soft-showering in my ears), and, (by the touch
Of scent,) not far from roses. Turning round
I saw an arbour with a drooping roof
Of trellis vines, and bells, and larger blooms,
Like floral censers, swinging light in air ;
Before its wreathed doorway, on a mound
Of moss, was spread a feast of summer fruits,
Which, nearer seen, seem'd refuse of a meal   30
By angel tasted or our Mother Eve ;

For empty shells were scattered on the grass,
And grape-stalks but half bare, and remnants more,
Sweet-smelling, whose pure kinds I could not know.
Still was more plenty than the fabled horn
Thrice emptied could pour forth, at banqueting
For Proserpine return'd to her own fields,
Where the white heifers low. And appetite
More yearning than on Earth I ever felt
Growing within, I ate deliciously ;   40
And, after not long, thirsted, for thereby
Stood a cool vessel of transparent juice
Sipp'd by the wander'd bee, the which I took,
And, pledging all the mortals of the world,
And all the dead whose names are in our lips,
Drank.   That full draught is parent of my theme.
No Asian poppy nor elixir fine
Of the soon-fading jealous Caliphat ;
No poison gender'd in close monkish cell,
To thin the scarlet conclave of old men,   50
Could so have rapt unwilling life away.
Among the fragrant husks and berries crush'd,
Upon the grass I struggled hard against
The domineering potion ; but in vain :
The cloudy swoon came on, and down I sank,
Like a Silenus on an antique vase.
How long I slumber'd 'tis a chance to guess.
When sense of life return'd, I started up
As if with wings ; but the fair trees were gone,
The mossy mound and arbour were no more :   60
I look'd around upon the carved sides
Of an old sanctuary with roof august,
Builded so high, it seem'd that filmed clouds
Might spread beneath, as o'er the stars of heaven ;
So old the place was, I remember'd none
The like upon the Earth : what I had seen
Of grey cathedrals, buttress'd walls, rent towers,
The superannuations of sunk realms,
Or Nature's rocks toil'd hard in waves and winds,

45 in our lips *Houghton : this looks corrupt.   A more likely reading would be* on our lips.
48 soon-fading] death-doing *MS. rejected, fide Woodhouse.*
55 sank *Houghton :* sunk *Woodhouse.*

Seem'd but the faulture of decrepit things   70
To that eternal domed Monument.—
Upon the marble at my feet there lay
Store of strange vessels and large draperies,
Which needs had been of dyed asbestos wove,
Or in that place the moth could not corrupt,
So white the linen, so, in some, distinct
Ran imageries from a sombre loom.
All in a mingled heap confus'd there lay
Robes, golden tongs, censer and chafing-dish,
Girdles, and chains, and holy jewelries.   80

    Turning from these with awe, once more I rais'd
My eyes to fathom the space every way ;
The embossed roof, the silent massy range
Of columns north and south, ending in mist
Of nothing, then to eastward, where black gates
Were shut against the sunrise evermore.—
Then to the west I look'd, and saw far off
An image, huge of feature as a cloud,
At level of whose feet an altar slept,
To be approach'd on either side by steps,   90
And marble balustrade, and patient travail
To count with toil the innumerable degrees.
Towards the altar sober-paced I went,
Repressing haste, as too unholy there ;
And, coming nearer, saw beside the shrine
One minist'ring ; and there arose a flame.—
When in mid-way the sickening East wind
Shifts sudden to the south, the small warm rain
Melts out the frozen incense from all flowers,
And fills the air with so much pleasant health   100
That even the dying man forgets his shroud ;—
Even so that lofty sacrificial fire,
Sending forth Maian incense, spread around
Forgetfulness of everything but bliss,

---

89 slept] *perhaps corrupt. The supposition to which I lean is that Keats wrote* stept, *meaning by a " stepped altar " an altar approached by steps, and that he had in his mind rejected that phrase by the time he wrote the next line, but failed to revise line 89 so as to do away the pleonasm.*

97 As in mid-day *Houghton.*

And clouded all the altar with soft smoke ;
From whose white fragrant curtains thus I heard
Language pronounc'd : "If thou canst not ascend
"These steps, die on that marble where thou art.
"Thy flesh, near cousin to the common dust,
"Will parch for lack of nutriment—thy bones   110
"Will wither in few years, and vanish so
"That not the quickest eye could find a grain
"Of what thou now art on that pavement cold.
"The sands of thy short life are spent this hour,
"And no hand in the universe can turn
"Thy hourglass, if these gummed leaves be burnt
"Ere thou canst mount up these immortal steps."
I heard, I look'd : two senses both at once,
So fine, so subtle, felt the tyranny
Of that fierce threat and the hard task proposed. 120
Prodigious seem'd the toil ; the leaves were yet
Burning—when suddenly a palsied chill
Struck from the paved level up my limbs,
And was ascending quick to put cold grasp
Upon those streams that pulse beside the throat :
I shriek'd, and the sharp anguish of my shriek
Stung my own ears—I strove hard to escape
The numbness ; strove to gain the lowest step.
Slow, heavy, deadly was my pace : the cold
Grew stifling, suffocating, at the heart ;   130
And when I clasp'd my hands I felt them not.
One minute before death, my iced foot touch'd
The lowest stair ; and as it touch'd, life seem'd
To pour in at the toes : I mounted up,
As once fair angels on a ladder flew
From the green turf to Heaven—"Holy Power,"
Cried I, approaching near the horned shrine,
"What am I that should so be saved from death ?
"What am I that another death come not
"To choke my utterance sacrilegious, here ?"   140
Then said the veiled shadow—"Thou hast felt
"What 'tis to die and live again before
"Thy fated hour, that thou hadst power to do so

---

140 sacrilegious *Houghton* : sacriligeous *Woodhouse, fide de Sélin-court.*

"Is thy own safety ; thou hast dated on
Thy doom."—"High Prophetess," said I, "purge off,
Benign, if so it please thee, my mind's film."—
"None can usurp this height," return'd that shade,
"But those to whom the miseries of the world
"Are misery, and will not let them rest.
"All else who find a haven in the world,   150
"Where they may thoughtless sleep away their days,
"If by a chance into this fane they come,
"Rot on the pavement where thou rottedst half."—
" Are there not thousands in the world," said I,
Encourag'd by the sooth voice of the shade,
"Who love their fellows even to the death,
"Who feel the giant agony of the world,
"And more, like slaves to poor humanity,
"Labour for mortal good ? I sure should see
"Other men here ; but I am here alone."   160
"Those whom thou spak'st of are no vision'ries,"
Rejoin'd that voice—"They are no dreamers weak,
"They seek no wonder but the human face ;
"No music but a happy-noted voice—
"They come not here, they have no thought to come—
"And thou art here, for thou art less than they—
"What benefit canst thou, or all thy tribe,
"To the great world ? Thou art a dreaming thing,
" A fever of thyself—think of the Earth ;
"What bliss even in hope is there for thee ?   170
"What haven ? every creature hath its home ;
"Every sole man hath days of joy and pain,
"Whether his labours be sublime or low—
"The pain alone ; the joy alone ; distinct :
"Only the dreamer venoms all his days,
" Bearing more woe than all his sins deserve.
"Therefore, that happiness be somewhat shar'd,
"Such things as thou art are admitted oft
"Into like gardens thou didst pass erewhile,
"And suffer'd in these temples : for that cause   180
"Thou standest safe beneath this statue's knees."
"That I am favour'd for unworthiness,

144 thy *Woodhouse :* thine *Houghton.*
167 *Woodhouse inserts* do *in brackets after* thou : *Houghton adopts* do.

" By such propitious parley medicin'd
" In sickness not ignoble, I rejoice,
" Aye, and could weep for love of such award."
So answer'd I, continuing, " If it please,
" Majestic shadow, tell me : sure not all
" Those melodies sung into the World's ear
" Are useless : sure a poet is a sage ;
" A humanist, physician to all men.   190
" That I am none I feel, as vultures feel
" They are no birds when eagles are abroad.
" What am I then : Thou spakest of my tribe :
" What tribe? " The tall shade veil'd in drooping white
Then spake, so much more earnest, that the breath
Moved the thin linen folds that drooping hung
About a golden censer from the hand
Pendent—" Art thou not of the dreamer tribe ?
" The poet and the dreamer are distinct,
" Diverse, sheer opposite, antipodes.   200
" The one pours out a balm upon the World,
" The other vexes it." Then shouted I
Spite of myself, and with a Pythia's spleen
" Apollo ! faded ! O far flown Apollo !
" Where is thy misty pestilence to creep
" Into the dwellings, through the door crannies
" Of all mock lyrists, large self worshipers
" And careless Hectorers in proud bad verse.
" Though I breathe death with them it will be life
" To see them sprawl before me into graves.   210
" Majestic shadow, tell me where I am,
" Whose altar this ; for whom this incense curls ;
" What image this whose face I cannot see,
" For the broad marble knees ; and who thou art,
" Of accent feminine so courteous ? "

Then the tall shade, in drooping linens veil'd,
Spoke out, so much more earnest, that her breath
Stirr'd the thin folds of gauze that drooping hung
About a golden censer from her hand
Pendent ; and by her voice I knew she shed   220
Long-treasured tears. " This temple, sad and lone,

216 linens *Woodhouse :* linen *Houghton.*

"Is all spar'd from the thunder of a war
"Foughten long since by giant hierarchy
"Against rebellion: this old image here,
"Whose carved features wrinkled as he fell,
"Is Saturn's; I Moneta, left supreme
"Sole Priestess of this desolation."—
I had no words to answer, for my tongue,
Useless, could find about its roofed home
No syllable of a fit majesty   230
To make rejoinder to Moneta's mourn.
There was a silence, while the altar's blaze
Was fainting for sweet food: I look'd thereon,
And on the paved floor, where nigh were piled
Faggots of cinnamon, and many heaps
Of other crisped spice-wood—then again
I look'd upon the altar, and its horns
Whiten'd with ashes, and its lang'rous flame,
And then upon the offerings again;
And so by turns—till sad Moneta cried,   240
"The sacrifice is done, but not the less
"Will I be kind to thee for thy good will.
"My power, which to me is still a curse,
"Shall be to thee a wonder; for the scenes
"Still swooning vivid through my globed brain,
"With an electral changing misery,
"Thou shalt with these dull mortal eyes behold,
"Free from all pain, if wonder pain thee not."
As near as an immortal's sphered words
Could to a mother's soften, were these last: 250
And yet I had a terror of her robes,
And chiefly of the veils, that from her brow
Hung pale, and curtain'd her in mysteries,
That made my heart too small to hold its blood.
This saw that Goddess, and with sacred hand
Parted the veils. Then saw I a wan face,
Not pin'd by human sorrows, but bright-blanch'd
By an immortal sickness which kills not;
It works a constant change, which happy death
Can put no end to; deathwards progressing   260
To no death was that visage; it had past

227 Priestess *Woodhouse*: goddess *Houghton*.

The lilly and the snow ; and beyond these
I must not think now, though I saw that face—
But for her eyes I should have fled away.
They held me back, with a benignant light,
Soft mitigated by divinest lids
Half-closed, and visionless entire they seem'd
Of all external things ;—they saw me not,
But in blank splendor, beam'd like the mild moon,
Who comforts those she sees not, who knows not
What eyes are upward cast.   As I had found   271
A grain of gold upon a mountain's side,
And twing'd with avarice strain'd out my eyes
To search its sullen entrails rich with ore,
So at the view of sad Moneta's brow,
I ask'd to see what things the hollow brain
Behind environed : what high tragedy
In the dark secret chambers of her skull
Was acting, that could give so dread a stress
To her cold lips, and fill with such a light   280
Her planetary eyes ; and touch her voice
With such a sorrow—"Shade of Memory !"—
Cried I, with act adorant at her feet,
" By all the gloom hung round thy fallen house,
" By this last temple, by the golden age,
" By great Apollo, thy dear Foster Child,
" And by thyself, forlorn divinity,
" The pale Omega of a withered race,
" Let me behold, according as thou saidst,
" What in thy brain so ferments to and fro !"   290
No sooner had this conjuration pass'd
My devout lips, than side by side we stood
(Like a stunt bramble by a solemn pine)
Deep in the shady sadness of a vale,
Far sunken from the healthy breath of morn,
Far from the fiery noon and eve's one star.
Onward I look'd beneath the gloomy boughs,
And saw, what first I thought an image huge,
Like to the image pedestal'd so high
In Saturn's temple.   Then Moneta's voice   300
Came brief upon mine ear—" So Saturn sat
When he had lost his Realms—" whereon there grew

277 environed] *probably a transcriber's misreading of* envisioned.

A power within me of enormous ken
To see as a god sees, and take the depth
Of things as nimbly as the outward eye
Can size and shape pervade. The lofty theme
At those few words hung vast before my mind,
With half-unravel'd web. I set myself
Upon an eagle's watch, that I might see,
And seeing ne'er forget. No stir of life   310
Was in this shrouded vale, not so much air
As in the zoning of a summer's day
Robs not one light seed from the feather'd grass,
But where the dead leaf fell there did it rest:
A stream went voiceless by, still deaden'd more
By reason of the fallen divinity
Spreading more shade ; the Naiad 'mid her reeds
Prest her cold finger closer to her lips.

Along the margin-sand large footmarks went
No farther than to where old Saturn's feet   320
Had rested, and there slept, how long a sleep!
Degraded, cold, upon the sodden ground
His old right hand lay nerveless, listless, dead,
Unsceptred ; and his realmless eyes were clos'd,
While his bow'd head seem'd listening to the Earth,
His ancient mother, for some comfort yet.

It seem'd no force could wake him from his place ;
But there came one who, with a kindred hand
Touch'd his wide shoulders after bending low
With reverence, though to one who knew it not. 330
Then came the griev'd voice of Mnemosyne,
And griev'd I hearken'd. "That divinity
"Whom thou saw'st step from yon forlornest wood,
"And with slow pace approach our fallen King,
"Is Thea, softest-natur'd of our Brood."
I mark'd the Goddess in fair statuary
Surpassing wan Moneta by the head,
And in her sorrow nearer woman's tears.

307 At *Woodhouse :* Of *Houghton.*

308 set] sat *Houghton, following Woodhouse (?) ; but this must be a
mistranscription from Keats's manuscript.*

315 voiceless *Woodhouse :* noiseless *Houghton.*

320 farther *Woodhouse :* further *Houghton.*

There was a listening fear in her regard,
As if calamity had but begun ;   340
As if the vanward clouds of evil days
Had spent their malice, and the sullen rear
Was with its stored thunder labouring up.
One hand she press'd upon that aching spot
Where beats the human heart, as if just there,
Though an immortal, she felt cruel pain ;
The other upon Saturn's bended neck
She laid, and to the level of his hollow ear
Leaning with parted lips, some words she spake
In solemn tenor and deep organ tune ;   350
Some mourning words, which in our feeble tongue
Would come in this-like accenting ; how frail
To that large utterance of the early Gods !

  "Saturn ! look up—and for what, poor lost King ?
" I have no comfort for thee ; no not one ;
" I cannot say, wherefore thus sleepest thou ?
" For Heaven is parted from thee, and the Earth
" Knows thee not, so afflicted, for a God ;
" And Ocean too, with all its solemn noise,
" Has from thy sceptre pass'd, and all the air   360
" Is emptied of thine hoary majesty :
" Thy thunder, captious at the new command,
" Rumbles reluctant o'er our fallen house ;
" And thy sharp lightning, in unpracticed hands,
" Scorches and burns our once serene domain.
" With such remorseless speed still come new woes,
" That unbelief has not a space to breathe.
" Saturn ! sleep on :—Me thoughtless, why should I
" Thus violate thy slumbrous solitude ?
" Why should I ope thy melancholy eyes ?   370
" Saturn, sleep on, while at thy feet I weep."

  As when upon a tranced summer-night
Forests, branch-charmed by the earnest stars,

341 vanward *Woodhouse, as in 1820 :* venom'd *Houghton.*

348 hollow ear *Woodhouse :* hollow *omitted by Houghton as in 1820.*

356 cannot cry, *Wherefore thus sleepest thou : Woodhouse, fide de Sélincourt.*

359 And] The *Houghton.*   361 thine] thy *Houghton.*
365 Scorches] Scourges *Houghton.*

Dream, and so dream all night without a noise,
Save from one gradual solitary gust,
Swelling upon the silence ; dying off ;
As if the ebbing air had but one wave ;
So came these words, and went ; the while in tears
She prest her fair large forehead to the earth,   379
Just where her fallen hair might spread in curls,
A soft and silken mat for Saturn's feet.
Long, long these two were postured motionless,
Like sculpture builded-up upon the grave
Of their own power. A long awful time
I look'd upon them : still they were the same ;
The frozen God still bending to the earth,
And the sad Goddess weeping at his feet,
Moneta silent. Without stay or prop,
But my own weak mortality, I bore
The load of this eternal quietude,   390
The unchanging gloom, and the three fixed shapes
Ponderous upon my senses, a whole moon.
For by my burning brain I measured sure
Her silver seasons shedded on the night,
And every day by day methought I grew
More gaunt and ghostly.—Oftentimes I pray'd
Intense, that Death would take me from the Vale
And all its burthens—gasping with despair
Of change, hour after hour I curs'd myself ;
Until old Saturn rais'd his faded eyes,   400
And look'd around and saw his kingdom gone,
And all the gloom and sorrow of the place,
And that fair kneeling Goddess at his feet.
As the moist scent of flowers, and grass, and leaves,
Fills forest dells with a pervading air,
Known to the woodland nostril, so the words
Of Saturn fill'd the mossy glooms around,
Even to the hollows of time-eaten oaks,
And to the windings of the foxes' hole,
With sad low tones, while thus he spake, and sent
Strange musings to the solitary Pan.   411
"Moan, brethren, moan ; for we are swallow'd up

381 mat *Woodhouse, as in 1820 :* net *Houghton.*
410 spake *Woodhouse :* spoke *Houghton.*
411 musings *Woodhouse :* moanings *Houghton.*

"And buried from all Godlike exercise
"Of influence benign on planets pale,
"And peaceful sway above man's harvesting,   415
"And all those acts which Deity supreme
"Doth ease its heart of love in. Moan and wail,
"Moan, brethren, moan; for lo, the rebel spheres
"Spin round, the stars their ancient courses keep,
"Clouds still with shadowy moisture haunt the earth,
" Still suck their fill of light from sun and moon;
"Still buds the tree, and still the sea-shores murmur;
"There is no death in all the Universe,   423
" No smell of death—there shall be death—Moan, moan,
"Moan, Cybele, moan; for thy pernicious Babes
"Have changed a god into an aching Palsy.
"Moan, brethren, moan, for I have no strength left,
"Weak as the reed—weak—feeble as my voice—
"O, O, the pain, the pain of feebleness.
"Moan, moan, for still I thaw—or give me help;
"Throw down those imps, and give me victory.   431
"Let me hear other groans, and trumpets blown
"Of triumph calm, and hymns of festival,
"From the gold peaks of Heaven's high-piled clouds;
"Voices of soft proclaim, and silver stir
"Of strings in hollow shells; and there shall be
"Beautiful things made new for the surprise
"Of the sky-children." So he feebly ceas'd,
With such a poor and sickly sounding pause,
Methought I heard some old man of the earth   440
Bewailing earthly loss; nor could my eyes
And ears act with that pleasant unison of sense
Which marries sweet sound with the grace of form,
And dolorous accent from a tragic harp
With large-limb'd visions.—More I scrutinized:
Still fix'd he sat beneath the sable trees,
Whose arms spread straggling in wild serpent forms,
With leaves all hush'd; his awful presence there
(Now all was silent) gave a deadly lie
To what I erewhile heard—only his lips   450
Trembled amid the white curls of his beard.

415 above *Woodhouse* : upon *Houghton*.
426 an aching *Houghton* : a shaking *Woodhouse*.
442 pleasant unison *Woodhouse* : unison *Houghton*.

They told the truth, though, round, the snowy locks
Hung nobly, as upon the face of heaven
A mid-day fleece of clouds. Thea arose,
And stretched her white arm through the hollow dark,
Pointing some whither: whereat he too rose
Like a vast giant, seen by men at sea
To grow pale from the waves at dull midnight.
They melted from my sight into the woods ;
Ere I could turn, Moneta cried, "These twain 460
" Are speeding to the families of grief,
" Where roof'd in by black rocks they waste, in pain
" And darkness, for no hope."—And she spake on,
As ye may read who can unwearied pass
Onward from th' Antichamber of this dream,
Where even at the open doors awhile
I must delay, and glean my memory
Of her high phrase:—perhaps no further dare.

END OF CANTO I.

CANTO II.

" MORTAL, that thou may'st understand aright,
" I humanize my sayings to thine ear,
" Making comparisons of earthly things ;
" Or thou might'st better listen to the wind,
" Whose language is to thee a barren noise,
" Though it blows legend-laden thro' the trees.—
" In melancholy realms big tears are shed,
" More sorrow like to this, and such like woe,
" Too huge for mortal tongue, or pen of scribe.
" The Titans fierce, self hid or prison bound, 10
" Groan for the old allegiance once more,
" Listening in their doom for Saturn's voice.
" But one of our whole eagle-brood still keeps
" His sov'reignty, and rule, and majesty ;
" Blazing Hyperion on his orbed fire
" Still sits, still snuffs the incense teeming up

454 Thœa *Woodhouse.*
465 th' Antichamber *Woodhouse :* the antechamber *Houghton.*
13 our *Woodhouse :* the *Houghton.*

"From Man to the Sun's God: yet unsecure.
"For as upon the earth dire prodigies
"Fright and perplex, so also shudders he:
"Nor at dog's howl or gloom-bird's Even screech, 20
"Or the familiar visitings of one
"Upon the first toll of his passing bell:
"But horrors, portioned to a giant nerve,
"Make great Hyperion ache. His palace bright,
"Bastion'd with pyramids of glowing gold,
"And touch'd with shade of bronzed obelisks,
"Glares a blood-red thro' all the thousand courts,
"Arches, and domes, and fiery galleries:
"And all its curtains of Aurorian clouds
"Flush angerly; when he would taste the wreaths 30
"Of incense breathed aloft from sacred hills,
"Instead of sweets, his ample palate takes
"Savour of poisonous brass and metals sick.
"Wherefore when harbour'd in the sleepy West,
"After the full completion of fair day,
"For rest divine upon exalted couch
"And slumber in the arms of melody,
"He paces through the pleasant hours of ease
"With strides colossal, on from hall to hall;
"While far within each aisle and deep recess   40
"His winged minions in close clusters stand
"Amaz'd, and full of fear; like anxious men,
"Who on a wide plain gather in sad troops,
"When earthquakes jar their battlements and towers.
"Even now, while Saturn, roused from icy trance,
"Goes, step for step, with Thea from yon woods,
"Hyperion, leaving twilight in the rear,
"Is sloping to the threshold of the West.—
"Thither we tend."—Now in clear light I stood,

---

17 unsecure *Woodhouse, as in 1820*: insecure *Houghton*.
20 Even *Woodhouse*: hated *Houghton, as in 1820*.
21 visitings *Woodhouse*: visiting *Houghton*.
22–23 *Between these lines Houghton inserts from the "Hyperion" of 1820 the Virgilian reminiscence*—

    Or prophesyings of the midnight lamp.

25 glowing *Woodhouse, as in 1820*: shining *Houghton*.
30 Flush *Woodhouse*: Flash *Houghton*.
45 while *Woodhouse*: where *Houghton*.

Reliev'd from the dusk vale. Mnemosyne   50
Was sitting on a square-edg'd polish'd stone,
That in its lucid depth reflected pure
Her priestess-garments.—My quick eyes ran on
From stately nave to nave, from vault to vault,
Through bow'rs of fragrant and enwreathed light
And diamond-paved lustrous long arcades.
Anon rush'd by the bright Hyperion ;
His flaming robes stream'd out beyond his heels,
And gave a roar, as if of earthly fire,
That scared away the meek ethereal hours,   60
And made their dove-wings tremble. On he flared.

56 diamond-paved] diamond-paned *Houghton.*

THE CAP AND BELLS

OR THE JEALOUSIES

A FAERY TALE—UNFINISHED

THE CAP AND BELLS

OR THE JEALOUSIES

A FAERY TALE—UNFINISHED

I.

In midmost Ind, beside Hydaspes cool,
There stood, or hover'd, tremulous in the air,
A faery city, 'neath the potent rule
Of Emperor Elfinan ; fam'd ev'rywhere
For love of mortal women, maidens fair,
Whose lips were solid, whose soft hands were made
Of a fit mould and beauty, ripe and rare,
To pamper his slight wooing, warm yet staid :
He lov'd girls smooth as shades, but hated a mere shade.

II.

This was a crime forbidden by the law ;
And all the priesthood of his city wept,
For ruin and dismay they well foresaw,
If impious prince no bound or limit kept,
And faery Zendervester overstept ;
They wept, he sin'd, and still he would sin on,
They dreamt of sin, and he sin'd while they slept ;
In vain the pulpit thunder'd at the throne,
Caricature was vain, and vain the tart lampoon.

III.

Which seeing, his high court of parliament
Laid a remonstrance at his Highness' feet,
Praying his royal senses to content
Themselves with what in faery land was sweet,
Befitting best that shade with shade should meet:
Whereat, to calm their fears, he promis'd soon
From mortal tempters all to make retreat,—
Aye, even on the first of the new moon,
An immaterial wife to espouse as heaven's boon.

IV.

Meantime he sent a fluttering embassy
To Pigmio, of Imaus sovereign,
To half beg, and half demand, respectfully,
The hand of his fair daughter Bellanaine ;
An audience had, and speeching done, they gain
Their point, and bring the weeping bride away ;
Whom, with but one attendant, safely lain
Upon their wings, they bore in bright array,
While little harps were touch'd by many a lyric fay.

V.

As in old pictures tender cherubim
A child's soul thro' the sapphir'd canvas bear,
So, thro' a real heaven, on they swim
With the sweet princess on her plumag'd lair,
Speed giving to the winds her lustrous hair ;
And so she journey'd, sleeping or awake,
Save when, for healthful exercise and air,
She chose to *promener à l'aile*, or take
A pigeon's somerset, for sport or change's sake.

VI.

"Dear Princess, do not whisper me so loud,"
Quoth Corallina, nurse and confidant,
"Do not you see there, lurking in a cloud,
Close at your back, that sly old Crafticant ?
He hears a whisper plainer than a rant :
Dry up your tears, and do not look so blue ;
He's Elfinan's great state-spy militant,
His running, lying, flying foot-man too,—
Dear mistress, let him have no handle against you !

VII.

"Show him a mouse's tail, and he will guess,
With metaphysic swiftness, at the mouse ;
Show him a garden, and with speed no less,
He'll surmise sagely of a dwelling house,
And plot, in the same minute, how to chouse

V 1–2 As in old Pictures Cherubs bear aloft
The souls of children *Holograph, rejected.*

The owner out of it ; show him a "— "Peace !
Peace ! nor contrive thy mistress' ire to rouse !"
Return'd the Princess, "my tongue shall not cease
Till from this hated match I get a free release.

VIII.

"Ah, beauteous mortal !" "Hush !" quoth Coralline,
"Really you must not talk of him, indeed."
"You hush !" replied the mistress, with a shine
Of anger in her eyes, enough to breed
In stouter hearts than nurse's fear and dread :
'Twas not the glance itself made nursey flinch,
But of its threat she took the utmost heed ;
Not liking in her heart an hour-long pinch,
Or a sharp needle run into her back an inch.

IX.

So she was silenc'd, and fair Bellanaine,
Writhing her little body with ennui,
Continued to lament and to complain,
That Fate, cross-purposing, should let her be
Ravish'd away far from her dear countree ;
That all her feelings should be set at naught,
In trumping up this match so hastily,
With lowland blood ; and lowland blood she thought
Poison, as every staunch true-born Imaian ought.

X.

Sorely she griev'd, and wetted three or four
White Provence rose-leaves with her faery tears,
But not for this cause ;—alas ! she had more
Bad reasons for her sorrow, as appears
In the fam'd memoirs of a thousand years,
Written by Crafticant, and published
By Parpaglion and Co., (those sly compeers
Who rak'd up ev'ry fact against the dead,)
In Scarab Street, Panthea, at the Jubal's Head.

XI.

Where, after a long hypercritic howl
Against the vicious manners of the age
He goes on to expose, with heart and soul,
What vice in this or that year was the rage,
Backbiting all the world in every page ;

With special strictures on the horrid crime,
(Section'd and subsection'd with learning sage,)
Of faeries stooping on their wings sublime
To kiss a mortal's lips, when such were in their prime.

XII.

Turn to the copious index, you will find
Somewhere in the column, headed letter B,
The name of Bellanaine, if you're not blind ;
Then pray refer to the text, and you will see
An article made up of calumny
Against this highland princess, rating her
For giving way, so over fashionably,
To this new-fangled vice, which seems a burr
Stuck in his moral throat, no coughing e'er could stir.

XIII.

There he says plainly that she lov'd a man !
That she around him flutter'd, flirted, toy'd,
Before her marriage with great Elfinan ;
That after marriage too, she never joy'd
In husband's company, but still employ'd
Her wits to 'scape away to Angle-land ;
Where liv'd the youth, who worried and annoy'd
Her tender heart, and its warm ardours fann'd
To such a dreadful blaze, her side would scorch her hand.

XIV.

But let us leave this idle tittle-tattle
To waiting-maids, and bed-room coteries,
Nor till fit time against her fame wage battle.
Poor Elfinan is very ill at ease,
Let us resume his subject if you please :
For it may comfort and console him much
To rhyme and syllable his miseries ;
Poor Elfinan ! whose cruel fate was such,
He sat and curs'd a bride he knew he could not touch.

XV.

Soon as (according to his promises)
The bridal embassy had taken wing,
And vanish'd, bird-like, o'er the suburb trees,
The Emperor, empierc'd with the sharp sting
Of love, retired, vex'd and murmuring

Like any drone shut from the fair bee-queen,
Into his cabinet, and there did fling
His limbs upon a sofa, full of spleen,
And damn'd his House of Commons, in complete chagrin.

XVI.

" I'll trounce some of the members," cried the Prince,
" I'll put a mark against some rebel names,
I'll make the Opposition-benches wince,
I'll show them very soon, to all their shames,
What 'tis to smother up a Prince's flames ;
That ministers should join in it, I own,
Surprises me !—they too at these high games !
Am I an Emperor ? Do I wear a crown ?
Imperial Elfinan, go hang thyself or drown !

XVII.

" I'll trounce 'em !—there 's the square-cut chancellor,
His son shall never touch that bishopric ;
And for the nephew of old Palfior,
I'll show him that his speech has made me sick,
And give the colonelcy to Phalaric ;
The tiptoe marquis, moral and gallant,
Shall lodge in shabby taverns upon tick ;
And for the Speaker's second cousin's aunt,
She sha'n't be maid of honour,—by heaven that she
      sha'n't !

XVIII.

"I'll shirk the Duke of A. ; I'll cut his brother ;
I'll give no garter to his eldest son ;
I won't speak to his sister or his mother !
The Viscount B. shall live at cut-and-run ;
But how in the world can I contrive to stun
That fellow's voice, which plagues me worse than any,
That stubborn fool, that impudent state-dun,
Who sets down ev'ry sovereign as a zany,—
That vulgar commoner, Esquire Biancopany ?

XVIII 9 Biancopany = Whitbread.

XIX.

"Monstrous affair!   Pshaw! pah! what ugly minx
Will they fetch from Imaus for my bride?
Alas! my wearied heart within me sinks,
To think that I must be so near allied
To a cold dullard fay,—ah, woe betide!
Ah, fairest of all human loveliness!
Sweet Bertha! what crime can it be to glide
About the fragrant pleatings of thy dress,
Or kiss thine eyes, or count thy locks, tress after tress?"

XX.

So said, one minute's while his eyes remain'd
Half lidded, piteous, languid, innocent;
But, in a wink, their splendour they regain'd,
Sparkling revenge with amorous fury blent.
Love thwarted in bad temper oft has vent:
He rose, he stampt his foot, he rang the bell,
And order'd some death-warrants to be sent
For signature:—somewhere the tempest fell,
As many a poor felon does not live to tell.

XXI.

"At the same time Eban,"—(this was his page,
A fay of colour, slave from top to toe,
Sent as a present, while yet under age,
From the Viceroy of Zanguebar,—wise, slow,
His speech, his only words were "yes" and "no,"
But swift of look, and foot, and wing was he,—)
"At the same time, Eban, this instant go
To Hum the soothsayer, whose name I see
Among the fresh arrivals in our empery.

XXII.

"Bring Hum to me! But stay—here, take my ring,
The pledge of favour, that he not suspect
Any foul play, or awkward murdering,
Tho' I have bowstrung many of his sect;
Throw in a hint, that if he should neglect

XX 1 So saying his eyes one minute's while were soft
Holograph, rejected.

One hour, the next shall see him in my grasp,
And the next after that shall see him neck'd,
Or swallow'd by my hunger-starved asp,—
And mention ('tis as well) the torture of the wasp."

XXIII.

These orders given, the Prince, in half a pet,
Let o'er the silk his propping elbow slide,
Caught up his little legs, and, in a fret,
Fell on the sofa on his royal side.
The slave retreated backwards, humble-eyed,
And with a slave-like silence clos'd the door,
And to old Hum thro' street and alley hied;
He "knew the city," as we say, of yore,
And for short cuts and turns, was nobody knew more.

XXIV.

It was the time when wholesale houses close
Their shutters with a moody sense of wealth,
But retail dealers, diligent, let loose
The gas (objected to on score of health),
Convey'd in little solder'd pipes by stealth,
And make it flare in many a brilliant form,
That all the powers of darkness it repell'th,
Which to the oil-trade doth great scaith and harm,
And supersedeth quite the use of the glow-worm.

XXV.

Eban, untempted by the pastry-cooks,
(Of pastry he got store within the palace,)
With hasty steps, wrapp'd cloak, and solemn looks,
Incognito upon his errand sallies,
His smelling-bottle ready for the allies;
He pass'd the Hurdy-gurdies with disdain,
Vowing he'd have them sent aboard the gallies;
Just as he made his vow, it 'gan to rain,
Therefore he call'd a coach, and bade it drive amain.

XXVI.

"I'll pull the string," said he, and further said,
"Polluted Jarvey! Ah, thou filthy hack!
Whose springs of life are all dried up and dead,
Whose linsey-woolsey lining hangs all slack,
Whose rug is straw, whose wholeness is a crack;

And evermore thy steps go clatter-clitter ;
Whose glass once up can never be got back,
Who prov'st, with jolting arguments and bitter,
That 'tis of modern use to travel in a litter.

XXVII.

"Thou inconvenience! thou hungry crop
For all corn! thou snail-creeper to and fro,
Who while thou goest ever seem'st to stop,
And fiddle-faddle standest while you go ;
I' the morning, freighted with a weight of woe,
Unto some lazar-house thou journeyest,
And in the evening tak'st a double row
Of dowdies, for some dance or party drest,
Besides the goods meanwhile thou movest east and west.

XXVIII.

"By thy ungallant bearing and sad mien,
An inch appears the utmost thou couldst budge ;
Yet at the slightest nod, or hint, or sign, ·
Round to the curb-stone patient dost thou trudge,
School'd in a beckon, learned in a nudge,
A dull-eyed Argus watching for a fare ;
Quiet and plodding, thou dost bear no grudge
To whisking Tilburies, or Phaetons rare,
Curricles, or Mail-coaches, swift beyond compare."

XXIX.

Philosophizing thus, he pull'd the check,
And bade the Coachman wheel to such a street,
Who, turning much his body, more his neck,
Louted full low, and hoarsely did him greet:
"Certes, Monsieur were best take to his feet,

XXVIII 5 As courteous to a Cobler as a Judge
        MS., cancelled.

XXIX *The following stanza is cancelled in the MS. after XXIX.*
 "Ho! Ho thought Eban so this Signor Hum
 A conversazione holds tonight
 Whene'er he beats his literary drum
 The learned muster round all right and tight

Seeing his servant can no further drive
For press of coaches, that to-night here meet
Many as bees about a straw-capp'd hive,
When first for April honey into faint flowers they dive."

XXX.

Eban then paid his fare, and tiptoe went
To Hum's hotel; and, as he on did pass
With head inclin'd, each dusky lineament.
Show'd in the pearl-pav'd street, as in a glass;
His purple vest, that ever peeping was
Rich from the fluttering crimson of his cloak,
His silvery trowsers, and his silken sash
Tied in a burnish'd knot, their semblance took
Upon the mirror'd walls, wherever he might look.

XXXI.

He smil'd at self, and, smiling, show'd his teeth,
And seeing his white teeth, he smil'd the more;
Lifted his eye-brows, spurn'd the path beneath,
Show'd teeth again, and smil'd as heretofore,
Until he knock'd at the magician's door;
Where, till the porter answer'd, might be seen,
In the clear panel more he could adore,—
His turban wreath'd of gold, and white, and green,
Mustachios, ear-ring, nose-ring, and his sabre keen.

XXXII.

"Does not your master give a rout to-night?"
Quoth the dark page. "Oh, no!" return'd the Swiss,
"Next door but one to us, upon the right,
The *Magazin des Modes* now open is
Against the Emperor's wedding;—and, sir, this
My master finds a monstrous horrid bore;
As he retir'd, an hour ago I wis,
With his best beard and brimstone, to explore
And cast a quiet figure in his second floor.

Drest in best black to talk by candle light."
E'en while he thought, for eighteen penny fare
He paid a half penny by cuning sleight
Made argent; then with self-contented Air
Broke through the Crowd to Hums, and all the world was there.

XXXIII.

"Gad! he's oblig'd to stick to business!
For chalk, I hear, stands at a pretty price;
And as for aqua vitæ—there's a mess!
The *dentes sapientiæ* of mice,
Our barber tells me too, are on the rise,—
Tinder's a lighter article,—nitre pure
Goes off like lightning,—grains of Paradise
At an enormous figure!—stars not sure!—
Zodiac will not move without a sly douceur!

XXXIV.

"Venus won't stir a peg without a fee,
And master is too partial, *entre nous,*
To"— "Hush—hush!" cried Eban, "sure that is he
Coming down stairs,—by St. Bartholomew!
As backwards as he can,—is't something new?
Or is't his custom, in the name of fun?"
"He always comes down backward, with one shoe"—
Return'd the porter—"off, and one shoe on,
Like, saving shoe for sock or stocking, my man John!"

XXXV.

It was indeed the great Magician,
Feeling, with careful toe, for every stair,
And retrograding careful as he can,
Backwards and downwards from his own two pair:
"Salpietro!" exclaim'd Hum, "is the dog there?
He's always in my way upon the mat!"
"He's in the kitchen, or the Lord knows where,"—
Replied the Swiss,—"the nasty, yelping brat!"
"Don't beat him!" return'd Hum, and on the floor
        came pat.

XXXVI.

Then facing right about, he saw the Page,
And said: "Don't tell me what you want, Eban;
The Emperor is now in a huge rage,—
'Tis nine to one he'll give you the rattan!
Let us away!" Away together ran

XXXV 8 yelping] whelping *MS. and Houghton.*

The plain-dress'd sage and spangled blackamoor,
Nor rested till they stood to cool, and fan,
And breathe themselves at the Emperor's chamber
    door,
When Eban thought he heard a soft imperial snore.

XXXVII.

"I thought you guess'd, foretold, or prophesied,
That's Majesty was in a raving fit?"
"He dreams," said Hum, "or I have ever lied,
That he is tearing you, sir, bit by bit."
"He's not asleep, and you have little wit,"
Replied the page: "that little buzzing noise,
Whate'er your palmistry may make of it,
Comes from a play-thing of the Emperor's choice,
From a Man-Tiger-Organ, prettiest of his toys."

XXXVIII.

Eban then usher'd in the learned Seer:
Elfinan's back was turn'd, but, ne'ertheless,
Both, prostrate on the carpet, ear by ear,
Crept silently, and waited in distress,
Knowing the Emperor's moody bitterness;
Eban especially, who on the floor 'gan
Tremble and quake to death,—he feared less
A dose of senna-tea or nightmare Gorgon
Than the Emperor when he play'd on his Man-Tiger-
    Organ.

XXXIX.

They kiss'd nine times the carpet's velvet face
Of glossy silk, soft, smooth, and meadow-green,
Where the close eye in deep rich fur might trace
A silver tissue, scantly to be seen,
As daisies lurk'd in June-grass, buds in treen;
Sudden the music ceased, sudden the hand
Of majesty, by dint of passion keen,
Doubled into a common fist, went grand,
And knock'd down three cut glasses, and his best ink-
    stand.

XL.

Then turning round, he saw those trembling two:
"Eban," said he, "as slaves should taste the fruits
Of diligence, I shall remember you
To-morrow, or the next day, as time suits,
In a finger conversation with my mutes,—
Begone!—for you, Chaldean! here remain!
Fear not, quake not, and as good wine recruits
A conjurer's spirits, what cup will you drain?
Sherry in silver, hock in gold, or glass'd champagne?"

XLI.

"Commander of the Faithful!" answer'd Hum,
"In preference to these, I'll merely taste
A thimble-full of old Jamaica rum."
"A simple boon!" said Elfinan; "thou may'st
Have Nantz, with which my morning-coffee's lac'd."
"I'll have a glass of Nantz, then,"—said the Seer,—
"Made racy—(sure my boldness is misplac'd!)—
With the third part—(yet that is drinking dear!)—
Of the least drop of *crème de citron*, crystal clear."

XLII.

"I pledge you, Hum! and pledge my dearest love,
My Bertha!" "Bertha! Bertha!" cried the sage,
"I know a many Berthas!" "Mine's above
All Berthas!" sighed the Emperor. "I engage,"
Said Hum, "in duty, and in vassalage,
To mention all the Berthas in the Earth;—
There's Bertha Watson,—and Miss Bertha Page,—
This fam'd for languid eyes, and that for mirth,—
There's Bertha Blount of York,—and Bertha Knox of
    Perth."

XLIII.

"You seem to know"—"I do know," answer'd Hum,
"Your Majesty's in love with some fine girl
Named Bertha; but her surname will not come,
Without a little conjuring." "'Tis Pearl,
'Tis Bertha Pearl that makes my brains so whirl;

And she is softer, fairer than her name!"
"Where does she live?" ask'd Hum. "Her fair
    locks curl
So brightly, they put all our fays to shame!—
Live?—O! at Canterbury, with her old grand-dame."

XLIV.

"Good! good!" cried Hum, "I've known her from
    a child!
She is a changeling of my management;
She was born at midnight in an Indian wild;
Her mother's screams with the striped tiger's blent,
While the torch-bearing slaves a halloo sent
Into the jungles; and her palanquin,
Rested amid the desert's dreariment,
Shook with her agony, till fair were seen
The little Bertha's eyes oped on the stars serene."

XLV.

"I can't say," said the monarch; "that may be
Just as it happen'd, true or else a bam!
Drink up your brandy, and sit down by me,
Feel, feel my pulse, how much in love I am;
And if your science is not all a sham,
Tell me some means to get the lady here."
"Upon my honour!" said the son of Cham,
"She is my dainty changeling, near and dear,
Although her story sounds at first a little queer."

XLVI.

"Convey her to me, Hum, or by my crown,
My sceptre, and my cross-surmounted globe,
I'll knock you "—"Does your majesty mean—*down?*
No, no, you never could my feelings probe
To such a depth!" The Emperor took his robe,
And wept upon its purple palatine,
While Hum continued, shamming half a sob,—
"In Canterbury doth your lady shine?
But let me cool your brandy with a little wine."

XLVII.

Whereat a narrow Flemish glass he took,
That once belong'd to Admiral de Witt,
Admir'd it with a connoisseuring look,
And with the ripest claret crowned it,
And, ere one lively bead could burst and flit,
He turn'd it quickly, nimbly upside down,
His mouth being held conveniently fit
To catch the treasure: "Best in all the town!"
He said, smack'd his moist lips, and gave a pleasant
      frown.

XLVIII.

"Ah! good my Prince, weep not!" And then
      again
He fill'd a bumper. "Great Sire, do not weep!
Your pulse is shocking, but I'll ease your pain."
"Fetch me that Ottoman, and prithee keep
Your voice low," said the Emperor; "and steep
Some lady's-fingers nice in Candy wine;
And prithee, Hum, behind the screen do peep
For the rose-water vase, magician mine!
And sponge my forehead,—so my love doth make
      me pine.

XLIX.

"Ah, cursed Bellanaine!" "Don't think of her,"
Rejoin'd the Mago, "but on Bertha muse;
For, by my choicest best barometer,
You shall not throttled be in marriage noose;
I've said it, Sire; you only have to choose
Bertha or Bellanaine." So saying, he drew
From the left pocket of his threadbare hose,
A sampler hoarded slyly, good as new,
Holding it by his thumb and finger full in view.

L.

"Sire, this is Bertha Pearl's neat handy-work,
Her *name*, see here, *Midsummer, ninety-one*."
Elfinan snatch'd it with a sudden jerk,
And wept as if he never would have done,

Honouring with royal tears the poor homespun ;
Whereon were broider'd tigers with black eyes,
And long-tail'd pheasants, and a rising sun,
Plenty of posies, great stags, butterflies
Bigger than stags,—a moon,—with other mysteries.

LI.

The monarch handled o'er and o'er again
These day-school hieroglyphics with a sigh ;
Somewhat in sadness, but pleas'd in the main,
Till this oracular couplet met his eye
Astounded—*Cupid I, do thee defy!*
It was too much. He shrunk back in his chair,
Grew pale as death, and fainted—very nigh !
"Pho ! nonsense !" exclaim'd Hum, " now don't
          despair ;
She does not mean it really. Cheer up hearty there!

LII.

"And listen to my words. You say you won't,
On any terms, marry Miss Bellanaine ;
It goes against your conscience—good ! Well, don't.
You say you love a mortal. I would fain
Persuade your honour's highness to refrain
From peccadilloes. But, Sire, as I say,
What good would that do ? And, to be more plain,
You would do me a mischief some odd day,
Cut off my ears and hands, or head too, by my fay !

LIII.

"Besides, manners forbid that I should pass any
Vile strictures on the conduct of a prince
Who should indulge his genius, if he has any,
Not, like a subject, foolish matters mince.

LI *In the MS. the first word of line 2 is unquestionably* These : *the*
These *of the Houghton text is likely to be unauthorized.   In line 5 the*
" *oracular couplet*" *has the comma after* I *instead of after* Cupid *as in
the Houghton text.   Keats's own punctuation preserves what we editors
failed to bring out, that Bertha's sampler made two lines of her defiance—*

CUPID I
DO THEE DEFY.

Now I think on 't, perhaps I could convince
Your Majesty there is no crime at all
In loving pretty little Bertha, since
She 's very delicate,—not over tall,—
A fairy's hand, and in the waist, why—very small."

LIV.

"Ring the repeater, gentle Hum!" "'Tis five,"
Said gentle Hum; "the nights draw in apace;
The little birds I hear are all alive;
I see the dawning touch'd upon your face;
Shall I put out the candles, please your Grace?"
"Do put them out, and, without more ado,
Tell me how I may that sweet girl embrace,—
How you can bring her to me." "That 's for you,
Great Emperor! to adventure, like a lover true."

LV.

"I fetch her!"—"Yes, an 't like your Majesty;
And as she would be frighten'd wide awake
To travel such a distance through the sky,
Use of some soft manœuvre you must make,
For your convenience, and her dear nerves' sake;
Nice way would be to bring her in a swoon,
Anon, I'll tell what course were best to take;
You must away this morning." "Hum! so soon?"
"Sire, you must be in Kent by twelve o'clock at noon."

LVI.

At this great Cæsar started on his feet,
Lifted his wings, and stood attentive-wise.
"Those wings to Canterbury you must beat,
If you hold Bertha as a worthy prize.
Look in the Almanack—*Moore* never lies—
April the twenty-fourth,—this coming day,
Now breathing its new bloom upon the skies,
Will end in St. Mark's Eve;—you must away,
For on that eve alone can you the maid convey."

LVI 7 Now spreading its yo[u]ng bloom upon the sky,
MS., rejected.

Two rejected readings in this stanza are of unusual interest:

        April the twenty fifth this very morn
        Is sacred to St. Mark

and

        Ends quiet in St Agnes E[ve].

LVII.

Then the magician solemnly 'gan frown,
  So that his frost-white eyebrows, beetling low,
Shaded his deep-green eyes, and wrinkles brown
  Plaited upon his furnace-scorched brow :
Forth from the hood that hung his neck below,
  He lifted a bright casket of pure gold,
Touch'd a spring-lock, and there in wool, or snow
  Charm'd into ever-freezing, lay an old
And legend-leaved book, mysterious to behold.

LVIII.

"Take this same book,—it will not bite you, Sire ;
  There, put it underneath your royal arm ;
Though it's a pretty weight it will not tire,
  But rather on your journey keep you warm :
This is the magic, this the potent charm,
  That shall drive Bertha to a fainting fit !
When the time comes, don't feel the least alarm,
  Uplift her from the ground, and swiftly flit
Back to your palace, where I wait for guerdon fit."

LIX.

"What shall I do with this same book ?" "Why
    merely
Lay it on Bertha's table, close beside
Her work-box, and 'twill help your purpose dearly ;
  I say no more." "Or good or ill betide,
Through the wide air to Kent this morn I glide !"
  Exclaim'd the Emperor. "When I return,
Ask what you will,—I'll give you my new bride !
  And take some more wine, Hum ;—O Heavens !
    I burn
To be upon the wing ! Now, now, that minx I spurn !"

LX.

"Leave her to me," rejoin'd the magian :
  "But how shall I account, illustrious fay !
For thine imperial absence ? Pho ! I can
  Say you are very sick, and bar the way

To your so loving courtiers for one day ;
If either of their two archbishops' graces
Should talk of extreme unction, I shall say
You do not like cold pig with Latin phrases,
Which never should be used but in alarming cases."

LXI.

"Open the window, Hum ; I'm ready now !"
"Zooks !" exclaim'd Hum, as up the sash he drew,
"Behold, your Majesty, upon the brow
Of yonder hill, what crowds of people !" "Whew !
The monster 's always after something new,"
Return'd his Highness, "they are piping hot
To see my pigsny Bellanaine. Hum ! do
Tighten my belt a little,—so, so,—not
Too tight,—the book !—my wand !—so, nothing is
        forgot."

LXII.

"Wounds ! how they shout !" said Hum, "and
        there,—see, see !
The Ambassadors return'd from Pigmio !
The morning 's very fine,—uncommonly !
See, past the skirts of yon white cloud they go,
Tinging it with soft crimsons ! Now below
The sable-pointed heads of firs and pines
They dip, move on, and with them moves a glow
Along the forest side ! Now amber lines
Reach the hill top, and now throughout the valley
        shines."

LXIII.

"Why, Hum, you're getting quite poetical !
Those *nows* you managed in a special style."
"If ever you have leisure, Sire, you shall
See scraps of mine will make it worth your while,

LXII 6 The sable heads of pointed firs and pines *MS., rejected.*
    7 They dip and fill the forest with a glow *MS., cancelled.*

Tit-bits for Phœbus!—yes, you well may smile.
Hark! Hah! the bells!" "A little further yet,
Good Hum, and let me view this mighty coil."
Then the great Emperor full graceful set
His elbow for a prop, and snuff'd his mignonnette.

LXIV.

The morn is full of holiday; loud bells
With rival clamours ring from every spire;
Cunningly-station'd music dies and swells
In echoing places; when the winds respire,
Light flags stream out like gauzy tongues of fire;
A metropolitan murmur, lifeful, warm,
Comes from the northern suburbs; rich attire
Freckles with red and gold the moving swarm;
While here and there clear trumpets blow a keen alarm.

LXV.

And now the fairy escort was seen clear,
Like the old pageant of Aurora's train,
Above a pearl-built minster, hovering near;
First wily Crafticant, the chamberlain,
Balanc'd upon his grey-grown pinions twain,
His slender wand officially reveal'd;
Then black gnomes scattering sixpences like rain;
Then pages three and three; and next, slave-held,
The Imaian 'scutcheon bright,—one mouse in argent
    field.

LXVI.

Gentlemen pensioners next; and after them,
A troop of winged Janizaries flew;
Then Slaves, as presents bearing many a gem;
Then twelve physicians fluttering two and two;
And next a chaplain in a cassock new;
Then Lords in waiting; then (what head not reels
For pleasure?)—the fair Princess in full view,
Borne upon wings,—and very pleas'd she feels
To have such splendour dance attendance at her heels.

LXVII.

For there was more magnificence behind :
She wav'd her handkerchief. "Ah, very grand !"
Cried Elfinan, and clos'd the window-blind ;
"And, Hum, we must not shilly-shally stand,—
Adieu ! adieu ! I'm off for Angle-land !
I say, old Hocus, have you such a thing
About you,—feel your pockets, I command,—
I want, this instant, an invisible ring,—
Thank you, old mummy !—now securely I take wing."

LXVIII.

Then Elfinan swift vaulted from the floor,
And lighted graceful on the window-sill ;
Under one arm the magic book he bore,
The other he could wave about at will ;
Pale was his face, he still look'd very ill :
He bow'd at Bellanaine, and said—"Poor Bell !
Farewell ! farewell ! and if for ever ! still
For ever fare thee well !"—and then he fell
A laughing !—snapp'd his fingers !—shame it is to tell !

LXIX.

"By'r Lady ! he is gone !" cries Hum, "and I—
(I own it)—have made too free with his wine ;
Old Crafticant will smoke me. By the bye—
This room is full of jewels as a mine,—
Dear valuable creatures, how ye shine !
Sometime to-day I must contrive a minute,
If Mercury propitiously incline,
To examine his scrutoire, and see what's in it,
For of superfluous diamonds I as well may thin it.

LXX.

"The Emperor's horrid bad ; yes, that's my cue !"
Some histories say that this was Hum's last speech ;
That, being fuddled, he went reeling through
The corridor, and scarce upright could reach
The stair-head ; that being glutted as a leech,
And us'd, as we ourselves have just now said,
To manage stairs reversely, like a peach
Too ripe, he fell, being puzzled in his head
With liquor and the staircase : verdict—*found stone dead.*

LXXI.

This as a falsehood Crafticanto treats ;
And as his style is of strange elegance,
Gentle and tender, full of soft conceits,
(Much like our Boswell's,) we will take a glance
At his sweet prose, and, if we can, make dance
His woven periods into careless rhyme ;
O, little faery Pegasus ! rear—prance—
Trot round the quarto—ordinary time !
March, little Pegasus, with pawing hoof sublime !

LXXII.

Well, let us see,—*tenth book and chapter nine,*—
Thus Crafticant pursues his diary :—
" 'Twas twelve o'clock at night, the weather fine,
Latitude thirty-six ; our scouts descry
A flight of starlings making rapidly
Towards Thibet. Mem. :—birds fly in the night ;
From twelve to half-past—wings not fit to fly
For a thick fog—the Princess sulky quite
Call'd for an extra shawl, and gave her nurse a bite.

LXXIII.

" Five minutes before one—brought down a moth
With my new double-barrel—stew'd the thighs
And made a very tolerable broth—
Princess turn'd dainty ;—to our great surprise,
Alter'd her mind, and thought it very nice :
Seeing her pleasant, tried her with a pun,
She frown'd ; a monstrous owl across us flies
About this time,—a sad old figure of fun ;
Bad omen—this new match can't be a happy one.

LXXIV.

" From two till half-past, dusky way we made,
Above the plains of Gobi,—desert, bleak ;
Beheld afar off, in the hooded shade
Of darkness, a great mountain (strange to speak),
Spitting, from forth its sulphur-baken peak,
A fan-shap'd burst of blood-red, arrowy fire,
Turban'd with smoke, which still away did reek,
Solid and black from that eternal pyre,
Upon the laden wind that scantly could respire.

KEATS   * R

LXXV.

"Just upon three o'clock a falling star
Created an alarm among our troop,
Kill'd a man-cook, a page, and broke a jar,
A tureen, and three dishes, at one swoop,
Then passing by the Princess, singed her hoop:
Could not conceive what Coralline was at,
She clapp'd her hands three times and cried out
    'Whoop!'
Some strange Imaian custom. A large bat
Came sudden 'fore my face, and brush'd against my hat.

LXXVI.

"Five minutes thirteen seconds after three,
Far in the west a mighty fire broke out,
Conjectur'd, on the instant, it might be
The city of Balk—'twas Balk beyond all doubt:
A Griffin, wheeling here and there about,
Kept reconnoitring us—doubled our guard—
Lighted our torches, and kept up a shout,
Till he sheer'd off—the Princess very scar'd—
And many on their marrow-bones for death prepar'd.

LXXVII.

"At half-past three arose the cheerful moon—
Bivouack'd for four minutes on a cloud—
Where from the earth we heard a lively tune
Of tambourines and pipes, serene and loud,
While on a flowery lawn a brilliant crowd
Cinque-parted danc'd, some half asleep reposed
Beneath the green-fan'd cedars, some did shroud
In silken tents, and 'mid light fragrance dozed,
Or on the open turf their soothed eyelids closed.

LXXVIII

"Dropp'd my gold watch, and kill'd a kettledrum—
It went for apoplexy—foolish folks!—
Left it to pay the piper—a good sum—
(I've got a conscience, maugre people's jokes;)
To scrape a little favour 'gan to coax
Her Highness' pug-dog—got a sharp rebuff—
She wish'd a game at whist—made three revokes—
Turn'd from myself, her partner, in a huff;
His majesty will know her temper time enough.

LXXIX.

"She cried for chess—I play'd a game with her—
Castled her king with such a vixen look,
It bodes ill to his Majesty—(refer
To the second chapter of my fortieth book,
And see what hoity-toity airs she took).
At half-past four the morn essay'd to beam—
Saluted, as we pass'd, an early rook—
The Princess fell asleep, and, in her dream,
Talk'd of one Master Hubert, deep in her esteem.

LXXX.

"About this time,—making delightful way,—
Shed a quill-feather from my larboard wing—
Wish'd, trusted, hop'd 'twas no sign of decay—
Thank heaven, I'm hearty yet!—'twas no such
    thing:—
At five the golden light began to spring,
With fiery shudder through the bloomed east;
At six we heard Panthea's churches ring—
The city all her unhiv'd swarms had cast,
To watch our grand approach, and hail us as we pass'd.

LXXXI.

"As flowers turn their faces to the sun,
So on our flight with hungry eyes they gaze,
And, as we shap'd our course, this, that way run,
With mad-cap pleasure, or hand-clasp'd amaze;
Sweet in the air a mild-ton'd music plays,
And progresses through its own labyrinth;
Buds gather'd from the green spring's middle-days,
They scatter'd,—daisy, primrose, hyacinth,—
Or round white columns wreath'd from capital to plinth.

LXXXII.

"Onward we floated o'er the panting streets,
That seem'd throughout with upheld faces paved;
Look where we will, our bird's-eye vision meets
Legions of holiday; bright standards waved,
And fluttering ensigns emulously craved
Our minute's glance; a busy thunderous roar,
From square to square, among the buildings raved,
As when the sea, at flow, gluts up once more
The craggy hollowness of a wild reefed shore.

LXXXIII.

" And ' Bellanaine for ever !' shouted they,
While that fair Princess, from her winged chair,
Bow'd low with high demeanour, and, to pay
Their new-blown loyalty with guerdon fair,
Still emptied, at meet distance, here and there,
A plenty horn of jewels.   And here I
(Who wish to give the devil her due) declare
Against that ugly piece of calumny,
Which calls them Highland pebble-stones not worth
        a fly.

LXXXIV.

"Still ' Bellanaine !' they shouted, while we glide
'Slant to a light Ionic portico,
The city's delicacy, and the pride
Of our Imperial Basilic ; a row
Of lords and ladies, on each hand, make show
Submissive of knee-bent obeisance,
All down the steps ; and, as we enter'd, lo !
The strangest sight—the most unlook'd-for chance—
All things turn'd topsy-turvy in a devil's dance.

LXXXV.

"''Stead of his anxious Majesty and court
At the open doors, with wide saluting eyes,
Congées and scape-graces of every sort,
And all the smooth routine of gallantries,
Was seen, to our immoderate surprise,
A motley crowd thick gather'd in the hall,
Lords, scullions, deputy-scullions, with wild cries
Stunning the vestibule from wall to wall,
Where the Chief Justice on his knees and hands doth
        crawl.

LXXXVI.

" Counts of the palace, and the state purveyor
Of moth's-down, to make soft the royal beds,
The Common Council and my fool Lord Mayor
Marching a-row, each other slipshod treads ;

Powder'd bag-wigs and ruffy-tuffy heads
Of cinder wenches meet and soil each other ;
Toe crush'd with heel ill-natur'd fighting breeds,
Frill-rumpling elbows brew up many a bother,
And fists in the short ribs keep up the yell and pother.

LXXXVII.

"A Poet, mounted on the Court-Clown's back,
Rode to the Princess swift with spurring heels,
And close into her face, with rhyming clack,
Began a Prothalamion ;—she reels,
She falls, she faints ! while laughter peals
Over her woman's weakness. 'Where !' cried I,
'Where is his Majesty ?' No person feels
Inclin'd to answer ; wherefore instantly
I plung'd into the crowd to find him or to die.

LXXXVIII.

"Jostling my way I gain'd the stairs, and ran
To the first landing, where, incredible !
I met, far gone in liquor, that old man,
That vile impostor Hum,——"

                   So far so well,—
For we have prov'd the Mago never fell
Down stairs on Crafticanto's evidence ;
And therefore duly shall proceed to tell,
Plain in our own original mood and tense,
The sequel of this day, though labour 'tis immense!

     *   *   *   *

LINES SUPPOSED TO HAVE BEEN ADDRESSED
TO FANNY BRAWNE

THIS living hand, now warm and capable
Of earnest grasping, would, if it were cold
And in the icy silence of the tomb,
So haunt thy days and chill thy dreaming nights
That thou would[st] wish thine own heart dry of blood
So in my veins red life might stream again,
And thou be conscience-calm'd—see here it is—
I hold it towards you.

SONNET

Written on a Blank Page in Shakespeare's Poems,
facing "A Lover's Complaint."

BRIGHT star, would I were stedfast as thou art—
   Not in lone splendour hung aloft the night
And watching, with eternal lids apart,
   Like nature's patient, sleepless Eremite,
The moving waters at their priestlike task
   Of pure ablution round earth's human shores,
Or gazing on the new soft-fallen mask
   Of snow upon the mountains and the moors—
No—yet still stedfast, still unchangeable,
   Pillow'd upon my fair love's ripening breast, 10
To feel for ever its soft fall and swell,
   Awake for ever in a sweet unrest,
Still, still to hear her tender-taken breath,
And so live ever—or else swoon to death.

Lines] *These were written in the margin of a page of the holograph*
manuscript of " The Cap and Bells," and were published in my sixth
one-volume edition of Keats's poetry (1898).
  Sonnet 1] Bright star ! *Houghton and Pocket Dante.*
  7 mask *Houghton ;* masque *Shakespeare's Poems and Pocket Dante.*
  8 moors ! *Pocket Dante.*   9 No ! *Pocket Dante.*
  11 fall and swell *Houghton :* swell and fall *Shakespeare's Poems.*
  14 Half-passionless, and so swoon on to death.
                                 Variant, Houghton.

INDEX OF FIRST LINES

THE END.

THE END